Navigating Conflict

THE CHICAGO SERIES IN LAW AND SOCIETY

Edited by John M. Conley and Lynn Mather

Also in the series:

The Sit-Ins: Protest and Legal Change in the Civil Rights Era
by Christopher W. Schmidt

Working Law: Courts, Corporations, and Symbolic Civil Rights
by Lauren B. Edelman

The Myth of the Litigious American: Or, Why We Don't Sue
by David M. Engel

Policing Immigrants: Local Law Enforcement on the Front Lines
by Doris Marie Provine, Monica W. Varsanyi, Paul G. Lewis, and Scott H. Decker

The Seductions of Quantification: Measuring Human Rights, Gender Violence, and
Sex Trafficking
by Sally Engle Merry

Invitation to Law and Society: An Introduction to the Study of Real Law, Second Edition
by Kitty Calavita

Pulled Over: How Police Stops Define Race and Citizenship
by Charles R. Epp, Steven Maynard-Moody, and Donald Haider-Markel

The Three and a Half Minute Transaction: Boilerplate and the Limits of Contract Design
by Mitu Gulati and Robert E. Scott

This Is Not Civil Rights: Discovering Rights Talks in 1939 America
by George I. Lovell

Failing Law Schools
by Brian Z. Tamanaha

Everyday Law on the Street: City Governance in an Age of Diversity
by Mariana Valverde

Lawyers in Practice: Ethical Decision Making in Context
Edited by Leslie C. Levin and Lynn Mather

Collateral Knowledge: Legal Reasoning in the Global Financial Markets
by Annelise Riles

Additional series titles follow index

Navigating Conflict

How Youth Handle Trouble in a High-Poverty School

CALVIN MORRILL
AND MICHAEL MUSHENO

The University of Chicago Press
Chicago and London

The University of Chicago Press, Chicago 60637
The University of Chicago Press, Ltd., London
© 2018 by The University of Chicago
Published 2018
Printed in the United States of America

27 26 25 24 23 22 21 20 19 18   1 2 3 4 5

ISBN-13: 978-0-226-53876-1 (cloth)
ISBN-13: 978-0-226-52373-6 (paper)
ISBN-13: 978-0-226-52387-3 (e-book)
DOI: 10.7208/chicago/9780226523873.001.0001

Library of Congress Cataloging-in-Publication Data

Names: Morrill, Calvin, author. | Musheno, Michael C., author.
Title: Navigating conflict : how youth handle trouble in a high-poverty
    school / Calvin Morrill and Michael Musheno.
Other titles: Chicago series in law and society.
Description: Chicago ; London : The University of Chicago Press, 2018. |
    Series: The Chicago series in law and society
Identifiers: LCCN 2017033943 | ISBN 9780226538761 (cloth : alk. paper) |
    ISBN 9780226523736 (pbk. : alk. paper) | ISBN 9780226523873 (e-book)
Subjects: LCSH: Peer mediation. | Poor teenagers—Conduct of life. |
    School violence. | Social conflict.
Classification: LCC HQ799.2.P44 M677 2018 | DDC 371.7/82—dc23
LC record available at https://lccn.loc.gov/2017033943

To Aaron, Haley, and Micah

*With the invaluable engagement of the fieldwork team of
Cynthia Bejarano, Christine Yalda, Madelaine Adelman,
Jerlyn Jones, and Billy Gray*

CONTENTS

CASES

This book tells two interrelated stories about youth conflict at a diverse, high-poverty public high school in the urban American Southwest. We ground these stories in sixteen years of ethnographic fieldwork, as well as archival research that historically locates the school in more than a century of local, state, and national change. These unusually long time horizons give us a unique window onto both the lived experience of youth conflict and the changing school contexts and control practices in which it unfolded. The first story challenges the conventional, violent-centered focus in most studies of urban youth conflict, revealing the social ingenuity with which teens informally and peacefully navigate potentially strife-ridden peer trouble. The second story tells a tale of resilience in the face of administrative changes to assert carceral-like school control practices, aligned with the national "safe schools" movement, which interrupted, but did not destroy, the very historic capacity for social trust and fluid peer relations across diverse groups that made campus peace possible. Taken together, these narratives offer the framing for what we call a "trouble perspective" on urban youth conflict.

Our first story emerged during the initial ethnographic fieldwork we conducted at the school in the late 1990s. Taking cues from anthropology and sociology, we analyzed hundreds of trouble cases—extended accounts of peer conflict told in young people's own voices and directly observed by our diverse fieldwork team during everyday campus life. Violence and aggression were known ways of dealing with peer conflict but not the default practices youth reported or that we observed, especially among older students. On a daily basis, students engaged in multiple moves to reconcile trouble while protecting their identities and relationships. They alternately modified their own behaviors, enacted deft moves to avoid troublesome parties and situations, or carefully talked with allies and antagonists. We also learned how and when youth took the initiative as engaged third parties to help de-escalate problematic situations. Although not without texture contingent upon race, ethnicity, and gender, students expressed trust in their teachers, their school as a place that mattered to their lives and futures, and across the diversity of peer groups that populated their campus. This trust became a sociocultural anchor, facilitating students' efforts to handle peer troubles in the ebb and flow of everyday school life as they moved and assembled across school grounds without fear of peer retaliation. School staff played important roles in these dynamics by both supportively monitoring young people and mobilizing formal discipline in relatively equitable ways when needed. Teachers who voluntarily opened their classrooms to students during lunch and before and after school further underscored trust on campus. In these sanctuaries, as students and teachers sometimes called them, youth could compose themselves away from the more public and "downtown" spaces of the campus, often working out their interpersonal troubles in the process.

Our second story also begins in the late 1990s at the end of a decade during which teachers and the administration championed the school as a striving, multicultural success and worked to expand social trust across the most marginalized students on campus, especially Mexican immigrants and African American young men. The narrative arc of this story came into focus as we explored the historical origins of social trust at the school in the early twentieth century. A significant Latino and white presence characterized the student body from the school's founding in the late Arizona territorial period, which was a period of relatively fluid social relations among land- and business-holding local European- and Mexican-descent families. During the first several decades of statehood, the school sustained its modest diversity despite state and federal laws that racially segregated schools. Black students enriched the school's diversity without collective trauma when they enrolled in sizable numbers during the 1950s and 1960s in the wake of the Supreme Court's 1954 *Brown v. Board* school desegregation decision. And in small numbers, Mexican immigrant youth and young people from other diverse ethnic groups began arriving to the school beginning in the 1980s.

Over the school's century-long history, we found evidence of its capacity to sustain social trust through continuous, adaptive commitments to inclusive academic opportunities and extracurricular activities. Student clubs in particular helped break down stereotypes associated with students of different ethnic and racial identities, and develop alliances and know-how among students and teacher-mentors collaborating on common goals. These practices enabled the school to adapt to a changing environment and student body into the late 1990s even as the campus experienced bouts of contestation as social trust and distrust coexisted side by side, waxing and waning with the rise and decline of student clubs.

But these conditions gave way to a major interruption early in the first decade of the twenty-first century. A moral panic about urban youth of color and violence had swept the nation, even as crime rates and youth violence declined on and off urban school grounds. Labels, such as "super-predator," cursed through popular and policy discourse, depicting urban African American and Latino male youth as lethal and uncontrollable. Poverty, joblessness, fractured families, failed schools, street gangs, and illegal markets in guns and drugs figured into these images as causes and consequences of urban youth violence. Neoliberal interventions into the social problems experienced by marginalized populations privileged public disinvestment and intensive, racialized policing and mass incarceration. Consonant with these developments, a variety of securitizing, carceral-like control technologies spread across American education, with the safe schools movement among the most visible due to its federal funding in the 1990s.

Locally, a new school administration, supported by a small group of teachers, reframed the campus from a striving, multicultural success to a "ghetto school" in need of tougher security and disciplinary policies, even as multiple strands of evidence showed the school as safe, if not safer, than most schools in its district, and quite safe by state and national standards. This coalition, with support from the school district, brought safe schools to the school. Under its tight grip the campus changed seemingly overnight. School policies prevented student movement on and off campus during lunch and other free periods as youth perceptions of campus territoriality tied to race and ethnicity intensified. The presence of inclusive student clubs declined dramatically. Racial inequities marked school discipline, and local police played an increasingly visible role in handling peer troubles on campus with youth conflict turning more violent. Social trust eroded as the lines among racial and ethnic peer groups hardened, although the relative demographic proportions of those groups did not substantially change during this period.

Safe schools policies began to wither only a few years after they were adopted, straining under the weight of their implementation as teachers who spanned the pre and post safe schools era on campus significantly reasserted the school's historic capacities. Taking these cues, a new school administration further relaxed safe schools in the latter half of the first decade of the twenty-first century. Fluid relations across different peer groups and space also reemerged, as did a considerable student club presence on campus. Youth on campus once more turned to predominantly conciliatory actions to handle interpersonal and intergroup peer trouble. Social trust, similar to what we had observed prior to the strident administrative commitment to safe schools practices, emerged as well.

Our two stories point to a larger thesis that ethnic and racial differences do not automatically generate social distrust or lead to aggressive peer conflict on school grounds with predominantly poor, diverse student populations. That our evidence led us to this thesis does not make us romantics who deny the importance of fair and consistent official school authority. We also do not deny the pressing need for effective administrative leadership and material resources for inclusive academic and other opportunities in high-poverty and other kinds of public schools. Such efforts are not enough, however. Our empirical evidence points to the foundational significance of meaningful, inclusive student organizations for sustaining social trust and collective peer dignity on high-poverty, urban campuses. Such projects require serious attention to how youth and adults use space on and off school grounds, and reliance on bottom-up, middle-out youth and teacher agency. At the high school we studied, their combined agency enabled freedom of assembly and spatial movement without retaliation. These processes are key, we argue, for sustaining peaceful peer and adult control practices in a school that works.

Acknowledgments

A book with this long a gestation needed the support and care of a multitude of individuals and institutions for which we are incredibly thankful. Most importantly, we thank the youth who took time out of their school and work days to let us hang out with them and teach us about their worlds in sometimes surprising, yet always insightful and authentic ways. We also thank the adults—teachers, administrators, security guards, police officers, and school support staff—who allowed us access to their campus over the many years this project unfolded and patiently answered all our questions. We owe a special thanks to those long-time teachers who gave us access to the school archives and put us in touch with former teachers and students to help us gain a long view. Finally, we thank the people working in multiple municipal organizations where this research occurred, especially those in the police department, library and city archives, and school district, for their openness and cooperation.

This book would not have been possible without extensive scholarly support for which we are enormously grateful. We are most indebted to a diverse fieldwork team composed of students then in graduate school—Cynthia Bejarano, Christine Yalda, Jerlyn Jones, and Billy Gray—and one additional faculty member, Madelaine Adelman, all of whom devoted many months to this project in its earlier phases. We give special recognition to them on a separate page preceding this preface. We also thank doctoral students then in the Department of Sociology at the University of Arizona, Jennifer Earl and Mary Nell Trautner, who worked on early qualitative and quantitative analyses of youth-authored trouble cases and youth-drawn sketch maps, respectively. We benefited from the efforts of Jamie Rowen, then a doctoral student in Berkeley Law's Jurisprudence and Social Policy (JSP) Program, and two Berkeley undergraduate students, Julia Chang and Sareen Tak, who helped code the youth-authored and ethnographic trouble cases. Two JSP doctoral students, Chase Burton and Kelsey Mayo, read an early draft of the entire manuscript, offering brilliant comments that importantly shaped our thinking and writing. We are grateful to Eleanor Williams, an undergraduate at the University of Oregon, for the insight that eventually led to the title of this book. We especially thank Kaitlin Jaffe for drawing the official campus plot maps, and Alisa Wabnik Morrill for her technical help in preparing the photos that appear in this book. Over the years, scores of graduate and undergraduate students in our classes at Arizona State University, the University of Arizona, the University of California, Berkeley, the University of California, Irvine, and the University of Oregon offered us perceptive feedback on our ideas and findings.

At the press, we thank our editors, Doug Mitchell and John Tryneski, for their unflagging support and encouragement, and Chuck Myers, who now leads the Chicago Series in Law and Society in the wake of John's retirement. Doug Mitchell was especially valuable in guiding us through the review process with his deep experience, nudging us when necessary and humoring us when we needed a boost. John Conley, coeditor of the Chicago Series in Law and Society, and two outside reviewers, Robert Emerson and Torin Monahan, carefully read the entire manuscript at critical moments, offering keen insights and supportive feedback that greatly improved it. Kyle Wagner, editorial associate at the press, provided supportive administrative guidance throughout the review process. Caterina MacLean kept us on point with her careful editing of the manuscript.

Along the way, numerous colleagues raised important questions and suggestions to advance this project, including: Kathryn Abrams, Catherine Albiston, Elijah Anderson, Richard Arum, Ron Avi Astor, Nina Bandelj, Stephen Barley, Timothy Bartley, Frank Bean, Jeannine Bell, Amy Binder, Albert Bergesen, Donald Black, Elizabeth Brown, Kenly Brown, Kitty Calavita, Prudence Carter, Mark Chaves, Elisabeth Clemens, Philip Cohen, Mark Cooney, Jared Curhan, Gerald Davis, Frank Dobbin, Mitchell Duneier, Jane Dutton, Jennifer Earl, Lauren Edelman, Christopher Edley, Mustafa Emirbayer, William Fabricius, Malcolm Feeley, Martha Feldman, Roberto Fernandez, Gary Alan Fine, Claude Fischer, Benjamin Fleury-Steiner, Neil Fligstein, Marion Fourcade, David John Frank, Robert Garot, Laura Gómez, Rosann Greenspan, Michael Grossman, Bernard Harcourt, Heather Haveman, Michael Hechter, Carol Heimer, Ruth Horowitz, Michael Hout, Iza Hussin, Curtis Jackson-Jacobs, Jack Katz, Valerie Jenness, Nikki Jones, Aaron Kupchik, Michèle Lamont, Jennifer Lee, Taeku Lee, Kristin Luker, William Lyons, Robert MaCoun, Michael Macy, Peter Marsden, Steven Maynard-Moody, Doug McAdam, David Meyer, Debra Meyerson, Mark Mizruchi, Laura Nader, Andrew Nelson, Katherine Newman, Jason Owen-Smith, Andrew Penner, Dylan Penningroth, Charles Perrow, Francesca Polletta, Walter Powell, Hayagreeva Rao, Diana Shivakamini Reddy, Victor Rios, Rubén Rumbaut, Martín Sánchez-Jankowski, Lance Sandelands, Marc Schneiberg, Evan Schofer, Gay Seidman, Carroll Seron, Susan Silbey, Jonathan Simon, Lynn Smith-Lovin, David Snow, Sarah Song, Jesper Sørenson, Sarah Soule, Rachel Stern, Mitchell Stevens, Mark Suchman, Ann Swidler, Christopher Tomlins, Judith Treas, James Tucker, Lars Tummers, Karolyn Tyson, John Van Maanen, Diane Vaughan, Marc Ventresca, Isaac Waisberg, Dana Wang, Christopher Winship, Alford Young, Mayer Zald, Viviana Zelizer, Frank Zimring, and Ezra Zuckerman.

We also benefited from audience feedback to our presentations at: the annual meetings of the American Sociological Association and the Law & Society Association; the Center for Law, Society, and Culture, Maurer School of Law, Indiana University; the Center for the Study of Law and Society, University of California, Berkeley School of Law; the Conference on Fieldwork in Contemporary Society, University of California, Los Angeles; the Department of Criminology, Law and Society, University of California, Irvine; the Ethnographies Working Group, Department of Sociology, University of California, Los Angeles; the Jurisprudence and Social Policy Program, University of California, Berkeley School of Law; the Metropolitan Policy Center, American University; the Organizational Studies seminar, Sloan School of Management, MIT; the Scandinavian Consortium for Organizational Research, Stanford Graduate School of Education; the School of Education and Ross School of Business, University of Michigan; the School of Education and Social Policy, Northwestern University; the Udall Center for Studies in Public Policy, University of Arizona; the University of Oregon Law School; and departments of sociology at Harvard University, the University of Arizona, the University of California, Berkeley, the University of California, Irvine, the University of Michigan, and the University of Wisconsin–Madison.

A project of this duration and complexity required flexible funding from multiple, generous sources, which we cobbled together from: the Arizona State University Multidisciplinary Initiative on Conflict and Its Management (co-awarded to Michael Musheno and Bob Dauber); the Center for the Study of Law and Society, University of California, Berkeley School of Law; the Center for Urban Inquiry, Arizona State University; the Dean of Behavioral and Social Sciences Research Fund, San Francisco State University; the Dean of Law School Research Fund, University of Oregon; the School of Social Sciences and Center for Organizational Research, University of California, Irvine; the Social and Behavioral Sciences Research Institute and Udall Center for Studies in Public Policy, University of Arizona; and the Wayne Morse Center for Law and Politics, University of Oregon.

We owe the greatest thanks to our immediate families—Alisa, Aaron, and Haley Morrill and Birgit and Micah Musheno—for their continual insights and support that buoyed our spirits while we completed this book. Without our families, not only would this project have been impossible, but it also would be far less meaningful.

Calvin Morrill and Michael Musheno
Berkeley and Eugene
September 2017

ONE

Rethinking Youth Conflict

Popular and scholarly imagination casts youth violence and aggression as taken-for-granted aspects of poor, urban high schools, with students of color playing central roles as predatory threats to social order.[1] Missing in this vision is a systematic look at how youth make sense of social dissonance while contributing to civility on school grounds. This book fills that gap by locating violence and aggression—what conventionally stands for urban youth conflict—as a narrow slice of a broader range of peer responses to interpersonal and intergroup trouble. We find social trust acts as a cultural resource tilting peer relations toward inclusive, group boundary crossing, and ways of handling peer trouble toward peaceful improvisation. At a more general level, our findings shed light on the conditions under which urban youth become solutions to social problems rather than treated as social problems themselves.

The research reported here spanned three decades, 1997–2013, a period of intense fear about violence in American schools, yet also a period of overall decline in rates of school violence and widespread adoption of carceral-like school discipline and security under policy rubrics related to the criminal justice–leaning "safe schools" movement.[2] Our focal research site, a high-poverty, urban public school in the American Southwest we call "New West High School" (NWHS), offers an illuminating window into these dynamics since multiple benchmarks characterized the school as safe *before* succumbing to the lure of resources and hard-edged legitimacy linked to the adoption of safe schools policies. We tracked peer responses to interpersonal trouble before, during, and after these policy changes through a combination of ethnographic, archival, and institutional evidence. This strategy offered a rare, in-depth view of how youth respond to personal enmities on a safe, high-poverty campus, and a longitudinal view of how administrative adoption of carceral-like control policies disrupts but fails to dismantle these practices permanently. To begin, consider these representative illustrations of how NWHS students and staff gave voice to these dynamics over the course of this study.

Voices of Peer Trouble

Troy Johnson, José Rodriguez, and Pamela Boynes, three students who attended NWHS in 1997, talked about how they approached peer trouble on campus in discussions with Cynthia Bejarano and Jerlyn Jones, two members of our diverse fieldwork team.[3] Their views were commonly voiced among students during our first two years of fieldwork in the late 1990s:

JERLYN: Ever had any trouble with another student on campus?

TROY: Yeah. A friend, well, someone I was with [dating]. . . . You know, sometimes you get these little dramas.

JERLYN: What did you do?

TROY: I got outta her face. Let things cool down. It was okay for a while. Then the dramas start again. . . . I went right up and talk with her, try to work it out. . . . You can find a place outta the way at lunch or after school sometimes to talk it out. . . .

†

CYNTHIA: What about trouble with another student on campus?

JOSÉ: A little. Had someone I don't know talkin' shit to [insulting] me in the cafeteria.

CYNTHIA: What'd you do?

JOSÉ: I fight him.

CYNTHIA: Why?

JOSÉ: Someone talks shit, you can't back down. Other kids was watching. You do what you gotta do. Not my first way to go. . . . [G]et your rep. Be strong. . . .

†

JERLYN: Any trouble with another student on campus?

PAMELA: Not too much. Sometimes.

JERLYN: What do you do when you have trouble with another student?

PAMELA: Most of the time you handle stuff yourself. Like if it's someone you don't have to be with you can avoid 'em. . . . Kids here are okay, they can work it out on their own. . . . Sometimes you can go to adults, like a teacher or a coach. You're having problems with another kid, the adult can help.

These students each illustrate different aspects of handling peer trouble in descending prevalence on campus: youth talking with or avoiding troublesome peers, engaging in verbal or physical aggression, or mobilizing school staff. Troy, a black eleventh grader who played team sports and was into graphic arts, took us inside the tensions ("little dramas") he faced with his girlfriend from whom he temporarily distanced himself to "let things cool down." When the tensions resurfaced, he tried to "talk with her" about the trouble in an "outta the way place" where they would not be disturbed. José, a ninth grader who came to the United States from Mexico as a toddler with his mother, noted that violence was not his "first way to go." Yet he resigned himself ("gotta do what you gotta do") to not "back[ing] down" from a peer who insulted him ("talkin' shit"), thus evoking well-worn images of urban youth conflict as affairs of intimidation and violence. Pamela was a twelfth grade honor student of mixed black, Mexican, and white descent, who played multiple varsity sports. She pointed out that youth on campus are "okay" and "work . . . out" much of their interpersonal troubles without adult intervention, although they "sometimes" seek adult "help" on campus.

Three years later and several months into a new administration's commitment to implement a bundle of safe schools practices heavy on surveillance and control, student responses to similar questions about handling interpersonal trouble on campus dramatically changed. In 2001, Christine Yalda, another member of our fieldwork team, spoke with Rachel, a black eleventh grader active in several student clubs, about her experiences with peer trouble on campus:

> . . . [I]t's more tense now. You gotta stay in one part of campus at lunch so they [school staff] can see you. People mark their spaces more. . . . Makes it hard to meet for a club because things really tense if you gotta walk somewhere or put up a sign or something [for a club]. You might get in the wrong place and people be like "what'cha doin' here?" There were fights before [safe schools] but you could find some place to work things out too. Hard to do that now always lookin' over your shoulder. Don't seem too safe.

Rachel signaled a heightened sense of territoriality and anxiety among students and the constraints they faced in finding places to "work things out" with one another. She observed how these developments undermined out-of-class activities, such as meeting in student clubs. Similar worries emerged in a diverse male-female focus group composed of black, Latino, and white youth from the tenth and eleventh grades that Christine and

Cynthia conducted, including statements like: ". . . . students . . . they can't even breathe sometimes," "maybe we go for while without any fights [on campus] and then it's like wham, bam, people kickin' ass all over," or "people don' work it out like they use to, they got to defend theyself any way they can or wait for guards." Increased personal and social anxieties, handling interpersonal trouble aggressively, and the heavy shadows of school surveillance and control all marked these accounts.

Late in the first decade of the twenty-first century, a change in the NWHS administration dramatically relaxed safe schools practices, demonstrating an adaptive, local organizational response to formal policies enacted from above. In 2008, Cal and Michael asked a diverse, representative group of students drawn from the eleventh and twelfth grades about their experiences with peer trouble. This group responded with accounts that paralleled what we found a decade earlier when students navigated their way through trouble, including: "people find a place to work it out here without gettin' too messed up," "sometimes they fight, but mostly not," and "if you got a real problem with someone or a group, talk it out or let it go, see a teacher you trust, if not."

We also observed changes over time in the ways school staff talked about youth trouble and conflict on campus. Prior to safe schools, Mrs. Robinson, a veteran teacher and black, voiced sentiments similar to many teachers on campus in speaking with Michael, noting that she "put[s] her ear to the ground to hear what the youth are saying." She pointed out that "there's mostly good kids here . . . even though they face so much challenge in their lives like poverty, racism." She cautioned that teachers "have to be real, to know when . . . to discipline 'em . . . [or] . . . give guidance, support, when to trust 'em and let 'em [youth] work it out on their own." Other teachers, such as Mr. Brown, a veteran white teacher who spoke with Cal, took a dimmer view of NWHS students, noting that "there's no real violence much of the time . . . real violence could happen" because there are ". . . a lot of immature kids on this campus . . . [who] can be a problem with kids in groups and if gangs are involved." He voiced an opinion shared by a group of teachers that "tougher policies . . . would give us better control."

When we checked in with these and other teachers three years later, the full-blown engagement of safe schools had further divided the NWHS faculty. Some, such as Mr. Brown, in a follow-up conversation with Cal, expressed strong convictions that safe schools policies worked "to reduce problems on campus." Many teachers, such as Mr. George, another veteran white teacher, expressed concerns that the new disciplinary policies themselves might be creating problems. He told Michael that the new policies, especially the spatial confinement of students in certain parts of the campus during lunch and other free periods, might even "encourage fighting" because they stripped away students' capacities to move out of the public spotlight to handle peer trouble. We learned how the new policies fomented trouble among teachers staffing the new policies and compelled some to modify their identities as educators, becoming, as one teacher put it, "a cross between a prison guard and a cop." Several years later, Cal and Michael uncovered yet another sea change in teachers' perceptions. A diverse focus group of veteran and neophyte teachers discussed how "well meshed" the students appeared on campus compared to earlier in the decade during the "high" safe schools period. They talked about what they learned from that period, including how disciplinary patterns and academic tracking that "favor one group over another" diminished students' trust in each other and the staff, at the same time "hardening" social divisions among students.

Explaining Youth Conflict in Schools

The student and staff accounts above point to a shifting social landscape at NWHS through which youth navigated peer conflict. Their perspectives on peer conflict hinted at the importance of youth agency and trust, staff orientations and commitments to their students, and the administrative focus of the school. What clues does the existing literature on urban youth conflict, particularly related to schooling, offer in aiding the translation of these hints into grounded explanations?

Criminological research on youth conflict in and around urban schools primarily focuses on the delinquency and criminality of student populations, especially incidences of rape, nonsexual forms of assault, and theft. This line of inquiry views much of what goes on in schools as reflections of social contexts off school grounds and deficiencies in school resources, linking higher rates of criminality to schools with higher concentrations of students of color from lower-income households, impoverished larger public schools, and unstable neighborhoods that result in constant student transfers in and out of schools.[4]

A stream of sociological inquiry into interpersonal conflict in urban public schools examines the importation of what Elijah Anderson calls "the code of the street" from impoverished neighborhoods onto school grounds. The code emerges in socially disorganized neighborhoods beset by joblessness, family fragmentation, and institutional distrust, especially of law enforcement, that result in young poor people of color having few avenues for developing self-worth and peer respect as they transition from childhood to adolescence to adulthood. Under these conditions, Anderson and other researchers argue that the code operates as a cultural script for personal honor and rough justice, compelling youth to handle disputes aggressively in order to protect themselves and garner a "tough front."[5] Nikki Jones argues that young women of color in high-poverty contexts can face particular burdens in this regard, as they negotiate interpersonal power relations with female and male peers based on code-of-street, masculinized senses of control.[6] Although Anderson notes that schools become places of "relative order" in high-poverty neighborhoods, he observes that peer conflict in schools under the strong grip of the code sometimes "can only be settled by death."[7] Victor Rios agrees with Anderson that the code has roots in the social and economic conditions of high poverty neighborhoods but finds that urban school authorities engage in a "re/production of street culture and identity," first mimicking gang-associated youth to gain their attention and then "when mimicking failed, authority figures defaulted to mocking youths' language and style."[8]

Sociological and criminological research on intergroup conflict in poor urban schools concentrates on the intersecting dynamics of street gang competition in illegal markets, neighborhood rivalries, and interethnic group tension, sometimes identifying the role of code-of-the-street mentalities. In these contexts, violence becomes a mechanism for settling intergang disputes, maintaining group solidarity, and disciplining wayward customers. Disputing gangs identifying with different ethnic or racial groups may stimulate or compound these conflicts.[9] Neighborhood rivalries, whether tied to formal gangs or not, have been associated with violent defenses of neighborhood turf on school grounds.[10] Recent research by Martín Sánchez-Jankowski takes such analyses several steps forward by linking interpersonal and intergroup violence in schools to the arrival in mass of new ethnic groups, the intersection of territoriality with ethnic identity, and intense interethnic competition over scarce academic and other vital resources.[11]

Schools can play key roles in creating or exacerbating interpersonal and intergroup violence and aggression. Criminologists find that schools in which students perceive greater fairness and clarity of official rules experience lower rates of delinquency and victimization, including rape, other forms of assault, and bullying.[12] The research proves mixed on the relationship between school violence and administrative commitments to carceral-like security, including armed personnel, zero tolerance, hardware screening, surveillance systems, and strict channeling of student spatial mobility on school grounds. Some research finds that such systems deter violence, particularly involving guns.[13] Yet these systems are themselves shaped by racialized, gendered, and classed images of youth, which define the everyday realities of school life along carceral lines.[14] For students already marginalized due to their ethnic, racial, and/or social class identities, such systems can produce dramatic social inequities, even becoming "toxic" in generating a variety of health and social maladies.[15] They also set in motion dynamics that can alter life-course trajectories, making male youth, particularly African Americans and Latinos, more susceptible to the "school-to-prison pipeline."[16] The risks faced especially by young women of color in such systems are just being documented. Kimberlé Crenshaw and colleagues, for example, use Department of Education national school disciplinary enforcement data from 2011–12 to find that all female students of color are at greater risk for exclusionary school discipline in US schools than white female students, but that African American female students face the greatest risk.[17] In follow-up focus group interviews, student and adult participants observed that teachers and administrators distrust African American female students as a group, which feeds into punitive "overdisciplining" for peer conflict and their separation from school.[18]

Taken together, studies of urban youth conflict and school control offer further direction, but not explanations for the longitudinal shifts in the shape of youth conflict at NWHS, nor how to understand reports from youth and adults that the campus experienced extended periods where youth "worked out" their conflicts through conciliatory practices. The guidance gained from the existing literature points to tracking the intersection of racial, ethnic, gender, and social class inequalities among the students, including the arrival of new ethnic groups and intergroup competition, which might increase or decrease the importation of street codes and gang defenses of neighborhood turf on campus. Previous research also underscores how shifts in the dependence on carceral-like and racialized school discipline can affect safety and security on campus. At NWHS, some of these changes, such as the arrival of new ethnic groups, particularly new immigrants crossing from the state's southern border with Mexico, occurred during periods when the campus was safest. Other dynamics appeared constant, such as the moderate presence of street codes and gangs. The biggest change we observed occurred with the dramatic shift in school discipline early during the first decade of the twenty-first century.

Most importantly, previous research does not offer a clear picture of how and why social and school environments facilitate or constrain a

range of peer practices for handling disputes beyond a treatment of the social forces that trigger aggressive and violent conflict. Much less is known,
as well, about how gender, race, ethnicity, and social class matter across
the myriad practices youth use to handle peer conflict. Prior research does
indicate that carceral-like school discipline disproportionately affects students of color while leading to fear and anxiety among all students, but
not how it conditions the ways in which youth handle their problems with
one another. To overcome these shortcomings, we recalibrated the object
of inquiry for the study of youth conflict, shifting from the conventional
concentration on urban youths' resort to intimidation, aggression and violence. We focus instead on how youth imagine and act on the *trouble* they
experience with one another.

Toward a Trouble Perspective of Youth Conflict in Schools

Developments in the anthropological, sociological, and sociolegal study of
social conflict and control provide the foundations for a trouble perspective.[19] Karl Llewellyn and E. Adamson Hoebel's classic work, *The Cheyenne
Way*, offers a point of departure by introducing *trouble cases* as the raw materials with which to analyze breakdowns and disruptions in "taken for
granted modes of interaction" that reveal the contours of cultural expectations as well as relational and institutional power.[20] Trouble can begin
as an ambiguous perturbation made sense of over time or as a definitive
act immediately tied to particular kinds of issues like problems with peers,
teachers, school structures, neighborhoods, or law enforcement. As Robert
Emerson argues, the give-and-take of ongoing action orientations for handling wayward persons, problematic events, or social structures deemed
unjust ultimately defines the kind and stakes of trouble.[21] A trouble perspective thus opens up a processual, panoramic view of social control in
ongoing, lived experience, inclusive of navigating conflict through the exercise of aggression and violence, and practices that can flow top-down and
bottom-up, from school administrative processes to contingent practices
embedded in campus youth cultures.

Scholars have devised multiple frameworks for understanding social
control across a broad range of social and cultural contexts, historical
periods, and legal systems. Early approaches conceptualized social control as all "human practices and arrangements that . . . influence people
to conform," including those associated with primary socialization, social
organization, such as families or workplaces, and law.[22] A highly visible
stream of sociolegal research defines social control as "transformational

stages" or "branches" in the mobilization of law, underscoring the discontinuous ways that responses to trouble can lead to or away from law.[23] Other scholars, such as Donald Black and Laura Nader, move beyond legal mobilization models by offering cross-cultural typologies and theories that encompass and explain the conditions under which disputants: do nothing, tolerate (including cope), or engage in self-help (including violent vengeance, avoidance, and control of the self), negotiation, and third-party settlement (including arbitration, adjudication, mediation, and peacemaking).[24]

Whether couched as stages, branches, or cross-cultural typologies, the preceding models focus on social control dynamics after a definitive identification of trouble has occurred and a grievance formed. Rather than fixed as a grievance tied to some definitive normative breach, trouble among young people may be especially fluid and ambiguous, owing to youth being at a time of personal exploration and change.[25] Schools can further magnify such ambiguities because inferences about trouble occur in punctuated episodes, disjointed by the temporal and spatial organization of the school day.[26]

We conceptualize the social processes wherein youth engage in sense making and respond to disruptions in their everyday lives as *trouble strings*. Strings constitute the interactional spines of trouble cases by charting how youth navigate or make their ways through interactional disruptions that occur in and around everyday public school life. For each case, a string traces contingent interactions and alternative lines of action by young people intended to control and transform social dissonance through manipulations of meaning, emotions, space, and time. The youth at the core of a disruption in relations and the stakes they attribute to it define the boundaries of a string, although neither is fixed. Youth who are core participants may give structure to a string by pursuing unilateral lines of action directed at either themselves or other parties. Pairs of students interacting among themselves constitute bilateral action, and trilateral action occurs when third parties, students or adults on campus, engage in partisan support or act as settlement agents.[27]

Trouble strings unfold over time in fits and starts with the suspension and resumption of problematic interactions and varying degrees of satisfaction by those involved. Some strings last only a few seconds or minutes while others can stretch on for days, weeks, months, or even years. Some strings stay in one geographic spot while others move among places. The normative meanings of trouble in strings are cobbled together from heterogeneous stocks of cultural knowledge that shift among "conciliatory-remedial" orientations framing trouble as mistakes, annoyances, or has-sles, and inviting mutual repair and minimal disruption of social routines, to "moralistic" orientations casting trouble as misconduct and intentional transgressions of definitive normative boundaries associated with ongoing social relations or formal rules, including law.[28] The code of the street rep-resents an archetypal approach to urban youth conflict constructed from moralistic stocks of knowledge in which normative breaches are definitive and their control tied to aggressive, if not violent, responses. Moralistic orientations also can yield senses of injustice, both personal and societal, that shape and are shaped by responses to trouble. Conciliatory-remedial stocks of knowledge resonate with religious and humanistic perspectives that teach to "live and let live" and can operate within and outside formal institutions. In practice, youth sometimes blend these orientations, such as when a sense of moralistic harm is met with conciliatory actions. Finally, trouble strings can shift in their emotional tone, coupled with shifts in normative orientations. Conciliatory-remedial orientations tend to be as-sociated with cooler emotions, such as frustration or mild anxiety, and can intensify if trouble persists. Moralistic orientations tend to link with hotter emotions, such as anger, fear, hostility, shame, or disgust.[29]

Peer relations are highly salient in shaping how trouble strings develop, especially with respect to what trouble means in any given situation.[30] Ad-olescence is a liminal, transitional social experience in the life course, a time of intense identity seeking in which peer relations become particu-larly important for young peoples' sense of self and well-being.[31] As a re-sult, youth continually take into account relational obligations in friend-ships and surrounding networks as they navigate trouble.[32] Parallel to what Donald Black and colleagues theorize about adults, we propose that youth embedded in dense-knit, interdependent networks may be especially sensi-tive to disrupting them and prone to move in conciliatory-remedial direc-tions, repairing trouble via bilateral interaction with troublesome parties. In these settings, third parties, often networked youth not directly engaged in a conflict, are likely to help to repair or keep the peace. Settings in which youth have few connections may lead to conciliatory-remedial orientations accomplished via minimal interaction as individuals unilaterally cope or avoid troublesome parties. Third parties may be less available in these settings.[33]

Where youth group together in tight-knit cliques and bridging ties be-tween groups are sparse or nonexistent, we propose that trouble is more likely to be perceived moralistically, fueled by negative stereotypes of mem-bers in opposing groups. In such settings, third parties linked to cliques will likely act as partisans while third parties disconnected from cliques, particularly adult authorities, may fill the void to settle conflict. Teachers, law enforcement, or on-campus security personnel may act as third parties and suppress trouble, with some drawing on their relational capital with youth and others invoking formal authority, a move that can escalate trouble toward violence and produce the unequal application of school rules and law.[34] How youth and adults consider their social relationships with one another as they respond to trouble in schools is bound up in the distinctive character of school campuses as defined by their formal structures and informal climates.

Brick-and-mortar schools are emplaced in that they occupy identifiable geographic space collectively invested with concentrated meaning and material forms.[35] As places, schools appear to be stable entities, but they are not atomistic wholes but instead continually made and remade through contestations over and collaborations in school structures and climates. By formal structures, we mean the social processes that constitute the official contours of the organization, including its material forms, geographic and temporal boundaries, and bureaucratic, academic, and disciplinary policies. School climate refers to the day-to-day cultural practices, symbols, identities, and expectations shared by students and staff, to which they refer and use as the bases for daily social interaction and informal control.[36] Both school climates and structures are importantly spaces in which, as Na'ilah Suad Nasir and colleagues observe, dominant storylines "take up life" about race, gender, social class, and other identities that influence how youth position themselves as they learn in and out of classrooms and interact with peers.[37] Climate is not monolithic and includes the heterogeneous ways youth on campus make sense of and use social groups and physical space. Sociospatial relations thus become a part of climate and the storylines of different social groups, such as whether students cut up campus space into finite territories attached to particular social identities or define and use space more fluidly. School climates extend into the local community through the way its members collectively view a school as a whole—its organizational identity—and the identities of subgroups of students. Finally, local and global youth-centered "cultures" networked via social media and stimulated by far-flung economic forces can influence school climates, informing different subgroup styles on and off school grounds in terms of rituals, dress, music, and bodily adornments.[38]

Social trust that undergirds school climates can operate as a sociocultural anchor, offering a firm storyline with which youth and adults can create durable interpersonal relationships, develop faith in administrative practices, and sustain a sense of ontological continuity in social life.[39] In urban public schools, multiple and sometimes conflicting forms of trust exist, associated with distinctive scales of expectations about mutual regard and support. Interpersonal trust figures prominently in close-knit groups, such as youth cliques, friendship groups, and some school clubs, or can emerge between students and particular school staff members. Intergroup trust may be more difficult to accomplish yet can develop in perceptions of mutual dignity and respect among and across diverse social networks of youth. Institutional trust involves beliefs in the fairness and effectiveness of social institutions—in our case, schools—and overlaps with legitimacy.[40] Each of these forms of trust can coexist with social distrust, and contestation on an urban school campus often revolves around tensions between trust and distrust. These tensions prove especially palpable for black and Latino urban youth in impoverished neighborhoods and schools as they live in the institutional shadows of constant suspicion, navigate distrust across different social groups, and, when they can, find solace in the interpersonal trust of their tight-knit peers and families.[41] For Latino youth in the American Southwest near border areas with Mexico, trust and distrust also involve contested storylines about what it means to be "Mexican," "Mexican American," "Chicana," "Chicano," or other Latino-inflected identities.[42]

The configuration and practice of school discipline can shape images of youth, how youth internalize authority and their own identities, and the meanings of social order and disorder on school campuses.[43] The dominant storylines for school discipline across the United States marries demonization of nonwhite youth, especially black and Latino males, with carceral-like discipline. This dynamic aligns with Michel Foucault's general observations that contemporary punishment transforms youth into both "docile bodies" and bodies, by definition, in need of policing and control.[44] By contrast, fair, school disciplinary policies and practices, where administrative structures take cues from a school climate infused with inclusive student-teacher trust, flips the moral script on this well-known argument by recognizing youth as agents who can improvise civilly and effectively as they regulate themselves and peers while sometimes turning to youth-centered teachers for help. Bottom-up and middle-out processes for handling trouble by students and teachers, respectively, thus contribute to building and sustaining trust in the climate of a school.

This perspective of building trust points to processes analogous to what

Robert Sampson and Doug McAdam call "collective civic action"—the ways neighborhood residents participate in sustained, meaningful activities for the public good. In neighborhoods, collective civic action can have explicit social change goals while manifesting as mundane collective activities, such as pancake breakfasts, intended to raise consciousness about the dearth of secure public places for urban children to interact and money for safe playground equipment. Collective civic action, to the degree that it includes diverse community members, can generate social trust in promoting regard toward others and facilitating the recognition of diverse members working together on common goals.[45] When divergences arise over goals and tactics of civic engagement, neighbors can draw upon collected social trust to handle trouble and sustain their work.

On urban school grounds, collective civic action is equally purposive and unfolds in before-, during-, and after-school interactions between students and school staff, often taking place in and around teachers' classrooms, as well as the social lives of school clubs and activities. As Hava Rachel Gordon observes, "student clubs have the potential to galvanize students into active social change campaigns that may ultimately work to improve their experiences of education and their schools as institutions."[46] To do so, they need not only the committed agency of diverse young people to interact for collective purposes, but also teachers, volunteering their time, to negotiate the adult terrain of the school on behalf of club members, garner resources for the club, and provide guidance to club members to understand how to define and act on their agendas. Clubs are useful places within which young people can meaningfully interact among themselves and with adults to bridge sociocultural, generational, and political differences as they pursue collective civic action. These practices sometimes convey mutual authenticity that enables the growth of interpersonal and intergroup trust among students and between students and staff.[47]

But, Nina Eliasoph notes, voluntary organizations that bring diverse young people together can experientially teach members how to work with others without carrying the burden that they must already "know . . . much about each other's [cultures] and home habits."[48] Indeed, youth may learn enough about each other in student organizations to inoculate them against narrowness and dogmatism as they begin breaking down stereotypes about diverse social categories while working to achieve common goals collaboratively with staff amidst the complex realities of public schools. Youth in such organizations can acquire bits of institutional trust and senses of collective efficacy if they experience their goals translating into ongoing practices—such as helping to establish an on-site childcare center or a meaningful role in governance—that become part of the structural fabric of a high school.[49]

Public schools are contested places where structures and climates rarely pull fully in tandem due, in part, to being political hubs in which local activist teachers and students, school administrations and boards, and constituencies in broader fields clash. Although these dynamics constantly play off one another, in particular historical moments they can align. For example, inclusive school structures can cultivate a climate of institutional trust that counters dominant storylines about racial, gender, and social class exclusion and inform collaboration among students, administrators, teachers, and parents. Inclusive collective civic action in student clubs and around classrooms not in session cultivates interpersonal and intergroup trust among students and teachers. Our sense is that bottom-up, inclusive collective civic action and fair, supportive top-down structures, especially regarding academics and discipline, ultimately must pull in the same direction to sustain trust across young people and adults in and around a school.

Sparse collective civic action and exclusionary school structures, such as racially disparate, carceral-like control and many forms of academic tracking, exacerbate racial and class inequalities, undermining social trust while seeding conflict among youth and between youth and school staffs. Under these conditions, a school climate can emerge rooted in sticky sociocultural and sociospatial relations grounded in zealously guarded, exclusionary, and territorialized boundaries. These conditions become breeding grounds for social distrust, as they are more likely to hem youth into peer identities and statuses residing in moralistic deterrent threat and force, or a dependence on school structures that can stimulate discriminatory overpolicing by school authorities and law enforcement agencies. Such conditions can harden ethnic and racial lines on campuses, creating fateful differences between how youth handle trouble within and across these divides. Youth trouble responses in this way integrally relate to school structures and climates, as well as to broader institutional and cultural arrangements.

Conversely, sustained trust operating at multiple levels provides a broad sociocultural anchor for young people's comfort and experimentation to build diverse relationships across social boundaries. Diverse relationships in turn are associated with crosscutting social ties, multiple kinds of obligations, and the mitigation of negative stereotypes associated with ethnic, racial, and gender differences. These dynamics can weaken geographic territoriality associated with particular groups and social identities. When these social and spatial qualities are evident, we would expect peer trouble, especially aggressive responses to conflict, to be less prevalent on school grounds. But trust is not a static social good that operates without texture and nuance. In particular, race and ethnicity can influence how trustful youth may be of one another, their teachers, and the school. Where deep cultural divides exist, such as in neighborhoods of high school catchment areas defined by new migrants, all levels of trust can be especially challenging to generate and sustain.[50] Trust among youth also can thicken in particular situations, such as when faced with matters they deem as serious and in need of adult intervention or when they fear another peer is veering into dangerous behaviors (e.g., drug use, criminal behavior, or as a victim of sexual harassment and/or violence) and mobilize either third-party peers or adults for help.[51]

School structures and practices that facilitate youth conducting peer relations with relative freedom of movement and association across groups and school grounds stimulate climates in which youth can exercise their agency to connect, reconnect, and disconnect relational ties. These dynamics create opportunities for improvising conciliatory-remedial trouble responses that accent negotiated problem solving, such as "talking it out" or temporary avoidance, as illustrated earlier by Troy and Pamela. Conciliatory-remedial trouble responses, in turn, help strengthen the campus as a place of trust.

We would expect historical moments when fair, inclusive structures and climates of trust align in a school to produce what Ann Swidler calls "coherent cultural strands" in the lines of action on that campus.[52] This kind of alignment can empower students and staff to act as agents drawing from and moderating the influences of the neighborhood and statewide policies to sustain campus vibrancy. Admittedly, such circumstances may never fully be realized in any particular school, especially a high-poverty school with significant material challenges and sociocultural heterogeneity. But when a high-poverty school constitutes a climate that promotes relative harmony among youth negotiating everyday relations, it offers a counternarrative to popular discourses demonizing urban youth of color through carceral-like control.[53] At the outset of our research, we did not know NWHS would offer such a counternarrative.

New West High School

Located in an Arizona metropolitan area, NWHS is similar to many high-poverty schools in the American Southwest yet stands apart from the typical high-poverty schools in Eastern, Midwestern, and Pacific Coast cities where much of the research on youth conflict has occurred.[54] Since its founding in the early twentieth century, NWHS has always enjoyed a sizable Latino student population relevant to its overall student body. In the 1990s, the proportion of Latinos in the student body grew from two-fifths to over one-half by the end of the decade. This proportion remained constant through much of the first decade of the twenty-first century until the student body in a few years in the late 2000s and early 2010s rose to over 60 percent Latino. Diversity marks the Latino population, with about two-thirds tracing their family lineages back several generations to pre-statehood days and one-third newly arrived from Mexico. Indeed, much of the change in the student population in the 1990s and again late in the first decade of the twenty-first century resulted from newly arrived Mexican immigrant families. During our study, the proportion of black students held steady at one-fifth, while small proportions of Native American and Asian American students remained at less than a tenth of the student body. The white population (mostly of Irish, English, and German descent), which stood at nearly two-fifths in the 1990s, decreased to one-third by the end of the 1990s, held steady during much of the first decade of the twenty-first century, and then diminished to less than one-fifth by the end of that decade. The vast majority of all NWHS students come from neighborhoods that range from 35 to 55 percent of households at or below the poverty line, and many of these neighborhoods have the highest crime rates in the city. More than three-quarters of the NWHS student body is eligible for free and reduced lunch (FRL)—the federal standard to be considered a high-poverty school—even as many students work in addition to their schooling.[55]

NWHS also displays school structures and a climate of ethnic and racial inclusion *and* exclusion. This combination includes a long history of opportunities for male and female youth of color to attain high academic achievement and leadership and participation opportunities across a full spectrum of student clubs, sports, and government. Over the course of the study, persons of color comprised 30 to 35 percent of the NWHS faculty, compared to a statewide average of 18 percent.[56] At the same time, NWHS tracked students through its English as a Second Language program (ESL; now relabeled as English Language Learners, or ELL, programs) and offered limited opportunities for students to join accelerated math and science programs. Teachers and administrators confronted the contradictions in these programs as they related to full student access late in the first decade of the twenty-first century, when the school systematically reduced tracking and expanded access in languages, accelerated math, and sciences for all.

Without knowing anything else about NWHS, prior research would predict that high poverty, changing ethnic and racial demographics, and academic tracking would lead to deleterious social outcomes on campus: low standardized test scores, low graduation rates, and a high rate of interpersonal violence, especially among nonwhite youth.[57] During the 1990s, NWHS graduation rates and standardized test scores stood well above the median for schools in the district and were higher than some schools with largely white, middle-class student populations. These rates dipped somewhat early in the first decade of the twenty-first century and rose again later in the same decade and in the early 2010s. By official measures, NWHS also is a safe campus. During 1997–2000 and 2006–2010, official counts of "serious campus incidents" at NWHS—including interpersonal violence, theft of cars and school equipment, and possession of narcotics—were the lowest in the district, an average of three per academic year compared to a median of sixteen incidents per year for other district high schools. During these same two periods, calls to the police from campus were in the lowest quintile for police calls in New West. In addition, black and Latino students appeared no more likely than white and other students to be involved in serious incidents or the subject of police calls on campus. Between these two periods, 2001–2005, NWHS administration embraced safe schools practices, including increasing the use of in-school and out-of-school suspensions, reducing student mobility on campus, and enhancing surveillance systems. The number of serious incidents and police calls increased precipitously, and the administration and some staff drew harder lines among youth of different ethnic and racial identities as black and Latino youth experienced higher rates of disciplinary actions than whites and other groups on campus.

Modes of Inquiry and Inference

NWHS chose us as much as we chose it, when a small group of teachers reached out to Michael to see if he or someone at the university where he worked would be willing to help resuscitate the school's peer mediation program. Rather than focus on peer mediation, he asked the teachers to consider a study of how youth "handle peer troubles on their own" and brought together a small group of faculty members from his home university and teachers from NWHS to brainstorm possible directions for such a project. He asked Cal, who then worked at another university, to join the initial meetings given his expertise in ethnographically studying organizational conflict, and he and Cal emerged as coleaders of the project.

Our study design emerged as less a grand blueprint than as systematic, flexible improvisation. We layered multiple kinds of data to first deeply dive into peer relations and official and peer practices for handling trouble on a safe campus undergoing significant demographic change during the years from 1997 to 2000. We situated that baseline historically by moving back to the founding of the school in the early twentieth century through means of an archive we constructed of faculty-mentored, student collective civic action on campus, and then forward in time documenting the changes in official and peer control with additional fieldwork and institutional evidence from 2001 to 2013. These stages of inquiry created the opportunity for investigating the intense safe schools period of 2001–2005 as part of a natural experiment with a focus on how it impacted everyday peer trouble and relations.

At a more abstract level, we conceive of our project as a "relational case study" in multiple senses. First, our approach pays particular attention to the relationships and meanings produced through interaction among people in a setting bounded by time, place, and social membership—a hallmark of ethnographic case studies.[58] At the same time, we attend to the interplay among individuals and groups occupying different social categories—with power always in play—across youth in culturally heterogeneous peer groups and student clubs as well as adults in roles as teachers, administrators, school/district staff, alumni, and law enforcement that is distinctive to what Matt Desmond calls "relational ethnography."[59] A third sense of the relational character of our study emerged as we explicitly tied modes of handling trouble on campus to previous periods in the history of the school and broader educational and legal fields.

This study presented multiple challenges, chief among them, as Amy Best frames it, concerning "the varied ways age intersects with other axes of power and difference and its consequence for research practice."[60] Once on campus, the spatial and temporal organization of the school day raised questions about how to represent our identities, placements, and movements. Youth are a vulnerable population, but they wield enormous power and sophistication in granting or withholding access to the interiors of their social worlds, especially about the nuances of peer trouble. Yet adults can alter peer interactions simply by their visible presence in school contexts because they represent, in some broad sense, "adult authority." Cal and Michael's race, ethnicity, social class, positions as professors, and experience further complicated these challenges.

To meet these challenges, we adopted a team fieldwork strategy, which sharply contrasts with the traditional ethnographic lore of the lone fieldworker, the solitary "conquering hero" bearing the burden of site access, data collection, and analysis.[61] Team fieldwork is a preeminently collective enterprise that enables flexibility, including developing field relations with diverse informants and broadly covering spatial and temporal aspects of field sites. Team fieldwork also comes with tradeoffs, including the possibility that no single team member will be as immersed in a field setting as would a solo fieldworker and the need for team members to engage each other at every turn.[62]

The original members of our fieldwork team—Billy Gray (then a graduate student in anthropology), Cal, Cynthia (then a graduate student in justice studies), Jerlyn (then a graduate student in public administration), and Michael—built on the initial meetings Michael and Cal held to brainstorm about the project.[63] Christine Yalda (then a doctoral student in justice studies) and Madelaine Adelman (a justice studies faculty member) joined a year later. We worked with several youth and teacher collaborators to whom we frequently turned for insider perspectives and with whom a subset of the team created a pilot workbook intended to help ninth graders imagine alternatives to violence and aggression in dealing with problematic peers.

Alone and in pairs, team members visited campus during and after school hours on a regular basis from fall 1997 through spring 2001, engaging in participant observation. During this period, we pushed back from the places where adults held the greatest sway (classrooms and administrative offices) to observing niches where students held defining powers over their interactions, including at some of the nearby fast food restaurants and public-street spots off campus. Our general strategy involved sitting with youth as they ate lunch and walking with them on their regular routes from class to class and within free periods on and off campus. Along the way, we helped youth hang posters and prepare food for student clubs and other activities; attended sporting events, plays, and art presentations; sat in empty classrooms and the room designated for In School Suspension (ISS) talking with teachers and students; sat with youth as they awaited appointments with a school counselor, teacher, or administrator; and talked with youth, teachers, security guards, and police officers as we parked our cars or exited public buses and walked in together in the campus parking lots. Along the way, we did not identify with any one group nor pass gossip along lest we be seen "spies" or untrustworthy. We attended alumni association meetings and occasionally met parents when they came on campus. Our "go-alongs"[64] with students afforded us a sense of youth spatial practices and their perceptions of the physical environment. Our movement with teachers, some of whom regularly traversed much of the campus and others who engaged the physical and social territory of NWHS more narrowly, enabled us to understand the social and spatial rhythms of staff. Most teachers anchored their movements around their classrooms, spaces in the hallways and between buildings near their classrooms, and places accessible only to teachers and other staff, such as the staff lunchroom or particular administrative offices.

As we walked and hung out with youth, team members listened to them talking among themselves and engaged in casual discussions with young people about what we were "really" doing on campus (e.g., "a study of how youth deal with trouble on campus"). We asked whether youth would like to participate in our collective interviews, assured their confidentiality, and talked about what we planned to do with what we learned about youth trouble and conflict ("help the school, especially staff and ninth graders, better understand and handle peer trouble on and related to NWHS"). Gradually, the presence of team members became a routine part of daily life on campus. The longer we worked in the field, the more we found that youth interpreted our interest in learning from them about their campus and taking seriously their perspectives on peer trouble as a sign of dignity and respect. Team members focusing on students appeared young in age, and they each found contexts reflective of their social backgrounds and interests to gain rich access to youth life at NWHS. We did field jottings in notebooks while sitting at picnic tables, on the ground between buildings," or in the library, much as we saw students do. We then converted our field jottings into full-fledged typed fieldnotes after leaving the school. We e-mailed fieldnotes on a team listserv moderated by a team member for ease of retrieval in the collective database.

Our understandings of youth trouble grew in tandem with the ways youth make sense of their problems, namely by immersing ourselves in the social geography of the campus. The rapport we cultivated with youth became especially important when talking with them about peer trouble. In conversation, we rarely asked students if they had experienced any "conflict," instead asking about specific troubles we observed or knew about on campus or letting youth lead the conversation. This strategy moved away from representations of youth as "perched at the threshold of adulthood" to reveal the complexities and socially constructed sense of youth meanings of trouble.[65] We quickly learned that for most youth at NWHS, the word "conflict" typically meant any form of physical violence or heated verbal argument over an issue deemed "serious" by those involved. By contrast, the words "trouble" and "problems" included conflict and pointed to a broader range of issues and behaviors that could range from minor annoyances, hassles, and mistakes to fights and near-fights (with or without weapons) to bullying, gossip, threats, sexual and racial harassment, intimidation, theft, and concerns about the behavior of friends and acquaintances, including alcohol and/or drug use/abuse, sexual promiscuity, and cheating in class.

Whenever we witnessed peer interactions that youth appeared to regard as problematic, we followed up with those involved to understand how the situation emerged, how those involved made sense of and defined it, and how the situation unfolded. Early in our fieldwork we found that youth tended to bound particular hitches with their peers, adults, or school and law enforcement officials as threads linking these participants to what they "did" or "said to each other" across different situations involving time, space, and relational contexts. In navigating through their troubles, youth nearly always took into account peer relations. This bounded, youth-centered sensibility dovetailed well with the construct of the trouble case and inspired us to conceptualize the internal organization or spine of cases as trouble strings. Through these methods, Cal and Michael identified ninety-four "ethnographic" trouble cases constructed from multiple vantage points, including direct observation by team members and the voices of relevant actors in the field.

Perhaps the greatest challenge to learning about youth trouble occurred when we uncovered potentially illegal or dangerous activities. We recognized from the outset that our study intended to deeply and confidentially engage young people on multiple dimensions, which could make us privy to potentially dangerous and illegal behavior engaged in by youth. By law, we were required to report such actions. The demands of confidentiality and legal reporting created "communication dilemmas"—occasions when our individual and collective judgments about confidentiality conflicted with obligations to disclose information to adult authorities.[66] Our solution to these dilemmas involved processing the issues through weekly research team meetings and via daily e-mail and phone conversations to get a read on what others on the team knew about the situation. On other occasions, we sought out our teacher collaborators to get quick and confidential reads of the situation (without divulging any identities). In every instance, they already knew of the situation and advised us on a course of action and/or reported on ongoing interventions. With the exception of one instance, an intense bout of collective violence we report on in chapter 7, youth and adults averted harm.

In addition to fieldnotes generated from observations and informal conversations during our first few years on campus, we collected other types of data to engage youth voice both verbally and visually, including: (1) taped in-depth and focus group interviews of youth and staff; (2) "youth-authored" trouble cases written by students in classroom exercises; (3) youth-drawn social-sketch maps of the campus completed in classroom "mapping exercises"; (4) open-ended survey responses from students on "how [NWHS] works for you"; and (5) youth-made photos and youth-authored essays of places and people on campus in the "photo-narrative exercise." These data-collection efforts enabled us to engage active participation by youth in different ways.[67] Interviews and written narratives concentrated on verbal accounts of school structures, climate, youth relations, and trouble. Maps and photo essays engaged how youth "see" the campus and themselves through visual images they made—what Sarah Pink generally calls "spatial discourse[s] of place and self."[68]

As safe schools tightly gripped the school from 2001 to 2005, a new administration showed little interest in our project and, at the same time, most members of the fieldwork team moved on to new opportunities. Cal and Michael kept tabs on the school through local contacts on and off campus, as well as numerous site visits and peripheral observation without being able to embed themselves in the school. Another administration took charge of NWHS in the latter part of the decade and was dedicated to relaxing safe schools policies. Two teachers operating as long-term advisors to the project took positions in this new administration. With this change, Cal and Michael returned to campus from 2008 to 2013 for a second round of observations and interviews on campus, replicating as much as possible the strategies we deployed a decade earlier. Our primary goal involved understanding what lasting impact, if any, safe schools had on the campus, paying particular attention to youth social and spatial movement on campus, trust, and the interplay between formal control and informal trouble handling among youth. We engaged in go-alongs with school staff and positioned ourselves in many of the vantage points we discovered a decade earlier in order to observe youth. Without a larger fieldwork team, we relied more extensively on these observations, interviews, and maps sketched and discussed by youth. We deepened our historical and institutional perspectives of the school by collecting police call and institutional data and constructing a historical archive of a century of NWHS yearbooks and other materials. Appendix A contains additional notes on the internal organization of the fieldwork team, data collection and analysis, and our interview guides. The list below summarizes these modes of inquiry and our original textual, visual, and institutional data sets.

Data Streams Summary

Textual data

- Observational fieldnotes and analytic memos
  - o 1,524 single-spaced pages of observational fieldnotes produced by Adelman, Bejarano, Gray, Jones, Morrill, Musheno, and Yalda, 1997–2001
  - o 247 pages of observational field notes and analytic memos produced by Morrill and Musheno, 2002–2007
  - o 481 single-spaced pages of observational fieldnotes and analytic memos produced by Morrill and Musheno, 2008–2013
  - o 94 ethnographic trouble cases and strings based on observational fieldnotes, 1997–2001
- Interview transcripts and notes
  - o Transcripts and notes from semistructured interviews with youth (n = 27) & staff (n = 19), 1998–2001
  - o Transcripts and notes from focus groups (n = 5) with youth, 1999–2000
  - o Transcripts and notes from focus groups with youth (n = 8) and staff (n = 8), 2008
- Youth-authored trouble cases
  - o 9th grade (n = 267), 1997
  - o 9th grade (n = 259), 1998
  - o 12th grade (n = 51), 1998
- Survey
  - o "How NWHS Works for You" open-ended survey of 11th and 12th graders (n = 72), 1999
- Archives
- NWHS student club descriptions from yearbooks and newspaper articles, 1913–2013
  - o NWHS student club diaries and student handbooks, 1938–2013
  - o Local newspaper articles, obituaries, and textual website materials, 1900–2013
  - o Review of *New York Times* for articles on the national criminal justice–leaning safe schools movement, 1980–2013

Visual data

- Maps
  - o 11th grade mapping exercise (map n = 122), 1999
  - o 11th and 12th grade mapping exercise (map n = 8), 2008

- Photos
  - o Youth-made photographs and essays from the photo-narrative project (n = 61), 1999
  - o Researcher-made photographs, 2000–2001
  - o Youth-made photos posted on youth websites, 2000–2013
- Archives
  - o NWHS and New West School District visual website materials, 2000–2013
  - o NWHS yearbook photos and essays, 1913–2013

Institutional data

- NWHS demographics from district and school, 1913–2013
- New West Police call data, 1995–2009
- US and state reports on school demographics and safety, 1990–2013

Examples provided in this manuscript, unless otherwise specified, are representative of typical patterns in the data. One counterexample to this convention involves the aforementioned violence that we discuss in chapter 7—an incident in late 1999 during our third year of fieldwork, referred by those on campus as "the Fight" or "the October Fight," and which we came to capitalize in our fieldnotes to emphasize its singularity in our observations up to that point. The Fight involved violence to a level that had not occurred in our first years on campus and helped justify the safe schools policies already adopted. It gave us collective pause and ultimately acted as a critical incident spurring us to further link peer trouble to changes in school structures, providing a route for understanding the longitudinal interplay between formal administrative and informal peer controls on the campus.

A Note on Language and Difference

Throughout this book, we draw on a lexicon that students and adults deployed to describe and explain difference, identities, peer relations, space, and trouble, linking this lexicon to relevant theoretical constructs. Our reasons for this approach are threefold. First, the close attention to language enables an understanding of how youth represent local meanings in comparison to adults, which points directly to power relations. For example, youth and the teachers they trusted framed safe schools very differently than the administration and their allies, particularly during the period of its intensive implementation. Second, our attention to language helps chart continuities and discontinuities in school structures and climates over time. As noted earlier in this chapter, for example, youth and adults used similar language to talk about handling trouble a decade apart, even as they parsed the language they used during the intense safe schools period that divided those two periods on campus. Third, our tracking of language enables us to understand how social differences, especially based in age, gender, race, ethnicity, and/or social class, intersect to reproduce and interrupt social inequality in everyday school life.[69] Language in use, deployed unofficially and officially, thus offers a window for understanding how youth and adults constituted power relations, trust, and change.[70]

We regard "ethnicity," "race," "gender," "social class," "youth," "gay," "trans," "straight," and "disability" as among many of the lived, socially constructed categories at NWHS and many high schools in the US and elsewhere. These categories appear in everyday and official language, helping to situate youth in social and institutional hierarchies, as well as relational and spatial contexts.[71] In the text, when we deploy and interrogate these categories, we draw directly from how NWHS students and staff use such labels in English and Spanish (when possible).[72] Short quotes from participants derive, unless otherwise noted, from our fieldnotes, while longer quotes come from taped, in-depth interviews. In some contexts, we use panethnic labels found in common parlance at NWHS, such as "African American," "Asian," "black" (which included all African Americans and the few youth who identified as black but not African American), "Native American," or "white." Youth and adults typically used the panethnic label "Latino" to refer to groups of female and male youth with ties to or ancestry from Latin America. By contrast, when referring to particular female youth with ties to Latin America, youth and adults used "Latina." During our fieldwork, older staff sometimes used the term "Hispanic" to refer to male and female Latino youth, although youth rarely used this term. An earlier generation of staff from the 1930s to the 1950s used "Spanish" to refer to Latino youth and the earliest generation, from the 1900s to the 1920s, used the term "Mexican," paralleling youth usage in the 1990s and early in the twenty-first century. Youth and adults at NWHS used the term "mixed" to denote identities that crossed categories, such as "Latino," "black," or "white." We note when we use official ethnic categories from institutional data.

The intersection of the concepts "race" and "ethnicity" depended upon whose perspectives and which groups became involved in any given social

situation. The diverse student body at NWHS facilitated youth consciousness of social identities, including white youth, who did not generally express their "whiteness" as a "normalized," default category of difference.[73]
Youth at NWHS generally referred to persons identified as "black" and
"white" as belonging to different "races," although within each group,
youth recognized different national and regional origins, as in "she's Irish"
or "I think his family's from the Caribbean." Youth also recognized peers
with multiple racial or ethnic identifications, often referring to them as
"mixed" or by identifications that comported with the peer group with
which they were hanging out at the time (e.g., peers might identify a mixed
Latino/white youth as Latino in one group and as white in another depending upon the composition of the group).[74] Latino youth sometimes
referred to themselves and other Latinos in racial terms (especially in
contrast to black youth), yet opted to a greater degree for national identities, for example, as "Mexicans," "Mexicanas," "Mexicanos," or "Salvadore-
ños." To a much lesser extent, US-born youth of Mexican descent referred
to themselves as "Mexican Americans," preferring the terms "Chicana" or
"Chicano". As we document in the next chapter, NWHS students crossed
ethnic and racial lines in their peer relations with great regularity, yet contributed to the divide in the student body between US-born Latinos and
newly arrived Mexican immigrant youth. How youth used language with
regard to racial and ethnic categories thus reinforced and bridged group
boundaries.

Gender categories, and especially heteronormative senses of masculinity and femininity, loom large on any US high school campus, and NWHS
proved no exception.[75] We detail how youth talked and wrote about these
norms as they related to peer relations and trouble, at times linking these
dynamics with issues concerning sexual identity when they arose. We ge-
nerically chose to refer to male and female students as "young men" and
"young women" to reflect the liminal status of youth at this age—older than
"boys" and "girls" yet younger than adult "men" and "women." NWHS students did not refer to social class differences among themselves with great
regularity, most likely due to the relative lack of variation in household
incomes among the largely poor or near-poor neighborhoods where they
lived. Yet they did discuss the material constraints and stigma they faced
individually and collectively as NWHS students. These references occurred
especially among black and Latino youth as their identities intersected with
social class and gender.

What Lies Ahead

Chapter 2 establishes a baseline for peer relations, meanings of campus space, and social trust during the late 1990s. We first identify a form of freedom of association and spatial movement on campus that youth call "hangin' out" and "movin' around," which we came to label analytically as *anchored fluidity*. This dynamic refers to youth grounding themselves in meaningful peer relations while engaging in mobility across diverse peer groups and space. We argue that anchored fluidity is the key social mechanism that links social trust to conciliatory-remedial responses to peer trouble. The second half of chapter 2 directly examines the language youth use to articulate trust on campus. We then explore the historical underpinnings for trust at NWHS by drawing from a century of archival evidence pointing to the role of student organizations in collective civic action on campus.

Chapters 3–6 investigate how youth made sense of and responded to interpersonal trouble during a period of high trust and anchored fluidity in the late 1990s. In chapter 3, we introduce the local lexicon that youth (and adults) used to describe the issues that spark trouble. For many youth, the language of dignity and respect tied more to gender dynamics than ethnic and racial identities or neighborhood loyalties. Next, we inventory a repertoire of actions in ongoing peer relations that constitute the stakes, processes, and potential outcomes of peer control: how young people navigate conflict, in their own words, to "work out" trouble without escalation; how youth "put" peers "in their place" in ways that sometimes spill into violence; and how youth deal with and mobilize "the system" of official authority. Taken together, youth tend to work out peer trouble and conflict rather than put peers in their place or turn to the system. Chapters 4 and 5 take a more nuanced look at how youth pursue conciliatory-remedial responses to trouble and what happens when peer trouble involves moralistic orientations and conflict. Chapter 6 explores how youth position themselves vis-à-vis formal rules on campus, focusing especially on the inequities experienced by black and newly arrived Mexican immigrants.

Chapter 7 examines the unanticipated dynamics associated with carceral-like safe schools implementation early in the first decade of the twenty-first century, documenting how youth language and images of trouble at NWHS changed, increasing rates of police calls, and contestation and normalization of departures from official policy. The chapter uses the Fight as a lens to unpack the relationship between changes in formal and informal control on campus. In chapter 8, we move more than a decade after the arrival of safe schools to the campus, offering evidence for how informal and formal control recoupled on campus and with it an alignment of trust and peer relations. This final chapter concludes with implications for our findings, including the significance of knowledge and authority on the frontlines of schools, the role of trust in moderating conflict among diverse young people, and local social resilience in a neoliberal-paternal era.[76]

Much of this book can be read as evidence supporting an observation made by Erving Goffman that a great deal of social order ". . . is sustained from below . . . in some cases in spite of overarching authority not because of it."[77] We are not making a blanket case that young people should be left entirely to their own devices, or that they will always find a way. Nor are we dismissing the importance of adult authority and control, particularly on the frontlines of a school. We are, instead, making a case that the creation and maintenance of a rich educational environment on a high-poverty or any school campus requires a commitment to youth agency. This means attending to youth sociospatial mobility and organizational sensibilities; respecting the local knowledge of teachers as a force in social ordering from the bottom up and middle out; and facilitating collaboration among youth and adults to channel trust into continuous social adaptation and change.

TWO

Anchored Fluidity and Social Trust

Scholars typically investigate youth conflict on high-poverty campuses with climates dominated by social distrust, including zealously guarded ethnic territories, public defenses of neighborhood or gang turf, and huge gaps in relational ties between students and teachers.[1] This chapter reveals a different slice of peer and spatial relations at NWHS during our first years of fieldwork, the period from 1997 to 2000, when students handled most trouble with one another through a variety of nonviolent strategies. At the heart of these relations is what students called "hangin' out" and "movin' around" campus apart from scheduled class time, like lunch or before and after school. Hangin' out and movin' around—analytically, anchored fluidity—involves finding places within and across spatial and sociocultural lines, and going on and off the "frontstages" of peer relations, sometimes relocating in and around "sanctuaries" or classrooms of trusted teachers. The concept of anchored fluidity emerged inductively from our fieldwork, theoretically moored to research on teens' tendencies to anchor their peer relations around social similarities and space in order to assert identity and autonomy while engaging in fluid relational and spatial movement.[2] We found anchored fluidity to be a key relational mechanism linking social trust with youth practices of informal trouble handling on campus, built up over decades through collective civic action on campus.

A First Look at Anchored Fluidity

A representative fieldnote from Cal offers an initial sense of anchored fluidity during a typical day at NWHS:

Just before lunch, a trickle of students walks through the main quad from the east, with a few turning up the breezeway to head north. Almost all these students carry something—manila folders, notebook-sized papers or, in one instance, what looks to be a rolled-up poster. They walk in quick, purposive clips, suggesting that they are on errands of some kind, perhaps trying to finish up before lunch. . . . .With the loud ringing of the lunch bell, the main quad, what students call "downtown," comes alive, filling up with hundreds of youth flowing in from all parts of campus. Instantly, lines of students snake out from the small cafeteria and the snack shack. The thick aroma of cooking meat wafts over the quad from the vent on the cafeteria roof.

Some students sit closely together at the few picnic tables on the large concrete pad in the center of the quad, but most sit on the dusty, dirt/grassy areas just off the quad or on the low-slung, wide concrete walls that border the quad. Students sitting on the ground in small groups of four to six arrange themselves in circles and semicircles; sometimes crowded so closely together that their shoulders almost touch. A few students sit alone, eating, reading books, writing in notebooks, wearing headphones listening to music, or reclining on their elbows, staring up at the sky. Larger groupings, each with three dozen or more youth, sit in interlaced (reticulated) circles with their belongings scattered about, chatting and laughing in animated ways. Students call groups "mixed" that include youth of various social, ethnic, and gender identities. Multiple mixed groups sit in smaller and larger groupings throughout the quad. Perhaps the largest group on the quad is what students call the "black group," which includes fifty to sixty black students sitting together with approximately a dozen nonblack youth on the dusty, dirt/grassy area just off the concrete pad. Students sit and stand in small groups in the shade cast by the edge of administrative building roof. Further out from the concrete pad away from the cafeteria and administration building toward the band building lay multiple, musical instrument cases. Two youth—one young woman with pale skin and long brown hair pulled back in a ponytail and the other a dark skinned male with flowing dreadlocks—play an impromptu, jazzy duet on alto saxophones. Other students in the same vicinity, some wearing blue "NWHS Falcons Band" t-shirts, begin keeping beat with the sax players by tapping on band cases, underscoring the social and aural rhythm of the scene.

On the opposite side of the quad, students sit at folding tables with signs identifying clubs for which they are recruiting members and advertising activities, such as "S.T.A.N.D." [Socially Together and Naturally Diverse], "Entrepreneur Club," or "BSU" [Black Student Union]. There is constant movement among all the groups, as youth move across space occupied by others, often greeting those they see or simply nodding their head and saying "excuse me" as they move through. Students sitting at tables and on the ground constantly look around, dividing their attention from their own groups to peers walking through to other groups sitting near and far. I see a group of five stocky male youth dressed in football jerseys walking in an exaggeratedly slow strut (heads and shoulders back, lifting their feet deliberately) across the middle of the quad. Three look to be black, judging from their skin tones and hair, one has pale skin and light blond, wavy hair, and a fifth could be Latino with very dark skin and slicked-back, black hair. Many students watch them walk through, a few shouting out greetings and others merely acknowledging them with a nod.

I walk thirty yards west into the "Q" building quad, which is less than half the size of the main quad. The density of bodies grows greater. Nearly everyone I hear speaks Spanish in the high-energy, staccato characteristic of Northern Mexico. Youth constantly circulate among a myriad of small groups within the "Q" quad but only a few students pass me coming into that quad—mostly carrying food from the cafeteria or snack shack. As with the main quad, students sit close together in small and larger groups, constantly surveilling their own groups and those around them. I walk out the back of the "Q" quad further west and see two male students playing pingpong at a table set up by the security guards. A cheer or collective laugh from a dozen or more youth onlookers sometimes breaks up the click-clack, click-clack of the game. A group of young men stroll in by the ping-pong table from the multi-acre, dirt/grassy open area that dominates the western side of campus—what youth call the "fields." One of the strolling young men idly bounces a soccer ball on top of his head—a soft thump, thump, thump—laughing as he speaks Spanish to another peer in the group. Several yards from the ping-pong table, the portable basketball hoop the security guards set up hosts a spirited half-court game among mixed youth with several groups of youth milling around just off court. As the game ends, one youth off the court shouts, "We got next."

Now it's only a few minutes until the end of the fifty-minute lunch period and I turn to walk up the main breezeway into what students call the "refuge." Much quieter than downtown, multiple, small groups of three and four young people sit on the dirt/grassy areas between the buildings. I pause to watch a mixed group of two young men and two young women sitting under a lone shade tree between the "J" and "K" classroom buildings. They chat and eat, their backpacks, a couple of thick textbooks, and an open, spiral-bound notebook lay open nearby. They are engrossed in each other and none of them notice me. I remembered a few days ago seeing a

different mixed group sitting under this same shade tree. . . . .I cut over by
"P" building to see small groups of students sitting far apart from each other
in the vast expanse of the fields, and another group of more than a dozen
youth milling around a distant stand of oleander trees, smoking. The bell
sounds, ending the lunch period. . . . .I hover briefly near "P" and overhear
one student anxiously tell another in English that "Roberto" is "out on the
fields somewhere smoking" and "hopes" that he "comes to class with my paper.". . . . .I walk the two minutes it takes to get back to the main breezeway,
which has become clogged with students heading to their classes. I go north-
ward with the flow of students toward "L" building where I will conduct an
interview with a teacher.

Most striking from this scene is the high volume of social interaction and
number of students in downtown, coupled with the public consciousness
of youth as they "constantly look around" in both the main and the "Q"
quads. Youth alight in groups and constantly move from group to group
and place to place. Downtown exhibits many attributes that urban design-
ers use to draw people to outdoor areas to sit alone or in groups, stand and
talk with others, and/or watch others. It has multiple areas and surfaces on
which to sit—a few picnic tables with benches, ledges at sitting level, open
spaces, and shady spots near the school's first buildings on which people
lean, a small basketball court, and ping-pong tables brought out by the security guards that always draw participants and onlookers during lunch.[3]
Downtown offers food, which perhaps accounts for the biggest draw of all.
Different scales of anchored fluidity can be detected in Cal's fieldnote. There
is movement everywhere, but more circulation within the "Q" quad than
between it and the rest of downtown. Youth in the "Q" quad appear more
anchored spatially and socially. Informal lunch activities in and around the
quads are bracketed by gender; male students of different ethnic and racial
identities play ping-pong, soccer, and basketball while females in the vicinity mostly watch, talk, or eat. The exception to this pattern unfolds in the
school band, composed of slightly more young women than young men.

Cal's fieldnote excerpt also illustrates how youth manage and perform
their identities for different kinds of audiences. Here we invoke Erving
Goffman's distinction between the "front" and "backstage."[4] At stake on
the frontstage is public standing, identity, and expectation—"how everyone
sees me," as a Latina senior put it to Cynthia. Youth described the backstage
as contexts "where I can wind down" or "take some time to think a little."
For youth, frontstage performances carried consequences for emotional
well-being, social relations with peers and adults (including the handling

of conflict), and even life chances. During school days on campus, youth-constituted backstages are provisional given the official organization of time and space.[5] In a high-poverty, urban high school, moving on and off frontstages, whether by physically moving to more private locales or momentarily transforming public spaces into more intimate backstages, lowers the stakes for youth and takes them out of the heat of public expectations. These sociospatial moves can broaden opportunities for reflection and alternate lines of action, especially in the context of trouble and conflict.

An epicenter of frontstages constituted the campus downtown and evoked some of the qualities of urban places where diverse people gather to interact and people-watch without fear of predation—what Elijah Anderson calls a "cosmopolitan canopy."[6] In a conversational interview with Michael and Jerlyn, Kendra, a black junior, noted about the quad that "It's where you get you grub on. All kinda students there hangin' out, see what up, enjoyin' each other." The vast majority of students we talked with in the late 1990s emphasized these two qualities of downtown—it offered food and a place for diverse cross-sections of the student body to socialize. Downtown and, more specifically, the quad also evoked qualities of "staging areas," in Elijah Anderson's sense, where the environment promotes youth engagement and observation of code-of-the-street "campaigns for respect."[7] In staging areas, youth generally remain wary of peers with whom they do not have close ties and regard such places as potentially dangerous. The youth wearing football jerseys, slowly strutting through the quad, signaled a sense of a campaign for respect, although their personas ironically linked to institutionally condoned football violence rather than the street. Some students, such as Lincoln, a black sophomore who proved especially keen on cultivating a "street image," articulated a strong sense of the quad as a staging area when he responded to a question from Jerlyn in an interview about how he walks through downtown: "You walk there [downtown] you gotta represent, you know. The way you carry you head, a little cocked, you know. You gotta walk strong. I mean, everybody watchin'."

Backstages formed in downtown typically last for only a few moments until peer groups disrupt them seeking space or by the myriad frontstage performances that draw youth attention away from intimate moments. Moreover, backstage interactions among youth are time sensitive. They occur in the temporal interstices of the school day: quick, punctuated bursts between classes or stolen, out-of-class moments with few other students or adults present. To create more durable backstages that last for several minutes or as much as an entire lunch period (or before and after school), youth seek out sparsely populated and/or physically occluded spaces. In downtown, such space can be found in hallways and staircases leading in to "Q" building and beyond "Q" to the west near the vocational classrooms.

North up the breezeway, as Cal's fieldnote illustrates, the refuge offered more opportunities for backstages less prone to interruptions, fewer people, and more amenable architecture, including multiple spaces between buildings and empty interior classroom hallways. Youth distinguish backstages from the public frontstages in downtown and the crowded main breezeway after lunch and between classes. Two youth-made photos from the photonarrative exercise in which two dozen students, representing a cross-section of the student body, received cameras to make pictures and write essays about "scenes around campus that mean something to you [them]" offer a sense of how youth saw these places. In the first, Bill, a white senior, made a picture of the main breezeway after lunch (figure 2.1), which illustrates an aspect of the frontstages that youth constitute and navigate on a daily basis. He titled his brief narrative about why he made the picture "Humanity on the Breezeway." Bill, standing at nearly 6′6″, wrote that he ". . . wanted to give people a sense of my perspective. After lunch it's intense on the breezeway, like a rushing stream of humanity. Everyone can see everyone. I can look out over everyone but I still get swept up in the stream."

Figure 2.1. "Humanity on the Breezeway": NWHS students fill
the main breezeway on their way to class, 1999

Figure 2.2. "Simple Life": Students on the backstage in a
New West High School building hallway, 1999

In figure 2.2, Lupita, a Chicana junior, depicts a backstage scene from the refuge in which three youth eat their lunch in an empty indoor, classroom hallway. She titled her picture "Simple Life" and wrote that she made the picture

> to show the lighting coming through the window shining down on [Jack] while he was eating with [Carol] and [Maria]. It created a kind of silhouette. Then I started thinking about what the picture really shows. It shows that not all teenagers are wild and crazy during their free time. Sometimes things are simpler. We eat sitting down in a hallway and have conversations. Then the bell rings. Next class. Simple.

Consistent with Lupita's account, we rarely witnessed or uncovered stories about youth acting "wild and crazy" in the refuge. As idyllic as this pattern seems, we do not romanticize seclusion in high schools. We recognize that on many urban high school campuses, youth and adults regard deserted, dark hallways, classrooms, and restrooms, as well as the nooks and crannies between buildings, as potentially dangerous places and, sometimes, as places where violence occurs. At NWHS, youth and adults regarded these potentially vulnerable areas as relatively safe opportunities for solitude and repose. Sarah, a white senior, talked with Billy Gray (a fieldworker) about how she understood the refuge in a conversation about social groups on campus: "I've never been afraid hanging out with friends or alone between the buildings, in the buildings at lunch or after school. I mean, stuff can happen on this campus, for sure. But people look out after each other here."

Classrooms, official frontstages for much of the day, become important backstage places before and after the school day, and during lunch. Although many teachers eat in the staff lunchroom near the quad or leave campus shortly after the official school day ends, more than two dozen teachers, well attuned to youth, stay in their classrooms during lunch as well as before and after school to prep or wrap up their work. These teachers keep their empty classrooms open to groups of students who wish to eat lunch, hang out, or meet in their clubs. As they host students in their classrooms informally, teachers sporadically walk through the areas around their classrooms, into the hallways, and even outside into the open areas between classroom buildings to "keep an ear to the ground," as Mrs. Robinson says in chapter 1.

Observations of Michael Rupp offer a poignant illustration of these teachers and their actions. During lunch periods, a dozen or more students routinely hung out in Mr. Rupp's "K"-building classroom, draped over student desks, eating their lunches in smaller groups of two or three. He typically sat at his "back-of-the-room" desk—the one with all the supplies and records—correcting papers for his tenth-grade history classes or preparing exercises for his junior-level social studies class. When he needed something from his "teaching desk," he shared a laugh with students about campus gossip or the entertainment world and made his way forward. Mostly, students kept to themselves and he to himself. As Mr. Rupp put it, "You get some regulars and you get some newcomers who come for the first time with friends to hang for a while. It's a pretty diverse group, probably more young women than guys, but maybe not." Occasionally, he asked students talking "too loud" to "take it outside." And he sometimes took it outside himself, eating his lunch on the scraggly, brown grass between "K" and "L" buildings and enjoying a few minutes of sunshine. Mr. Rupp had taught at NWHS for nearly a decade. With a ruddy-light complexion, pale blue eyes, and a shock of red hair, he looked a bit younger than his early forties. In a discussion with Billy about his approach to students, Mr. Rupp described his classroom as having an "an open-door policy" during free periods, which meant "a lot of students hang out in my room during lunch or after school if I don't have Key Club (an international youth organization, with chapters in hundreds of high schools, dedicated to facilitating high school students engaging in social projects to help children in local communities); I guess it's a bit of a sanctuary, a cocoon from the commotion of the day."

Mr. Rupp's sanctuary illustrates a key set of resources on campus that enables the creation of backstages for youth (with adults in supportive, moderating roles). Aside from Mr. Rupp's "sanctuary," we identified four others in the refuge (in "D," "J," "K," and "M" buildings) and one comprising two adjacent classrooms in "Q" building. Teachers on the faculty who created "sanctuaries" formed an important veteran core of the NWHS faculty, some having taught at NWHS since the 1970s. Teachers who sustained these practices and orientations not only brought important elements of the past to inform the present, but also responded to new student populations in ways that signaled space as mutually available to staff and students, thus strengthening and instantiating trust into the school's everyday culture.

Focusing on Space and Movement

To gain a broader and deeper visual sense of space and youth movement at NWHS, we examined two kinds of maps of the campus, the first an official representation and the second drawn by students. Figure 2.3 represents an official map of the current, open-air campus of low-slung brick buildings, which opened in the mid-1950s. This campus replaced the original three-story building that housed the old campus, built early in the twentieth century. Two of the city's busiest streets, Rio Leon Road and New West Road, bound the southern and eastern borders of the current campus, respectively, with railroad tracks on its northern and western borders. Some of the poorest neighborhoods in the metro area lie off the edges of campus among strings of warehouses, small factories, and a few strip malls leading to a local college.

In the southeast corner of the campus stands a hub of original buildings dating from the 1950s that frames the main quad. These buildings include the administrative/security offices that officially designate the entrance to the school (building "B"), student guidance offices ("C"), the staff lunchroom ("O"), cafeteria ("N"), and library ("J"). Additional construction in the 1960s resulted in: two large parking lots along Rio Leon and New West Roads; an auditorium and adjacent classroom buildings ("A," "H," and "I"); a two-story building ("Q") that frames the "Q" quad and contains

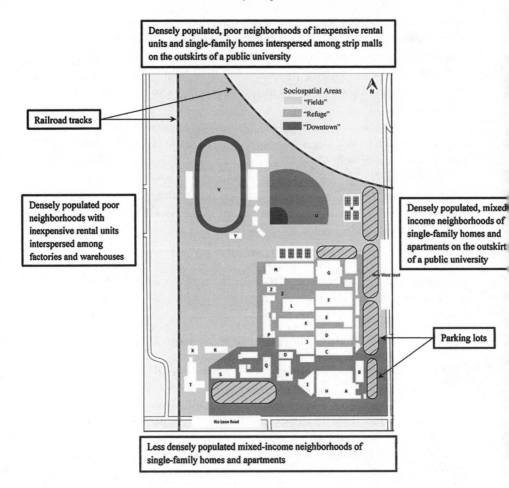

Figure 2.3. Official map of New West High with student-perceived sociospatial areas, 1999

the humanities and English as a Second Language (ESL) programs; vocational education classrooms ("S" and an unlabeled building north of "Q"); the unlabeled snack shack east of "O"; art and science classrooms ("P"); several all-purpose classroom buildings ("D," "K," "E," "L," "F," "M") arrayed south to north along the outdoor main breezeway in the refuge; the electrical plant ("Z"); and, on the northeastern side of campus, the gymnasium ("G"), a parking lot, and tennis courts ("W"). A few small storage buildings dot the fields on the western side of campus.

Now consider how NWHS students visualized campus space and peer relations during our first few years of fieldwork. We asked a cross-section of eleventh graders in required English courses (which also included some Mexican immigrant youth) to sketch maps of the parts of campus they knew well and place on their maps where they hung out when not in class (identifying themselves as "me") and the peer groups they typically saw during free periods, such as lunch or before and after school.[8] Of the 120 students asked to complete the exercise, 114 drew maps, of which seventy-seven offered representations of individuals and groups in physical space, what we call "sociospatial maps."[9] Susana, a junior born in the United States whose

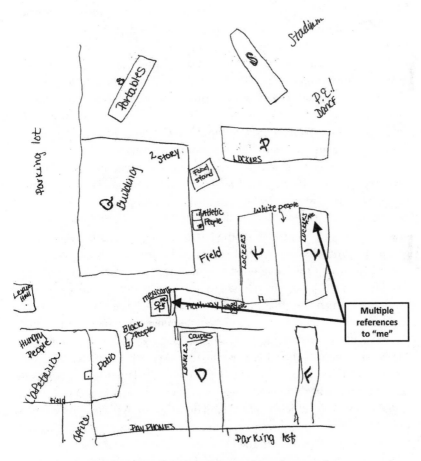

Figure 2.4. Susana's sociospatial map of a southeast portion
of the New West High School campus, 1999

parents emigrated from Mexico, drew a typical sociospatial map, which appears in figure 2.4. In the lower left of her map appears the administration "office," "cafeteria," a "field" (the dirt/grassy area to the east of the cafeteria that borders the main quad), and a "patio." Dominating the center of her map is a "2 story" structure ("Q") with a "Food stand" (a temporary cart) next to its northwest corner near a "field." Susana's rendering includes several places where we observed youth congregating during free periods and between classes, including "Lockers" in "D," "K," and "L" and a bank of "Pay Phones" between "D" and the "Office."

Multiple peer groups appear on Susana's map, including what social psychologists of adolescence call "crowds"—large groups of young people with shared identities.[10] Among the crowds Susana identifies, three reference ethnic and racial identities: "Black People" and "Mexicans" appear in the open space between the cafeteria and "Q" building, while "white people" congregate outside the western end of "K" building with a small arrow indicating their movement into the outdoor space between "K" and "L." She identifies two additional crowds, one associated with school-based activities ("Athletic People" outside of "Q") and the other, emotional and physical states ("Hungry People" in the "Cafeteria"). Susana identifies "couples" who appear inside "D" near some "Lockers."

Across the seventy-seven sociospatial maps, youth generated 151 identity categories that they applied to their maps 379 times. We coded these labels according to how youth identify peer groupings on campus and arrived at percentages of labels (based on 379) appearing on the sociospatial maps: (1) 42 percent of the labels referenced youth-centered peer groupings primarily created and sustained by youth without adult moderation (of which the three most common were "friends," "stoners," and "couples"); (2) 25 percent of the groupings referenced ethnicity, race, or gender (of which the three most common were "Mexicans," "Black People," and "mixed group"); (3) 22 percent referenced student clubs (of which the three most common were "club members," "S.T.A.N.D. people," and "Anytown people"—the latter two clubs are explicitly oriented toward ethnic and racial inclusion); and (4) 11 percent of the labels referenced adult-centered/official activities and categories (of which the three most common were "freshmen," "athletes," and "band nerds"). Youth placed 69 percent of the 379 labels in downtown, concentrated in the main quad; 21 percent in the refuge; and 10 percent in the fields and parking lots.[11]

Susana's sociospatial map provides a useful point of departure for further exploring anchored fluidity. Susana placed herself in her map twice:

first in a "Mexicans" peer crowd (identified as a bubble on the quad) and by the "Lockers" in "L" building. In response to a question from Cal about why she placed herself in her map multiple times, she said:[12]

> I'm friends with some Mexicanas. We met in MEChA (Movimiento Estudiantil Chicano de Aztlán or, in English, Chicano Student Movement of Aztlán, a national youth organization dedicated to promoting pride in Mexican culture). We camp out for a while on the quad, always a lot to see, or walk up the breezeway and eat on the grass between buildings. It's quieter there. Sometimes when I'm bored, I walk up all the way to see white friends eating lunch in L by the lockers. It's even more quieter there. It's like, we trade food. Sometimes my Mexicana friend, her *abuela* [Grandma], she makes these killer tamales, she come with and one of my Jewish friends bring this noodle thing with raisins [an Ashkenazi Jewish dish, commonly called kugel].

Susana illustrated how she brackets her friends as "Mexicanas," "white," and "Jewish" and locates them in particular places on campus, speaking as well to relational and spatial fluidity as she and her friends move back and forth among places and groups.

Aggregate analysis of the sociospatial maps offers additional evidence for anchored fluidity among youth on campus, apart from the school bell-driven movement of class changes. In 68 of the sociospatial maps, youth included themselves at least once as "me," and total self-references numbered 164 "me"s with an average of a little more than two per map. Overwhelmingly, youth placed themselves within social groups, most often in broad, social crowds, such as the "Mexicans" label in Susana's map, rather than in small social cliques or romantic pairings. In fifty-five of the sociospatial maps, youth located themselves in at least two places, with one-third of those maps locating a "me" within the same group that appears in multiple locales. These maps signal that peer social life on campus takes place on the move from place to place; it is literally walked or, for students with physical disabilities, rolled by wheelchair, aided by the flat physical plane of the campus. For other youth, everyday social life on school grounds is walked or rolled, but in more constrained spaces. Among the twenty-one youth who placed a single "me" in their maps, thirteen appear in or near "Q" building, with most of these self-references linked to labels referring to "Mexicanos" or "Mexicanas." Of the six maps drawn by youth identifying as Mexican immigrants, four have a single "me" in the "Q" quad.

Facilitating and Constraining Crossing Sociocultural Lines

In addition to spatial movement, anchored fluidity involves the routine crossing of social and cultural lines. Carlos, a mixed Chicano/white senior, described to Cynthia what facilitates and constrains crossing sociocultural lines on campus:

CYNTHIA: Do kids hang out with people different from them or only the same?

CARLOS: Both. Some kids hang in racial groups. Black kids hang with black kids; you see them at lunch on the quad. Mexican kids hang with Mexican kids. You see them around Q. Kids who don't speak Spanish give Mexicanos a hard time so maybe they [Mexicanos] closer to Q where the ESL classes are. . . . [W]hite kids hang out with white kids in the quad and in the buildings.

CYNTHIA: So kids have places they like to hang out on campus?

CARLOS: Yeah. Kids have spots they like, like favorite places. No one's got a territory totally staked out. Like if you cross here, you're not gonna get beat down or nothin'. ESL folks, they hang by Q, but I hang out with different kinda people over there too because there's a lot of stuff happening. There's the ping-pong tables, you know. Some teachers are cool too; sometimes I eat my lunch with my friends in the classrooms over there. Sometimes I'm on the computers in the library. . . . People move around.

CYNTHIA: Do people get to know people in different groups on campus?

CARLOS: Yeah.

CYNTHIA: How does that happen?

CARLOS: It happens in class a lot. You get in a group with different kids and you do a project, study with them. Science and math programs get different kids together. Kids mix in clubs a lot. Football, mostly black and white. Baseball, Mexican, white, and some Asians. Band's mixed.

CYNTHIA: What about after school on the weekends? Do kids hang out with particular groups then?

CARLOS: You mean like parties and such? You know, there are parties that're racial, only black kids or only Mexican kids or only white kids. But the big parties are pretty mixed. . . . My friends and I are more into the after-parties than the main parties. We hang out, listen to music, little drinking, talk about what's going on, no dancing. Just our friends; sometimes it's kids I know from the neighborhood, sometimes from campus. There's always mixes of different races, you know.

CYNTHIA: What about close friends or couples? Do they mix?

CARLOS: They do. You know, love takes you wherever. Some kids get family pressure to have a girlfriend or boyfriend the same as them. . . . You see mixed couples all over campus.

From Carlos's perspective, race and ethnicity mark the key social and cultural divides on campus. Yet he recognized how academic structures can bring diverse youth together or reinforce peer stigma through school tracking policies. Like Susana, Carlos evoked the importance and abundance of student clubs as contexts in which diverse youth came together. Off-campus, such mixing varies, in that some ". . . parties . . . are racial," but he again noted that the "big parties are pretty mixed," and friendships and social cliques in the "after-parties" cross ethnic, racial, and/or neighborhood lines. With regard to romantic relationships, Carlos saw "love" as a powerful motivator carrying youth across social and cultural lines except when "family pressure" compelled young people to develop relationships with peers of similar cultural backgrounds.[13]

Abelena and Roberta, two eleventh-grade Mexicanas who arrived in the United States only a few years before attending NWHS, added to Carlos's observations about "Q" in a separate, representative conversation with Cynthia:

CYNTHIA: Do you hang out with people different from you or the same?

ABELENA: I'm around Q mostly so I don't see other parts of campus. People I see hang out there are mostly with their own, Mexicanos, Mexicanas. . . . Boys hang with their own more than girls.

ROBERTA: Yeah, guys are more close-minded; they stay with their own. A girl, she might have at least a few friends in another group. You know . . . I hang out with Mexicanas mostly. I do have some friends who aren't Mexicanas.

CYNTHIA: Other than differences between guys and girls, are there any other circumstances when people hang out on campus with different youth?

ROBERTA: Yes. You have kids with different backgrounds who hang out together because they're in the same class or in the same club and doing a project together or like the same things. Like if you're into music. There's some [break] dancers from different groups. They dance by M. They're Asian, white, black, maybe some Mexicanos. Other clubs mix people. At MEChA the teachers try to bring us together too. Sometimes works and sometimes not.

CYNTHIA: What do you mean?

ROBERTA: On this campus, people who are different can be respectful and become friends. But if you're Mexicana or Mexicano it can be hard. You get in ESL classes mostly. Not everyone treats you with respect. Some Chicanos or

Chicanas, they make jokes and call you bad names. Most other students are good with us. Some teachers think we're smart and help us. Others don't.

Both Roberta and Abelena discussed how student clubs facilitated crossing social and cultural divides, referencing social tensions on campus between newly arrived immigrants from Mexico and Chicanos. Roberta pointed to tracking, especially ESL, which perpetuated these differences, reducing the proximity of immigrants from Mexico to other students on campus. Her observations pointed as well to different expectations and practices among teachers with regard to Mexican immigrant youth.

Youth perspectives of crossing social and cultural divides on campus reflected their own biographies and social positioning in the school. Carlos's panoramic descriptions of social groups on campus signals features in his biography, especially his embrace of his mixed identity as Chicano and white. At the same time, Carlos described himself as a high academic achiever, a "smart kid," as did several other youth and teachers familiar with him. In many ways, Carlos epitomizes what Prudence Carter calls a "multicultural navigator"—a youth who effectively negotiates different youth- and adult-centered cultural milieus.[14] To us, he is a sociospatial navigator, highlighting his mobility across campus and capacity to understand the cultural and social complexities of space. By contrast, Abelena and Roberta's descriptions resonate with a more focused horizon anchored strongly to their close "Mexicana" friends and the "Q" quad. These two youths' biographies link strongly to their identities as Mexicanas, rather than as Chicanas, opening a window into what Cynthia calls a "spectrum of Mexicanness," which school structures reinforce to produce sociospatial bracketing of Mexican-immigrant youth at NWHS.[15]

Carlos, Abelena, and Roberta's accounts, coupled with our findings from the sociocultural youth maps, raise questions about how pervasively students meaningfully move across sociocultural lines among peers. A consistent finding among scholars who study youth is the anchoring of close peer friendships in homophily—the tendency to form meaningful social attachments with those who are socially similar. Homophily structures much of social life, including interpersonal networks, romantic dyads, job hiring, and residence.[16] As we came to know the campus, we observed homophily in action, especially in downtown, where youth daily checked in and hung with socioculturally similar peers. Our aggregate analyses of the sociospatial maps also show youth on the grounds of NWHS crossing sociocultural lines with considerable regularity, a relational dynamic not commonly reported in the discussion of high-poverty schools.[17] An aggregate analysis of our fieldnotes during the first two years of fieldwork adds further confirmation of the fluid choreography of youth movement across the lines of social similarity.

In our first semester in the field, we counted sixty-six unique "hang out" groups in our fieldnotes, ranging in size from triads to nine youth.[18] Where we could identify youth from two or more ethnic or racial groupings evident on campus, such as "Mexicano" or "Mexicana" (born in Mexico), US-born Latinos (e.g., Chicano, Chicana, or Mexican American), or "African American/black," we coded those groups as "mixed" (multicultural), the term that youth use to refer to diverse groups. We coded groups composed of culturally similar youth using the term "own," which youth use to refer to internally homogenous ethnoracial and/or neighborhood peer groups.[19] Using these criteria, we coded forty-one groups (62 percent) as "mixed" and the rest as "own" (reflective of social similarity or homophily). Three kinds of mixed groups dominated these hang-out cliques in order of their prevalence: youth who identify as white and US-born Latinos, followed by black and US-born Latino-white groups, and groups made up of newly arrived Mexicanos or Mexicanas and US-born Latino youth with active connections to Mexico. The intra-Latino "mixed" groups typically occurred in the context of MEChA events and activities, suggesting that such crossings are facilitated by combined adult and youth agency to bridge this vexing boundary at NWHS and build trust through club formation.

Twenty-one peer groups of the original sixty-six disappeared entirely by the end of our first two years of fieldwork. In another forty groups at least one member left and/or joined the group, and only five groups stayed wholly intact. These findings further substantiate the fluidity in peer relationships on campus. In some instances, two groups formed a single group with a different sociocultural composition, illustrated by Susana's Mexicana and white friends. Another example occurred when two mixed break dancing crews came together at the end of our first year in the field after engaging in informal duels and competitions during much of that year. Each of the sixty-six groups moved across campus on nearly a daily basis, with a subset of fifteen claiming particular places as their "regular spot." However, none of these groups treated their spatial claims as inviolable, often moving their group within large crowds and to alternative spaces both in the quad and to less densely populated areas in the refuge and fields.

Anchored fluidity, including prevalent crossing of sociocultural lines, stands out as distinct when compared to most prior studies of high-poverty schools that show them beset by intense ethnic and neighborhood territoriality and social distrust at the intergroup and institutional levels. To explore why anchored fluidity rather than territoriality defines the socio-spatial life of NWHS, we turn to a direct consideration of trust on campus, first examining evidence of it during the late 1990s and then contextualizing these findings historically.

Student Perceptions of Social Trust

The most concentrated evidence of student trust in NWHS emerged from a representative subsample of students (drawn from the mapping exercise) who responded with brief written answers to our query "How does the school work for you?" Of the seventy-two students in the subsample, sixty-seven answered the question, producing a total of 119 comments. One hundred and three of the comments referenced how the school worked for participants and sixteen comments expressed negative views, or that the school did not work for them.

Many of the positive comments focused on the intersection of inter-group and interpersonal trust. They included forty-seven comments that referenced mutual regard within and respect across diverse peer groups, linking trust most pointedly to anchored fluidity, including: "This school works for me because kids trust each other on campus and there's not alotta [sic] fights like my other school"; "It works for me because people of different backgrounds can count on each other here"; "[NWHS] works for me cause divers [sic] kids get along and work together in clubs on campus"; "I like to be with different kinds of people and different races chill in the quad"; "It works for me becuz [sic] I can move around campus to different friends"; and "It works for me because I'm accepted for who I am." A second cluster of twenty-nine comments gave weight to the intersection of interpersonal and institutional trust among teachers and students, for example: "The school works for me because the teachers trust us and we trust them"; "The school works for me because Teachers care about kids on campus"; or "Teachers think [student] clubs are good and give time." These latter responses dovetail with our discovery of a substantial group of teachers at NWHS who mentored students in clubs and provided informal sanctuaries in and around their classrooms for students to gather in small groups off the frontstages of campus. As we report above, the clubs and sanctuaries are places that enabled spatial movement and the crossing of the ethnic and racial lines of identity. A third cluster, made up of twenty-seven comments, associated the school working for students exclusively with institutional trust. Many of these responses referred to ethnic, racial, and social class inclusion, such as: "The school works for me because it's good for different kinds of kids"; "It works for me because different races get opportunity [sic]"; or "We poor here but that dont [sic] mean it [NWHS] bad. It works."

Of the sixteen negative comments, nine came from young people who also wrote that the school works for them, and seven only wrote how the school does not work for them. The mixed comments included two mentions of social tension between US-born Latino youth and newly arrived immigrants from Mexico (e.g., "It work for me most of the time. It don't work when Chicanos think were [sic] dumb"); two mentions of institutional distrust based in academics by youth identifying as Mexican (e.g., "Mexicanos only get ESL courses"); and one reference to administrative discrimination faced by "Black guys" ("The school work and don't for me. I gotta lot of friends here. Teachers okay. Administration think Black guys always up to something"). Among the seven negative comments without positive comments, one student pointed to tensions among US-born Latinos and Mexican immigrants, one referenced tensions between black students and the administration, and one referenced construction "hassles" on campus. These negative responses revealed that Mexican immigrant and black male students perceived trust less uniformly. Our field research, as reported above, indicated that components in school structures and aspects of the campus climate constrained Mexican immigrant youth from fully participating in anchored fluidity, with many staying close to the "Q" building where most of their classes took place. At the same time, our field observations and mapping data showed black males as significant participants in the sociospatial practices of anchored fluidity.

Overall student responses to the question about how NWHS works for them suggested an alignment of inclusive trust, ranging from the interpersonal to the institutional, among the youth of NWHS. A substantial number of students associated both trusting social ties and institutional trust with school clubs and the teachers who mentored students in these settings, including granting access to their classrooms. But how did these dynamics develop at NWHS? This question led to our historical inquiry of NWHS, which further revealed the importance of clubs and the teachers associated with them over several decades.

A Brief History of Inclusive Collective Civic Action at NWHS

In the latter years of the Arizona Territory in the late nineteenth and early twentieth centuries, white settlers comingled with Mexican-descent settlers, treating them as "near-" and "nonwhite," in part contingent upon whether their families owned ranches, farms, or other businesses.[20] Traces of these blurred ethnic boundaries within social class privilege marked NWHS from its founding by land- and business-holding Mexican-descent and white families during the late Arizona Territorial years early in the twentieth century. Consistent with these practices, the first decade of school yearbooks and newspapers reported a student body "glibly conversing in Spanish and English between classes." These blurred ethnic boundaries, however, did not extend to black, Native American, or Chinese-descent students, who, if they attended school at all, attended segregated schools in a neighboring town.

In the first NWHS yearbook, *The River*, youth with Spanish surnames appear in nearly every extracurricular activity on campus, including the school newspaper, *The Falcon*, academic honor society, orchestra, and several sports teams. The academic honor society, comprised of youth with both Spanish and non-Spanish surnames, raised the first cash prize, donated by an "esteemed," wealthy local farmer, for the Senior Award given to students achieving the highest "grade averages" in the senior class. Carmelita Diaz and Barbara Walsh each received inaugural Senior Awards. Diaz was the daughter of a cotton farmer and textile mill owner who emigrated from Mexico to Arizona with his wife in the last quarter of the nineteenth century and helped organize interstate commercial associations that brought together business owners of Mexican descent from the American Southwest with those from northern Mexico. Walsh was the eldest daughter in a second-generation immigrant family of Irish descent; her family owned the town's flour mill and several other businesses in New West. Diaz and Walsh symbolize the early mix of ethnic and gender inclusion, important building blocks of campus collective civic action.

Other evidence of early collective civic action materialized in the form of NWHS resistance to statutes passed by the newly formed Arizona state legislature that strengthened educational segregation for "African," "Indian," "Chinese," and "Mexican" youth in the 1910s and 1920s.[21] New West City built its first "Mexican" primary (K-8) school in the late 1910s. The nexus of the new "Mexican" school reified the categories of "white" (sometimes referred to as "Anglo" by both whites and Mexicans) and "nonwhite Mexican" persons, in turn sparking legal disputes during the 1920s and 1930s as long-time, land-holding families of Mexican descent contested their exclusion from the original, now "white" New West primary school, where earlier generations of students of Mexican and white youth had attended. Local judges initially ruled in favor of Mexican-descent plaintiffs in multiple cases, recognizing them as legally "white" and therefore eligible to send their children to the New West primary school. A state appeals court, however, overturned these rulings, drawing from the "separate but equal" tenets in the landmark 1896 US Supreme Court case *Plessy v. Ferguson* and redefining youth of Mexican descent as "nonwhite." Until the *Brown* desegregation decision in 1954, segregated public schools operated throughout Arizona.[22]

Despite segregation of New West K-8 schools throughout the 1920s into the early 1950s, NWHS continued to enroll youth of Mexican descent. The uniqueness of NWHS resulted from the strong connection of Mexican-descent families to the school, their legal activism, and the city holding off on building a second high school until the 1960s. Twenty to twenty-five percent of NWHS students depicted in student class photos had Spanish surnames in the 1920s and 1930s as the overall NWHS student population grew from a few dozen youth to more than 300 students. By the late 1930s, the first faculty-mentored student clubs formed apart from sports, drama, music, newspaper, and student government activities. The Spanish Unity Club (SUC) formed in 1939 and first gained entry to *The River* in 1942, becoming the most visible of these clubs. This description appeared under its inaugural group photo:

> This club is a member of the Mexican Youth Organization, which includes members of the states of New Mexico, Arizona, and California. This club is composed of college and high school students who meet regularly with delegates of the other clubs at the college. The [NWHS] club, since its organization three years ago, has been growing in membership and efficiency in carrying out its purposes, which are as follows:
>
> (1) Social and Service, (2) To promote scholarship, (3) To inspire close collaboration with the majority group, (4) To help underclassmen understand the meaning of "unity" with the majority group.
>
> "We wish to extend our deep and sincere thanks to [Mr. Gallagher], who has been our sponsor since this club was organized."

The first two goals in the SUC's mission statement commonly appeared for other student clubs on campus at the time, while the latter two goals broke new ground by signaling a place controlled by Latino youth while simultaneously recognizing the importance of cultural bridging ("collaboration") and assimilation with the dominant white student population. Indeed, the thirty-three-member SUC included a majority of Spanish-surnamed students (twenty-five) and eight students with non-Spanish surnames. Equally apparent in this entry is the US-based character of the NWHS SUC as part of a network of clubs springing up throughout the American Southwest and Mexico, as well as student recognition of a teacher-mentor, Mr. Gallagher.

Throughout this era, articles and editorials in the school newspaper, *The Falcon*, constantly referred to the SUC as among the most "important" and "efficient" clubs on campus, known for organizing successful fund-raising events and cultural, college, and job fairs attended by most NWHS students. The SUC organized the most important extracurricular events, such as the spring dance, either in collaboration or on a rotating basis with other student clubs. By the early 1950s, the SUC had expanded to sixty members—10 percent of the total student population—with two-thirds of its members with Spanish surnames. By the end of the decade, and only a few years after the school moved to its new (and present) campus, SUC membership included one-quarter of the student population, which by then stood at more than 800 students. Nearly half of SUC members had non-Spanish surnames and its group photos include what appears to be black youth.

Aside from its singular importance as an inclusive student club signaling ethnic identity and culture, and involving a broad swath of the student body, the SUC proved important for at least four other reasons. First, the SUC's founding teacher-mentor, Mr. Gallagher, signaled the bridging of cultures in that he was the son of Irish immigrants and married to a US-born Latina. Second, his example of dedication to such a successful club led to a tradition of teachers becoming involved in the SUC and student clubs, including keeping their classrooms open for club activities and garnering resources from the administration. Third, the success of the SUC led to the founding and sustaining of several other clubs over multiple decades that emphasized both ethnic identity and inclusiveness, as well as sustained growth in active clubs tied to skills and opportunities, such as the "Future Farmers of America," "Future Accountants of America," "Aerospace Club," "Computing Club," and the "Car Club." Many of the most popular clubs that emerged in the 1960s and 1970s signaled explicit political and/or ethnic pride agendas, such as the "Young Republicans" (of all white youth) or the "Goldwater Youth" (supporting the conservative presidential campaign of Arizona Senator Barry Goldwater in the early 1960s). Other clubs espoused progressive agendas aimed at social change, such as the Afro-American Club that emerged in the 1960s and became the Black Student Union in the 1970s, MEChA, which emerged from the SUC in the 1970s, and "Anytown," with the mission to "promote brotherhood, unity, and membership open to all students." And fourth, student clubs offered early leadership opportunities for young women. The SUC, for example,

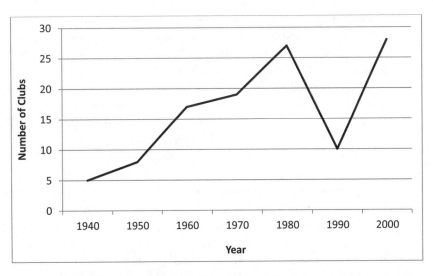

Figure 2.5. Number of student clubs listed in the New West High School yearbook, 1940–2000

elected young women as president multiple times in the 1940s, perhaps initially owing to the depletion of young men in the student body during World War II, and continued to do so on a regular basis after the war. These early leadership opportunities included the student body electing young women to key posts in student government during the 1940s and 1950s, which continued in subsequent decades. During the 1990s, when the campus experienced its highest volume of collective civic action, young women founded multiple student clubs with explicitly inclusive agendas, and the student body elected young women to positions of formal leadership in the largest student clubs and as class presidents every year. Figure 2.5 tracks the volume of student clubs appearing in *The River* from 1940 to 2000. From the 1940s through the 1970s, clubs grew at a steady rate, reaching as high as twenty-seven in 1979 before declining in the 1980s and surging again in the 1990s.

During this same period, the New West city population, economy, housing development and new school construction grew dramatically, but outward from the city center where NWHS is located. Increasingly, the school's catchment area took on the features of low-wage work, warehouses, small factories, and strip malls with single-dwelling housing replaced by low-income apartment buildings. By the 1970s, NWHS grew to more than 1,200 students with increasingly more drawn from lower-income households. The number of Latinos on campus grew steadily in the decade to nearly one-third and whites to just over two-fifths of the student population. Black students, who had barely been a presence on campus owing to the legal segregation in the state until the 1954 *Brown* decision formally desegregated schools nationally, increased their numbers to one-fifth of the NWHS student population.

The vibrancy of student club life on campus continued through the 1960s and 1970s. An alumnus from the early 1970s, and later an NWHS teacher from the 1980s into the 2000s, remembered that "white students outnumbered Hispanics and blacks . . . [with] all being active in student council, sports, and student clubs." Another alumnus remembered "protesting the Vietnam War" during the early 1970s with "white, Latino, and black" students drawn from student clubs. These recollections parallel articles and editorials from *The Falcon* and local community newspapers, which portray the NWHS campus as both a hotbed of organized protest with student clubs often at the forefront and a school with significant career clout with occupational and academic clubs across a broad spectrum of fields.

As NWHS experienced these changes, the district added a second high school in the 1960s and two more in the 1970s to accommodate the city's growth. These newer schools drew increasingly diverse students, especially with Latino and some black families moving into white, middle-class neighborhoods. Fine-grained historical analyses of how youth handled interpersonal and intergroup trouble during these years are not possible, and nor are estimates of gang presence at NWHS available. Local newspapers of the 1960s and 1970s, however, reported at least one instance of inter-ethnic, collective violence involving Latinos, whites, and blacks occurring nearly every year at every school in the district except NWHS. *Falcon* articles reported social tensions among different groups on campus and occasional interpersonal fights, but no reports of collective violence at NWHS. Local newspapers ran articles on the "changing face" of NWHS, noting that the school had a reputation as a "tough urban school." Student editors of *The Falcon* noticed the irony of the growing public reputation of NWHS despite its continuing safety relative to other schools in the growing school district. Throughout the 1970s, *The Falcon* ran editorials and letters to the editor decrying the school's reputation, sometimes linking it not only to the shrinking white population on campus, but also to students' organized political protests, which sometimes joined with student organizations from the local college and drew condemnation from school administrators and some local authorities.

The 1980s marked a period of a dramatic decrease in the school population at NWHS prompted by the arrival in the school's catchment area of increasingly poor Mexican immigrant and black families to fill low-wage jobs and the exit of middle-class Latino and white households to neighborhoods on the periphery of the city. Accompanying this demographic shift, the district diverted resources from NWHS and the older high schools in the district to the construction of new high schools on the peripheries of the town where middle-class planned "communities" emerged. By the middle of the decade, the school shrunk to under 900 students and then, within a three-year period, grew briefly to as high as 1800 students as youth (mostly middle class), waiting for new schools to open closer to their homes, spent one or two years on campus. While a core of dedicated teachers remained, the school experienced considerable turnover as teachers dealt with wildly fluctuating class sizes and temporary appointments at NWHS prior to joining the new high schools elsewhere in the district. This tumult led to a sharp decline in student club presence, reaching a low of ten clubs represented in *The River* by the end of the decade. Moreover, the number of teachers listed as student club mentors declined, reaching a low of three in 1989 from more than thirty-five a decade earlier.

As reported in *The Falcon*, the campus experienced an upsurge in interpersonal and intergroup conflict, which the school administration attempted to manage through an expansion of formal school control and the policing of students in areas just off campus. Local newspapers reported an upsurge in fear of NWHS students by merchants in nearby strip malls as the school came to be referred to in newspapers as a "ghetto school." On campus, the student handbook dramatically expanded from its long-time orientation to student life as a whole to be dominated by an extensive listing of punishments and rules in a matrix that listed categories of offenses, including "possession of alcohol, drugs, or drug paraphernalia," "theft," "assault," "insubordination," "cheating," "parking in unauthorized areas," and "tardiness." Each of these offenses drew different punishments, such as "after-school detention," "suspension" or "expulsion from school," and/ or "referral to the police," depending upon whether they fell under "minor" or "major" offense categories. Although definitive data on how staff applied these rules do not appear in available materials, scores of articles from *The Falcon* reported the constant application of school discipline on campus, and local newspapers reported an intense police presence at New West and its surrounding neighborhoods.

As collective civic action on campus waned and social disorder on and around the NWHS campus became a public issue, the district school board and administration considered closing the school. Alumni, working with what remained of committed teachers and student clubs on campus, managed to keep the campus open through numerous well-organized protests and highly visible public school board meetings reported on by the local press. NWHS alumni, major civic players in the town, and teachers, always had been well organized and active, supporting everyday campus activities and engaging in collective civic action. In the early 1990s, the alumni's capacity for collective mobilization reached deeply into the local community, ultimately generating private and public financial support for campus renovations, rather than closing. These renovations, however, would not begin until later in the decade due to a long planning process with their most visible aspects reframed around safe schools securitization—a dynamic we explore in chapters 7 and 8.

The renewal of NWHS attracted new administrators and teachers, many themselves alumni, who joined with those veterans who remained from the pre-1980s tumult to lead the school in a new direction in the 1990s. NWHS continued experiencing significant demographic change, ultimately becoming a Latino-majority school by the end of the 1990s, and within the Latino population, approximately one-fifth comprised newly arrived Mexican immigrants. Black students held steady at one-fifth the total student body, with a continually shrinking one-fifth composed of white students. During this period, student clubs grew dramatically, reaching an all-time high of twenty-nine in 1999 with more than forty teachers participating in one way or another as club mentors or supporters. A highly visible coalition called "S.T.A.N.D." ("Socially Together and Naturally Diverse") emerged later in the decade, which brought together multiple clubs focused on ethnic and sexual identity, politics, and other political issues. They organized multiple cultural heritage days, community events (working off campus with community organizations), fundraisers, job fairs, dances, and the "Unitown" youth camp "where each member of the community was a human being first, and an important person in his/her own right."

Administrators during this period encouraged, supported, and piggybacked on the upsurge in on-campus collective civic engagement by turning the school's reputation as a "ghetto school" on its head to reposition it in the collective imagination of the local community. In multiple local media reports, teachers, administrators, and reporters championed both the bottom-up and "multicultural" aspects of the school—a place composed of students and teachers "doing good" with few resources and a diverse student body. One long-time teacher, quoted in a mid-1990s local newspaper article, observed: "It's an administration that lets the staff do what it takes. . . . It takes a lot of trust to let go and resist the temptation to . . . rule things from the top." An editorial in the same newspaper opined that the school's academic performance and safety exceeded many of the schools in the district:

> [New West High] is the city's . . . inner-city school. You know, one with a lot of—whisper—minority students. . . . What people don't whisper—probably don't even know—is that [New West High] boasts some of the highest test scores [in the district] on the Scholastic Aptitude Test, the college entrance exam. . . . And [New West High] puts out as many—and often times more— National Merit Scholars than its four sister schools [in the district]. It's also a safe school that students don't fear and like attending. . . . [E]very parent should want to send their child to a school like [New West]. It is a beloved school that uses its diversity to its advantage.

On campus, the complex formal rules and punishments established during the previous decade still existed, but *The Falcon* and local newspapers reported a decline in intense policing and fear of students by nearby merchants, replaced by reports and editorials reframing the public identity of the campus as a striving school that works. School district and police-call data paralleled media reports: As we noted in chapter 1, "serious campus incidents" (including interpersonal violence and theft) and police calls from campus for intervention into fights and other collective violence ranked as the lowest in the district in the latter half of the 1990s.

Social Trust, Anchored Fluidity, and Cultural Flexibility

Each successive NWHS cohort of students and teachers adapted old clubs to new conditions and founded new clubs. This constant invention and reinvention resulted in the reframing of trust as traditional ethnically oriented clubs waned in the 1960s to be reborn in more actively political modes in the 1970s. The overall decline in student clubs in the 1980s proved equally important as it coincided with a deterioration of social trust surrounding NWHS both on and off campus. Without clubs and the solidity of the teaching staff at NWHS, the school's historic capacity to adapt to new conditions diminished, and media reports suggest that social disorder increased on campus, spurred partially by district-level actions and strong bias in favor of new schools in the growing middle-class enclaves of the town's suburbs. Alumni, well versed in collective civic action and with continuous local knowledge and presence on campus, prevented the closing and enabled the renewal of NWHS during the 1990s, even leading to the allocation of much-needed funds for material upgrades on the campus. Active student clubs dedicated to inclusiveness and academic achievement, backed by engaged teachers and alumni, became crucial elements of bottom-up collective civic action for building and sustaining social trust at NWHS.

When we began fieldwork on campus in 1997, we did so amidst a period when inclusive structures and the school climate aligned, revealing social trust as a sociocultural bedrock enabling anchored fluidity to flourish. Such alignment did not perfectly encompass the entire student body in that Mexican-immigrant and black male youth, together comprising approximately one-quarter of the total student population at NWHS, perceived and experienced social trust at lower levels than the rest of the diverse student body. Drawing on the spanning social trust evident at the school during this historical moment, NWHS students routinely practiced anchored fluidity as they traversed the front- and backstages of social interaction, crossing sociocultural lines. For many students, hanging out and moving around enabled familiarity with many different groups and places, which both signaled and supported social trust on campus. In turn, student networks constantly connected and disconnected, which helped students avoid both sticky identities that can lead to embattled efforts to retain or climb to favorable status positions and the harmful social psychological alienation of peer hierarchies.[23] Anchored fluidity thus facilitated what Prudence Carter calls "cultural flexibility"—the willingness of youth to "navigate across diverse social environs" and "step out of one's skin."[24] In schools, cultural flexibility breaks down barriers, reducing the probability of the stigmatization or stereotyping of any single group, which in turn reduces the likelihood of hostile responses to conflict. Although it is difficult to tease out the causal relationship between anchored fluidity and cultural flexibility, each dynamic reinforces the other, and we would expect to see a decline in one when the other wanes. This chapter, then, sets the stage for exploring how youth managed conflict on a high school campus when the underlying conditions of trust were in place and anchored fluidity operated as routine practice. We turn next to a panoramic view of youth trouble issues and responses evident under these conditions.

THREE

Trouble

What do youth call peer trouble? How do they handle it? What makes peer trouble difficult to handle, or, for that matter, easier to manage? In a school context, young people have to grapple with these issues in a place where peer relations matter most, and yet adults hold considerable sway over them. At NWHS, students drew on a multitude of catch phrases from popular discourse and the local scene to describe the issues that define trouble and the practices deployed to handle it. Our early fieldwork between 1997 and 2000—a time of relatively high social trust and anchored fluidity—revealed a school where code-of-the-street orientations were substantially muted as to how youth perceived the stakes and responded to trouble with peers.

When schools draw from neighborhoods characterized by high poverty and the defense of neighborhood turfs through the deployment of the retributive code of the street, previous research finds that older students recruit younger students into their neighborhood-based campus turf groups and intimidate youth who resist membership or pass through their turf.[1] Fieldwork at NWHS during this period uncovered few such peer formations in and around turf and relatively little interpersonal aggression. Juniors and seniors routinely socialized younger students into the campus climate of trust and perspectives of conflict management that favored, as youth put it, "live and let live," problem solving, and, when needed, adult help. While social trust on campus moderated the impact of aggression and turf claiming, it did not erase street codes from the consciousness or practices of youth and adults. Ninth graders embraced street code discourse more than older students, and some young people, especially first-generation immigrant youth from Mexico, disproportionately experienced social distrust and put-downs from other youth.

With close attention to the campus climate, we discovered a gap between how youth narrate the issues that spark peer trouble and how they responded to it. With time, we recognized that the space between naming trouble and responding to it creates an opportunity to deepen an understanding of what youth take into account as they de-escalate or escalate troubling encounters. This chapter first explores how youth characterized various trouble issues, ranging from personal to collective social problems; we then unearth the range and social distribution of peer trouble responses. We offer an analytic strategy, through the use of trouble strings, to represent how youth trouble responses transform the meanings of conflict that combine attention to the relational, spatial, and temporal dynamics in play. Along the way, we consider how youth include adults in their navigation of trouble.

Trouble Issues

One morning on campus, Paul, a senior living in a densely populated poor neighborhood of largely black families west of campus, gave Jerlyn his views of the kinds of peer trouble he faced at NWHS:

JERLYN: What kinds of situations are there on campus where people aren't getting along? Any trouble?

PAUL: Some of it is with gettin' treated right, you know. A guy hooks up with another girl and his girl, like, she pissed. She gettin' treated like shit, you know. You get some drama. . . . I seen beefs with guys in the cafeteria over a dirty look. It's respect, you know. With adults, maybe a teacher's a hardass or whatnot. Treat us like little kids; do this, don' do this with no clear reason or just cuz they say it. . . . .Most teachers is alright, you know. Some not.

JERLYN: What about trouble off campus? Can that cause trouble on campus?

PAUL: People don' bring bad stuff on campus too much. Nobody want it here, kids, teachers, guards. . . . If you got bad stuff going on outta school with kids you see at school, you can give 'em room or even talk, you know. You can move around. Not like some places [in the community] where you go. Somebody say, "Who you? Where you from?" I ain't afraid here.

Paul's observations highlighted what youth called "drama"—concerns about interpersonal dignity ("gettin' treated right" or "gettin' treated like shit") intertwined with romantic relationships.[2] He observed that most teachers were "alright" but mentioned arbitrary exercises of authority from some teachers ("cuz they can") that left youth feeling like "little kids." All young people experience these concerns at some level given their liminal position, as neither children nor adults, and the asymmetrical power that adults in authority hold over them. The challenges of this contradictory position and adult authorities, cops to teachers, ruling over them are particularly pronounced for youth in high-poverty schools, and sharpened by anxieties about social distrust and peer violence.[3] Paul, whom we came to know as a shrewd and keen observer of the campus, suggested how the campus climate muted these anxieties ("nobody want it here") while constituting a place of security ("I ain't afraid here"). At NWHS, social trust moderated the suspicion and anxiety students face in many parts of their lives off campus, while everyday manifestations of anchored fluidity ("you can move around . . .") interrupted off-campus defenses of neighborhood turf that could be imported to campus, or, as Paul noted, situations in which personal and neighborhood identity can fuse into conflict ("Who you? Where you from?").

Youth and adults at New West High used drama to refer to a broad range of trouble involving campus-based: (1) interpersonal relationships among male and female young people, especially involving romantic "breakups," triangles, and sexual exclusivity; (2) competition among young women without male involvement; (3) unwanted sexual attention involving only youth or youth and adults; and (4) youth perceptions of discrimination by adults based on sexual, racial, ethnic, and gender identities.

The stakes in campus-based drama revolved around normative breaches and reputational challenges to heteronormative gendered or sexualized standing as well as power dynamics among youth in friendships and romantic relationships. For example, Monica, a black junior, described the drama created by a sophomore named David, also black, who had "feelings" for one of her friends but did not "know what to do about it." Monica explained to Jerlyn with a wan smile and in a slightly exasperated tone that "there's constant drama with [David] and all us [among her girlfriends]. Constant. He spread nasty rumors about us." She elaborated on the trouble with David, noting that "Kiona [her friend] is hot. We know that. I understand why he afraid; not fair to the rest of us to havin' him drag us through crap. He gotta cut the drama; ask her out." Monica's acknowledgement of Kiona as "hot" spoke to a girl's ability to attract young men as a key power dynamic and status marker integral to heterosexual relations among female and male youth on campus. At the same time, Monica acknowledged David's fear, even putting herself in his shoes for a moment. She also implicated the lack of dignity David afforded her and her friends by spreading gossip that was "not fair" and noted how his inability to "ask her [Kiona] out" undermined David's ability to conform to stereotypical masculinity norms. Male youth used the term "drama" to trivialize the concerns by female youth about their competition over male youth, highlighting stereotypical heterosexual norms of teen masculinity based on mastery of young women.[4] Troy, whom we met in chapter 1, illustrated this tendency as he experienced "little dramas" with his girlfriend who was irritated by him spending "more time with my homies [male friends]" than with her.

Brittany and Cheryl, two black juniors, illustrated female-only drama surrounding Brittany's still-contentious and bitter disappointment over receiving the "second-highest" grade to Cheryl in a class they both took during their freshman year. According to Cheryl, "We've been friends a long time. It's like middle school all over again. The drama continues. Sometimes we joke and sometimes we treat each other badly. I guess that's friendship." Brittany, meanwhile, described Cheryl "as funny" yet "not getting over herself" for earning a slightly higher grade. This example also underscored how youth use drama, as youth researchers Alice Marwick and dana boyd put it, to "blur distinctions between the serious and frivolous . . . [and] what is just joking and what truly hurts."[5] In Cheryl and Brittany's accounts, drama slid back and forth between trouble and nontrouble and could be difficult to discern without a sense of context. Unlike adult-centered terms, such as bullying, that denote fixed roles and power asymmetries between perpetrators and victims, for youth, drama involves agency wrapped up with dynamic interruptions of power in interpersonal relationships.[6]

When drama involved unwanted sexual attention or unfair treatment by peers or adults due to one's ethnicity, race, sex, and/or sexual identity, youth gauged and negotiated power asymmetries carefully. Youth referred to such situations that occurred without public visibility as "personal dramas" or those that cursed through the gossip circuits of the school with great fanfare as "messy dramas." We uncovered a personal drama that involved a male teacher who made offensive asides in class about gays and lesbians that compelled a closeted gay male student to stop attending the class. In this incident, the student never confronted the teacher directly but privately consulted with another teacher on campus who sponsored the "Gay-Straight Alliance" (GSA) student club. The GSA faculty sponsor eventually convinced the teacher in question to cease his remarks in class, all without the student-in-question becoming directly involved, and attend some GSA meetings to, in the sponsor's words, "see what the GSA is accomplishing." The offending teacher did attend multiple GSA meetings and, while never becoming GSA faculty sponsor, became known among students as a teacher who, in the words of one GSA member, "treats LGBTQ kids with respect in his classes."

Off-campus drama pushed beyond interpersonal relationships to encompass code-of-the-street altercations intertwined with neighborhood ethnic and racial identities. This sense of drama resonates with David Harding's findings about how black and Latino male youth in high-poverty urban areas in Boston used the term to describe neighborhood violence.[7] On-campus evidence for these kinds of social tensions occasionally appeared in graffiti on the outsides of campus buildings and walls or in students' notebooks, but we uncovered few conflicts associated with neighborhood drama. As described in chapter 2, youth hung out together in groups assorted by peer relationships and different identities (especially race, ethnicity, and gender) on the main quad during lunch, but these crowds constantly shifted their specific locales and membership. We rarely discerned crowds staunchly defending turf via force or intimidation.[8]

If drama at NWHS largely referred to cross-sex, on-campus trouble with occasional references to off-campus conflict, "beefs" demarcated a stereotypical masculine world of trouble largely devoid of female youth. How male youth at NWHS used beefs seemed even closer to Harding's findings regarding male drama minus the strong linkage to the "protection of . . . home turf."[9] Unlike campus-based drama, beefs typically did not blur the boundaries between trouble and everyday interactions. To be in a beef, according to Pablo, a Mexicano junior, was "to mean business." Moreover, youth typically described beefs at NWHS playing out on the frontstages with audiences that extended beyond proximate peer groups or interpersonal networks.

Although drama and beefs could be racially charged, youth infrequently invoked these terms to refer to peer trouble shaped by ethnic or racial animus—what youth referenced as "racial stuff" (with "shit" often substituted for "stuff" in everyday student parlance) when it was in play. The exception to this pattern were tensions related to what a broad range of youth called "Mexican issues" among newly arrived Mexican immigrant youth and some US-born Latinos. Such trouble typically involved peers demeaning each other for their limited English or Spanish skills, respectively, all the while ironically asserting their pride in being "Mexican." In so doing, Latinos instantiated, crossed, and blurred the identity boundaries of Mexicanness through interpersonal relationships. Such boundaries also were crossed and reproduced in student clubs, especially MEChA, even as some members on both sides of this divide claimed they would "never work together." Moreover, some youth (especially those who migrated to the United States from Mexico as young children) moved across multiple Latino identities fluidly, in part due to their fluency in English and Spanish. One such youth was Carlos, whom we met in chapter 2. Carlos moved back and forth across sociocultural lines and constituted a bridging tie among US- and Mexican-born Latino youth.

In addition to interpersonal racial stuff, youth also recognized and recounted ethnic and racial trouble that blended interpersonal slights with systemic failures and injustices—what youth generally called "system stuff."[10] Recall Abelena and Roberta's observations about the constrained academic opportunities outside ESL for Mexicanos and Mexicanas. Black males also discussed systemic aspects of discrimination and institutional racism they faced on campus. Black males referenced, for example, their sense of the school using them for their athletic prowess and giving them preferential treatment only to pass them over for academic placement or disciplining them more harshly than their peers. In addition to the intersection of ethnic and racial dignity and discrimination, youth asserted that system stuff created multiple kinds of trouble in their lives, especially if they were undocumented. For example, youth who moved to residencies outside the school's catchment area, but who wanted to continue attending NWHS, found themselves caught up in endless streams of bureaucratic paperwork and appearances in district offices to explain their situation. Such appearances created fear because they could lead to questions of legal status of them or their parents or other adult family members acting as their guardians. Students also faced trouble involving academic issues not involving discipline, such as running afoul of graduation requirements.

Finally, youth associated trouble with the material world, including what they called "hustling" (entrepreneurial activities in illegal and legal markets), "not paying up" (debt), and "rip-offs" (theft). One kind of hustling referred to youth who brought food and other goods, such as inexpensive jewelry, to sell on campus, while another related to marijuana selling and use among some students. Whether in legal or illegal markets (and the blurred boundaries between the two), hustling could lead to disputes for market share and among "customers" and "hustlers" who did not "pay up" because they could not either afford or deliver goods, respectively. Some of these same hustlers also supplied access to alcohol or marijuana and much less often crack, heroin, or crystal meth. A Latina senior discussed hustling on campus in response to a question in an interview with Cynthia about social tensions among hustlers and their clients:

Hungry people want their food. Druggies want their drugs. Drunks want their alcohol. People want their jewelry. Hustlers wanna sell stuff. If one hustler thinks another is coming on his scene [client base], it gets tense. Nobody's gonna do nothing on campus. They work it out.

Not paying up and rip-offs also occurred apart from informal markets. One white student, for example, told a story about a peer "ripping off" food, a radio, and other items from her school locker. A Chinese-descent student talked about having "paid off" a debt to a "friend" for "concert tickets," but that the "friend spread rumors" that she didn't "pay up," which embarrassed her. As this last example illustrates, becoming known as someone who does not pay up or rips off peers becomes an identity marker, signaling a lack of dignity and disrespect for others.

Teachers understood and invoked the terms "drama" and "beef" to refer to interpersonal trouble among youth, and sometimes discussed with us racial issues on campus or hustling and rip-offs. The biggest difference between adult and youth depictions of trouble issues, not surprisingly, concerned academic and disciplinary issues. Some teachers associated disciplinary problems with "problem kids" as the primary lens through which they viewed youth trouble. Mr. Brown, whom we met in chapter 1, noted in an interview with Cal that he constantly thought about youth conflict in this way:

> I seem to spend a lot of time dealing with or thinking about disciplinary issues, problem kids. I guess kids think I'm a hardass or something. . . . I spend a lot of time on drama; you know, he said, she said stuff. There's constant drama among these kids and it percolates up to something that you have to deal with. If you don't, kids get outta line. They'll take advantage and you'll have real problems like fights and what not.

In these comments, we see social distrust that resonates with what Victor Rios calls the "code of the state"—a "labeling hype" and constant punishment through which youth misbehavior and peer aggression become self-fulfilling prophecies even when youth often tagged as disciplinary problems do not engage in such behaviors and deal with most drama and beefs among themselves in nonaggressive ways.[11] Classes where teachers strongly held this view often appeared on the brink of collapse, animated by anxiety, if not uncertainty, by both students and teachers.[12] Mrs. Robinson, whom we also met in chapter 1, talked about "keeping an ear to the ground" to learn about current dramas and beefs but did not automatically tie them to failures of discipline: "Kids are going to have drama and beefs, going to get into it. That's just human nature, not because they're bad or the school's not keeping them in line."

The Social Distribution of Trouble Issues:
Race, Ethnicity, Sex, and Grade Level

To examine the social distribution of trouble issues on campus, we analyzed the focal trouble issues in 539 youth-authored trouble cases and ninety-four ethnographic trouble cases. Ninth and twelfth grade students wrote youth-authored trouble cases in required humanities classes while ethnographic cases emerged from our direct observations of and discussions with youth and adults on and just off campus.[13] Neither type of trouble case is more valid than the other, or reflects "reality" in unmediated ways, instead offering different perspectives of social action, both influenced by interactional and institutional contexts. Student storytellers narrate youth-authored trouble cases from their perspectives, voicing how they make sense of their identities and express expectations of events and places, and what, if anything, they believe they can and should do about situations and persons they find troubling. Stories are particularly salient for youth, who narrate the negotiation of their social worlds as trial-and-error interactions. Institutional dynamics also shape youth-authored trouble cases in that storytellers recount their navigation of hierarchies and discipline that cut across formal educational and legal institutions, and bring into play intersecting social institutions of race, ethnicity, social class, gender, disability, and place.[14] Ethnographic trouble cases are stories, as well, but formed through the interaction of multiple researcher and participant perspectives, underlying institutional hierarchies and discipline, and the norms current in social scientific (especially sociological) narrative analysis.[15] The collection of youth-authored and ethnographic trouble cases enabled us to examine the continuities and discontinuities among youth and researcher representations. As Kitty Calavita and Valerie Jenness remind us, "Much current research . . . on disputing relies on interviews, but . . . an altogether different picture emerges and interesting fluidities and shifts are uncovered by looking *across* data sources, from interviews to written documents and back [emphasis in the original]."[16]

Aggregated together, dramas and beefs accounted for two-thirds of focal trouble issues framing youth-authored and ethnographic trouble cases, with system stuff, racial stuff, and hustling/rip-offs/not paying up making up the remaining one-third.[17] The high prevalence of drama and beefs in both kinds of trouble cases comports with prior research demonstrating the salience of interpersonal tensions around friendships and heterosexual dating relationships for youth conflict in high schools.[18] Troubles reported in the youth-authored compared to ethnographic cases tracked similarly with two exceptions: (1) beefs animated the youth-authored cases (24 percent) at a higher rate than in the ethnographic cases (16 percent), and (2) system stuff appeared at a considerably lower rate in the youth-authored cases (15 percent) when compared to ethnographic cases (28 percent). The higher percentage of beefs in the youth-authored cases may underscore how ingrained stereotypical images of masculinity are in the minds of youth, especially males. We examine this possibility more closely later in the chapter. The differential rates of trouble related to system stuff may relate to the historical context when we collected both kinds of cases. At the time when we began our fieldwork, NWHS administrators, working with teachers and security personnel, had relaxed the security regime begun in the 1980s. By the end of our first three years of fieldwork at the beginning of the twenty-first century, a new security regime, safe schools (the focus of chapter 7), was gradually pulling the school into the grips of tighter, carceral-like discipline. While we collected youth-authored cases prior to the full-blown imposition of the new security regime, our first three years of observations on campus took place across the relaxed and the earliest period of the heightened security, thus reflecting greater involvement of school discipline in the everyday lives of youth.

Only 12 percent of the youth-authored cases explicitly focused on racial trouble with peers. Although there is not an abundance of research quantifying perceptions of ethnic and racial conflict in American urban high schools, studies that do exist report substantially higher rates. In a survey study of New York City public high schools during the late 1990s, for example, 71 percent of student participants reported they had been the object of "peer prejudice based on race or ethnicity" and 70 percent reported witnessing youth violence that was "definitely" or "probably" motivated by racism or racial prejudice.[19] In another study of student perceptions of discrimination in an urban high school during the 1990s, 50 percent of self-identified non-Latino (white), 47 percent of Latino, and 36 percent of black youth reported being "called racially insulting names" by peers in school.[20]

To unpack the patterns at NWHS, we examined ethnic and racial differences across different trouble issues in youth-authored cases.[21] Regardless of their racial or ethnic identification, the vast majority of youth authors focused on drama or beefs. As for racial and system stuff, we uncovered significant differences among youth in terms of what these trouble issues signal to them. Black youth authored 103 trouble cases, of which 19 percent focused on racial stuff involving themselves and white peers and a Latino grouping they referred to as "Mexicans." Latinos authored 183 trouble cases, of which 20 percent involved ethnic and racial trouble. Of the Latino-authored cases about racial stuff, most centered on tensions between US-born Latinos and newly-arrived Mexican immigrant youth. Of the 210 youth-authored cases authored by white youth, only five cases focused on ethnic or racial tension involving nonwhite peers. Of the 43 remaining cases authored by Asian, Native American, Pacific Islander, and a handful of youth with identities not covered by these categories, only four dealt explicitly with ethnic and racial tension involving peers.

The picture sharpens when tracking what black or Latino youth wrote about when they recounted trouble with the system. Of the twenty-two and twenty-six cases about system trouble written by black or Latino youth, five and four, respectively, recount perceived racial discrimination by teachers or administrators related to disciplinary and/or academic issues, a narration more prevalent when compared to other identities on campus. In their written cases, Latino students place themselves at the intersection of ethnic status and social class, especially those who are newly arrived to the United States, and report getting in trouble with school authorities because of the demands on them to support their families through work. Among the cases authored by white youth, the focus on system trouble is narrated at a rate equal to Latinos, but their academic and disciplinary trouble issues lack social class framing and none focus on ethnic or racial discrimination. That black youth write about racial discrimination at higher rates than either Latino or white youth parallels prior research.[22] NWHS youth *do* experience discrimination and ethnic and racial trouble with peers, and especially black and Latino youth bear an extra burden in this regard. Equally important, however, NWHS students report ethnic and racial trouble at far lower rates than in other studies to date.[23] These lower rates may indicate a lowered sensitivity to ethnic and racial trouble or a reluctance to write about such issues in a classroom setting. However, youth wrote about a range of sensitive issues, which suggests a feeling of safety in expressing themselves. A more plausible explanation is that this pattern represents empirical traces of the long-term, evolving commitment by campus youth and adults to sociocultural diversity and cultural signifiers that trust on campus runs deep across diverse student groups, as depicted in chapter 2.

Turning to sex differences, female youth-authored cases focused on drama involving heterosexual dating relations substantially more than male youth narrations (56 percent compared to 32 percent), whereas the reverse is true with regard to beefs: male youth framed their youth-authored cases around beefs far more than female youth (43 percent compared to 8 percent).[24] Here again, this pattern comports with earlier research suggesting the salience of heterosexual dating relations as grist for youth conflict in American high schools.[25] Moreover, female youth-authored cases were twice as likely to invoke system stuff (19 percent compared to 9 percent) than male youth cases, and focused on academic concerns involving grades, attendance, and eligibility while nearly all the male youth-authored cases of system trouble hovered around disciplinary actions.[26] This pattern also held constant across youth-authored cases by Latina and black female students, which differs from more recent findings regarding young black female student fears of and vulnerability to school discipline.[27] Whatever a writer's grade level, youth-authored cases focused on drama and beefs, with fewer cases invoking ethnic and racial trouble by twelfth compared to ninth graders. At the same time, twelfth grade youth-authored cases focused on problems with authority and material exchange at a greater rate than ninth grade cases.[28]

An Inventory of Trouble Responses

Trouble issues offer a useful index of what youth perceive as the spark of peer trouble, but yield less insight into how youth gage the intensity of or responses to trouble. Not all drama or beefs, for example, rise to the level of serious transgressions. When researchers rely only upon trouble issues, they can conflate tropes with action and treat conflict as a discrete event rather than as social interactional processes among the conflicting parties and others who are not antagonists. Our perspective, as described in chapter 1, demands inquiry into how youth (and adults) respond to trouble, not only what they call different kinds of it. Meanings and stakes of peer conflict can be transformed through lines of action, revealing potential trajectories of escalation and de-escalation. To begin addressing these complexities, we first examine an inventory of trouble responses on campus. The bulk of this inventory involves bottom-up, informal control efforts by youth. Also contained in this inventory are formal control efforts mobilized by youth or initiated by school staff members to intervene into youth trouble and/or sanction youth for infractions of school rules.

Trouble responses are interactional accomplishments, ranging from highly visible to barely perceptible efforts, embedded in ongoing social relations. We identified three broad repertoires of trouble responses that youth and adults recognized at NWHS: "workin' it out," "puttin' 'em in their place," and "dealing with the system." Different local vocabularies demarcate each repertoire, the stakes underlying trouble issues, and emotional linkages that tie persons and acts together.[29] These repertoires were distributed across youth and campus spaces, connecting in different ways to social trust and anchored fluidity. Table 3.1 represents this repertoire in summary form.

When youth "worked it out," they treated trouble as the result of an unintentional mistake or an ambiguous situation in which it was unclear

Table 3.1   Youth trouble response repertoires

Trouble response repertoire → Components ↓	"Workin' it out" (conciliatory-remedial)	"Puttin' 'em in their place" (moralistic)	"Dealing with the system" (rule-oriented)
What is the underlying definition of trouble?	"Screwing around": hassle, mistake, bother	"Crossing the line": intentional disrespect and violation of dignity	"Getting jammed up": Becoming ensnared in official disciplinary or academic sanctions and constraints
What emotional linkages typically emerge?	"Upset, "kinda pissed," "concern": annoyance, frustration, mild anger, empathy, care	"Super-embarrassed," "totally pissed," and/ or "scared shitless": humiliation, indignation, extreme anger and/or fear	"Feeling disrespected," "dissed," "worried," "freaked": fear, anxiety, worry, care
What trouble responses constitute each cluster?	"Chillin'": coping/ lumping/ accommodating/ignoring, self-directed changes, deflecting, friendly denial, apologizing, biographical storytelling, temporary avoidance, complaining to a third-party sounding board, mobilizing third-party friendly support or friendly peacemakers "Educating": complaint making to and attempts at correcting a troublesome party, therapeutic counseling, informal negotiation ("talking it out")	"Beat down": bothering, hostile accusation, hostile command, verbal and nonverbal threat/ insult, hostile denial, hostile declaration, physical jostling, physical fighting, third-party partisan support, third-party enabling "Goin' undercover": malicious gossip, hidden transcript, covert third-party mobilization, investigating a deviant, sabotage, punitive theft "Movin' on": ostracism or exit	"Playing by the rules": active/passive compliance; therapeutic referral/advice "Playing the rules": mobilizing overt or covert 3rd party adult support or intervention (either verbally or nonverbally) "Played by the rules": subject to discipline, surveillance, third-party settlement by adults "Played against the rules": noncompliance, resistance, sabotage, hidden transcript, mass mobilization

who was at fault—a "screw-up" or something "weird," as youth and adults sometimes put it. Such hassles carried emotional consequences, as youth spoke about being "upset" or "kinda pissed" with their peers, yet rarely rose above feelings of annoyance, frustration, or mild anger. In many instances, workin' it out involved displays of empathy and caring. Adults recognized workin' it out by youth, but usually added "on their own" to signal the lack of adult intervention. Adults, teachers, and security guards also referred to workin' out trouble with youth when they handled a problem without reference to their disciplinary authority. These practices carried greater benefits than merely solving the problem at hand as they bolstered the legitimacy and moral authority of a teacher or security guard while leaving youth with a sense of dignity and trust in knowing their voices were heard. Such actions illustrate the intertwining of trust and control flowing less through official school structures and more through the capillaries of everyday relational work among youth and frontline staff.[30]

One set of responses youth deployed to work out trouble with peers involved what young people called "chillin'"—reconciling problematic situations, as one twelfth grade Latina put it, by "keeping the temperature down." A second set of actions associated with workin' it out moved in more corrective and remedial directions, involving what youth called "educating" or communicating one's complaints and feelings directly to a troublesome party in an effort to change that person's behavior. Whether chillin' or educating, youth proceeded cautiously under the assumption (and hope) that the trouble would not, as one Latino twelfth grader put it, "get out of hand."

On campus, youth chilled trouble, in their own words, by: (1) "coping" with troublesome situations, peers, and adults without much outward action; (2) self-directed changes that led to "stopping doing stupid stuff" or "thinking about it [the trouble] in a new way," in which the "self" reference could be an individual or a small group;[31] (3) "denying" in a friendly way knowledge of or responsibility for trouble;[32] (4) "changing the subject" by "making a joke" or "laughing a bit" in a way that deflects attention away from trouble; (5) "saying sorry" even though it may be unclear who is responsible for the trouble;[33] (6) "talking about where I come from" or biographical storytelling as a way to create shared empathy with or validate the perspectives and identity of a troubling party; (7) temporary avoidance by "getting outta there for a while" to curtail discussion about a troubling situation and/or interaction;[34] (8) "talking with friends" to seek their advice as third-party sounding boards without getting friends directly involved in the trouble; and/or (9) "gettin' other people involved" by mobilizing third-party supporters or peacemakers who can directly intervene.[35] Youth or adults sometimes opted into third-party roles, aiding the navigation of trouble through humorous asides, a story that casts a troubled party in a positive light, or by facilitating movement away from a troublesome situation. When adult staff members—often teachers or security guards—acted as third-party peacemakers among youth, they straddled the line between invoking official authority and relying on their informal standing as responsive to youth concerns—as being youth-centered. For youth-centered teachers, such as Mrs. Robinson or Mr. Rupp, their capacity to invoke official authority in managing conflict among youth peers played less of a role than their moral authority as adults whom youth trusted and respected. Although youth might test that trust in the heat of the moment, such teachers' credibility operated as an orienting benchmark in social interaction with youth. Youth (and adults) facilitated such responses by moving to the backstage either to reflect on and rehearse further proceedings or to have more private footings on which to deal with troubling parties.

Youth educated peers when they directly engaged the source of trouble and walked a fine line between escalating trouble to open conflict and workin' it out. Among youth at NWHS, "saying sorry" entailed communication between troubled and troubling parties, but the focus stayed on forgiveness, sometimes even occluding the character of the trouble in question. Educating, by comparison, identified trouble, its sources, and attendant feelings through voicing complaints to those deemed responsible.[36] Such responses did not necessarily unfold linearly. Youth often circle around a situation, attempting to discern what was definitively trouble or merely an unfortunate occurrence without a responsible party. If youth identified what they believed to be a source of trouble, their attempts at educating were muted at first and only over time developed into direct complaints to a troubling party with associated encouragement to make constructive changes to ameliorate or end the trouble.[37] Youth engaged in talk that resembled informal counseling, "talking it out" as they put it, when trying to find out what troubled a peer and help them correct wayward behavior. Such efforts might initially be met with denials that anything was "wrong," which could lead away from intervention or, over time, to repeated attempts to persuade a troubled peer to "get with the program" and seek help and/or change their behavior.

For adults, educating involved brief or longer interactions in which they directly or by referral engaged in therapeutic attempts to ameliorate youth trouble. Educating also veered into explicit adult concerns about younger students' understandings of basic civility, as Mr. Jacobs, a physical education teacher, noted in an interview with Cal about how he handled trouble in his classroom: "Kids need to be educated on how to treat other people. They don't always know the norms of good behavior, especially when they are just coming out of middle school."

The contours of trouble appeared blurry and in the background when youth attempted to work it out, whereas normative breaches operated in the foreground with clearer demarcations when youth attempted to put 'em in their place. Such actions often involved youth projecting a sense of self-righteousness and asserting moral high ground with troublesome parties "placed" on the deviant underside.[38] Puttin' 'em in their place was sometimes associated with peers cultivating identities as "badasses" linked less to the social trust of campus than the imagined or real outlines of neighborhood turf challenges and conflicts.[39] Peers often viewed students who continually engaged in moralistic activities as pariahs, with only a few garnering the narrow respect of the street tough. The emotional patterns associated with puttin' 'em in their place also ran hotter than workin' it out as youth talked about being "totally pissed" or "superembarrassed," which could rise to humiliation, extreme anger, or indignation. Youth put 'em in their place through three sets of trouble responses, specifically through "beat downs" that invoked the street in literal and aspirational senses; by "goin' undercover" to covertly pursue grievances; or by "movin' on" to ostracize troubling persons.

In beat downs, male and female youth projected stereotypical images of masculinity via force as they attempted to establish, in their words, a "rep." Even in urban settings dominated by the code of the street and higher rates of street violence, beat downs typically occur without physical force.[40] Parallel to this pattern, beat downs at NWHS typically did not escalate beyond bluster. Targeted youth might initially try to chill the trouble by turning the offending aggression into a good laugh by all involved. If chillin' the trouble did not work, the targeted youth might try to stop the bothering via a hostile command laced with profanity, such as "don' be doin' that shit" or "cut that shit out." Beat downs also began via "call outs" (hostile accusations) that named and condemned a peer for a particular normative breach, again laced with profanity. Although youth often greeted call outs with friendly denials of wrongdoing, they could lead to youth responses in kind, such as in "I din't do nothin', asshole!" (a hostile denial of cheating with a male youth's girlfriend), "Don' be saying no mo' shit 'bout it!" (a hostile command), or an angry denial of disbelief in Spanish like "¿Chingao?!" ("What the fuck?!"). Other verbal beat downs involved threats and names that attempted to lower the moral standing of the accused, as in "I gonna whip his pussy ass!" Subtle, nonverbal manipulations of the body that were unmistakable in their intended menace also constituted beat downs, depending upon who else was present: the long stare or sneer or making a fist by one's side as if ready to strike were decidedly different actions depending upon the context. Aside from verbal beat downs resonant with the code of the street, youth also engaged in ritualistic beat downs, the most common of which involved competitions among break dancing "krews" who practiced in empty building hallways or between buildings to loud hip hop and rap music played on portable sound systems.

The most common physical beat down involved what youth called "pushin'" or "bumpin'" (physical jostling). Pushin' occurred with the hands and unmistakably signaled aggression, whereas bumpin' occurred via the torso often without hands. Although rare, "kickin' ass" (physical fighting) on campus took one of two forms, involving aggressive wrestling among either male or female youth with a few physical blows, usually to the face, followed by either wrestling or kicking. The latter form of fighting often produced the most blood and injuries. Although we collected youth-authored and ethnographic cases of youth carrying and having access to knives or guns (in the trunk of a car, for example) or using makeshift weapons (a baseball bat or bottle), the fieldwork team never observed the actual use of weapons on campus.

When youth went undercover to respond to trouble moralistically, they engaged in malicious gossip ("spreadin' shit"), portraying the troublesome party either as a willful miscreant engaging in egregious behavior or as someone caught up in a drama blurring victim and predator roles. Youth also "laugh at 'em when they don' know" or "put it in a notebook" to assert the moral superiority of a subordinate group—a kind of hidden transcript, to borrow from James Scott's analytic lexicon for understanding covert resistance to power and authority.[41] For example, Mexican immigrant youth ornately wrote profane statements in Spanish (e.g., "¡Chingan Chicanos!" [Fuck Chicanos!"]) or told jokes in Spanish underscoring their perceptions of US-born Latinos' arrogance and lack of authenticity as true "Mexicans."

In some instances, youth talked about engaging in undercover actions without the troublesome party "ever knowing what hit them" or with an ally "delivering a message that you can't fuck with me." Youth also went undercover to steal possessions from transgressors that the latter valued highly, such as a gift from a family member, romantic partner, or close friend. A final way that youth put 'em in their place was via "movin' on," which carried a sense of finality in exiting a peer group or the school permanently.[42] In the former situation, youth talked about peers "crossing the line," which led them to be cut off from contact with relevant peer groups. Movin' on differed from, yet played off, non-trouble related movin' around campus, often leading to such tactics being camouflaged from all but the discerning eye.

Compared to the close normative dynamics involved in workin' it out or puttin' 'em in their place, youth viewed the system as a web of local and far-flung rules, organizations, and actors. Trouble issues surrounding system stuff were often depicted by youth as "getting jammed up," which meant becoming ensnared in academic, disciplinary, or legal sanctions. Students who were arrested, for example, got jammed up, as did students who found out toward the end of their senior years that they fell short of the required course credits to graduate. When youth referenced trouble with each other, getting jammed up referred to the consequences of system intervention into peer conflict in the form of on- and off-campus suspensions, the mobilization of parents or guardians to help enforce sanctions, or arrest and/or time in juvenile detention, should the police become involved. Youth who mobilized the system to help them handle peer trouble or problems with the system itself, like filing a formal grievance of sexual harassment against a teacher, became ensnared in the system even as the "system worked for them" in the end. Emotions swirling around dealing with the system ranged from fear and anxiety to positive emotional ties students felt toward NWHS teachers and some security guards, who, as one Latino senior put it, "look after us."

Youth invoked a series of overlapping phrases to describe trouble responses related to dealing with the system. When youth "played by the rules," they either habitually or actively complied with the normative parameters of a particular set of rules or procedures. Habitual compliance involved relatively unreflective action, such as sitting quietly with a notebook at the ready in a classroom as a teacher began class. While such actions could be interpreted as a form of pandering to the adult world, we found little evidence of youth recognizing their peers as causing trouble because of habitual compliance. Active compliance, by contrast, involved youth engaging in reflective, conscious action to conform or urge peers to conform to rules and adult directives, such as when youth aided teachers in gaining control of a classroom in the wake of peer disruptions. Active compliance of this sort could lead to retaliatory peer trouble; active compliers sometimes were labeled as "snitches" or "ass kissers," especially if they were involved in "ratting out" (signaling) to a teacher or security guard peers who committed minor rule infractions.[43] In both kinds of actions, youth stood "before" the rules, yet in very different ways.[44] In habitual compliance, youth experienced the rules as inevitable in the same nonrational way that one takes a breath under most circumstances without thinking. Situations of active compliance interrupted that "naturalness" and created contingency, if not uncertainty and anxiety, among both youth and adults. The rules did not appear as "natural," delivered whole cloth to youth; they came in piecemeal fashion, stitched together by everyday youth and adult interactions and with trouble swirling around.

Active compliance also was evident in "playing the rules"—trouble responses by youth that engaged the system strategically, a phenomenon akin to what Patricia Ewick and Susan Silbey call "playing with the law."[45] To "play the rules" was to find something in the system for one's self, to use the rules as a tool and a strategic site for action. When youth played the rules, they did not necessarily break rules or misrepresent their own behavior or goals. Instead, they asked questions, used information, or assembled facts in ways that enabled them to achieve a particular strategic goal, like finding a way to remain a student at NWHS despite living outside its catchment area. Adult supporters providing advice often facilitated such navigation, vouching for a youth's credibility or bringing the problem to higher authorities. Such support also occurred more nefariously, such as when a peer "set up" another to take the fall for initiating a fight. The risks for playing the rules could be high for youth, particularly if peers discovered the "game."

Students spoke of "getting played by the rules" when they experienced unilateral discipline, discipline coupled with the settlement of peer disputes, or direct surveillance. In these situations, adults often exercised authority in response to trouble that disturbed youth, and young people made fine distinctions between who intervened: teachers and guards— adults who mixed with youth on a daily basis—or administrators, whom students perceived as more distant, inscrutable, and prone to unfairness.

Finally, youth "played against the rules" when they resisted or subverted both the official authority of adults on campus and their peers in governance roles, especially the student council. As with resistance to authority across multiple types of organizations, mass mobilizations rarely occurred on campus and only in reaction to dramatic policy shifts or threats to the school, such as in the late 1980s when the district threatened to close the school or in the early twenty-first century when students attempted to mobilize against the administration's turn to intensify surveillance and strict enforcement of safe schools policies. On an everyday basis, resistance more commonly occurred as students acted alone or in tacit coordination with each other to defy an adult's directions, or engaged in covert actions that were difficult for adults to discern as challenges to their authority. In these efforts, youth took advantage of the situation at hand, turning their knowledge of school structures to sabotage classroom procedures when, for example, teachers were perceived as "hardasses" or "unfair."[46] Youth also turned to hidden transcripts in the form of pantomimes, imitations, jokes, cartoons, and profane writings in notebooks to tacitly express grievances against the system.

Image and Action in Trouble Responses

With this inventory of trouble responses in mind, we turn to an aggregate analysis of trouble responses in youth-authored compared to ethnographic trouble cases. A starkly differentiated pattern emerges, with puttin' 'em in their place dominant in the youth-authored cases while ethnographic cases lean substantially in the direction of workin' it out. Specifically, in figure 3.1, we show that 62 percent of the trouble responses in the youth-authored cases compared to 31 percent in the ethnographic cases involved youth puttin' 'em in their place; 20 percent of the responses in the youth-authored cases compared to 48 percent in the ethnographic cases involved workin' it out; and 18 percent of the responses in the youth-authored cases compared to 21 percent in the ethnographic cases involved dealing with

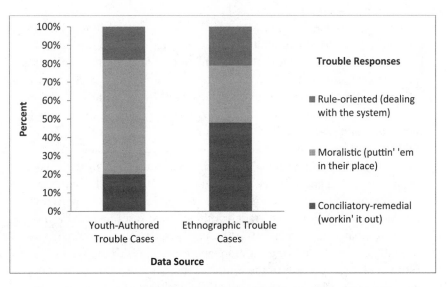

Figure 3.1. Trouble responses in youth-authored and ethnographic trouble cases, 1997–1999 (based on table B.5)

the system.[47] The marked differences in the patterns of ethnographic and youth-authored cases hold when we consider how youth write about and respond to different kinds of trouble issues.[48] When we examined ethnic, racial, and sex differences in how youth wrote about responding to trouble, we found a predominance of moralistic responses regardless of ethnic or racial identification, although conciliatory-remedial responses were a bit more prevalent in female- compared to male-authored cases. At the same time, we did not find relationships in the ethnographic cases among trouble responses and the principals' sex or their ethnic or racial identifications.[49]

In the three years of our fieldwork before the safe schools regime gained a full grip on campus, we rarely uncovered aggressive intimidation among youth. During this period, an average of three physical fights per year occurred on campus. Young women were more likely than young men to be involved, and neighborhood identities were implicated in only two fights. The number of fights we observed on campus during this period comported with official New West School District statistics. In this three-year period, as noted in chapter 1, NWHS experienced the lowest rate of on-campus serious incidents in the district. Both the number of physical fights we observed and the official number of violent incidents at NWHS compare favorably to national statistics during the same period, which reported seven "serious violent incidents" per 1,000 students per year on US high school campuses from 1997 to 2000.[50]

One explanation for the disjuncture between youth-authored and ethnographic cases could be that we misinterpreted our observations. This explanation is unlikely given the triangulation of findings across multiple data streams and fieldworkers, including consulting youth and adults in the field about local meanings of actions in different contexts. An alternative explanation appears in figure 3.2, revealing striking differences in how ninth and twelfth graders represent how they respond to peer trouble in youth-authored trouble cases.[51] Sixty-seven percent of trouble responses in ninth grade youth-authored cases involved puttin' 'em in their place, compared to 22 percent in the twelfth grade youth-authored cases. Nearly the opposite ratio appears with regard to workin' it out: 54 percent of trouble responses in twelfth grade youth-authored cases involved workin' it out compared to 16 percent in the ninth grade youth-authored cases. Twelfth graders also wrote a bit more about dealing with the system than ninth graders: 24 percent of the trouble responses in twelfth grade youth-authored cases referenced aspects of official authority compared to 17 percent in ninth grade youth-authored cases. These patterns, coupled with the

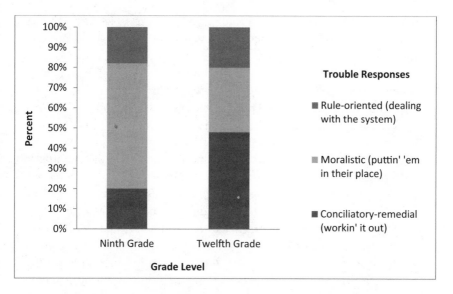

Figure 3.2. Trouble responses by grade level in youth-authored
trouble cases, 1997–1999 (based on table B.12)

large proportion of the cases written by ninth compared to twelfth graders,
may account for the overall skewing of youth-authored cases in the direction of moralistic trouble responses.

Also, we compared ethnographic trouble cases by grade levels. Fifty
ethnographic cases involved only eleventh and twelfth graders and produced a total of 586 trouble responses, of which 422 (72 percent) were
conciliatory-remedial, twenty-seven (5 percent) were moralistic, and 137
(23 percent) were rule-oriented actions. By contrast, twenty-nine cases involved only ninth or tenth graders and produced 237 trouble responses, of
which 161 (68 percent) took a moralistic turn, forty-nine (21 percent) were
conciliatory-remedial, and twenty-seven (11 percent) were rule-oriented.
The remaining fourteen cases involved mixtures of younger and older students, who together produced a total of 168 trouble responses. Of these
responses, eight-six (51 percent) were conciliatory-remedial, sixty-four
(38 percent) were moralistic, and eighteen (11 percent) were rule-oriented.
Eleventh and twelfth graders accounted for fifty-nine of the conciliatory-
remedial actions. That eleventh and twelfth graders, compared to ninth
and tenth graders, turned more often to adults to help manage peer trouble
comported with their increased likelihood of representing such directions
in their youth-authored trouble cases.

Consistent with other research, these patterns may reflect common difficulties of transitioning from middle to high school, when youth face physiological, psychological, and social change. Key challenges in this transition include the management of peer relations (including trouble) and seeking viable personal identities.[52] In schools that draw from high-poverty neighborhoods, ninth grade students draw upon experiences in and expectations derived from their local middle schools and neighborhoods, as well looking to parental, familial, media, and cultural influences for cues about how to manage the challenges they face. Parental and other familial influences in these communities include significant attention to the importance of education and also teach young people to be wary of strangers and ready to defend themselves, including a willingness to fight if necessary.[53] Along with stock images that highlight social distrust and the code-of-the-street lens from media and entertainment sources, youth coming to NWHS have cultural and experiential grounding for seeing puttin' 'em in their place as a first-order response to trouble. Our interpretation that ninth graders are more likely to come to NWHS with the imprint of a street orientation toward conflict also resonates with more general understandings of narratives, as suggested in the literature on cognition and memory. Narratives about personal experience can certainly express many things, including fictional representations. But they also tend to be structured by long-term patterns and experience such that what is recalled and woven into a recounting of any particular event is what an individual expects will be typical, whether it actually happened or not.[54] Added to these cognitive processes are normative demands in high-poverty urban settings for particular kinds of masculinities and femininities residing in physical and symbolic force. Thus, narratives authored by the ninth graders of NWHS are likely to be as much about cognitive and normative expectations as they are experiential representations.

These expectations, genuinely felt by ninth graders, and the actions they sometimes stimulated were moderated by the climate of trust sustained through collective civic action in clubs and introduced to new students, especially at the ninth and tenth grade levels, through peer socialization. Even as ninth and tenth graders brought with them cognitive and normative expectations imported from their communities and middle schools, they also looked to and were pulled toward their older peers—youth living in many of the same neighborhoods and negotiating the same school campus—for clues and direction in how to treat peers and handle peer trouble at NWHS. With academic classes and sports teams largely segregated by age, younger peers most often mixed with older students in student clubs, which they joined in great numbers toward the second semester of their first year and first semester of their second year at NWHS. Family ties also facilitated access to older youth; many entering students in the 1990s had older siblings attending NWHS. And older youth sometimes included younger peers in their small groups, facilitated by the constant flow of anchored fluidity and a responsibility felt by older youth to socialize younger youth into the ways of the campus, to make sure, as one Chicano senior put it, "kids comin' in . . . know how it's done here [at NWHS]." These experiences on school grounds created opportunities for what David Harding calls "cross-cohort" socialization, in which older youth socialize younger youth about how to handle peer conflict. In the high-poverty Boston setting that Harding studied, older youth socialized younger youth into neighborhood-based, code-of-the-street perspectives. At NWHS, our evidence points to cross-cohort socialization that reproduces social trust and nonviolent conflict management.[55] Representative excerpts from conversations with two senior students, Paul and Maria, illustrated what these interactions looked like on the ground:

JERLYN: How do ninth graders deal with trouble on campus compared to say juniors or seniors?

PAUL: Different ways, you know. When I was just comin' into the school, you know, I would be thinkin' about kickin' ass. Now, I don' do that. No fightin', you know? I let it slide, work it out somehow. They ain't a lot who'll get into it, you know. Everybody know. We all chillin', you know.

JERLYN: How did you learn to do that?

PAUL: You watch older kids. How they handle themselves. You know, I hang out with the older guys sometimes. You can do that here. They tell me "cut that fightin' shit out," educate me on that. They grew up with me in [his neighborhood] and they almost ready to graduate. They know what up, you know.

†

CYNTHIA: How do youth deal with trouble on campus? Say, ninth graders compared to eleventh or twelfth graders?

MARIA: That depends.

CYNTHIA: Depends on what?

MARIA: Like, ninth graders are more likely to get into it here, fight. Now, I'm not going to let someone rope me into that. I have a friend who's a senior at [Eastern High] and there's a lot of fighting there even with seniors. You really gotta watch your back. By the time you're a junior or senior here, you know better. You try to work it out. It's safe here. I wish my friend could transfer here. She'd do better here.

CYNTHIA: How did you learn to handle trouble without fighting? Did anyone tell you not to do that?

MARIA: I don't think anyone told me. I guess I watch older students sometimes. Sometimes I would get to know them in a club [she is in various student clubs]. I ate my lunch sometimes by lockers in a building when it's hot outside and after a while the older girls, they ate their lunch in the same hall, they talk with me and my friends when we were freshmen. I didn't ask them what was up. I guess I listened. I kinda learned it on my own.

Paul charted a career in trouble handling, from ninth grade inclinations about "kickin' ass" to a senior who "work[s] it out." He noted that NWHS students do not expect to "get into it" (escalate trouble)—another nod to the underlying social trust on campus—as older generations "educate" younger generations into the school culture. Maria's account resonates with Paul's, signaling both a cross-cohort socialization and comparative perspective. She noted that older students on campus "know better" than to handle interpersonal conflict in hostile ways, contrasting her experiences at NWHS to her friend's at neighboring Eastern High where "there's a lot of fighting . . . even with seniors." Like many students with friends at other schools in the district, Maria emphasized her campus as "safe" and even hoped that her friend could "transfer" to NWHS. Maria also recognized how older students model trouble handling by recounting the small group of older students she and a friend joined during their first year on campus, from whom Maria learned how to "work out" trouble "on her own." Maria and Paul's comments thus suggest, as do the patterns in the youth-authored and ethnographic cases, that the variety of trouble responses among students narrowed the longer they were at NWHS during the late 1990s. Over their time at NWHS, youth tended to work out trouble with peers, turned a bit more to the system, and sidestepped puttin' 'em in their place.

Trouble Strings: Handling Problems across Ties, Place, and Time

Until now, we have treated trouble responses as discrete analytic units that coalesce into youth-identified repertoires of action in order to understand their common properties and associations with youth social attributes. At the heart of each trouble case, however, is a sequence of contingent interactions—what we call a trouble string—through which youth make sense of and handle experiences of discontent or being upset within and across relationships, geographic space, and time. Trouble strings represent the microprocesses of navigating conflict, ranging from youth-centered actions without adults to more formal, adult-centered actions including therapeutic and legal interventions. An analysis of trouble strings tracks the temporal interplay between the meanings young people give to trouble and how it is handled, including the evolution of action from or toward hostility and open conflict, or shifts from being personal to collective problems. Some strings contain "response clusters"—trouble responses tightly coupled together in compact periods of time and space—while other strings contain responses that stretch out over longer periods of time and greater space. Response clusters are important because they underscore how trouble responses can gather momentum and limit the possibilities for deviation from a particular course of action. To illustrate what we mean by a trouble string, consider an incident of peer trouble as told to Cal by Joni, a white eleventh grader, as she finished her map for the in-class mapping exercise:

I was eating lunch with my boyfriend and my friend, Katie, on the quad. So many people coming through the quad; ya know, prying eyes. He was sorta quiet; kinda grunted a couple of times, had this look on his face when I asked him something. Maybe he was pissed 'bout me going out on Friday without him. Not sure. Kinda bein' an ass with the dirty looks. We're sorta sitting there for a while. I'm not saying nothin', just chillin'. He's giving me the look. I got outta there for a minute; move away from him. Coulda gone bad. Maybe he thought I crossed the line. Then Katie says, "Let's go eat lunch in Mr. Rupp's." That was perfect. We go to the classroom; hung out, just eating. It was quiet. Mr. Rupp was working on something at his desk; there was a few other kids there just eating or reading. Really mellow. I told a story about my sister; she's good for a laugh. He [the boyfriend] was still doing the dirty look then he laughed a little. We did that for a while. Didn't [Joni and her boyfriend] see each other the rest of the day. We talked on the phone that night; went on and on till midnight. . . . We said things gotta change between us. No more dirty looks.[56]

We can consolidate Joni's trouble case as a sequence of actions in a trouble string with each response as a numbered node: smooth-line circles refer to workin' it out (conciliatory-remedial responses) and dashed-line triangles represent puttin' 'em in their place (moralistic responses). In addition, the increased size of the circle indicates an important turning point in the string, such as a moment of escalation or de-escalation or intervention by a third party. Also included in the string are geographical

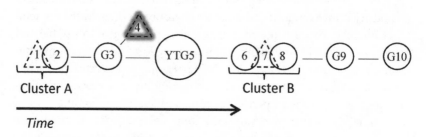

Figure 3.3. Trouble string for "Joni's Story"

moves (G), third-party youth intervention (YT), and potential behaviors as a shadowed node above the string.

Viewed as a trouble string, the trouble case recounted by Joni contains eight different trouble responses: two moralistic responses (one enacted and one contemplated), six conciliatory-remedial responses, and four geographic moves, three on- and one off- campus. The string began as an ambiguous situation: Joni was uncertain about whether her boyfriend was "pissed" about her going out without him on a Friday night. Here, the string oscillated (represented by response cluster "A," involving nodes 1 and 2) between the boyfriend's moralistic "dirty looks" (1) and Joni "chillin' . . . not saying nothin'" (2). She then engaged in temporary avoidance that broke out of cluster A by moving away from her boyfriend (G3; "got outta there for a minute") that led her to think her boyfriend might respond moralistically (4; "coulda gone bad" and "maybe he thought I crossed the line"). A key turning point occurred when Joni's friend, Katie, intervened by suggesting that the three friends walk to Mr. Rupp's classroom to fin-ish eating lunch (YTG5; "Let's go eat lunch in [Mr. Rupp's]"), which Joni remembered as reducing the tension ("lightened up stuff"). Once in the classroom, the three friends ate lunch, and cluster B emerged as Joni told a story (6) to further deflect the trouble she suspected influenced the situ-ation, which first drew a "dirty look" (7) and then a small laugh from her boyfriend (8) as he aligned himself with the conciliatory-remedial orienta-tion of Joni's story. Joni and her boyfriend temporarily avoided one an-other during the rest of the school day (G9; "Didn't see each other the rest of the day") and the string dissipated in the aftermath of a long talk on the phone about changing their relationship, an instance of educating (G10; ". . . things gotta change between us. No more dirty looks.").

Fifty-two of the ninety-four ethnographic trouble cases contain trouble strings in which conciliatory-remedial responses comprised the modal action, with an average of 9.71 responses (nodes) per string and more than six geographic moves across different campus areas. In thirteen strings, youth engaged in moralistic responses as the modal response, averaging 15.69 responses with fewer than three geographic moves per string. Seventeen ethnographic trouble cases contain strings in which rule-oriented responses predominate, averaging 7.82 responses with fewer than two geographic moves per string. Twelve of these strings involved youth trying to put 'em in their place and the other five involved peers trying to work it out. A dozen strings were multimodal, with a mean number of trouble responses of 12.50. Appendix A offers schematic visualizations of two additional strings, one dominated by moralistic trouble responses and the other by rule-oriented responses.

Among the fifty-two strings dominated by conciliatory-remedial responses (workin' it out), thirty-six contain only conciliatory-remedial responses. In these strings, youth patiently, if not tenaciously, focused on multiple ways of workin' it out with peers, interacting in tight-knit response clusters to deal with a troubling party (or friends) to figure out and handle trouble. Of the remaining sixteen strings dominated by conciliatory-remedial responses, thirteen include moralistic responses, two contain rule-oriented responses, and one contains all three kinds of responses. In nine of these thirteen, when youth turned to workin' it out via multiple responses, they interrupted moralistic actions but did not return to them, suggesting that when youth attempted to work out trouble, their efforts could reorient trouble handling and rarely unraveled or re-escalated in moralistic directions.[57]

How trouble strings unfolded hinged importantly on peer relationships as suggested by our analysis of strings with different modal control efforts—strings with a predominance of conciliatory-remedial, moralistic, or rule-oriented trouble responses. Conciliatory-remedial modal strings comprise seventy-one percent of the strings involving youth who hung out on a regular basis compared to 38 percent of the strings among youth who did not hang out regularly (see table 3.2). By contrast, youth without strong ties were more likely than youth with strong ties to build moralistic trouble strings (20 percent compared to 8 percent) or strings with a predominance of rule-oriented responses (29 percent compared to 8 percent). This pattern comports with multiple studies of conflict management among both adults and youth that find conciliatory-remedial actions are more likely than moralistic or rule-oriented responses in contexts marked by strong ties with future orientations, that is, where people are invested

Table 3.2   Ethnographic case-based trouble strings by "hanging out"

Trouble strings dominated by . . .	Principal parties regularly "hang out" with each other	Principal parties do not regularly "hang out" with each other	Totals
"Workin' it out" (conciliatory-remedial responses)	71.4% (35)	37.8% (17)	55.3% (52)
"Puttin' 'em in their place" (moralistic)	8.2% (4)	20.0% (9)	13.8% (13)
Dealing with the system (rule-oriented responses)	8.2% (4)	28.9% (13)	18.2% (17)
Multimodal responses	12.2% (6)	13.3% (6)	12.7% (12)
Totals	100.0% (49)	100.0% (45)	100.0% (94)

Note: By percentage. Figures in parentheses are absolute frequencies. $X^2 = 12.77$; $dF = 4$; $p < .02$.

in each other and feel an obligation to preserve relationships.[58] While students at NWHS assembled in large groups in the most public places of the school, anchored fluidity meant that these clusters of youth rarely became the source of high-stakes confrontations and claims of exclusivity that can fuel violent moralistic and aggressive social control among peers. It is also telling that strings exhibiting ethnic and racial heterogeneity appeared just as likely to move in the direction of workin' it out as those in which there was homogeneity. Finally, the fact that seventeen strings featured attempts to work out trouble among youth who did not regularly hang out resonates with two underlying dynamics. In the majority (ten) of these strings, the youth involved did hang out together previously—a function of anchored fluidity on campus—and so may or may not have had residual personal regard for each other or relational obligations. In the other seven strings, relationally unconnected youth treated each other with mutual regard even amid trouble, perhaps a result of the social trust that generally informed everyday campus life at NWHS during the late 1990s.

The contingent character of trouble strings also related to the geographic origins of trouble and how and whether youth moved it across campus, as represented in figure 3.4. Although trouble began in many places on campus, trouble most often emerged (as denoted by the triangles in figure 3.4) (1) in downtown on the quad or in the cafeteria (fifty-eight strings began there); (2) in particular classroom buildings, especially "L"

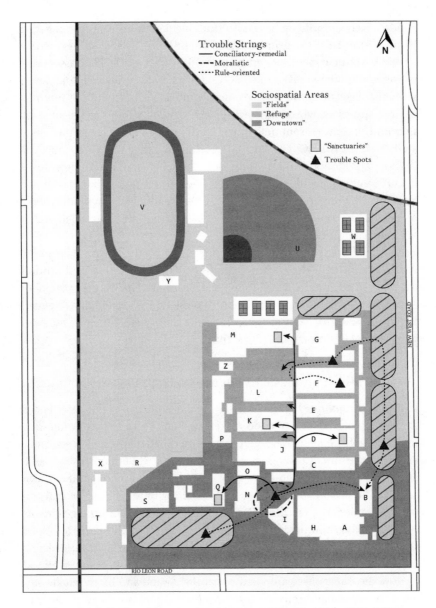

Figure 3.4. Stylized spatial routes of trouble strings at New West High, 1997–1999

and "F" (neither building has classroom sanctuaries; thirteen strings began there); (3) outside the gymnasium ("G" building; twelve strings) where multiple youth congregate, especially after ninth grade PE classes; and (4) on both parking lots in the half hour just before or after school (eleven strings).[59] Like well-worn trade routes, youth moved forty of the fifty-two trouble strings in which they attempted to work it out (represented by smooth lines) away from downtown up the main breezeway to the grassy areas between "J," "K," "L," and "M" buildings, where there are "sanctuaries" in "D," "K," and "M" buildings, or to the sanctuaries within downtown in "Q" building. Troubles with strings oriented toward workin' it out followed the flow of anchored fluidity as youth made their way to the refuge or sanctuaries, on to the backstages of the school for more relationally-sensitive interactions.

In ten of the thirteen strings dominated by puttin' 'em in their place, youth remained in downtown (represented by dashed-line oval around the main quad) or attempted to move off campus. Finally, the movement of strings oriented toward the system (represented by dotted lines) tended to travel toward the administration and the office maintained by the New West Police Department in "B" building.

Beyond Ethnic and Racial Violence on High-Poverty Campuses

In the late 1990s, much of the interpersonal trouble that youth experienced at NWHS revolved around concerns about dignity and respect in interpersonal relationships, trouble issues that youth called drama and beefs. Trouble grounded in ethnic and racial animus was a real and persistent issue on campus, especially between newly arrived, Mexican immigrant and US-born Latino youth, and for black male youth with the school administration. Yet ethnic and racial conflict did not define trouble among students at NWHS when compared to previous research in urban high schools. As real as the trouble issues were to both youth and school staff, these depictions of trouble did not determine what trouble responses youth deployed or how these responses unfolded over time. Latina and black female students, in particular, expressed fewer concerns about their vulnerability to school discipline than to bureaucratic constraints that could interfere with or limit their academic opportunities. Although difficult to quantify or link causally, this pattern may align with the long-standing tradition on campus of opportunities for young women in leadership positions and academic achievement (see chapter 2).

Contextual cues, including grade level, interpersonal peer relationships and groups, and spatial dynamics, all shaped how youth made sense of and acted on interpersonal trouble. Youth entering NWHS in the ninth grade tended to imagine peer conflict in code-of-the-street terms, a perception that clearly contrasted with the experience and narration of twelfth graders. Some of these discontinuities are undoubtedly linked to developmental differences between the two grades, although previous portraits of conflict among urban youth in the context of social distrust chronicle the increasing sophistication and deadliness of peer violence, especially tied to weapons and gangs, as young people enter their late teens and early twenties.[60] At NWHS, the predominant response to trouble during this period involved workin' it out with peers, which led away from or interrupted moralistic, aggressive actions. Social and geographic space also conditioned how youth handled peer trouble. Youth relationally closer to one another (even when identifying with different ethnic or racial groups) were more likely than socially distant youth to pacify their troubles or to problem solve. However, the constant social mixing that occurred via anchored fluidity moderated social and cultural distances. On the frontstages of downtown, especially on the quad, trouble was more likely to surface and to result in moralistic actions echoing the code of the street than on the backstages of the refuge or the broad expanses of the fields. Quick efforts at pacification or reconciliation occurred in the downtown area but were typically stretched out in time and space as youth walked their troubles up the main breezeway into the refuge or, less often, to the fields. Trouble strings involving the system, both on foot and by security golf cart, moved toward the main administration building in downtown.

Our development of trouble strings carries broad implications for process approaches to the study of conflict, particularly related to urban youth. Scholars have given substantial attention to the importance of examining the social interactional processes that constitute conflict and its management.[61] We take particular note of Robert Emerson, who argued that trouble unfolds through cycles of response and counter-response—a process of interactional co-construction.[62] We agree with the basic premises of Emerson's arguments regarding the cyclical character of a great deal of trouble and conflict. But we also find that among youth, interruptions, defined by spatial movement, third parties, and the structure of official school authority (the "school bell"), can enable de-escalation as much as escalation. Such interruptions allow youth to punctuate particular responses and reposition themselves both socially and emotionally for subsequent attempts at managing conflict.[63]

Ethnographers of urban youth conflict in high-poverty settings also have adopted process perspectives to examine how peers engage in and sometimes avoid interpersonal, "street" violence.[64] But too often this line of scholarship concentrates on violent episodes or those phases of dealing with trouble that are dominated by moralistic control, conflating all urban youth trouble and conflict *as* violence. Trouble strings provide conceptual and methodological tools to unpack this bracketing of code-of-the-street responses by examining sequences of trouble responses that lean toward or fall away from violence. Our intent is not to claim that previous researchers have "gotten it wrong" but instead to establish that tracking the flow of responses, through the plotting of trouble strings, provides a fuller picture of the interactional dynamics of youth conflict. This approach, then, visualizes the processual character of trouble responses over time and space, including alternative pathways not taken. Although trouble strings unfold over time, youth may return later in a string to trouble responses tried earlier but, as with all interactions, never in quite the same way. There are always improvisational aspects to navigating trouble, as youth adapt to new situations tied to surrounding contexts and previous, anticipated, or hoped-for actions by peers. The dynamics early in a trouble string, however, can constrain what is possible later in the string, limiting the improvisation of those involved. At NWHS, for instance, conciliatory-remedial trouble responses can gain such momentum that moralistic responses rarely derail them. By contrast, conciliatory-remedial interventions can derail moralistic responses in a trouble string. Attention to trouble strings thus enables a fine-grained guide to the microdynamics of shifting normative orientations and control efforts that may not be as apparent from only observing, reading, or listening to a trouble case.

Researchers in the code-of-the-street tradition argue that in high-poverty neighborhoods marked by territorial rivalries peer groups operate as mechanisms of protection and victimization.[65] The everyday realities of anchored fluidity at New West meant that many peer groups formed and reformed over time and space, so that youth had multiple places to perform identities and make meaningful relational peer connections. In this way, anchored fluidity embedded youth in particular peer groups at different moments in time and space and assured students multiple places to claim as their own geographically and socially. These dynamics helped youth develop empathy and relational connections across cultural difference. To be clear, peer groups can only accomplish these intersections in places where youth and adults operate together to build and sustain social trust. Such trust pervaded the campus throughout much of our initial field research, especially in the refuge, although this again was not without variation and asymmetry among some peer groups. Peers worked out their relationships in these places and teachers opened their classrooms as sanctuaries, often developing informal, supportive ties with students. While this chapter outlines the broad contours of the ways youth contributed to peace at NWHS before the intensive implementation of safe schools, it does not delve into the richness of interactions among youth responding to trouble on a daily basis. To explore these interactions in greater depth and offer a sense of the school as a place of its own during this period, we draw on representative trouble cases in the next chapter to reveal the nuanced choices and subtle actions youth embark on to work out their troubles in conciliatory-remedial ways.

FOUR

"Workin' It Out"

Trouble sometimes "went bad," as students would say, but hostility and violence were not habituated youth responses to peer trouble at NWHS during the late 1990s, a historical period on campus when social trust ran strong and forms of control, both youth- and adult-generated, were substantially aligned. Instead, students often improvised as they, in their own words, "worked out" trouble. Layers of adult authority officially structured school life and occasionally led to direct interventions into youth conflict. And a score of teachers informally opened their classrooms as sanctuaries, providing places for youth to hang out during free periods and manage conflict away from the public scrutiny of downtown. But, on a daily basis, workin' it out hinged on the capacity of young people to act in ways that at first glance did not appear to be conflict management at all.

"Chillin'"—from accommodation to deflection to temporary avoidance—blended into the ebb and flow of youth movement across different peer groups and campus geography. "Educating"—a bottom-up youth practice of teaching and learning corrective practices for sustaining peer relationships—was a second response strategy we observed. As youth enacted these repertoires of control practices to work out their troubles, they took into account relational ties. Youth who hung out with one another on a regular basis were more likely to move trouble to the backstages of the campus; youth who rarely or only occasionally hung out were more likely to posture initially with moralistic acts on the frontstages of school grounds.

Chillin'

Among peers who hung out on a regular basis, youth deployed chillin' to handle ambiguous or problematic situations, slipping back and forth among trouble, near-trouble, and not trouble without much notice by anyone except those directly involved. This apparent ambiguity also marked problematic situations that, as youth put it, "everyone knows about" but remained puzzling as to motivation and outcome. Youth chillin' trouble delicately balanced different social skills and emotions, often skirting direct engagement with peers whom they held responsible for or suspected were the source of trouble. These balancing acts proved particularly challenging for peers close to one another. Youth-authored trouble case 4.1, written by a NWHS senior, illustrates these subtleties, beginning with a slight occurring between two close girlfriends that could become a public drama without early recognition and action. Ethnographic trouble case 4.2, observed by Jerlyn, illustrates another common reality of trying to chill a little drama that began with a highly visible interaction on the quad slipping between teasing and insults, involving a boy with a "crush" on a girl in a group of girlfriends who hung out together at a regular spot on campus.

Case 4.1 "Gave Her Some Room"

The day school started and my best friend and I was tour guides for the new freshmen in school. We hang out all the time, she and I. The group we were touring needed to get a health screening from the nurse at the admin office. It was really crowded so we all just waited around outside the office while people went in to see the nurse. Took a while. The freshmen was asking questions when my friend was giving information about something. I stepped in to give some information. She looked down. Not sure if she was pissed a little because I stepped in. I was talking to the freshmen because there were other things to say. She answered questions to. The bell rang and we went to class. I gave her some room between classes when I would see her. She looked away when I saw her. I was worried didn't want any drama in front of everyone. I care about her too! I don't want to embarrass her or me. She's my best friend! I saw her at lunch on the quad and we walked up the breezeway to hang out. I told her about my brother getting in trouble last Saturday. Got a smile from her. We could talk. Maybe it was better not to. The next day we did more tours for freshmen. I made sure I didn't step in on her. My friend seemed her old happy self.

Case 4.2 "Gave Each Other Some Space"

On the quad early during lunch, Jerlyn sat down at a picnic table with several African American girls known on campus as the "WestSiders"—so named because they lived in the poor neighborhoods to the west of campus. They referred to the table as their "regular spot," which was part of a larger African American crowd that regularly gathered in the quad during lunch. The crowd sometimes grew so large that it spilled over from the quad on to a large, open grassy/dirt area just off the quad (framed by "A," "B," and "C" buildings). All juniors, the WestSiders consisted of Kiona and Monica, who sat on the side of the table where Jerlyn was sitting, and Vanessa, Evon, and Destinee, who faced Jerlyn and the other students across the table. As Jerlyn got comfortable, Monica greeted her warmly. Monica was interested in pursuing "higher ed," as she put it, and talked about joining her cousin, who attended Spelman College [a historically black college in Atlanta for women]. Monica's friends characterized her as "taking care of business" in school and in life with very high grades and a retail clerk's job at an outlet mall store. Sitting next to Monica was Kiona, petite yet curvy, who constantly greeted boys coming by the table to say hello during any given lunch period. Kiona was not as good a student as Monica but she still earned solid "B's and a few "A's" even though the girls said she was a bit "wild" and "likes to party." For most of the school year, Kiona was not dating anyone consistently, preferring, as she put it, "just to have fun." The other three girls chatted about a party they went to last Saturday. As Monica and Jerlyn start chatting, David, another African American junior, bustled over to sit down at the table next to Kiona. He was short and well-built with an unusually large mouth that seemed fixed in a perpetual grin. He too lived west of campus and often rode with the five WestSiders on the city bus they all took to school. On most days, David moved from table to table, talking fast and loudly cracking jokes in his high-pitched voice, constantly looking around to see who noticed him. Sometimes he would hit a nerve, drawing shouts of "move yo punk ass outta here," and sometimes he left a table laughing uproariously like a comedy club audience in the wake of a particularly good joke.

As David sat down at the table, he leaned into and touched Kiona's jacket, which was precariously draped on the table top, looking as if it might fall to the ground. David called out loudly to no one in particular, "Whose fake-ass leather coat is this?" Almost as soon as he delivered the comment, he laughed and got up to walk to a group of youth three tables over from the WestSiders. David's comment caught the girls' attention and Evon loudly said across the table to where Monica, Kiona, and Jerlyn were sitting, "Ooh, he call yo new coat fake! He ain't gonna get with that! Uh, uh!" Kiona shouted in the direction David walked: "Muthafucka, the coat not supposed to be leather. Always talkin' shit. No one likes yo short ass anyway! I gonna whip yo ass!" Although the quad was always noisy, Kiona's brief tirade attracted the attention of youth from the next table, who turned toward the commotion. Kiona frowned and chuckled as she looked down. Destinee, Evon, and Vanessa got up and formed a half circle around Kiona. Jerlyn could see David a few tables over, now without his usual silly grin. He cocked his head as if surprised by Kiona's seeming hostility and turned his back completely toward the WestSiders' table, seemingly engrossed with the youth where he sat. Back at the WestSiders' table, the girls told Kiona what a "punk ass" David was. Destinee said, "You [Kiona] could whup him. He don deserve the energy to beat down his ass." Vanessa said, "David's a little boy. You know he like you and don know what to do." Monica added quietly that Kiona "should pay him no mind if he's gonna treat you that way." Kiona, half frowning and half chuckling, almost whispered, saying, "He alright sometimes. His head big as a basketball though." The group erupted in laughter at Kiona's last comment.

After a few minutes the laughter subsided and the girls decided to walk up the breezeway, as Monica put it, to "get some peace." Monica and Jerlyn trailed a few steps behind the group and Jerlyn asked, "What's the deal with Kiona and David?" Monica shrugged her shoulders and said, "Constant little dramas with him. He gotta a crush on Kiona but he don't know what to do about it." Monica continued, "You wanna get pissed and you laugh too. He funny. She good at lettin' it go and chill, though." As they continued strolling up the breezeway, the noise on the quad receded into the background and Monica and Jerlyn found a grassy spot with the rest of the WestSiders where they could sit under a shade tree midway between "K" and "L" buildings. They saw Mr. Rupp (the history teacher), who held open his classroom for students during lunch, walking between the buildings. He often got some air for a few minutes before going back to his classroom. He waved and smiled. Another small group of youth sat near the end of "L" opposite the breezeway, with some youth sitting alone, sprinkled between the WestSiders and the breezeway. For the next twenty minutes before the bell rang, the girls chatted about what the weekend would bring. The topic of David only came up once when Vanessa said, "nice not to have the drama," to which all the girls nodded in agreement. In the coming weeks, David only encountered the WestSiders on the bus to school and Monica reported he was "quieter . . . not talkin' shit." Monica went on to tell Jerlyn that David and the WestSiders "gave each other some space." For his part, David shifted his attention away from the WestSiders' regular spot, saying to Jerlyn, "That part of the quad ain't too friendly to me right now."

Trouble cases 4.1 and 4.2 remind us how the trouble strings for each case might have unfolded but did not. Research on street code contexts demonstrates how interactional slights and insults among youth directed at persons or possessions can lead to hostile and violent altercations. The code of the street evokes strong cognitive and normative expectations about what will and should occur in public interactions.[1] Social trust at NWHS set different expectations in which the first reaction to an insult among peers was not automatically a hostile response. When insults did occur, as in case 4.2, youth experienced ambiguity and concern coupled with an underlying obligation to keep the peace, or, as in case 4.1, to treat a friend in a way that signaled care. To be sure, youth also drew on a cultural stock of knowledge that resonated with the code of the street, yet those expectations were tempered by social trust, especially among older students in the eleventh and twelfth grades.

Peer relationships and space both inhibited and facilitated workin' it out, playing off thick and thin social trust. Vanessa, for example, publically conveyed her tie to and support of Kiona via moralistic pronouncements of David's slight and its consequences for having a relationship with Kiona. In so doing, she signaled what it meant to be a friend and to openly "back up" and trust members of cliques with whom one hung out. Such public displays occurred primarily in the campus downtown where youth, more than any other place on campus, mixed a "tough" or "hard" public front with relational commitments and normative obligations to keep the peace. Indeed, in the classic street code/social distrust context, a proclamation of public support can escalate trouble to open conflict as it syndicates the risk of confrontation by any single person all the while eroding social trust with those beyond the friendship group such that there are few possibilities for backing down.[2] Although these possibilities could occur in the campus downtown, enough thin trust existed in socially distant peers at the school such that downtown was a place where diverse students were comfortable in each other's presence. In this regard, as Robert Putnam notes, thin trust in "the generalized other" is perhaps "more useful than thick trust" because it gives people beyond one's close ties "the benefit of the doubt."[3] The thin trust operating in downtown provided some social space in which Kiona's five friends created a provisional backstage that not only validated her capacity to escalate the situation and "do bad" vis-à-vis David but also shielded her from public scrutiny or retaliation from David, deterring further escalation from either direction. Her friends then piggybacked on to the dynamics of anchored fluidity by moving from downtown to the refuge, solidifying the peace for that day. Subsequent weeks witnessed yet more relational skill linked to anchored fluidity as David moderated his own behavior on the bus where Kiona sat with the WestSiders, moving to hang out with a new group on the quad.

There is, however, a potentially bleaker side to chillin' that research on interpersonal communication in close relationships has uncovered. Practices comprising chillin', such as those illustrated in case 4.1, can produce "chilling effects," which can undermine thick trust and lead to long-term anxiety among close friends and romantic partners, even feeding into asymmetrical power relations.[4] On the one hand, relational partners who withhold grievances in a relationship can become powerless to raise problems and effect needed change. On the other hand, chillin' can operate as a control strategy by higher-power relational partners to suppress open challenges to the status quo in a relationship. Power struggles of this sort are not immediately evident in case 4.1. Instead, the storyteller revealed a measure of empathy, seeing the world through the eyes of her friend and modifying changes to her behavior to sustain the relationship. In the aggregate on campus, chillin' was key to keeping the peace, but its impact on individual youth varied with the kinds of relational ties—long- compared to short-term and relatively equal compared to unequal—between participants dealing with trouble.

Case 4.2 provides a third insight about trouble responses under conditions of social trust, one that relates to the intersection of gender roles and expectations related to race and class. Nikki Jones argues that inner-city African American female youth constantly negotiate two bundles of normative expectations—the respectable "good girl" distanced from "behavioral displays of aggression and overt sexuality" and the "ghetto girl" aligned with the code of the street that leads to physical and verbal ripostes to deter "potential challengers on the street or in the school setting."[5] For African American girls from high-poverty neighborhoods, if not all urban core girls, on-campus social trust legitimizes "good girl" expectations but is not completely divorced from the tough front of the code of the street. Under such conditions, youth learn to "code switch," borrowing from Elijah Anderson, tacking back and forth between "good girl" and "ghetto girl" personae, but in a stylized way. Kiona's coarse retort to David resonated with the street, but her "situated survival skills," to borrow again from Jones, enacted a form of femininity that brought respect without succumbing to either street bravado or demure deference. In effect, the social trust on campus granted interpersonal license that enabled girls (and boys) to approach workin' it out with creative agency and face saving, all the while engaging in the flow of anchored fluidity.

In the opening two cases, relational ties between the parties to trouble had a history, were valued, and were grounded in common affiliations. Social trust and youth agency were especially tested in situations when students did not hang out with each other, were culturally distanced from one another due to different ethnic or racial identities, national affiliations, or neighborhoods, and did not or could not move trouble from the frontstages of downtown to other places on campus. Under such conditions, youth enjoyed little social or spatial room to maneuver and exercised extreme care as they attempted to chill trouble. Ethnographic trouble case 4.3, observed by Cynthia, poignantly illustrates these dynamics.

Case 4.3 "¡Esé?"

Cynthia walked through a part of the cafeteria where the long tables jam close together. It was lunch with everyone crowded together eating, chatting, laughing, moving about from table to table. The density of youth amplified the noise. She found Roberta and Gabriela eating lunch at the same table as always, greeted them, and sat down to chat. Only a minute or two later, Felix, a short, slight Mexicano junior with striking, dark brown eyes and very dark hair, came to sit at the table with Cynthia, Roberta, and Gabriela. Felix, as always, was dressed in a neatly pressed, white button-down shirt and a pair of brown slacks. He sat with Gabriela on his left and Roberta sitting on Cynthia's side of the table opposite him. Felix sometimes joined Roberta and Gabriela to eat lunch if he wasn't over in the "Q" quad or in one of the sheds on campus tinkering with old radios or other electronics. He was always very nice to both girls and had "a thing" for Roberta, according to Gabriela, although it was hard to tell since Felix was unfailingly polite to everyone he encountered, speaking quietly and carefully in both English and Spanish. Today, everyone chit-chatted in Spanish, which the two young women preferred. Felix told the group about an old, short-wave radio he was fixing, which he hoped to use to contact an uncle in Mexico who "liked fixing radios." Next to Roberta and Gabriela's table sat four African American male students also chatting and eating their lunches. Jerlyn talked occasionally with two of the four at the table, Anthony and Jalal, who were seniors and usually hung out on the quad. The other two young men at Anthony and Jalal's table were also seniors, but neither Cynthia or Jerlyn knew their names. No one ever observed these two small groups interacting with each other.

Jalal, sitting closest to Felix, turned to him and with a smirk, said in broken Spanish somewhat loudly above the cafeteria din, "¿Esé, [hey you]? Don't you live near Rio Leon and 93rd?" This intersection marked the border of two low-income areas on the west side of town, one primarily populated by newly arrived Mexicano households and the other by concentrations of poor African American households. At first, Felix ignored him, continuing to tell the group about the old radio he was fixing, although it was clear he heard the question because his head moved a little toward where Jalal was sitting. Jalal persisted, this time saying in English, "Hey" and tapping Felix on the shoulder, "I seen you 'round there, that's where I live. Don't you live there?" Anthony and the other two youth at their table now looked toward the table where Felix sat. It was unclear if Jalal was sincere and did not know how to engage Felix appropriately, if he was trying to insult him, or if this was some sort of neighborhood drama. Still no response from Felix. Jalal now took a different tack, saying in an agitated manner, "¡Orale!" [a Spanish colloquial exclamation used for encouragement as in, "Alright!"], pronouncing the word poorly in Spanish and laughing. Anthony turned back to Jalal and the other two guys at the table, saying, "maybe he don understand." Jalal was now practically standing up as he kept repeating, "¡Orale!," a bit louder.

After a couple more "¡Orales!" Felix stopped talking with the group and looked down at his food, sighing a little bit. He gathered himself, calming himself. Gabriela smiled a little at Felix, catching his eye but not Jalal's or the other boys at the next table. Felix looked concerned and then turned around slowly to Jalal, nodding his head affirmatively with a friendly smile as he quietly yet firmly said he lived near the corner of Rio Leon and 93rd and that "maybe I have seen you around there." Felix turned around to Cynthia, Gabriela, and Roberta so that Jalal and the other three guys could not see his face, and rolled his eyes and curled his lip as if he was disgusted. He then looked back to Jalal's table and smiled again. Jalal shrugged his shoulders, saying, "okay," as he turned to talk with his friends, seemingly losing interest in Felix, who turned back toward Cynthia and the rest of the group. After another sigh, he began talking again about the radio he was trying to fix.

Twenty minutes elapsed and the bell was about to ring, signaling the end of lunch. Gabriela and Roberta headed off to class and Jalal's table had long since cleared out. Felix had a few minutes to chat with Cynthia alone. She asked him in English, "What was up?" in the earlier interaction with Jalal. Felix smiled, shaking his head slowly from side-to-side. He then told Cynthia he did not want any kind of "problems to mess up lunch with his friends," so he just tried "to not let it get to me" and "let it go." He said sometimes one person "wanted to get through lunch with their friends" and another person "wanted" to prove how "bad ass they are." Cynthia asked Felix if he thought Jalal wanted to prove he is a "bad ass" and he replied that what Jalal did is "annoying" but that he was "probably not a bad guy." Felix added, "you don't have to worry too much about fights on campus" because youth "chill on campus." Cynthia also asked Felix whether it mattered that Jalal is black and he is Mexican. Felix answered that "blacks and Mexicanos are okay on campus," yet he said with a shrug, sometimes Mexicanos whose "English is not good get picked on." He added, "That's probably what was going on." More concerning for Felix was his other passion, amateur boxing, which not only gave him confidence that he "can handle himself" but also compelled him to be "extra careful" about not getting in a "pleito" [fight] and "hurting someone." He said that some of his friends know about his boxing and watch him in tournaments, although most people at school only knew him as a "Mexicano who likes radios." For Jalal's part, he told Jerlyn the next day that there were not any "problems" between "Mexican" and black youth at the school, but that the former are "sometime in their own little world," pretending "not to know English." Jalal and his friends sometimes played a "game" to "test" newly arrived youth from Mexico to see if they "can speak English" and added that they "don mean nothing by it." According to Jalal, Felix "got the game" and "passed the test."

In case 4.3, social trust and distrust, as well as cultural distance, came into play in multiple ways as youth navigated potential racial trouble implicating masculine identities. Students newly arrived from Mexico faced multiple difficulties on campus regarding their English-speaking abilities and cultural backgrounds, which Jalal and his friends' "game" underscored. As stigmatizing and potentially degrading as Jalal's "game" was, both Jalal and Felix tempered these tensions with a modicum of regard for each other, at least in their accounts to the fieldworkers. From Felix's standpoint, black youth were "okay" and from Jalal's perspective, Mexican immigrant youth were not "problems." Although these blanket statements signaled a sense of thin social trust, Jalal added that students from Mexico "sometime being in their own world," which conveyed cultural distance, if not distrust, and fueled interactional tensions. That the interaction unfolded in a second language for Felix may have facilitated the suppression of his own personal anxieties or annoyance, reducing the challenges posed by the cultural distance between him and Jalal. Albert Costa and colleagues, for example, have shown experimentally that persons operating in second languages tend to feel emotional distance from moral decision making, leading to a "utilitarian" calculus in their actions.[6] Jalal, on the other hand, conducted the interaction in English, his native tongue, which, in addition to Felix's attempts to ignore him, may have led to his heightened emotional engagement.

The potential for a beef between Felix and Jalal also involved a delicate balance of masculine power and assertion of personhood. Jalal's attempt to get Felix's attention constituted a form of interpersonal masculine power and conversational control in which the male asking a question expects to direct the particular interaction. In his constitution of masculine power, Jalal asserted his personhood as an actor who presumes the racial accounting on campus puts Mexican immigrant youth in the most marginalized positions and Felix, as a member of that category, as someone from whom he deserved an answer to his question. Felix responded to Jalal's attempts at control in two ways. He first ignored Jalal, rendering the power of Jalal's question impotent and thus denying him some of the personhood that Jalal attempted to project. Felix then attempted to assert his own control and personhood as he interacted on the backstage with his two female friends, Gabriela and Roberta, in order to save face and distance himself from Jalal's ongoing actions. Felix also pointed to social trust with his account that Jalal is "probably not a bad guy" despite only interacting with him in this problematic situation. Finally, Felix's status as a boxer both constrained and provided him a source of masculine control as he was careful not to escalate the situation lest it lead to a fight, while also feeding into his own sense of self as a strong male who can "handle himself" in a fight. Jalal's agitation occurred in response to Felix's lack of initial engagement, a potential public slight and undermining of masculine control that quickly evaporated with Felix's deference to Jalal.

This last point suggests how workin' it out can strengthen and weaken social ties in complex ways. The presence of supporters compelled Felix to minimize "problems" on the frontstage that could "mess up lunch with his friends." These same ties also enabled a momentary backstage for Felix to compose himself and express his disdain for Jalal while deferring to him on the frontstage. Felix's social skill in the interaction thickened the relational ties between him and his friends, as it let them in on his frontstage act with Jalal, building their solidarity with Felix when he rolled his eyes at them signaling their shared experience of being "picked on" as "mojados" [the Spanish for the English pejorative "wetbacks," or undocumented Mexicano immigrants]. Later, in a brief interaction with Cynthia, Felix shrugged, a sign of resignation to the stigma faced by Mexicanos on campus. From Jalal's perspective, his successful highly visible "game" with Felix strengthened his sense of power over Felix and perhaps Mexican immigrant youth, more generally, as it solidified interpersonal ties with his friends. And, in terms of the potential for intergroup trouble, social trust, even in this somewhat thin guise, operated as a touchstone for these youth in that the very different peer groups with which they identified both had a place at the school, albeit with Mexican immigrant youths' place more tenuous, particularly in the context of language competency.

Each of the first three cases focuses on how youth chilled drama on campus when dyads operated at the core of the trouble—the first two among youth who hung out together and the latter case involving two youth who did not hang out with each other and came from different ethnic and racial backgrounds. In case 4.4, observed by Jerlyn, we explore difference and cultural distance further by focusing on how chillin' played out between two youth cliques, each with sparse prior contact with the other.

Case 4.4. "Keep Some Distance"

Only a couple of days left to the end of the fall semester and holiday parties seemingly enveloped the campus. The lunch bell came and went, and the period just after lunch turned into a quasi-free period as most classes were, as Diego, a security guard, put it, "shut down for the holidays." Students enjoyed one another's' company either in their classrooms or in student clubs celebrating holiday parties. Toward the end of the period, the nice weather also brought many students outdoors to hang out and take pictures of each other on the quad. Jerlyn sat with three of the WestSiders, Monica, Kiona, Destinee, near their "regular spot." Today, two other youth sat with the West-Siders: Lawrence, a black junior, and William, a freshman who identified as "mixed" "African American" and "white," and Willie, the younger brother of a close friend of Lawrence's. Lawrence spent a lot of time with the WestSiders since he began dating Destinee.

As Jerlyn chatted with the WestSiders, Evon walked up to the group and announced, "They wanna jump us after school." Monica and Destinee both said simultaneously, "Huh? Who?" Evon pointed over to a group of six girls, all of whom were juniors, sitting further out on the grass off the quad. One member of the group, a Chicana named Catrina, held a large bouquet of balloons with "Happy Birthday" written on them. Catrina's group were known as the "SouthSiders" because three of the six members lived on the south side of town near the catchment area border for NWHS and South High School (SHS). According to another SouthSider, an African American named Kayli, the impacted enrollment at SHS enabled her, Catrina, and another SouthSider, Joyellen (who described her heritage as "mixed Irish-Mormon"), to enroll in NWHS. The remaining SouthSiders, an African American named Aleisha and two Chicanas named Rosa and Isabel, lived east of campus but shared part of the same bus line going into and from school. The SouthSiders started hanging out with each other near the end of the previous school year. Although only three of the six lived on New West's south side, all, according to Catrina, shared a "lot of pride" in the south side of town. The SouthSiders uniformly dressed in hip-hop style baggy jeans and flowing white t-shirts that draped over their bodies almost to their knees, accented occasionally with flashy gold necklaces. They sharply contrasted how the WestSiders dressed, who alternated between baggy hip-hop and tight jeans with colorful blouses that reflected whatever was on discount from the outlet mall where Monica worked.

Evon told the group that Kayli, whom she pointed out on the grass among the SouthSiders, was the same girl that she and Vanessa "had problems" with at a party the weekend before last. Jacob, a white senior with whom Kayli was going out, and one of his male friends, Billy, an African American, had struck up a conversation at the party with Evon and Vanessa, who were "pretty drunk," according to Evon. Several minutes into the conversation, Kayli came over with a couple of her SouthSide girlfriends to "pull" Jacob and his friends away from Vanessa and Evon. "They got them [Jacob and Billy] outta there," said Evon. All the youth involved then spent the evening trying "not to run into each other" as they circulated in and out of the house where the party was held. Evon and Vanessa did not have any classes with Kayli and her friends, so it was relatively easy on campus, as Vanessa put it, to "stay outta they [the SouthSiders'] way." Evon then recounted running into Jacob earlier in the day and his "warning" her that the SouthSiders had grown tired of "WestiSiders gettin' in their business."

"They crossin' the line. I got yo back, Evon," Vanessa volunteered and turned around to glare across the grassy area to where the SouthSiders were sitting. Joyellen and Kayli turned around to look toward the WestSiders as if sensing the glare from Vanessa. Destinee and Kiona added their support for Evon and the WestSiders, more generally. "We in it," says Destinee. Kiona added, "We gonna whup ass." Monica, always a voice of reason in the group, asked, "Those girls wanna fight us from what happened at a party like two weeks ago?" Evon nodded her head affirmatively, "Yep." "Nuthin' happened 'tween you and this Jacob since?" Monica asked Evon. "Nope," Evon said, "I ain't seen him 'til this morning." Jerlyn interjected, "But the trouble from the party was never settled?" "No it was not," Evon emphatically stated. Monica commented to no one in particular in reference to Catrina's balloons, "Looks they more gonna have a birthday party than fight. "They want pictures just like us." Over on the grass, Kayli and Joyellen and the rest of the SouthSiders began taking pictures of Catrina with her balloons.

A few minutes passed and the SouthSiders walked past the WestSide table toward the base of the breezeway, laughing. Jerlyn overheard someone in the SouthSide group, say, "Jacob and Billy gonna go for those skinny hoodrats?" [a degrading term for promiscuous young women]. Monica dryly said to Jerlyn, "It's like a movie. You seein' a little drama here." Everyone at the WestSide table ignored the SouthSiders by eating their lunches as Jerlyn noted tension at the table growing; it was so quiet at the table that only chewing and a lunch bag crinkling could be heard. After the South-Siders passed by and were out of sight up the breezeway, William said to no one in particular at the WestSide table, "Hoodrats? No hoodrats here. They the only hoodrats I see [referring to the SouthSiders]." "I wanna take a picture of everybody. Let's get outta the sun." Monica cut the tension with her suggestion, holding a small camera in her hand and motioning everyone at the WestSide table toward the front of "A" building where the indirect sunlight was better for snapping pictures. The group walked over to the spot near "A" and Evon invited Jerlyn to kneel down with the rest of the group as Monica started snapping pictures. Jerlyn volunteered to snap some pictures of the group with William and Lawrence also joining in and making jokes that cracked the group up. Everyone was more relaxed now. The WestSiders remained in the quad until the end of the free period and Jerlyn remained on campus until after last period, positioning herself near the quad where the two groups would mostly likely walk as they made their respective ways to their bus stops. Jerlyn caught up to the WestSiders walking out the south parking lot toward their stop on Rio Leon Road. Monica waved Jerlyn over to say it would be "better not to run in to nobody while waiting for the bus," referring to the SouthSiders. Within a few minutes they boarded their bus and were gone without incident. Jerlyn could see across the street where the SouthSiders waited for their bus to head south on New West Road. During the next two days, as Monica put it, both groups "keep some distance" during lunch by moving between the quad and the refuge, but there was not any "real tension no more." Jerlyn asked her why not and she said, "People moved on." Jerlyn chatted with Kayli on the quad the next day and the conversation came around to "a rumor about a possible fight between the WestSiders and the SouthSiders," which stemmed from an incident at a party involving Evon, Vanessa, and Jacob. Kayli said, "That was a while ago. Those girls was drunk. Fight? Nobody wanna bring that shit on campus." When Jerlyn asked about whether any trouble could occur off campus between the two groups, Kayli remarked, "Not likely; we chill." In response to a question about Jacob, Kayli remarked that, "He talk shit from time to time. He like drunk ones and that ain't no good," referring to Jacob's proclivity to talk with drunk girls at parties. For his part, Jacob told Jerlyn that he knew "nothing about no party problems or fighting," and did not remember whether he spoke with Evon on campus when she told the WestSiders that the South-Siders wanted to fight them. The two groups seemed to have forgotten the trouble by the end of the next week and, later in the year, the SouthSiders seemed to have turned over in their membership as Isabel and Rosa could be seen hanging out with friends they met through MEChA activities.

Case 4.4 underscores how social distance can intensify in-group/out-group dynamics marked by intragroup solidarity and intergroup derogation—all of which carries the potential of escalating peer conflict in the image of gang rivalry.[7] Scholars of urban youth conflict have long argued that such dynamics can transform interpersonal altercations into intergroup hostilities as youth in close social circles and street gangs from the same neighborhoods regard themselves as in-groups and peers from other neighborhoods as members of out-groups.[8] Under these conditions, groups are likely to make negative moralistic attributions as they make sense of and manage conflict.[9] All the ingredients for these dynamics appear in case 4.4 as Jacob played off these dynamics in passing on the SouthSiders' "threat," which fit intuitively with Evon and Vanessa's sense of the situation. As such, it is not surprising that at two different points in case 4.4 youth engaged in moralistic responses to trouble, the first when Evon delivered her news of the SouthSider threat and the second in response to the "hoodrat" comments as the SouthSider group passed by the WestSiders. At each point, these interactions stayed within the WestSider group and developed no further as they were interrupted by various kinds of chillin'. Avoidance played a key role in these dynamics yet did not alone mitigate the in-group/out-group dynamics of the situation.

Monica's intervention interrupted the first set of moralistic actions with an expressed skepticism about the SouthSiders' threats. Both the West-Siders and SouthSiders refocused on the benign reasons that brought them onto the quad ("snapping pictures") in a holiday atmosphere, which created a perceptual bridge between the two groups. Although tension still existed between them until the SouthSiders left the quad on the first day of the on-campus portion of the trouble, Monica compelled the WestSiders to return to their own activities without being consumed by the SouthSider threat, an act that diminished her group's fear and anxiety about the situation. On the other side of interaction, Kayli, in her comments to Jerlyn a few days later, shifted the source of threats from the SouthSider group to Jacob, which further defused the social tension between the groups, yet without direct communication between them. Monica's multiple interventions in the trouble string and Kayli's after-the-fact account certainly played off the two girls' own agency and social positions as informal leaders in their respective groups. The fluidity of groups on campus further diffused the possibility of long-term trouble as some SouthSider members became involved with other groups, revealing the porous quality of the group's boundaries and reducing the possibility of entrenched intergroup conflict. Their actions and accounts also resonated with the broader climate of trust on campus and that sociocultural difference need not automatically equal fear and derogation.

In the examples of chillin' above, all the youth involved eventually came to share a tacit, bridging understanding that the situation could be handled without escalation. Of course not all the parties viewed their respective situations identically nor did they validate each other's concerns in similar or equivalent terms. But youth held enough of a shared understanding of events that they approximated what Erving Goffman calls a "working consensus" of the actors and events involved.[10] The climate of social trust and anchored fluidity conditioned such understandings as much if not more than direct exchange among parties and the lessons learned from it. While tacit understandings formed a basis for students to work out their troubles through chillin', other instances featured youth approaching peers to voice grievances directly to educate them about annoyances and possible remedies for trouble.

Educating

When NWHS students used the term educating they turned official versions of this practice on their heads. In most schools, official educating unfolds in top-down ways from adult teachers, counselors, and administrators to students. A great deal of social learning also occurs in adult-moderated student clubs and in youth-centered peer relations. As a form of peer control, educating put youth at the center of teaching and learning processes that involved delivering and receiving voice about interpersonal, peer trouble. When youth at NWHS enunciated "educating" in conversation, they typically emphasized the ". . . ing" suffix instead of dropping into the more casual "n'" form characteristic of workin' it out or chillin'. This usage underscored the act of voicing concerns about trouble, even under difficult conditions.

Case 4.5 illustrates educating within a youth clique that suffered the death of one of their members in an automobile accident. In this case, the trouble string included moralistic talk but was brought back toward a conciliatory-remedial path by the efforts of two informal leaders of the peer group and in the presence of adults—a security guard and researcher—who did not directly intervene but offered relatively restrained assistance.

Case 4.5 "Gio Didn't Mean to Do It"

It was the first day back after the Thanksgiving break, about fifteen minutes after the last school bell had rung, and almost the entire student body had cleared out from campus. Jerlyn was sitting at a picnic table on the edge of the quad writing fieldnotes from observations earlier in the day. Robert (a Latino/Anglo security guard) pulled up in a golf cart and asked how she was doing. They started chatting and another security officer, an African American named Tyson, pulled up in another cart in what he jokingly called the "fleet"—the two decrepit golf carts that NWHS guards used to patrol the horizontal campus. He asked Robert and Jerlyn if they had seen the article in the local newspaper about Rosa Gonzalez, a NWHS senior who recently died. Robert slowly nodded his head up and down, noting in a low, sad voice that she died during the Thanksgiving break. Jerlyn nodded affirmatively too. She did not know Rosa but knew she died in an accident of some kind. The newspaper article discussed her life and her family's reaction but not the specific circumstances of her death. An awkward silence followed Robert's question, which Jerlyn filled with, "That's horrible, just horrible. What happened?" Robert said, "She was in a car accident. She was in an old truck driving and hit a wall not too far from here. She was about two blocks from home on her way back from the store when she crashed." Tyson added, "The guy she was with didn't die. I think he just has a broken leg and a bunch of cuts and bruises. He's in the hospital." "That's weird on a city street," Jerlyn commented. "Alcohol or drugs?" Tyson said, "No. From what I understand, they had the windows down and the guy who was with her had ashes from a cigarette in his hand. They blew into Rosa's eyes while she was driving. She lost control of the truck and ran into a wall at about thirty miles an hour. She hit her head." Jerlyn said, shaking her head, "Wow, she died due to cigarette ashes in her eyes. That's incredibly sad." Robert said, "She was a good kid. Was going to graduate soon. Her life hadn't even begun yet." Another awkward bit of silence; the three of them stared at each other processing the tragedy. Then Robert said, "Her friends like to sit on the fields at lunch, after school, talking, smoking. I saw 'em there a few minutes ago. I should bust 'em for smoking. Not today. I think I'll go see how they're doing. I know them pretty well." Jerlyn asked if he minded if she went with him." "No problem," Robert replied. As she hopped into the cart with Robert, Tyson took off in his cart going the opposite direction. While driving with Robert, Jerlyn learned that Rosa hung around with a group of sophomores and juniors known as "stoners" because they smoked cigarettes and pot on the far western edge of the fields. Robert told Jerlyn that Rosa was not known as a "stoner" but liked these youth because they were "easy going" and, at fifteen and sixteen, closer to her age. Rosa would not have turned seventeen until the summer after her graduation.

They arrived on the far edge of the fields to find a mixed group of eight male and female students. A few sat in blue, lightweight plastic chairs and the rest stood under a huge shade tree. Some had cigarettes dangling from their mouths. A guy held a cigarette in one hand and a slice of pizza in the other. A young woman ate a donut and sipped something from a large, paper coffee cup from a local donut shop. The air was thick with smoke from unfiltered cigarettes but no pot smoke. Cigarette butts, empty water bottles, soda cans, backpacks, and an old shoe were scattered about the area. Jerlyn recognized three youth from some of the Latinos she sometimes saw in or near the "Q" quad and two black guys (one with really dark skin and dreads whom she knew as Jamaal) that she sometimes saw eating lunch with the black crowd on the quad. A white young man and woman smoking sat close to each other with a lot of tattoos on their arms and some on their necks. Where they didn't have tattoos, their skin looked pale white, like they had never seen the sun (even though they were outside under a tree). Most of the group dressed in black from head to toe and some had their heads shaved very close in the back. Close up, Jerlyn could see that several members of the group, both young men and women, had their nails painted black. All the girls and two of the boys wore heavy black eyeliner, and many had various piercings of their ears, noses, and faces, which taken together appeared characteristic of the "goth" style.[11]

All eyes fixed on Robert and Jerlyn as they pulled up in the cart. Although the school prohibited smoking on school grounds at any time, as promised, Robert did not respond in any way to the youth smoking in front of him. One of the Latinas Jerlyn had seen in the "Q" quad asked Robert why the tree logs (on which they used to sit) "were moved." Robert replied it had "to do with the construction" just beginning on campus. He then asked how the group was doing with Rosa's death. He added, "I'm here if you need me or if you need to see someone." A couple of students mumbled "okay" and everyone looked either down or away from Robert or Jerlyn.

A young man Jerlyn did not recognize, who she later found out was named Jaime, sat on one of the chairs and said in somewhat high-pitched voice, "It's not fair. I can't believe she's not here anymore." Robert later told Jerlyn that Rosa was really close to Jaime in a "sister-brother way," including helping him with some of his schoolwork and talking with him when he was "down." Jaime lived with his "abuela" [grandmother] and was from Mexico, but it was not clear where the rest of Jaime's family was or even if he had other family in the United States. He originally met Rosa on the same bus they took to school from west of campus. Jaime raised his voice in an angry tone, saying he was "really fucking mad at Gio," the male member of their group whose ashes got in Rosa's eyes. He questioned Gio "smoking with the window down" and blurted out, "He shoulda known something could happen!" Then Jaime said he wanted to go "kick his ass, give that muthafucka a beat down real good." Jaime was almost crying now and repeated his threats again. Jerlyn and Robert listened attentively, nodding their heads occasionally, looking down and remaining quiet. It was an intense moment mixed with sadness, remorse, and anger. Jerlyn looked to her right and saw Jamaal scowling as if he was going to cry when he blurted out, "Damn right; mess up that muthafucka!" To Jerlyn, it felt as if Jaime and Jamaal were venting, although they sounded very sincere and very angry. The young, pale white woman with all the tattoos, who Jerlyn later found out was named Lacey, stood up and walked over to Jaime, bending down to put her arm around his shoulders. Jerlyn could hear Lacey gently telling Jaime how "Gio didn't mean nuthin'" and "how much" they "all miss Rosa." Lacey's touch and quiet words seemed to break the spell and Jaime looked down at his feet, now only sniffling a little. Lacey continued consoling him, saying something to him softly of which Jerlyn only picked up bits and pieces like "It's okay to be mad and sad" and that "We'll get through this together." Lacey then stood up and turned to Robert, assertively asking why an "admin announcement wasn't made about Rosa" that morning. All eyes turned to Robert and Jerlyn again; Lacey definitely got everyone's attention. Robert said, "I don't know," and suggested that the students "think of a tribute for Rosa they could say" during morning announcements. He also mentioned that tomorrow there might be "information from Rosa's family" about a "service" for her. Lacey responded with a more energetic "Okay. We can put something in." He and Lacey talked for a bit about what information might be coming from the family and to whom she and the group should talk to about an announcement. The tattooed young man sitting next to Lacey, who Jerlyn later found out was named Gordon, stood up rather deliberately and asked Jamaal if he wanted to see how Gio "is doing." "He's already pretty messed up, brother," said Gordon. Jamaal, quiet now and less animated than just a few minutes before, said, "Yeah I guess. He'll wanna see friends." "Jaime? Wanna go?" To which Jaime nodded affirmatively, not saying anything. The entire group fell silent. After what seemed like forever, but was probably closer to a minute, Robert said to the group, "Okay, hang in there." He and Jerlyn climbed back into the cart and set off toward the center of campus. In the days that followed, Lacey read a moving statement from "Rosa's friends" over the morning announcements celebrating Rosa's life, and Gio, on crutches, returned to school.

For several weeks after her visit to their spot, Jerlyn saw the group as a whole or in pairs (with Jaime or Jamaal helping Gio carry his stuff) hanging out by the fence on the outskirts of the fields. Midway into the spring semester, she had not seen the group for some time and learned from Lacey that they rarely hung out together anymore, having dispersed to different areas and groups on campus.

This case illustrates multiple bottom-up and middle-out ways through which socioemotional support and youth resilience occurred on campus in the course of working out trouble. Most apparent was the support and compassion among socially intimate peers themselves, first in the guise of the group's informal leader therapeutically calming (educating) an angry peer about the legitimacy of his emotions, which in turn led other members of the group to signal support for the group member blamed for the trouble. Robert, the security guard, offered additional support through his empathetic visit to the group, followed by an offer to talk informally with them about their distress, guidance on how to inform broader public audiences on campus about their friend, and encouragement to see the school counselor. As has been found in other studies of urban schools, security guards can develop meaningful social ties to youth, becoming de-facto advisors and often knowing as much or more than anyone else about the social lives of students.[12] In this sense, some NWHS security guards and youth-centered teachers replicated the informal roles that social workers and cops play in neighborhoods as they act as third-party peacemakers and supportive observers of trouble among social intimates—roles that we will explore more fully in chapter 6.[13]

Case 4.5 also points to how situational contingencies can mitigate whatever generalized distrust a particular group has of official policing authority. Monica Bell, for example, finds that in the context of generalized distrust and legal cynicism regarding the police in poor, urban African American communities, disadvantaged mothers still call the police to help them gain advantage over other sources of institutional authority, such as social welfare agencies, housing authorities, or schools.[14] Rosa's friends viewed the NWHS security guards and administration with suspicion because, as Jaime noted in a conversation with Jerlyn, "The guards they mostly okay with us, but you never know. They sometimes bust us for smoking cigarettes or pot, you know." Robert's relational outreach, including his empathetic decision to refrain from enforcing the antismoking rules, was generative of situational trust. His actions created an opening for Lacey to ask him for advice about getting a message out to the student body about Rosa and moved the conversation away from a digression into why the school had removed some old logs on which they used to sit. This interaction provided yet another glimpse of informal and formal control working in alignment on campus.

A final aspect of the case concerns Lacey's actions, illuminating the importance of peer group leaders, especially young women, on campus for keeping both inter- and intragroup peace. Her interaction with Robert focused on complaints about the "admin" not yet recognizing Rosa's death, signaling the group's lack of full trust in the school and perhaps the marginal acceptability of her group by school authorities. Robert closed this possible gap, at least related to these events, with his empathetic response and instrumental help. Lacey's question to Robert also played an important role in managing the trouble within the group, as it turned the attention toward the school, as embodied in Robert, over a perceived slight, then to Rosa's funeral service, and finally to an instrumental act in the composition of a statement about her for morning announcements. In this way, Lacey's actions both dealt with the trouble at hand and built solidarity among the group for future action. In the end, it is difficult to discern whether Rosa's loss ultimately led to the disintegration of the group or if its members, as is common among youth on campus, simply found other interests and groups.

Although educating among socially intimate peers is more common than among socially distant peers, it also occurred among those who did not hang out together, as the author of case 4.6, a twelfth grade Latina, illustrates.

Case 4.6 "Could I Educate Her?"

Well about a month ago I had a conflict with another student, she's a junior & I'm a senior. We don't hang out. I do see her sometimes at school. She's the type of person that has that natural mean look like if she's rolling her eyes at you. One day she gave me a crazy look that I didn't appreciate so from then on I let her know I didn't like her, and whenever she would see me I would roll my eyes, because I figured, okay. She must have a problem with me, so I'm letting her know that I could see that she has a problem with me, so if she wants she could come up to me & solve it because she was the one that had the problem with me first. So about a few days later when I was going to my last hour class (7th) with my friend, her & her friend stopped me & asked if she could talk to me real quick, so my friend and I went between a couple of buildings with her and her friend and she told me that she's been noticing that I was rolling my eyes so she just had come to find out why. Could I educate her? I told her that it seemed like she was dogging me first, so we talked about it & she said she didn't mean it that way cause she doesn't even know me & she was rolling her eyes because everything is so crowded, not because of me. So I made a mistake. We agreed on things & said sorry. End of story.

In many ways this case is unremarkable with regard to how youth represented workin' it out via educating in youth-authored cases: two youth engaged one another with allies present and in locales on campus ("between buildings") where they could more easily sustain a backstage without public scrutiny. The case also was unremarkable in its "all's-well-that-ends-well" feel, which signals a sense that youth can comport with adult-centered expectations about how one "should" handle interpersonal conflict ("said sorry . . . end of story"). From another vantage point, however, the string of trouble responses in case 4.6 underscores that even under conditions of relatively weak social ties—among peers who, as the author notes, did not "hang out" together—youth took the risk to voice their concerns to one another. The storyteller did not portray herself as the protagonist driving the trouble toward peaceful resolution. She waited for her antagonist to approach her, signaling a moralistic high ground and a sense that the antagonist was in the wrong and must initiate reconciliation. Once her antagonist approached, the author then became a coparticipant in problem solving, both piggybacking on anchored fluidity to find a quiet spot "between buildings" while playing off the expectations associated with social trust on campus.

Ethnographic trouble case 4.7 again addresses trouble among socially and culturally distant youth who attend different high schools and share only a loose connection via a set of common activities—street racing. Underscored in this beef are attempts to cultivate masculinity via violence and an undertone of racial competition, if not disdain, all refracted through the campus climate of social trust.

Case 4.7 "That's Not How It Works Here"

Cynthia was at the cafeteria on a mid-spring day and saw a white senior named Bill, who transferred to campus at the beginning of fall. He was hanging out with Pablo, a stout senior whose shirt always seemed to be untucked, and two of his Latino friends, both of whom were seniors. Bill always wore a t-shirt that showed off his muscular arms. He fancied cars and drove a "tricked out" Honda Civic on which he had installed large, shiny mufflers that amplified the engine's throaty growl. Pablo and Bill lived south of campus in mixed-income neighborhoods and came to know each other at school through their cars. Pablo also drove a Honda Civic that he "tuned" (modified) for street racing. That day he wore a work shirt that identified the small auto repair shop where he worked after school and enabled him to get discounts on parts for his and his friends' cars. When Pablo was not working after school, he, his friends, and Bill sometimes hung out in the east parking lot talking cars.

Cynthia sipped a soda while looking at the school newspaper, positioned between Bill and Pablo's table and another table where there was a group of three Cambodian youth who were known as serious "racers" or "tuners" because they street raced their Hondas almost every weekend. She overheard Bill talking loudly about the "rice rockets" he saw in the parking lot that he claimed were "all show and no go." Pablo made a gesture with his hands as if to quiet Bill down. The maligned racers, one of whom looked toward Pablo and Bill's table, did not respond to Bill's comments in any demonstrable way except to get up and leave, one of them saying "hi" to Pablo as he passed by but saying nothing to Bill. A "rice rocket" can be a derogatory or complimentary term for a Japanese car modified for street racing depending upon how the term is used. Although Pablo obviously knew a few of the racers, Cynthia had never seen Bill hanging out with them.

Three days later, Cynthia saw Pablo in the cafeteria. He agreed to hang out with Cynthia for a while to talk about "what's going on." He told her about a beef he experienced a couple of days ago after school [the timing of which places it after the cafeteria remarks Bill made in the presence of the racers]. The beef involved Tuy, a Cambodian guy who attended East High School, lived in the same southern neighborhood as the racers, and also raced cars with them. According to Pablo, he and Bill were standing near

Pablo's car talking and the racers were hanging out nearby in the parking
lot when Tuy pulled up in his car and parked in a space next to where Pablo
parked his car. As the racers began ambling over to Tuy's car, Bill let fly with
some unflattering remarks about Tuy's car that paralleled what he said about
"rice rockets" in the cafeteria. The Cambodians seemingly ignored Bill, but
Tuy got out of his car and, as Pablo recalls, said, "That's how it is?" Tuy then
walked to his trunk, opened it, and pulled out a gun so Bill, Pablo, and the
racers could see it. He did not point the gun at anyone, holding it buy his
side. Pablo said that everyone looked surprised, if not "shocked." According
to Pablo, he "let Tuy know" that "it's not how we do things here [i.e., have
a gun at NWHS and/or threaten someone with it]. Pablo remembered one
of the racers agreeing with him, saying to Tuy, "Come on man, let's not get
into it." Tuy did not say a thing, but looked somewhat disgusted, according
to Pablo, and slowly put the gun back in his trunk, closing the lid. The racers
hopped in Tuy's car and they all "took off" about the same time Diego, the
security guard, walked from the administration building into the parking lot
to do his usual afterschool "walkthrough." Neither Pablo nor Bill told Diego
about the incident. Since that time, Pablo had worked to, in his words, "educate" Bill to not "talk shit" about other youth's cars. Pablo also learned that
the racers told Tuy that it was "best if he didn't come to campus [NWHS] for
a while."

Case 4.7 involved moralistic insults that led to a potentially dangerous
situation. NWHS security guards or town police officers were not present
to intercede and nor did any NWHS staff member learn of this incident.
Clearly, the trouble could have taken a different turn, resulting in violence.
At the same time, it fit much of the interactional and cultural dynamics of
trouble handling on campus during this historical period in which adults,
even those monitoring situations, rarely interceded directly into peer conflict except in the most dramatically visible cases. It is not that adults on
campus were lax or did not care, but that the dynamics of youth trouble
at NWHS made it impossible to intervene on a minute-by-minute basis
given the constant sociospatial dynamics in play among youth, providing
the interactional foundations of peaceful peer control. Underneath these
microdynamics, case 4.7 illustrates multiple qualities of the campus climate relevant to trouble. The first consists of youth protecting the school
from violence. The second was our discovery that insults among peers
did not automatically demand a violent response—a clear counter to the
typical code-of-the-street dynamic in which affronts to personal or group
identity are met by force. Yet one might ask if this incident "really" oc-

curred. This question is reasonable, especially given our earlier findings that youth entering NWHS wrote about violent episodes of conflict at far higher rates than we observed on campus. Nevertheless, all the youth in Pablo's recounting were older, and we rarely observed or collected narrations of threats and violence among older youth. Also, note that the agent of potential violence, Tuy, did not attend NWHS. Whether the incident unfolded just the way Pablo told it or not, its form and substance demonstrate the stock of legitimated story elements out of which youth, especially older students, routinely narrated trouble on campus. Indeed, that Pablo believed he *could* intervene certainly signaled his own courage and conviction, emboldened by the social trust on campus even in a situation involving cultural difference. Moreover, his narration parallels the routine kinds of peacekeeping among youth that we observed at NWHS during this period.

Finally, it is important to note that tamping down trouble often involved third parties acting on behalf of their friends—Pablo for Bill and the Cambodian racers for Tuy. This pattern illustrates the importance of peer group communication on and off campus. In many ways, Tuy's support of his friends with a gun, an artifact of actual and symbolic force, comports strongly with street code logic.[15] Pablo counters this logic, absent adult monitoring, with a statement that illustrates how the campus climate moderates the potential for interpersonal youth violence. The statement "[I]t's not how we do things here," as Pablo reported saying, carried both descriptive and prescriptive connotations, yet another link to the climate of social trust and civility on campus.

Keeping the Peace in Everyday School Life

To work out their troubles, youth used a range of nonconfrontational tactics they referred to as "chillin.'" Their responses included various forms of lumping, accommodation, self-directed changes, deflection, friendly denials, nonspecific apologizing, biographical storytelling, temporary avoidance, and engagement with third parties as either sounding boards or peacemakers—all without explicit attachment to the trouble issues that were at stake. These practices occurred ubiquitously but operated in the shadows of official school control practices and blended into the everyday social and spatial movement across campus that constituted anchored fluidity. When youth "educated" each other, their tactical orientation alternated from carefully couching their complaints to voicing them directly, which led to various forms of informal negotiation (talking it out) and problem solving.

How youth used these two repertoires in trouble strings often hinged on contextual features, especially the social distance among peers, the ease of finding a backstage away from the scrutiny of public audiences, and the presence or absence of other peers, especially allies.

When youth engaged in these conciliatory-remedial responses to trouble, conflict rarely became stuck in the direction of moralistic or rule-oriented responses, underscored by our aggregate data in chapter 3. These two repertoires of responses aligned with both default expectations of social trust and the sociospatial practices of anchored fluidity. Workin' out trouble also involved multiple, delicate balancing acts. Chief among these, as students put it, was "keeping the trust" while "standing up for yourself"; the latter under some conditions did veer toward the code of the street and social distrust. Evidence of this balancing act appeared in trouble-response strings in which youth talked about engaging in potential moralistic acts with particular brio, often supporting friends outside of hearing range of troubling parties. This balancing act intertwined, as well, with complex senses of gender and race. How does one, for example, convey and cultivate masculinity or femininity, as conventionally understood among teens in this context, while keeping the trust and standing up for one's self? In these moments, youth exercised considerable and creative agency, oriented toward both a practical awareness of the present and an awareness of a future beyond the moment, an agency that underlying expectations of dignity also shaped.

A second balancing act involved moving trouble off the frontstages to the backstages of campus. When youth moved their troubles to a backstage with a supportive presence, as in a classroom sanctuary with supportive friends and a teacher monitoring from afar, they were more likely to approach conflict in a conciliatory-remedial fashion. Here again, youth drew on their knowledge of anchored fluidity to affect these moves in ways not easily observed by the adult world around them. In addition, when they could not do so, youth might remain stuck in moralistic directions with eroded social trust.

A third balancing act involved the maintenance of mutual regard and empathy in the face of strong emotions. The management of emotions proved difficult when youth attempted to handle trouble in places of thin social trust, such as on the frontstages of downtown or the convenience store parking lot across the street, among youth who did not hang out together, or among youth with great cultural distance between them, especially different ethnic and racial identities.

Youth also balanced the temporal uncertainties of workin' it out. They recognized that workin' it out is an ongoing process with relatively rare definitive resolutions, and at the same time told of peer trouble unfolding in episodes (orally and in writing) punctuated by recognizable beginnings and endings.[16] When trouble strings dissipated or dragged on without definitive resolutions, youth spoke about "trying their best" and being uncertain about "what just happened."[17] Youth who suspended or resolved troubles without escalation experienced little emotional dissonance or ambivalence, at times capturing their accomplishment with the phrase "that's how you do it."

The interplay between relational ties and workin' it out, especially avoidance, suggests another implication of our analyses in this chapter. Sociolegal scholars argue that the management of conflict via avoidance is especially likely under conditions of social distance because weak ties exert little behavioral, emotional, or materialistic grip on troubled parties, with the result that they are more likely to push away from ties fraught with trouble.[18] In some ways, much of the theory of avoidance focuses on "push" dynamics, in that it focuses on weaker parties' attempts to escape threats from more powerful, threatening parties. At NWHS, weak ties certainly exerted this push, but the dynamics of anchored fluidity also facilitated avoidance, opening other places and contacts that "pulled" youth from troublesome peers and created plausible relational conditions where youth escaped troubling parties and situations. In many ways, this "pull" dynamic resonates with Albert O. Hirschman's insights regarding the conditions under which voice (what youth call educating) and exit from relationships occur. Where alternative social relationships and places are available, as Hirschman puts it, exit will be more likely and voice less likely. This association may explain why chillin', especially temporary avoidance, was more prevalent than educating: Anchored fluidity created pull conditions that facilitated temporary avoidance, thus limiting confrontation as the defining feature of managing trouble among NWHS students.[19]

Yet another balancing act involved young women of color who not only tacked between the stereotypical expectations of what it means to be a "good" and "bad" young woman but also exercised considerable informal group leadership that led to workin' out trouble in peaceful ways. We collected multiple examples of this pattern, such as in case 4.4, when female leaders of two informal, all-female groups reframed and steered their peers away from conflict without directly interacting with each other, or in case 4.7, when a young female group leader moderated the moralistic responses of two young males in her group toward another male member responsible for the accidental death of a female group member. That female students, especially young women of color, would take on the mantle of peacekeepers in interpersonal and intergroup contexts is not surprising from an organizational perspective. Based on multiple studies of women in large, bureaucratic organizations, Deborah Kolb, for example, notes that women often assume behind-the-scenes peacekeeping roles: "Given the structure of contemporary organizations and the support roles in which women are represented in large numbers, they are likely to be major practitioners of behind-the-scenes peacemaking."[20] Hidden peacemaking thus aligns with power relations and female subordination in many large organizations. What is striking about NWHS is the visibility of peacemaking roles for young women, which underscores the empowered, agentic place of young women in the school, including their long-standing tradition of leadership in student clubs.

Finally, workin' it out among youth at NWHS symbolized the existence and maintenance of relationships over time. That is, workin' it out not only addresses particular instances of trouble in relationships but also symbolizes a dominant, distilled "rhetorical vision"[21] of peer relations and social trust within the school—a depiction that modeled how peers did and should create, maintain, and repair damaged relationships, as well as how relational work thickened or thinned social trust. As prevalent as such actions and vision was at NWHS, the aggregate analyses in chapter 3 demonstrated that youth responses to peer trouble did fall outside these parameters, moving in moralistic directions that evoked social distrust. It is to this side of peer trouble at that we turn in the next chapter.

FIVE

"Puttin' 'Em in Their Place"

Our deep ethnographic search for the ways youth dealt with trouble at NWHS under conditions of social trust and anchored fluidity uncovered a family of moralistic responses, or what the students called "puttin' 'em in their place." These actions departed from the usual ways youth managed peer trouble on campus, evoking practices akin to disputes in high-poverty neighborhoods dominated by the code of the street. Youth also used puttin' 'em in their place to refer to covert, moralistic actions cloaked in outward civility, revealing a nuanced picture of how students strategically used and sometimes distanced themselves from social trust on campus.[1]

As revealed in chapters 3 and 4, NWHS students worked out many of their interpersonal and intergroup troubles by relying on cross-cutting, yet fluctuating, peer ties and geographical mobility associated with anchored fluidity. When peer motives and anticipated actions seemed unclear, youth drew on the cultural bedrock of social trust to fill in uncertainties. In students' imaginations and experiences, puttin' 'em in their place focused on building interpersonal hierarchy, a vertical force of action that disrupted the horizontal flow of workin' it out as some youth pursued reputations tied to masculine and relational dominance. For young women, these dynamics took on additional meaning as a form of resistance to masculine, interpersonal domination even as they became entangled in it. One strategy used to put peers in their place is what students called the "beat down," accomplished through hostile accusations, threats and denials, physical violence, and the mobilization of third parties who might carry the fight to troublesome parties. As we demonstrated in previous chapters, physical altercations occurred infrequently on campus during this historical period and were rarely linked to neighborhood turf or street-gang tensions.

Nonetheless, male ninth graders often told tales of beat downs involving physical violence, fear, and social distrust. In practice, male ninth graders rarely pushed beyond bluster to violence, taking each other up to the brink of fighting, which was then constrained by assertive mentoring by senior peers, campus interpersonal ties, and intergroup comity, and by the pervasiveness of trust. On those rare occasions when physical violence did occur, it often manifested among male youth as quick affairs or among female youth as entanglement in multiple power dynamics, sometimes reaching physical violence with both males and females.

Beyond the beat down, youth talked about "goin' undercover" to handle moralistic trouble issues. These actions included covert malicious gossiping, poking fun at or excoriating objectionable parties via hidden transcripts, punishing peers by stealing or damaging their possessions, surreptitiously positioning third-party peers or adults to handle problematic situations, conducting "investigations" to determine the identities and actions of troublesome parties, or permanently cutting off (exiting from) ties with persistently troublesome parties. Goin' undercover revealed a duality on the backstages of campus social life, which were domains of repose and other-regarding, reasoned reflection, but also places for moralistic action that departed the trust within the school or used it to advantage. As youth went undercover, they maintained trusting fronts to cover their tracks, so to speak, whereas youth who attempted beat downs found themselves boxed into identities as "fighters" or "gangsters" that led to overt challenges while limiting the possibilities for backing down or goin' undercover. Beat downs constituted the most visible peer trouble on campus and prominently unfolded on the quads and cafeteria in the heart of the campus downtown. Social trust was thinnest in these places, peer audiences were readily available, and peer interactions could involve students with relatively weak preexisting social ties with each other.

The Beat Down

Two male ninth-grade authors, one white and the other black, take us into the ninth-grade male imagination of the beat down. Case 5.1, "Gave Him a Beat Down," offers a typical version of a physical altercation outside the cafeteria with a male peer unknown to the author, while case 5.2, "I Wasn't to Fight Him," explores a beat down with an uncommon antagonist in a common context—a fight between the author and his friend outside the crowded cafeteria.

Case 5.1 "Gave Him a Beat Down"

One day I had went to school everything was O.K. until lunch came. I went to get my food from the cafeteria. This dude I don't know start throwing trash in my face. I don't do nothing. Let it go. I got no beef with him. He keep throw something else in my face. He told me "you calling me names & stuff behind my back." I said "I don't calling you names you (mf bad name)." So everyone getting us to go outside in the quad. So like a few minutes go by when I went outside everyone was pushing me over there saying I was chicken. Like they was gonna fight. Some kid said "Whoa, why you doing this? Then I went over there by him. He hit me. I hit gave him a beat down. That's what peer pressure can do to you. A teacher caught us said we both go to the office. We had to fill out sheets. Then we had to go to ISS [in-school suspension] for 2 days. So that's it. For 2 days I had to stay in ISS.

Case 5.2 "I Wasn't to Fight Him"

Yes I knew the student. I was at lunch standing in line and he came up to my face and started saying stuff and then he pushed me. He was saying that I wasn't to fight him. I said I didn't say that plus I'm cool with you, I'm your friend and then he push me again and calling me names. I told him to please stop pushing me and then he push me hard and said something about my mom. And then he hit me, and I hit him back. After he fell I started kicking him.

These two cases resonate in part with accounts of revenge collected from urban youth in street code contexts where, as Elijah Anderson puts it, "the culture of the street doesn't allow backing down."[2] As we noted in chapters 3 and 4, street-based neighborhood and gang ties did not figure prominently in youth stories or our observations of youth conflict on campus. But social trust on campus was thinnest downtown, where one's public identity was most salient and students were most likely to encounter socially distant peers, dotted among crowds and small groups who supplied audiences for the latest drama or beef. Case 5.1's author explicitly discussed how the audience witnessing his altercation exerted "peer pressure" by calling him a "chicken"—a label from which the audience, as Jack Katz generally observes, could "develop and carry away its own version of the scene, staining the reputation beyond any visible limit."[3]

At the same time, both authors recounted their attempts to interrupt the flow of moralistic trouble responses, and the author of Case 5.1 reports an attempted intervention by a peer, "some kid." Previous research on urban youth conflict occasionally records observations of youth turning away from altercations and third-party peers attempting to keep the peace, even as social pressure compels violence, but the conditions under which peers de-escalate hostile conflict remain unclear.[4] As documented in the previous two chapters, we observed NWHS students, especially eleventh and twelfth graders, de-escalating trouble via a variety of conciliatory strategies. Ninth graders, who most frequently portrayed and pursued conflict in moralistic terms, included references in their stories to at least one attempt to work out trouble in over one-third of the 307 youth-authored trouble cases in which moralistic responses predominate. Many of these stories are like case 5.1 in that third-party peers not identified as socially linked to the authors or their antagonists attempt to keep the peace.

Case 5.2 also illustrates that NWHS students regard close social relationships as an inhibitor to aggression and violence, even if these ties do not always work as a braking force. In this way, "structural inhibitions" rooted in strong social ties, as Robert Garot calls them, lead to momentary digressions from escalation but are not enough to transform a moralistic to a conciliatory-remedial outcome, especially in the face of group peer pressure to fight.[5] The physical places where peer trouble begins and ends help explain why strong social ties alone cannot channel youth conflict away from escalation. Recall that the majority of moralistic or puttin'-'em-in-their-place trouble strings remained on the frontstages of the quad in the campus downtown and that conciliatory-remedial strings usually moved onto the backstages of the refuge. Without a move off the frontstage, away from the presence of broader peer audiences, strong ties or third-party attempts at peacekeeping are not always enough to redirect an altercation. The spatial move in case 5.1, for example, carried the conflict outside the cafeteria to the main quad, placing it even more squarely on the frontstage in full view of peer audiences.

In youth-authored cases, young people rarely portrayed themselves as initiators trying "to make a rep" (reputation), but rather worried about how they would be viewed by peers related to trouble visited upon them by others seeking to pick fights. Ninth and tenth graders who were caught up in altercations they described as beat downs often pointed out that the initiators of these acts were likely engaged in what Elijah Anderson calls "campaigns of respect" to garner or sustain reps as tough "fighters" and control power relations among peers.[6] At NWHS, students who attempted such campaigns of respect developed reputations as people to avoid, isolating them further from peer networks and denying them the dignified treatment afforded to the great majority of youth who moved across different groups and space in the punctuated flow of anchored fluidity. The tendency of NWHS students to deny reputational status to "fighters," coupled with broader sociocultural constraints on interpersonal violence, emerged in case 5.3, "I Gotta Rep," an altercation observed in the cafeteria between two US-born Latino ninth graders.

Case 5.3 "I Gotta Rep"

Billy watched Roberto, stocky with thick, closely cut black hair, sitting alone at a table in the crowded cafeteria on a late fall day. Roberto came to NWHS from middle school with a "rep" as a fighter, although no one, except some of his friends from middle school, could recall seeing him fight. A few tables away sat José (whom we met in chapter 1) who was about the same height as Roberto, but thin and wiry with his brow perpetually furrowed as if he was thinking hard about something. José enjoyed a reputation as a "peaceful" guy who fought if "provoked" but who did not look for trouble. Although José and Roberto came from the same poor neighborhoods west of the campus, they didn't hang out together. As he ate his burger near where Billy sat, José hunched a bit from the weight of his backpack, heavily laden with books. To José's right sat another boy eating a sloppy joe sandwich, the thin, brown sauce from the sandwich dripping on his chin and plate as he bit into it. Roberto dribbled some of his lemon-lime soda on one side of wadded-up pieces of paper about the size of golf balls that he lined up on the table bench where he sat. He was careful not to get the soda on his fingers so that when he began lobbing pieces of wadded-up paper in José's direction the projectiles came off his fingers cleanly and with accuracy.

A projectile landed on José's backpack, sticking just a bit on the top (the soda providing a little adhesive), which José did not notice. The next one bounced off José's backpack, tumbling on to the young man's plate to José's right, splashing a bit of sloppy joe sauce. José glanced in the direction of the young man's plate but then ignored him as he took the wadded-up paper ball off his plate and dropped it on the floor. José took off his backpack and set it by him, finding the other paper ball on top of his backpack, flicking it off. José and the guy next to him both continued eating without talking. Roberto lobbed another projectile, this time impossible to ignore as it hit José on the left side of his face. Surprised, his face flushed, he whirled around to his left, slightly stumbling as he stood up, glaring in Roberto's direction. No response from Roberto, but a group of ninth grade male and female students sitting at a table near José momentarily looked up from their meals toward José, glaring in Roberto's direction. Under the table where Roberto was sitting, he dribbled what seemed to be a lot of soda on a wad of paper. A few moments passed without incident. José shrugged his shoulders and turned away from Roberto to sit back down. He went back at his sandwich, taking a big bite. A fourth projectile, a bit bigger than the others, caught José's attention as it landed on the bench next to him with a splat.

Roberto now glared hard in José's direction and for another moment neither boy said anything. José broke the silence with an angry "What's yo fuckin' problem?!" "Nuthin', ¡Pito! [dick]" Roberto shouted back. Most of the conversations in that part of the cafeteria now stopped and all eyes fixed on José and Roberto. José, his brow more furrowed than usual, shouted, "¡Pito! You the ¡Pito!" Neither boy moved for a moment, glaring at each other, but then Roberto got up and began walking toward José. José, his brow still furrowed, got up too. They hurled different phrases at each other as they walked toward each other—"That's how it's gonna go!" or "You wan' somma me?!" Their voices pierced the air in high-pitched screeches, seemingly afraid yet trying to project bravado. They stopped far enough away from each other so that they could not physically touch but close enough so that a single large step from either one would bring them into physical contact.

Most youth sitting at the nearby tables vacated the area, others seemed to ignore the action unfolding nearby, and a few formed a semicircle around José and Roberto as the situation grew more tense. The young men continued shouting and gesturing until Roberto said gruffly, "Fuck it. I got 'em. Kick his ass later." Two male students sitting nearby where Roberto was sitting stepped in, said something to Roberto, and pointed toward the direction of Diego, a security guard, bustling toward that end of the cafeteria. In the thirty seconds it took Diego to reach that end of the cafeteria, the semicircle broke up and Roberto was walking away from the area, leaving José to respond to Diego's question of "What's up here?" with a few grunts that there was "no prob."

A day later, Cynthia followed up with Roberto about "what happened in the cafeteria" and he only volunteered that "I gotta rep. It's fun." In a separate conversation with Billy, José added that "Nobody like him [Roberto]. He's a crazy vato [dude]." But he then added, "You try to let it go. If you back down you can get beat down," so you have to "sometimes try to fight." When asked why the two young people did not actually fight, José responded, "People say shit. Sometimes fight. Mostly not." In the weeks subsequent to this incident, we witnessed Roberto sitting alone on several occasions in the cafeteria and quad and other students moving away from him if he sat near them.

Many of the aspects of the trouble strings appearing in youth-authored stories of beat downs, illustrated by cases 5.1 and 5.2, also appear in case 5.3: a provocation, a few attempts at toleration and coping (especially at the beginning) that failed to interrupt the momentum gained by multiple moralistic actions piling up one after another, including nonverbal threats and gestures, and a style of talk that became more exaggerated with verbal sparring dominated by hostile accusations and insults. The youth involved also alluded to some of the same motivations mentioned by male ninth graders, linked to peer audiences and eloquently summarized by José as "if you back down you can get beat down." But in case 5.3, the pressure to confront intensified as some youth formed a semicircle around Roberto and José, and Roberto seemed thrilled by the provocation, which he called "fun"—a somewhat unusual emotion for NWHS youth facing the potential of violent confrontation.

Brinkmanship did not result in physical violence in case 5.3, consistent with other ethnographic trouble cases. Of the thirteen trouble strings in ethnographic cases dominated by moralistic trouble responses, eight (six involving young men and two involving young women) resulted in the principal parties ceasing their aggression with one party declaring him- or herself a victor of sorts with an intention to finish the altercation physically in the future. What explains such outcomes? Did these campaigners simply "chicken out" at engaging in violence? Certainly fear played a role in these dynamics as illustrated by Roberto and José's emotions when they walked toward one another. At the same time, Roberto recounted the interaction as "fun," perhaps signaling how such bluster itself can constitute "thrilling action," which observers argue can characterize the experience of physical fights and near-fights, especially as documented among affluent youth.[7] Scholars of urban youth conflict and violence, more generally, argue that when youth verbally constitute the code of the street, it can act as a deterrent, taking antagonists up to the precipice of violence but, as Randall Collins notes, ultimately avoiding "violence by boasting and bluster, projecting an image of confidence in one's ability to fight well."[8]

This threshold effect may have been in play here, although we observed dynamics linked to social trust and what Collins argues are the emotional constraints on all interpersonal violence.[9] Thin social trust in downtown and interactions with relationally distant peers sometimes undermined these normative constraints and caused youth to perceive the opportunities for preemptory intimidation as greater than in other places on campus, thus creating the conditions for interactions that resembled the code of the street. Yet these interactions were embedded in the larger climate of social trust on campus, coupling a default mode of handling peer trouble via conciliatory-remedial actions with the substantial presence of adults in the cafeteria.

As we noted earlier, actions like Roberto's typically did not lead to an honored reputation or status among peers at NWHS, but rather social isolation. Youth commonly believed that individuals like Roberto were "immature" or, as José put it with regard to Roberto, "a crazy vato [dude]."[10] Such identities limited students' spatial and social mobility, leaving them in social isolation. The "winner," if there was one in this altercation, may have been José, who did not back down but also did not fight, thus upholding his reputation as a "strong" yet "peaceful" guy, which fit with the modal way of building a legitimate "rep" among NWHS students. As James Jimerson and Matthew Oware observe, for code-like acts to carry efficacy among urban youth they must "occur at certain times in certain settings in front of certain audiences for certain reasons."[11]

Case 5.4, "Jumped In," illustrates how young women engaged in campaigns for respect in the context of relational-boundary violations, particularly romantic, heterosexual triangles where third parties jumped in to defend another female peer. All six ethnographic cases with moralistic strings and young women as principal actors exhibited a relational dimension, which contrasted with the seven ethnographic cases with moralistic strings involving only male youth protagonists. Moreover, three of the moralistic strings involving young women campaigning for respect led to physical altercations, whereas only two of the seven moralistic strings involving young men exhibited these tendencies. Case 5.4 takes us into these dynamics as two Latina sophomores confront each other over a piece of jewelry regifted by an ex-boyfriend.

Case 5.4 "Jumped In"

Ramona grew up in El Dorado, a poor barrio of Mexican immigrant and Mexican-descent families west of campus. She was known as a "fighter" because she fought, as did members of her family, some of whom were known for fencing stolen cars across the US-Mexico border. Ramona was stout and pretty with deep brown skin, green eyes, and long amber-brown hair. According to Ramona, her father was especially keen on her "going to college" and "not following in the family business." Her ex-boyfriend was Harold, a black eleventh grader known as a bit of a "playa" [a male who flirts and may be simultaneously dating multiple female peers] and a football player. When they broke up, Ramona "accused Harold of taking [her] necklace" on which hung a large, gold-plated pendant that read "Number One Bitch." Ramona received the pendant as a "gag gift" from her mother and also, according to Ramona, "to remind me and anyone else not to mess with me." Ramona called Harold on the phone during a weekend to demand he return it, which he claimed was "impossible" because, as she put it, "he said it was superglued to the wall [in his house] to remind him of what a bitch I am." Ramona "hung up" in response to Harold's "rude remark" and, although she wanted the pendant returned, was willing to "give up on it to move on from Harold."

On a Wednesday afternoon the week after Ramona and Harold's phone call, Cynthia sat outside the administration building in the aftermath of a fight during lunch between Ramona and two other sophomores, Lourdes, a tall, light-skinned Latina SouthSider with long, wavy dyed blond hair, and Jenny, whose thin brown hair was pulled back in single ponytail and whose pale white skin appeared almost translucent in the sun. Jenny lived in a small, mixed Latino/white neighborhood east of campus and had been hanging out with Lourdes on campus, or with Lourdes and Harold, who since his breakup with Ramona had been "seeing" Lourdes. Lourdes used to "hang out" with Ramona when they were both in the ninth grade, but neither young woman had spoken to each other in more than a year, blending into very different groups that only overlapped through Harold.

As the young women waited for their one-on-one "interviews" with the principal—each sitting several feet away from one another on chairs outside the main office—Cynthia asked each one separately and quietly what happened in the fight. According to Ramona, the fight erupted at lunch in the wake of her seeing Lourdes between classes earlier in the day "wearing my necklace." Ramona tried to "let it slide" through her morning classes but "couldn't stop thinking about it" and planned to confront Lourdes at lunch when, as Ramona put it, "she'd have to own up to how she got it." According to Lourdes, Ramona confronted her on the quad during lunch about wearing "a necklace she said was hers [Ramona's]," calling Lourdes "a thief and a whore." Lourdes met this hostile accusation with a hostile denial, calling Ramona "a liar" and "bitch"—an irony that, according to Ramona, "pissed me off majorly." Lourdes then told Cynthia how she "got in Ramona's face," which prompted Ramona to push Lourdes hard, who stumbled backwards over a picnic table bench, almost tumbling to the ground. Lourdes claimed that the entire incident stemmed from Ramona being unable to "keep a man" but never specifically mentioned the pendant. According to Tyson, the security guard who saw the fight begin and intervened to break it up, Jenny "jumped in" for Lourdes as the latter lay sprawled over the picnic table bench, pushing and trying to hit Ramona, who then landed "several jabs to Jenny's face." Tyson noted that "it was clear" Jenny was "game" despite "not knowing how to fight." Tyson described Ramona hitting Jenny with one fist while using her other hand to grab Jenny's t-shirt sleeve and arm, gouging Jenny's arm with her finger nails as she threw her to the ground. When Tyson arrived, Ramona stood over both Jenny and Lourdes, repeatedly kicking Lourdes's leg.

While waiting for a turn with the principal, Jenny was quiet and appeared withdrawn, looking down at her shoes, a few pieces of dried grass still in her hair from being on the ground. Fresh bruises appeared on her face and a large, white gauze bandage was taped around one of her arms. In response to Cynthia's questions, Jenny mumbled something about "a rep ain't worth it" and looked away. In response to a question about why she "jumped in," she said, "I know Lourdes can fight but don't seem right to just stand there when she fell." When it was Jenny's turn to talk with the principal, Ramona returned outside and continuing talking with Cynthia while Robert, another security guard, escorted Lourdes to a security office for more questioning. Ramona explained that "[Jenny] don't know how to fight" but "seem pretty tough." She added, "I don't know why she jumped in for that weak-ass whore [Lourdes]. I wanna friend like that." Ramona also noted that she "don't know she was going to fight" or she would not have worn "short sleeves." (A tight, long-sleeve shirt can protect against cuts and prevent an adversary from grabbing one's shirt to gain an advantage as Ramona did to Jenny.) Ramona made it clear that she fought because the pendant was "important to her," rather than because of any lingering emotion for Harold. "I'm over him. He always stirring the drama; I gonna give him beat down too," said Ramona defiantly, her jaw set. She then softened her tone, speaking more quietly. "I'm not worried about suspension. . . . I'm scared my dad 'cuz he want me to go to college and he'll whip my ass." After this brief exchange, the principal, Ms. Adams, appeared and motioned Tyson to bring Ramona into the administration building to wait for her father to pick her up.

A day later, Ms. Adams held what she called "disciplinary hearings" with each young woman to ensure that she had "the facts correct" and that all three young women involved "understood" what the "next steps are" in the "process." She then held a group meeting with all three young women and their parents/guardians present at which she gave a brief lecture about "conflict escalation" and "choices." The three received three days of OSS [out-of-school suspension] plus some other on-campus penance. In the days after the incident, according to Ramona, her father was less angry and "physical" with her than "disappointed" and "sad" over her fighting.

In subsequent weeks, we saw the young women largely keep to themselves, eating lunch alone on the fields or occasionally in an empty classroom. During this period, Ramona mentioned to Cynthia that she was "determined" to leave her "fighting past" and her "bad choices in men and women" behind her. She also felt the stigma of her identity as a "fighter," remarking, "Sometimes it feels like people think I'm gonna attack them or something." Four weeks after the incident, we saw Ramona eating lunch with new friends she met from MEChA in the "Q" quad. Jenny, too, moved on, now eating lunch with a mixed group of Latina, black, and white members of the school softball team whom she knew through another young woman in her neighborhood. She remarked that she "don't wanna be friends with fighters." Lourdes, too, moved on to a mixed group of Mexican-immigrant and US-born Latino youth who hung out near the "Q" quad, remarking that she "needed to get with some sane people." Harold had taken up with a white female eleventh grader with whom he ate lunch in the company of several other black youth in the quad, citing the "need to be with people who ain't so into drama." The fate of the pendant remained unclear.

The stakes in case 5.4 ostensibly revolved around the possession and exhibition of a pendant, but at a deeper level touched on aspects of female resistance to masculine dominance and manipulation at the intersection of social class, ethnicity, and race. Harold's refusal to return the pendant that belonged to his ex-girlfriend, Ramona, and then regifting it to his new girlfriend, Lourdes, asserted his control over the jewelry, undermining Ramona's identity while momentarily elevating Lourdes. His actions set in motion the events that led to the fight and resulting disciplinary action. Yet the young women did not hold Harold directly accountable for their altercation, although Ramona viewed Harold as troublesome in general ("He always stirring the drama"). Ramona faced additional trouble, as she anticipated her father's anger and potential physical abuse, though she actually experienced a nonviolent yet emotionally wrenching rebuke from her father.

These gendered power dynamics among peers are not particular to this group of urban youth; in fact, they parallel what Nikki Jones reveals in her ethnographic explorations of power relations and coercion among black, high school-aged young women and men from high-poverty neighborhoods in Philadelphia. In that context, Jones explains: "Young men with few resources to enact mainstream notions of masculinity outside of their intimate relations find broad cultural acceptance for keeping the young women in their lives subservient with force, if necessary."[12]

In this way, young women can experience "multiple forms of oppression" as they manage the challenges of being poor, black, and female faced with male attempts to dominate them. Jones found that some young women responded to such oppression by engaging in campaigns for respect, projecting tough personae to "challenge both traditional and local expectations regarding femininity."[13] Ramona found herself at the intersection of multiple forms of oppression enacted by her ex-boyfriend, her father, and, more broadly, the expectations associated with coming from a "tough" Latina family where survival depended upon a "tough" front. Yet she also was expected to comply with her father's wishes of "not going into the family business" and therefore uphold the generalized, stereotypical gender expectations about appropriate, feminine, Latina behavior. Faced with these contradictory demands, her threat against Harold symbolized resistance to his oppression even as she fell prey to it, reflected in her violent attacks on Lourdes and Jenny. At the same time, the altercation represented what Jones calls a "test,"[14] signaling Ramona's identity as "tough" and strong, countering Lourdes's derisive labeling of Ramona as a "weak whore."

A tough reputation and fighting to back it up were among the limited avenues Ramona saw available to her in responding to Harold giving Lourdes the pendant. Her confrontation of Lourdes and Jenny carried less physical or emotional risk than confronting Harold or her father. The fact that this test was embedded in betrayal—the regifting of the pendant and the lies surrounding it—intensified the emotional nature of this trouble, overwhelming the local and more generalized constraints on interpersonal violence and thus creating the conditions for Ramona's physical beat down of Lourdes and Jenny. Similarities to these relational dynamics appear in every one of the campaigns for respect by young women that we collected ethnographically on campus.

Social trust on campus and the importance of anchored fluidity for settling troubles in a conciliatory-remedial manner carried negative consequences for young women who engaged in beat downs to deal with trouble. The aftermath of the fight represented in case 5.4 has parallels to

Nikki Jones's observation that in high-poverty situations young women with fighting reputations can become further isolated, inviting them to rely even more on code-of-the-street sensibilities in their interactions with peers. With her reputation as a fighter, Ramona was temporarily ostracized from the routines of anchored fluidity and thus temporarily frozen into a stigmatized identity that cut against the grain of social trust on campus. As Ramona put it, "people think I'm gonna attack them or something." Yet the identities of three young women were not inviolable or immutable in the context of anchored fluidity. Since youth hierarchies and social groups tended to be fuzzy and fluctuating at NWHS (with the exception among some Mexican immigrant and US-born Latino youth), all three young women found new friends in a few weeks' time. Harold, too, moved on to a new girlfriend, and we observed him engaging in the same manipulation that both Ramona and Lourdes suffered until his new girlfriend exited their relationship, moving on to a new network.

Goin' Undercover

Goin' undercover pointed to yet another, less publicly acknowledged slice of youth trouble and conflict on campus. Rather than the trouble playing out on the frontstages of NWHS with identities at stake for the principal participants, this kind of control involved youth pursuing covert practices to gain private satisfaction and even publically embarrass a peer while maintaining an air of civility. Such actions reach into what Erving Goffman calls the "underlife" of the school—those actions through which youth "hold [themselves] off from fully embracing all of the self-implications of [their] affiliations . . . while fulfilling . . . major obligations."[15] In this way, goin' undercover undermined *and* sustained campus expectations of social trust. Through such actions, youth sustained trust-oriented and other-regarding fronts pervasive on campus while deliberately pursuing troublesome parties in impactful, moralistic fashions. The behaviors that constituted goin' undercover operated metaphorically like the tip of an iceberg: much of the action occurred beneath the surface of everyday interaction. As such, many of our observations of goin' undercover emerged as behavioral traces filled in by accounts from youth. Case 5.5, "Keepin' Civil," illustrates goin' undercover as eleventh graders spread gossip about a peer they found "not bein' real" about her pregnancy, who, in turn, retaliated by spreading gossip about one of the principal gossiper's "STDs" (sexually transmitted diseases).

Case 5.5 "Keepin' Civil"

It was a Thursday morning during third period. Jerlyn hung out with a mixed group of four juniors who had been released from their history class to work on a group project in the library. At the table sat Makayla, a bubbly, stout black WestSider with long chestnut braids pulled up on top of her head, held in place by a wide, white band. Bettee, a tall, quiet black SouthSider with close cropped hair, sat next to her, carefully transferring notes from a stack of index cards into a spiral-bound notebook. Next to Bettee was Jone, a self-described "Italian-Irish" young woman with long, straight black hair, who lived in a small neighborhood east of campus populated by Mexican-descent and white families and college students who rented cheap apartments near the university campus. Ronelle, another black WestSider, was next to Jone and positioned herself so that she could sit at the table and turn around to type information supplied to her by Bettee into a desktop computer. Rounding out the group was Debbie, a SouthSider white young woman with bright red hair and freckles covering her face and arms, known for carrying all her books and several other belongings in a huge, worn satchel positioned on the table in front of her. She was partially hidden behind the satchel as she doodled in her notebook.

Another group from a different class also sat several tables over and was laughing at something. Francine, a heavy set black SouthSider wearing an oversized, multicolor windbreaker, got up from the second group and walked across the room toward Makayla. Francine and Makayla met in a dance class as sophomores, sometimes ate lunch together, and occasionally hung out after school. Various members of the group glanced over in Francine's direction and said some version of "How you doin', girl?" and then returned to various tasks, save for Makayla, who quietly said "Hi" and raised her eyebrows with a look of concern as Francine began whispering something in her ear. After approximately a minute of quiet whispering, Makayla and Francine left the table and walked to another part of the library to sit by themselves and speak quietly to each other. As they spoke, Makayla leaned toward Francine with her hand on Francine's arm, and Francine looked down at the table. Makayla, in a separate conversation with Jerlyn later, said she "helped her [Francine] work out some problems."

As soon as they left the table, Ronelle burst out laughing. In response to a question by Jerlyn about "What's so funny?" Ronelle continued laughing and, in between snorts and chuckling, said, "I don' know how big a baby is when you two months. They not that big! [using her hands to make a round shape near her stomach while puffing out her cheeks and laughing].

We keepin' civil until she [Francine] leave. She pregnant." Jerlyn said, "She's pregnant [referring to Francine]?" Everyone sitting at the table nodded their heads up and down in agreement. Ronelle added, "She say only two months. Everyone know she mo. Everyone talkin' about it. Tellin' stories 'bout how could be onena three daddies and at three different schools." Jerlyn asked, "Where are these stories coming from?" Ronelle laughed again. "Me. Maybe. Some other girls tole me at a party. I talkin' too. And, you know, it is a *good drama* [emphasis by the participant]." Jone also laughed as she said, "I was talkin' with people on the bus one day. We were gonna make bets on who the daddy is." Bettee looked up from her notebook and said dryly, without laughing, "I hate people lying. Especially about stupid shit. She pregnant—everyone know that. She not bein' real about the time." Francine and Makayla returned to the table, and the young women returned to their notebooks, not looking at Francine, except for Jone, who asked in a quiet, serious tone, "How you doin', girl?" Francine responded, "Off and on. Feelin' a little better." "Good," said Ronelle without a hint of sarcasm. "I'm glad."

A few days later, Jerlyn sat in the cafeteria with Bettee, Jone, Debbie, and Makayla. After a few minutes of chit-chat about clothes and how bad the sloppy joe sandwiches were that day, Ronelle joined the group in a huff, saying in an exasperated tone, "You can't believe it this mornin'!" Ronelle went on to tell the group how she walked into her math class and "girls [were] laughing at her, covering their mouths" and "sayin' you don' wanna to catch it." All during class Ronelle said she worried about "what was goin' on" and after class asked a classmate whom she "[rode] the bus with . . . what up." The young woman, according to Ronelle, was "laughing too, sayin' 'people sayin' you got STDs.'" The other young women at the table reacted in disbelief, Jone letting out a "What the hell?! Nah!" In response, Ronelle spit out angrily, "You got to have sex to have STDs and ain't having sex right now! I ain't got no STDs! Anybody who say it I whuppin' they ass!"

In the days following this revelation, Ronelle and her other friends conducted what they called an "investigation" across several peers who might be spreading the story about her having "STDs." They decided that to catch the "gossip" they needed to be subtle, goin' undercover to reveal who spread the rumors, including investigating Makayla about Francine's potential involvement with the rumors. Makayla claimed Francine was "worryin' about her own life" instead of "puttin' shit out about people." Although Francine's and other names came up from time to time, Ronelle never confronted her or anyone directly about the rumor. Two weeks into the "investigation" and again in the company of the five young women in the cafeteria, Jerlyn noticed that the group's conversation never veered into who might be spreading the rumor about Ronelle. Jerlyn asked Ronelle, "Did you ever figure out who spread those rumors about you?" Ronelle paused for a moment, as if trying to remember what Jerlyn was referring to and then said, "Oh, that. No, not really. I let it go." She also asked the group about the rumor and, like Ronelle, several had to be reminded of the rumor as the conversation quickly pivoted to another topic. Ronelle's "STDs" rumor never came up again as the conversation over Jerlyn's next several visits moved across the usual topics of young men, clothes, family, food, jobs, and parties/partying. Whenever the group encountered Francine, sometimes in the cafeteria and sometimes sitting under a tree in the refuge, Jone or Debbie asked politely how Francine was "feelin'" while Ronelle smiled warmly at Francine without saying anything and Makalya sometimes reached out to touch Francine's arm as she did two weeks previously in the library. Further out from the library encounter a few weeks later, suspecting that Francine or someone close to her had been behind the rumors because of the polite but strained interactions between her and the group (save for Makayla), Jerlyn asked Francine if "she knows anything about the gossip spread about Ronelle." Francine responded with a breezy, "Dunnoh. Goin' undercover people get shit back on 'em. You gotta get over it." When Jerlyn asked her what she meant, Francine responded, "People be nice to you like they friends sometimes. They not. I'm just sayin'."

Although this case ostensibly focused on youth spreading rumors about a peer who was not honest about the timing of her pregnancy and perhaps the identity (or knowledge) of the father, there were multiple instances when nearly all the key actors engaged in deception to protect one another or to put up a trusting front while pursuing moralistic actions on the backstage. At the same time, multiple forms of third-party support occurred, including Makayla's support of Francine and acquaintances who transitioned from feigned concern for Francine to gossiping behind her back to real concern. Once more we see that the dynamics of peer trouble handling among young women implicated relational connections in complex ways that led to both social division and cohesion.

This case also illustrated another dynamic regarding the ways "spoiled identities"—to borrow again from Goffman—did not stick to NWHS youth either in how they subjectively felt about themselves or in how others felt about them.[16] Anchored fluidity meant that youth were constantly on the move socially and spatially, which figured into the impact of gossip on identity and control. Sally Engle Merry generally argues that ". . . [G]ossip creates cognitive maps of social identities and reputations . . . [but]. . . . [t]he impact of gossip . . . is greater in more bounded social systems in which the costs of desertion or expulsion are higher and the availability of alternative social relationships less."[17] Although NWHS exhibited qualities of a bounded social system, its internal dynamics provided constant opportunities for new relationships to arise, diluting the effect of gossip and enabling youth to move quickly to new dramas as well as to other supportive relationships.

The fluidity of association among youth also appears in trouble case 5.6, "Gonna Get It," in which a male youth revealed his plot for covert revenge against peers in the context of a romantic triangle but then quickly reconciled with some of those against whom he had grievances.

Case 5.6 "Gonna Get It"

While walking up the breezeway one afternoon after lunch, Cynthia spotted Gerald carrying what looked like rolled-up white posters and a large roll of masking tape. A white twelfth grader, he stood over 6' 4" and was quite skinny, his oversized flannel shirt draped over his shoulders and a long ponytail pulled through the sizing strap of a baseball cap that he wore backwards. Gerald lived with his mother northwest of campus in a mixed neighborhood where lower-income Mexican immigrant and US-born Latino, black, and white families rented apartments in several rundown buildings. Cynthia had been talking with Gerald over the last several months and learned about a series of personal problems he was managing, ranging from anxieties about his future after graduation (he wanted "to go to college" but was anxious about whether "he can" because of his "low grades") to trouble with his mother (she worked "a lotta hours" and "drinks too much"). Cynthia said hello and learned Gerald was putting up posters to advertise a school play that he helped "produce" and in which he played "a small part." She asked if she could "help" hang the posters. "Great," Gerald responded, and they begin walking toward the quad where they affixed posters on the walls there and in "Q" quad next to several other posters advertising student club events and sporting events.

As they walked down the breezeway, Gerald told Cynthia how he "feel[s] better" because he had "a plan now" after his graduation from NWHS. In midsentence, they paused on the breezeway between "J" and "L" buildings as Gerald stopped talking. Gerald saw John in the distance coming out of "J" building and turning right to walk toward the quad. John did not see Gerald or Cynthia. John also was a white twelfth grader who hung out with Gerald. John lived east of campus in another small neighborhood of rental properties populated by lower-income Latino families and married college students. Like Gerald, John lived with his mother. Gerald watched John for a couple of moments until he disappeared from view. With a sigh, Gerald launched into a rambling story about his girlfriend, Diana, a US-born Latina twelfth grader who attended Eastern High, John, and Teddy, a US-born Latino twelfth grader who lived in Gerald's neighborhood. Gerald talked about John "always being high now" and that Teddy was "a dealer of weed, a little meth, other stuff." He then turned to "what happened on Saturday night."

On that night, Gerald, Diana, John, Teddy, and three other youth he did not mention by name went to "play pool at an all-ages pool hall." The next day Gerald spoke with Diana by phone and she seemed "really weird . . . distant. She said her and Teddy smoked a little weed. I think they hooked up." Gerald elaborated, "I got pissed so I say to her what the fuck!" when he visited her at her mother and aunt's apartment where Diana lived. "She says Teddy just a friend." Cynthia asked Gerald why he believed Teddy had sex with Diana and he replied, "Because Teddy drives us around in his brother's truck and he let me off at my place first 'cuz I got to work early on Sunday [at a gas station near NWHS] and he took John and her home. He [John] gonna know something. I mean you know like Teddy get her high and who know what the hell happens." Cynthia asked Gerald, "What are you going to do?" Gerald said he was going to "ask John" about the situation tomorrow in a "real nice way like he won't know nothin'." "If he [John] tell the truth, I'm gonna tell Teddy to stay the fuck away from her [Diana]. If he lies, I got many different ways to take down John, Teddy, and Diana, put 'em in their place." For John, Gerald said, now almost in a low growl, "I rat him out on the security phone [call the security guards]. He [John] always smoke weed on the fields by the [south] parking lot. He always reek. They probably bust him right there." For Diana, he "might do something to Diana's place" because he regarded her as "rich" and the "kinda girl you wanna stay with." Gerald says he also had "other ways goin' undercover" but did not elaborate." Gerald concluded his plan by saying, somewhat more forcefully, "I be all nice to 'em. They'll never know it was me."

Before Gerald and Cynthia finished talking, John came around the corner up the breezeway. When he reached Gerald and Cynthia, Gerald smiled and greeted him with a "Hey," nodding his head up and down. John said "Hey" back but did not say anything else, his eyes red and dilated and his clothes smelling of marijuana and cigarettes. John then excused himself, walking up the breezeway and out of earshot, turning left to walk between "M" and "L" buildings, which led back out to the fields. Cynthia finished up helping Gerald hang the posters and then bid him adieu as he returned to his last two class periods of the day.

.

The next day, Cynthia sought out John on the quad at lunch, asking him "How's it going?" He smelled of cigarettes but not pot. John replied, "Okay," but then added that "Gerald may be pissed at me" because his [John's] "girl-friend hung out with a friend on Saturday." Cynthia asked, "How is that a problem if two friends wanna hang out?" John replied, "They doing a little weed and Gerald doesn't smoke much." John patted his stomach, saying "I got to gets some food," and walked to the cafeteria line. A couple of minutes later, Gerald sat down next to Cynthia with his lunch. "How's it going?" she asked Gerald. He replied, "Okay," in an almost cheery tone. Yesterday, Gerald said he "was mad at the world" and "planning revenge on everyone." Today, he said he was "mellow" and mentioned he "talked it out" with Diana on the phone and "she says that she drank some beers and smoked some strong weed with Teddy. Made her sick for a day." So Gerald figured that Diana "saw a bit of this other life with Teddy and don't like it," so he "just trust her." He also said that he "never talked with John" and was "movin' on" from Teddy and the "whole group" [of regular drug users] to which Teddy belonged. While Gerald spoke, John returned to the table with some food, and he and Gerald began talking about their weekend plans, which did not include each other. During their conversation, they occasionally cracked a joke and laughed, never letting on about the tensions between them. In sub-sequent weeks, we did not see Gerald or John in each other's company, and Teddy disappeared from campus altogether. John and Gerald reported that Teddy "got busted for drugs." When Cynthia asked Gerald whether he knew "how Teddy got busted," Gerald replied, looking down at his shoes, "Lots o' people know he hustling, you know."

Unlike street or school contexts of social distrust in which youth shift among hostile, overt intimidation and avoidance, case 5.6 shows youth switching between overt reconciliation and covert revenge. In a sense, Ger-ald performed trusting frontstage behavior common among NWHS stu-dents to cover his intent and possibly his actions, although it remained un-clear whether he had anything to do with Teddy's arrest for drugs. Beneath Gerald's cynical manipulation was the authentic desire to move toward a more trusting sense of his girlfriend, as he exited from what he regarded as untrustworthy relationships with Teddy and John.

These interactions unfolded at the intersection of class difference and attempts at masculine control. Gerald believed Diana violated the promise of relational and sexual exclusivity, and he confronted her about the pos-sible betrayal of that exclusivity. Yet he also viewed her as beyond his di-rect control because of her social class position as "rich"; both her mother and aunt worked at bank branches as managers, and Diana did not work while attending school. From Gerald's perspective, Diana's class position elevated her to the "kinda girl [one] wanna stay with," which also evokes Nikki Jones's characterization of the "good girl" in inner-city contexts, only in this case as a young woman who enjoyed that status because of her tie to a material situation rather than a behavioral one. Gerald spun an elaborate revenge fantasy but never acted on it (except perhaps for tipping off school officials about Teddy or at least giving off impressions to that effect to Cynthia). Indeed, the only person he confronted, at least in his account, was his girlfriend, which underscored the attempts at masculinized control in many interpersonal dramas pursued overtly or covertly by male youth.

Power Relations, Gender, and Back- and Frontstages

Youth constituted a moralistic repertoire of peer control through actions that ranged from confrontations echoing campaigns for respect organized by the code of the street to covert actions on the backstages of student life with strategically cultivated veneers of trust and concern for the other. Neighborhood or gang affiliations, as well as ethnic and racial difference, did not appear to foment moralistic youth conflict on a routine basis. Yet in downtown on the frontstages of the campus, youth proved more prone to imagine and engage in beat downs with socially distant youth, against the backdrop of peer pressure and a kaleidoscope of cultural difference. Physical altercations and intimidation rarely occurred, as youth were more likely to reconcile trouble rather than engage in intimidation and violence.

Moralistic trouble strings in which young women are the primary players, however, were more likely to include some form of physical altercation, usually with a female peer. This pattern is also embedded in gendered power dynamics. Parallel to Nikki Jones's arguments, young women in impoverished urban neighborhoods face multiple, intersecting forms of oppression based on ethnic and racial identification, class position, experiences with male domination, and normative expectations.[18] Our evidence points to the ironic fact that these acts of oppression manifested around demands for relational and sexual exclusivity, which sometimes led to young women fighting *each other* rather than confronting the young men at the source of the trouble. In case 5.4, "Jumped In," we detailed how this dynamic led to a violent melee, set in motion by a boy's actions with his current and ex-girlfriends. This pattern seems to contradict our claims in the previous chapter that social trust and opportunities for leadership facilitate greater license and agency to work out conflict while saving face, especially with regard to young women. But it is important to note that such physical violence rarely occurred. And equally important, when it did, it almost always involved gendered power relations in which young women found themselves directly or indirectly manipulated by the men in their lives. To be clear, we are not implying that female peer relations are frictionless or that young women do not bear at least some responsibility for the choices they make. But the fact that gendered power relations among young women and men are associated with low-volume, but occasional, violence may signify the consequential capacities of social trust and sociospatial mobility (especially when extended to both young women and men) to hold down what otherwise would be more aggressive, street-oriented trouble responses surrounding male-female romantic relations.

Our exploration of covert peer control complicates our general story. Indeed, the covert actions that youth took could even suggest, in the extreme, that much of what we observed on campus during this period was a front for a bitter underlife of trouble simmering beneath the surface of social trust and concern. The triangulated character of our evidence leads away from this conclusion and points to the dual character of backstages, the provisional character of everyday social trust, and the intricacies of how youth approached peer trouble. Amid a school climate of working social trust, youth shifted back and forth from trusting to distrusting actions in which moral judgments were in play. In case 5.6, for example, Gerald refined his sense of trust, moving closer to his girlfriend and further away from Teddy and John. Violence did not erupt, despite Gerald's bluster and posturing about doing people in. Throughout the chapter, we noted instances in which adult authorities, both teachers and security guards, kept their ears to the ground and stepped in to mobilize official control when moralistic trouble responses gained visible momentum; a teacher intervened into a fight in case 5.1 and a security guard did the same in case 5.3. Our discussions thus far have only offered brief glimpses of official school control, often operating in the background with youth-led efforts of peer trouble handling in the foreground. We turn now to a more systematic look at how youth operated in and around official school control.

SIX

"Dealing with the System"

During the late 1990s, youth at NWHS handled a great deal of peer trouble without directly engaging adults or their rules. Teachers, administrators, and security personnel continuously circulated throughout the campus but often missed subtle trouble that broke out in high-trafficked areas, including the social tension in the cafeteria between Felix and Jalal in case 4.3 and the gun display in the parking lot a stone's throw away from the administration building revealed by Pablo and Bill in case 4.7. In both cases, NWHS students stamped out the potential for violence.

In this chapter, we reveal how young people positioned themselves in relationship to adult authority and school rules when weighing and acting on peer trouble. Much of the chapter examines how young people in a high-poverty school imagine, reason, and deal with institutionalized authority under conditions of trust and safety, including their consciousness and mobilization in and around adult power, rules, and legality. We also offer insights into how authority-in-action differences youth, bracketing and controlling particular behaviors and identities and locating perspectives of school-produced inequality from youth positioned below. Which NWHS students were marked by school rules and under what conditions? Who, if any youth, challenged adult authority and by what means? Who used adult authority to deal with interpersonal conflicts, why, and with what consequences? The chapter closes with an exploration of changes in the interplay between youth and school structures during the third year of our fieldwork in 1999–2000 as the school began to implement safe schools policies.

From Playing by the Rules to Playing the Rules

In youth parlance at NWHS, youth "played by the rules" when they reasoned about their options to comply with or invoked adult authority to resolve trouble with peers. On one level, we uncovered youth calculating whether following the rules would result in a salient gain or loss. Underneath instrumental calculation, however, lay students' symbolic judgments of what the rules meant in terms of fairness and, ultimately, social trust. Youth-authored case 6.1, "Didn't Want to Get Kicked off the Team," illustrates the instrumental quality of playing by the rules, while ethnographic case 6.2, "Mrs. Lopato, Alanza, and the *Payasos*," reveals both the instrumental and symbolic aspects of how students reasoned about school authority and discipline, how they attended to their relationships with peers and adults, and how they imagined their futures.

Case 6.1: "Didn't Want to Get Kicked Off the Team"

There was this time that in P.E. that there was a conflict. I knew the student because he was also in my P.E. class. We were in the gym annex playing basketball and the conflict started by just talking stuff about each other. Nothing really happened just a little pushing but nobody else was involved. While this was going on I was thinking I don't need make this decision and fight him because at that time football season had just started and I didn't want to get kicked of the team or get suspended. After the incident I was real satisfied with my decision and not fighting him because then I would just be going down to his level. It was resolved because I had gone and told my coach and after school the coach told him next time he does that to me or anybody on the team or in the school that he'll get kicked off the team and suspended.

Case 6.2: "Mrs. Lopato, Alanza, and the *Payasos*"

Nineteen students, thirteen young women and six young men, formed Mrs. Lopato's junior-level ESL class during third period. All but two of the students came from Mexico, with one female student from Cambodia and one from Russia. Cynthia observed the teacher, Mrs. Lopato, facilitating the students in small-group discussions at the beginning of class in which they spoke with each other in English about a short essay (written in English) they had completed the previous day. The assignment focused on what they "want to be when they grow up." The Spanish speakers slipped in and out of Spanish and English while they chatted about their essays as Mrs. Lopato reminded them to speak only in English "unless absolutely necessary." The Cambodian and Russian students spoke little and seemed to be looking over what they had written. Occasionally, they too spoke in mixed Spanish and English with their peers.

Mrs. Lopato transitioned from the group discussions to the principal class activity for the period, first in Spanish and then in English laying out some goals for the session. She then subtly looked over at the Cambodian and Russian students, and nodded to them supportively, signalling, "You okay? Do you understand?" Both students nodded back affirmatively with wan smiles. Two male students in the corner persistently said in loud Spanish whenever Mrs. Lopato spoke, "No comprendo" [I don't understand] or "No hablo inglés o español" [I don't speak English or Spanish]. They then began laughing loudly. Their comportment in class was never completely on point, and their unruliness had built up over the past few class sessions. Mrs. Lopato appeared to be trying to ignore the young men. Whenever they made noise, she barely paused and then simply spoke a little louder. Now speaking only in English, Mrs. Lopato asked the class to turn to their textbooks and begin an exercise in which each student read aloud a series of passages about how to approach career choices. She then asked them to use what they read to comment on some aspect of their essay. The students took turns reading from their textbooks and then commenting in halting English about their essays. One of the young women sitting at the front of class, Alanza, seemed eager to read, and when it was her turn she read in a strong, accented voice, adding her own comments about her essay. When Mrs. Lopato called on a male student near the front of the class, he was uncertain what to do and on what page he was supposed to be. Alanza, sitting near him, whispered to him in Spanish where to begin reading. He began reading in halting English and took a while to work his way through a short passage in the textbook. After completing his reading, he made one comment about his essay that was difficult to understand. Mrs. Lopato smiled in response at his effort and asked him a brief question in English to which he responded in Spanish.

As the exercise proceeded, one of the two students who earlier interrupted Mrs. Lopato begin saying loudly, "¡Orale!" (slang in Spanish meaning "OK" or "all right") whenever one of his classmates read. The students sitting near Cynthia began quietly whispering to each other that the two students who kept interrupting were "payasos" (clowns), but they did nothing more to signal their annoyance. Mrs. Lopato gave the *payasos* a "look"—a long, stern gaze, seemingly looking them up and down—but said nothing. Once more the *payasos* spoke loudly and once again Mrs. Lopato gave them a "look." A few minutes elapsed without any disruptions and then the *payasos* once again began making noise. Every time the *payasos* spoke out, Alanza, who was sitting near them, shifted nervously in her seat, grimaced, and moved her head very closely to her open textbook on her desk as if trying to lose herself in her studies. She also looked up in a quick, nervous glance at Ms. Lopato. Alanza's situation vis-à-vis the *payasos* was complicated in that all three are "tapatios"—that is, persons born in Guadalajara, Mexico—and so they had hung out together at MEChA once or twice but were not close. After yet another "¡Orale!," Alanza leaned over to the *payasos* and said quietly, but forcefully, in Spanish, "¡Cállate!" ["Shut up!"], giving them a stern look. After she did this, she turned to Ms. Lopato and nodded, subtly. Ms. Lopato looked back at her with a slight smile, gave the *payasos* yet another "look," and asked, in a pleasant voice, for the next student to begin reading. The two *payasos* kept looking at Alanza and then back at Mrs. Lopato, and then down at their shoes. They seemed embarrassed that Alanza told them to shut up, although several students looked relieved (as suggested by their loosened body language, such as not raising their shoulders and not looking down so closely at their texts). When it came time for them to read, each boy read a passage, then their essays, and then commented in no more than one or two short sentences about their essays. Mrs. Lopato smiled after each of them finished, saying "Good" and "That's coming along." Later, at the end of class, Mrs. Lopato took the two students aside as they began walking out to the hallway and talked with them in Spanish in a quiet yet firm tone. At the end of her conversation with them, she said, ". . . . no de nuevo en esta o en cual-quiera otra clase. . . ." [Not again in this or any other class].

The next day, while talking with Cynthia, Alanza noted that the *payasos'* disruptions in class were "disrespectful" to Mrs. Lopato and "make all the Mexicanos look bad." Alanza added that it was important to "play by the rules" (speaking in English) and that "she had to do something" since "disrespecting teachers is wrong [because] . . . the school is a good place." One of the two *payasos*, Juan, told Cynthia in Spanish later the next day that "Mrs. Lopato is nice," but he and his friend did not like the class because they feel "stuck away" in "those classes." They "do not care if they speak English" since they planned to work in his uncle's "shop" where "you don't need English." They also added that they didn't want "to make Alanza or Mrs. Lopato mad" so they stopped disrupting the class.

The settings, participants, and issues of cases 6.1 and 6.2 are distinctive, but the two together reveal a path where adult authorities and rules intersected with the ways youth imagined and acted on trouble among themselves. Certainly, youth compliance to rules was visible everywhere on campus. When the bells rang, most students routinely moved on to the next place called for by their schedules. A few stragglers wandered into classes late or loitered in the hallways, but virtually every student found his or her way to where he or she should officially be. When teachers called classes to order, most students quieted down and turned their attention to them. When teachers asked students to turn in their homework, most did so. Playing by the rules carried echoes of compliance in that youth recognized the authority of adults on campus and an awareness of the many layers of rules associated with any given activity from classroom to student club to team. When students invoked the authority of adults or school rules while engaging in trouble responses among themselves, drawing upon these sources of authority or lending support to them, they played by the rules to remedy troubles with one another.

As in case 6.1, students abided by the rules in part because they calculated the utility of doing so, realizing that escalation of trouble hindered short- or long-term aspirations. Their conscious calculations sometimes coupled with deeper judgments of the rules, particularly what they symbolized about their identities and their regard for the school. Alanza's decision to confront two male acquaintances certainly evoked a sense of instrumental purpose in securing an environment in which the students in Mrs. Lopato's classroom could learn English. It also anchored in her a deep commitment to Mrs. Lopato, an adult who earned Alanza's respect tied to a broader moral judgment—"disrespecting teachers is wrong"—itself linked to her sense of the school as "a good place."

Yet another element of playing by the rules emerged with Mrs. Lopato's class management practices in the mix of teacher-student interactions. Her conduct in the classroom involved a delicate balancing act in which youth and adults on campus engaged. For many NWHS students (if not all students everywhere), the act of reading aloud in front of one's peers in a class, even in one's native language, provoked palpable anxiety. In a second language that is entirely new or still developing, the experience could terrify youth. Mrs. Lopato could have scolded the *payasos* early on, which may or may not have prevented them from further disruption. Yet such discipline, while maintaining order, might have undermined the supportive environment that she had built for other students in the class. In doing so, Mrs. Lopato turned a classic insight into education from the theorist Émile Durkheim on its head. He argued that the effectiveness of formal school discipline resides in its "moral force," the capacity to stir feelings of sacredness if not legitimacy.[1] Rather than relying solely on the moral force of her official authority Mrs. Lopato instead piggybacked on the bottom-up moral force of peer control enacted by Alanza. As Mrs. Lopato pointed out later to Cynthia, she knew that "for the most part, I can count on the kids in my classes." So she made a bet that the trouble she experienced would ultimately die down through a mixture of expressive adult authority and peer control, giving them "a look," while continuing to work through the exercise with the students. She also invoked her authority coupled with the threat of formal control when she told the two disruptors privately "not again in this or any other class" but did so out of the earshot of the other students and in Spanish, not disrespecting them (even as they disrespected her earlier) while protecting the support of the class and Alanza. The effectiveness of this classroom management strategy can be debated and certainly depends upon the overall climate of particular classes, if not that of an entire school. However, we observed this same class later in the semester moving through in-class assignments with marked improvement in the English-reading abilities of all the students and with few disruptions by Juan and his friend or any other students.

As illustrated in cases 6.1 and 6.2, the process of playing by the rules often worked through the frontstages of the school, in the gym annex and classrooms, and among youth with weak ties to one another. At the same time, this means of control drew on backstage communication among teachers and students, verbally as in case 6.1 when the storyteller approached his coach about the altercation in the PE class, as well as when Alanza nonverbally caught Mrs. Lopato's eye with a quick nod of support after admonishing her classmates. These actions also revealed that when youth played by the rules, they often revealed meaningful ties with particular adults on campus whom they especially respected. Alanza demonstrated her ties to and trust in Mrs. Lopato by intervening into trouble to advance a purpose shared with an adult authority figure while potentially risking peer recrimination.

When students turned to adults to alleviate peer trouble or intervene into trouble between teachers and other peers, youth risked their own reputations among peers who could harm, scold, or isolate them. Common purposes—those shared by adults and youth alike—buffered such risks, as demonstrated in case 6.2. Student clubs, organized sports, and other officially sanctioned extracurricular activities often became a part of the story when youth played by the rules. Both youth and adults recognized that keeping the peace among club or team members is important. When members of the team or club, such as the storyteller of case 6.1, approached a coach about trouble, they acted in ways aligned with social trust and were buffered against what could otherwise become an accusation, as youth put it, of "ratting" (betraying a peer confidence). When playing by the rules, youth, such as Alanza or the author of case 6.1, initiated their engagement with adult authorities rather than being spotted by adults who watched for trouble in the gathering areas of the school including the cafeteria, main quad, "Q" quad, gym annex, and the main breezeway. Such initiation can be seen in youth-authored case 6.3, "If a Scout Sees Me Fighting," in which a black senior told the story of her altercations with a rival white player while playing for the NWHS women's varsity basketball team.

Case 6.3 "If a Scout Sees Me Fighting"

I'm on the basketball team with my friends. We played another school that was mostly white. Well we played them and it was the middle of the game and me and this other girl (from the other team) started going for the ball. I landed on top of her while they called jump ball, I got up and she got mad cause I landed on her. She called me a racial name, the N-word. I shouted at her, What did you say! Got up in her face ready to fight! My friends had to hold me back but she just kept going on. The conflict wasn't really resolved cause after that me and her would just go at it on the court but it would never be fighting on the court, because #1 I want to go to college for basketball and if a scout sees me fighting, I've just lost my chance to go to college. I talked to my coach. She told the refs before the next game that the girl was trying to go at me, get me mad, elbows, saying racial stuff. So they talked with the other team's coach, you know right before the start of the game. This player, she kept at me, elbows, saying stuff so only I could hear it. I ran by the refs one time and she was right behind me. I turned around to her and said real loud, You just call me the N word? The ref blew her whistle and the girl said she didn't say anything. Her coach took her out. She didn't play the rest of the game.

Youth who played by the rules sometimes developed sensibilities about legality that resonated with the practical adult knowledge gained by being regular users of dispute resolution forums. Sally Engle Merry, for example, found in her ethnography that working-class Americans using local courts for the first time "see the court as awesome and fearful."[2] As these adults gained experience with the court, they recognized it as a "pliant, if excruciatingly complex, institution" that can provide help if "played with skill and finesse"—an arena where one could gain strategic advantages over one's opponents. Merry recounts trouble cases in which adults initiated actions against neighbors and family members, as plaintiffs, to "pummel" adversaries, yielding favorable results and gaining dominance over them. Thus, there can be advantages to becoming a "repeat player" in court or any normative system, as Marc Galanter famously observed. In Galanter's formulation, repeat players not only develop advantageous practical knowledge of courts but also tend to be social organizations arrayed against single "one-shotters."[3] At NWHS, repeat players emerged, as youth put it, by "playing the rules" as they simultaneously played by the rules, often learning how to tacitly ally themselves with adults as they did so.

Experiential knowledge and an adult alliance became intertwined in case 6.3 with ethnic and racial boundaries in play with complex psychological responses to discrimination. These dynamics brought the storyteller into the interpersonal dynamics of the "victim-oppressor bond," as Kristin Bumiller calls it—a relationship that denies not only the dignity of victims but also their humanity.[4] Such dynamics can create enormous anxiety and uncertainty in victims' minds, resulting in powerlessness, if seen only as an isolated incident, tied in some way to victims' personal inadequacies. The storyteller faced yet another challenge, however, of not allowing herself to be seen as a would-be college player prone to emotional outbursts, intersecting with her identities as a young black woman. She needed to demonstrate that she was under control as a basketball player but, beyond that, also a person who conducted herself as a "good" young black woman even under the most trying circumstances.[5] Animated by future aspirations, the storyteller did not leave the altercation with the rival white player as an isolated incident. Instead, she transformed it into a triadic structure and a strategy, similar to the way one might develop a technical strategy to defeat a particular type of basketball offense or defense, by mobilizing her coach on the backstage, who created a context of readiness for mobilizing the referees on the frontstage.

In so doing, the storyteller imagined playing by the rules and playing the rules in that she both complied with official authority and used the rules to turn the tables on the racially inflected power dynamic with a peer. She also took us deep into youth imagination about back- and frontstage dynamics with regard to authority, difference, and power relations among peers. On the backstage, youth expressed their concerns and fears to adults with whom they enjoyed a trusting relationship, but on the frontstage they maintained their sense of autonomy: to be careful, as noted by Pamela, an eleventh grader and another athlete we met in chapter 1, of "getting adults too far into your business." The status earned by the storyteller as a star basketball player and an individual, as one coach put it, "above reproach" with good grades also mattered. As such, the story she told her coach was likely to be believed and to lead to a protective stance by the coach. A shift in emotion also occurred in the story, moving from anxieties about the future to the cool sophistication of playing the rules practiced by a young black woman who knows how to defeat an opponent without compromising either her future or her present identity.

In the brief yet poignant ethnographic case 6.4, "Playing the Rules Beautifully," Dalton, a white junior who is a self-described "hippie stoner kid," revealed another side of playing the rules with the help of one of his teachers, Mrs. Starks.

Case 6.4 "Playing the Rules Beautifully"

Dalton typically spent a few days in ISS every semester for minor disruptions in class and for smoking cigarettes on campus. He wore a tie-dyed t-shift and loosely fitting, ripped blue jeans with his long brown hair in a ponytail, nearly reaching the middle of his back. Mrs. Sparks was his eleventh-grade English teacher—a teacher he told Billy that he "trusted." Indeed, she invited Dalton to hang out with other youth who typically sat eating in her classroom during lunchtime.

One day in English, as Mrs. Starks held forth on Shakespeare's use of irony, Billy observed a couple of students making fun of Dalton's hair, laughing and saying in high, whispery voices, "Hey there, girlie, I bet your hair feels real nice." After finishing her comments, Mrs. Starks set the students to writing a short response essay on irony in Shakespeare, using excerpts from their Shakespeare reader. As the class settled into the assignment, Dalton motioned her over to his desk to quietly say that two students sitting near him were "screwing off so I can't write," adding, "I just wanna learn." Dalton knew Mrs. Starks's strict policy about students interfering with other students' in-class writing assignments, but he never specifically mentioned what they said. Mrs. Starks told the two male students that "if they can't do the assignment quietly" they could "step outside and complete it in the hallway" or "go to ISS—your choice." They opted to step out and spend the fifteen minutes for the assignment in the hallway, with Mrs. Sparks occasionally walking into the hallway to make sure they were still there and writing. At the end of class, Dalton smiled privately to Billy as he said that he was "playing the rules beautifully" to "get those dudes removed."

Dalton may be a student who drew less empathy than the two athletes in cases 6.1 and 6.3 or Alanza, but he, like the others, realized how to appeal to adult authorities and use the rules to his advantage. In subsequent conversations with Billy, Dalton told him over and over that "the system wasn't fair" and so he "play[ed] the rules to his advantage." He appealed to Mrs. Starks by invoking his desire to learn and, as a result, trumped his opponents, at least with regard to this particular incident. And, like the adults that Sally Engle Merry found playing the local courts, Dalton had logged multiple experiences with the adult disciplinary system, particularly ISS, and recognized its pliant qualities even as he sometimes became caught in it through acts of defiance.

Dalton shared a demographic trait with others who played the rules to their advantage. Male students identifying as and considered white, and female students of all racial and ethnic categories, commonly wrote stories about playing by the rules and playing the rules to manage interpersonal peer trouble. Unlike Dalton, most of the students engaging in these strategies offered underlying rationales that hinged on their having substantial future aspirations, often with college in their sights. These students realized that how they handled peer troubles on the frontstages of the school, where adult authority is preeminent, would impact their opportunities to achieve long-term aspirations. Playing by the rules and playing the rules were an exception in the stories by and trouble cases involving male Latino and black students. When these students recounted stories of peer trouble intersecting with the system they typically revealed how peer reputations came into tension with one's reputation in the world of official school authority and aspirations became more immediate even as consequences were weighed. These dynamics appear prominently in youth-authored case 6.5, "Going to ISS, but I Would Get My Respect."

Case 6.5 "Going to ISS, but I Would Get My Respect"

My conflict was a week ago. I had a conflict because Jorge was flirting with my girlfriend. He knew we were going out, so I got upset and went up to him and talked to him face to face we were yelling back and forth. The thing that was going through my mind was that if we fight I'm going to ISS [in-school suspension], but I get my respect. If I don't fight I lose respect and I would get laugh at, and other things were running through my mind like, I'm not going to fight over no female. What if I got beat up? But after all that Jorge walked away and he called me a "playa hata" [player hater, a derogatory name] so I push him and he kept on walking. Later on he came back and apologize for disrespecting me. After words I felt kind of bad because he was scared of me.

One can view action in this story as unfolding through a well-worn moralistic trouble string that evokes honor as a kind of instrumental "symbolic capital,"[6] the metaphorical currency fought over endlessly in code-of-the-street transactions. But case 6.5 occurred in the shadow of official authority on campus as the storyteller weighed his options for dealing with Jorge. He realized that if he fought, he might end up suspended, yet the fight could earn him "respect," unless he lost, in which case he would be "laugh[ed] at." The author also weighed the value of fighting over a girl and came to the conclusion that he was "not going to fight over no female." The youth in cases 6.1, 6.2, and 6.3 demonstrated considerable faith in the adult system, recognizing their opportunities, if not their future, in that system while not being blind to its considerable shortcomings. Dalton, in case 6.4, placed a cynical faith in a system he believed was unfair but could readily be manipulated to serve his short-term ends. By contrast, the storyteller in case 6.5 saw the adult system as threatening and as no guarantor of his future. He recognized the potential for deterrence if he oriented himself toward the code of the street and secured a reputation as a "fighter." That the author reported his adversary apologized for "disrespecting" him, rather than for the altercation itself or for flirting with his girlfriend, underscored this sense of deterrence. At the same time, he recognized that investing fully in the code of the street to deal with peer trouble would undermine his standing in the school, a place he wanted to hold onto even though he distrusted the adult system of rules and discipline.

The capacity to navigate regimes of adult control and maintain a place in peer relations is necessary for all youth, but especially so for black and Latino male students from high-poverty neighborhoods who receive the most intense gaze and control from school authorities. In his ethnography of Oakland youth in California, for example, Victor Rios finds that black and Latino males are "granted courtesy stigmas" due to their social identities and fall under constant suspicion by law enforcement and school authorities.[7] Aaron Kupchik likewise observes that stereotypes of black and Latino male youth "shape how [these] students are treated" and recounts discriminatory treatment (compared to white youth) even when young men in these categories engage only in "horseplay or bodily touching."[8] These marks appear in case 6.5 as the storyteller recounted his belief that if he did fight, he would almost certainly receive ISS, signaling his recognition that he was under the gaze of school authorities. Moreover, he saw ISS in immediate terms, which differs from the longer-term betterment logics articulated in stories and cases featuring young women of all backgrounds and young men identifying and identified as white.

In studying the intersections of ethnicity and gender in relation to educational success among Latinos, Heidi Barajas and Jennifer Pierce find that Latinas living in poor neighborhoods have more paths available to them, including those enabled through supportive relationships with other Latina peers.[9] They receive support through both peer and adult structures that give weight to their ambitions. This pattern held true for Latinas and black female students at NWHS as they negotiated their troubles with peers even as they navigated power relations with the males in their lives. The mutual continuous support among Abelena and her friends, whom we met in chapter 2 and will meet again in the current chapter, underscores this dynamic. In case 6.3, the teammates of the black female storyteller with strong college aspirations held her back from responding aggressively to a racial slur. She also recounted how her coach helped manage the situation when she and her antagonist encountered each other later in the season, which offers a counter narrative to the discriminatory, carceral-like control and lack of adult support that black female students frequently experience in urban US high schools.[10]

Barajas and Pierce further report that peer support networks are less evident for urban male Latino youth. They rely much less on one another for school success and instead are reliant upon adult mentors, particularly teachers and athletic coaches, to facilitate their formal educational success. Likewise, Victor Rios finds that the male youth he studied recognize the value of education, but the few young men whose lives were transformed through education had supportive adult mentors or "genuine caring relationships with adults who advocated for them and helped them develop their everyday resistance and resilience into navigational skills . . . which allowed them to desist [from delinquency], complete high school, and attend college."[11] The larger point here is that adult social support can play prominent roles in how youth handle trouble and their life-course trajectories. Adult social support, for example, can buffer black and Latino youth from social distrust and exclusion manifest in discriminatory institutional control, facilitating opportunities for youth agency related to peaceful trouble handling and broader life chances. It also can thicken interpersonal trust among diverse youth and adults, which may spill over into institutional trust in school structures if youth come to regard their treatment by adults in such relational contexts as emblematic of their school.

Played by the Rules

In chapter 1, we introduced Mrs. Robinson as one of several NWHS teachers who "keep their ears to the ground" and connected to the youth cultures of the school. These teachers were important mentors on campus both in their interpersonal relationships with students and through their sponsorship of student clubs. They generated interpersonal and institutional allegiances among students, including among black and Latino male students. Still, even with our observations of historical and broad-based adult mentorship and youth across the spectrum of identities reporting trust in the school, black and Latino male students at NWHS were most likely to be under surveillance and disciplined without due cause. These dynamics animated system-based trouble, which youth described as "getting jammed" or "being played by the rules." Consider Derrik in case 6.6, "Jammin' Us All the Time," a black male athlete and one of the stars of the successful NWHS football team, as he told Jerlyn about his trouble with the school administration.

Case 6.6 "Jammin' Us All the Time"

Three black male seniors were sitting and chatting at one of the tables in the library. Jerlyn recognized one of them as Derrik, powerfully built and on crutches due to an ankle injury he suffered while playing in last Saturday's rivalry game against Eastern High. Before she sat down, she said, "Do you mind if I join you guys?" Derrik nodded, "Okay," but the two other guys nodded in her direction politely and excused themselves from the table. She asked Derrik if she "scared them off" and he says, "Nah, they were gonna go to class anyway. I got study hall. I can talk for a few minutes." Jerlyn and Derrik previously had talked a couple of times on the quad in the company of some of the young women she hung out with. He was somewhat soft-spoken and appeared to be well liked by a broad range of peers, in part because he was a star player on the football team, but also because he treated everyone politely, especially the young women on the quad. They began chatting about how his ankle felt and whether he would be well enough to play in the state playoffs in two weeks. He nodded affirmatively and said he saw a doctor who called the sprain a "grade 1 or 2," meaning a mild to moderate sprain. Jerlyn transitioned to how he was "doing otherwise" and "how things are going in school." At first Derrik answered, "All good, you know," but then paused and said that he "don't like the school administration much . . . because we don't have a choice on the classes we take." This statement surprised Jerlyn and she asked what he meant. He said he and his two friends who were just sitting at the table, Toby and Elijah, were seniors and also played on the football team. "We all gotta take only some classes during the season 'cuz they want us to pass. Keep our eligibility. They think we're dumb and can't pass if we take other classes." He added in an animated way, "Only problem is we just found out that if you don' take some pre-reqs last year [junior year] you might not have the right credits to graduate so you goin' to summer school. If you still don' have the credits then you not goin' four-year [to a four year college], you at a JC takin' more classes to qualify for a four year." He ended his explanation with, "The system [is] jammin' us all the time. . . . [We] don't have a say in our education!"

Derrik paused again, took a deep breath, and smiled, saying, "It's worse if you black" and "male" because everyone "thinks you gonna cause trouble," such as getting into "fights" or "doin' drugs." Derrik paused yet again, collecting his thoughts, and spoke a little quieter so that Jerlyn had to lean in to hear what he was saying in his deep baritone voice: "Look, some of 'em, they scared of us. They not gonna deal with us unless there's some problem or we good in sports." He added that the teachers "are pretty good for the most part" and "got to know kids." The guards he counted as "helpin' me and other kids, too." He focused his frustration on the "administration [which] . . . wants to jam us up" but regarded many adults and youth at the "school . . . [as] . . . okay . . . treat you decent."

Jerlyn reassured Derrik that the project was not using anyone's real names. She asked him what he and his friends did when the administration "jams them up," and he said, "Like nuthin'. I play by the rules like they're given." He continued, "You gotta get to where you know how to move ahead. For me that's football and the classroom." Derrik then told Jerlyn that he was "gonna go to college after he graduates" and "try to play football. I guess at a JC for a while." He added, "If I make a complaint for discrimination or somethin', you think anyone gonna give me a scholarship? No way. No how!" Derrik then opened a book and said that he needed to complete some reading. Jerlyn thanked him for his time and bid him farewell as she walked out of the library.

While he expressed positive regard for the NWHS teachers ("pretty good for the most part") and guards ("helpin' me and other kids, too"), Derrik distrusted "the administration," which he saw as a monolith of adults "scared of us" (black males), treating him and other black male athletes one way when they were on the field or the court and another when moving about campus. Derrik viewed the administration jammin' him and his peers by limiting their selection of classes, a move that Derrik said pushed them into junior colleges instead of going directly to "four years" (universities). When going about their daily business on campus, Derrik believed official school authority was trained on them because they were "black" and "male" and, therefore, presumed to be the source of trouble on campus, including fighting and "doing drugs." Yet he balanced his critique with favorable perceptions about the decency with which adults and youth treated one another on campus.

In his four-school study of "unequal discipline," Aaron Kupchik reports that racialized fear shapes school administrators' perceptions of school disorder and, in turn, the differential treatment of students based on ethnic and racial identities. He "observed occasions when black and Latino students touched others [their ethnicity or race unidentified] and were reprimanded or given referrals . . . yet this is less often the case for white students, whose actions are viewed as harmlessly playful and therefore ignored."[12] Kupchik demonstrates that unequal discipline is "veiled and made to seem fair" by school authorities who claim that poor academic performance and differential behavior, not ethnic or racial identity, drives their targeting. Played by the rules, Derrik felt he had to lump his experience of discrimination—"if I make a complaint for discrimination or somethin', you think anyone gonna give me a scholarship? No way. No how!" Derrik said that a lot of the teachers and the security guards were different because they "got to know kids," but he did not refer to a trusted teacher or coach who might help him negotiate the position of being jammed by a distant administration. Derrik resigned himself to "play[ing] by the rules like they're given." Still, he weighed the totality of his situation and continued to plot a course toward university as a two-step process, beginning with junior college.

In their study of the rights consciousness and mobilization among US high school students, Cal and colleagues find that black and Latino high school students report higher rates of rights violations committed by adults on school campuses when compared to Asian American and white students. While black and Latino students' legal consciousness is highly sensitized to rights violations, they are no more likely than their white classmates to put the law to work to redress their grievances even as they report experiencing more discrimination. Consistent with other scholars' findings, this disjuncture results in a "paradox of rights and race" among male youth of color that becomes an integral part of the dynamics of social inequality they face in schools.[13]

Our aggregate analyses in chapter 3 suggest that black and Latino male students were the most likely to write in their narratives about racial trouble with school discipline, although at far lower rates compared with previous research. Being "jammed" or "played by the rules" characterized youth renderings of adult discrimination at NWHS visited upon primarily nonwhite males who come from low-income families—overlapping axes of disadvantage based in ethnicity, race, and social class that produced unique patterns of discrimination. Critical race scholars have drawn attention to compounding inequities or their "intersectionality," which includes gender as a chief component.[14] At NWHS, intersectional inequality and discrimination plays out somewhat differently than the treatment of intersectionality to date. Male youth of color are partially buffered against these adult-centered practices when they serve the interests of the school, particularly when participating in interscholastic athletics and when they have teachers and security personnel who vouch for them. Away from the football field or basketball court, this protection wanes, as Derrik revealed living in fear that adult authorities and school rules might undermine his future ambitions.

Playing Against the Rules

Under the gaze of school authorities, youth with intersecting stigmatizations infrequently resisted discrimination or mobilized against it. Usually, they lumped it, as Derrik illustrated in case 6.6. Yet, as youth sometimes put it, "playing against the rules" was not unheard of among students, including Derrik, who revealed hidden transcripts about the complex ways the school worked against and for them as they engaged in various acts of noncompliance. In such instances, as Erving Goffman described, youth would "decline in some way to accept the official view of what they should be putting into or getting out of [an] organization."[15] When youth revealed hidden transcripts, resisted, subverted and/or mobilized against formal authority, they, like students in many high-poverty schools, reasserted their sense of self-worth and identity by challenging the system.[16] In doing so, they found support in their closest peers and in the student clubs in which they participated, often with the involvement of teachers they knew and trusted, as illustrated in case 6.7, "Help Open the Doors."

Case 6.7 "Help Open the Doors"

Cynthia sat with a group she knew well from "ESL"—Abelena, Roberta, Victoria—at their corner table in the back of the cafeteria. They agreed to sit down with her and talk about whether they had ever had "experiences with

discrimination" at NWHS and "what was done about it." She first asked them
if they ever faced any kind of discrimination on campus and they all nodded
affirmatively. Roberta led off the discussion by saying she "faced it with some
teachers." Roberta added that "some teachers here [at NWHS] want to only
work with the American students" and they "don't want to bother with us."
Cynthia asked, "Do you mean immigrants?" To which Roberta and her three
friends nodded affirmatively.

Abelena then discussed an example involving Ms. O'Malley, whom she
described as an older white teacher who supervised study hall and ISS. Billy
observed Ms. O'Malley in study hall the previous year and noticed that she
was quite strict, including telling some students to stop "jabbering in Spanish" because they were "bothering the rest of students." He noticed that she
appeared more tolerant of students speaking in English even when the study
hall grew quite noisy. Ms. O'Malley did not have her contract renewed at
the end of the previous school year and took a job at Western High, another school in the district. According to Abelena, several students, including her, Roberta, and other students they knew from MEChA, had been in
Ms. O'Malley's study hall as sophomores and believed that Ms. O'Malley
"put Mexicanos in ISS for no reason." Victoria interjected that Ms. O'Malley
always spoke harshly to students "speaking Spanish."

Abelena and Roberta recounted how they had met with an assistant principal, Mr. Amado (a former graduate of NWHS), to tell him of their experiences and concerns about Ms. O'Malley. They also spoke with Ms. Goldstein,
who is white and bilingual and lived in Mexico and Central America when
she was younger. She taught history, including some sections for "ESL" students. They knew her from her work with MEChA and other student clubs,
although she had never taught them in a class. They told her, according to
Abelena, that Ms. O'Malley "is not fair to Mexicanos." Roberta interjected
that both Mr. Amado and Ms. Goldstein "listened carefully" to what she and
Abelena told them about the situation. Based on what Abelena and Roberta
told her, Ms. Goldstein unobtrusively observed Ms. O'Malley in study hall as
she ostensibly pored over some course syllabi stored in filing cabinets in the
back of the room. Ms. Goldstein, Abelena says, then spoke with Mr. Amado
about the situation. Cynthia asked Abelena how the situation made her feel
now and she said, "bad, very bad and maybe good," because teachers like
Ms. O'Malley made her feel "dumb" as if she could only "take ESL classes"
because she "can't speak English" very well. She added that the situation
made her feel "sometimes" as if "all the doors are closed to her" at NWHS. At
the same time, Roberta adds, there were "many" teachers like Ms. Goldstein
who "help open the doors" and "even having adults who will listen shows

you it's a good school." Victoria agreed that there are "good" teachers like Ms. Goldstein who "help." She added that "most teachers" at NWHS "do not act in this way." Roberta commented that early in the current year Ms. Goldstein had told Abelena and her that "she was glad they spoke up" and it "made a difference" with regard to Ms. O'Malley not returning to NWHS.

In a follow-up, in-depth interview with Michael, Ms. Goldstein did not specifically comment on the situation with Ms. O'Malley but did offer an extended response to a question about her relationship with students that seemingly touched on the situation and larger issues: "I think I have a good relationship. . . . I have one of trust and it's nothing I try to force. Sometimes students will come with problems, with trouble like with another teacher. You have to be careful but you have to try to help. Last year, I had a situation where I helped some students with a teacher who was probably—no, definitely—discriminating against them and other students. . . . I helped out as a confidant and talked it out with them, counseled them. I also carefully, confidentially brought the issue to the attention of the administration because it was serious. We resolved the problem so that it's no longer on campus and affecting the students. Doing that builds trust. They don't have to have a special problem, though. I make time for every student every day. . . . And I think that's real important, especially for kids in their adolescence. . . . In some homes I think it's great and you get a lot of parental support. I don't think you have that in every home. It's not an ideal situation. Earlier this semester I recommended some students from my classes . . . just learning English . . . for the new advanced math track because they're gifted. [NWHS began math tracking the previous year with the appointment of a new principal.] I was doing some assessments using different subject matter to test their English and I could see that I had three students who were really advanced analytically with how they approached solving various puzzles. So I spoke with them about how they were doing in their math. They were bored. I talked with our math track coordinator and he gave them the assessment. We don't . . . give advanced assessments to second-language learners. Sure enough they were gifted. So I think it's important that you see . . . them for everything they can bring . . . try to help them in every way you can so it keeps them going. Now we're considering giving everyone the gifted math assessment."

Cynthia invoked the term "discrimination" to jumpstart the conversation that revealed this trouble case. While Abelena, Roberta, and Victoria recognized this legal construct and recounted events that are commonly associated with ethnic and racial discrimination, they did not deploy or invoke legal constructs in their telling of the events. Rather, they drew more upon a discourse embedded in concerns about unfairness, particularly being denied voice—"stop jabbering in Spanish"—when other peers were not singled out for chatting among themselves. They also reported their perceptions of being denied opportunities because they were new immigrants from Mexico, leaving Abelena feeling that "sometimes all the doors are closed." Justice violations that deny voice and that block fair distributions of valued goods, including education, are often found to be the undergirding constructs that marginalized populations, including marginalized youth, draw upon when asked to articulate their experiences with wrongdoing, even when led to do so through the invocation of legal discourse by researchers.[17]

Concerns about a lack of voice and opportunity because of their social identities animated core grievances for these young Mexicanas yet existed side by side with trust in particular staff and the school. Abelena and her friends bridged the divide between trust and distrust by using relational ties to Ms. Goldstein, who brought not only cross-cultural experiences that facilitated the relationship, but also empathy and authentic respect for the challenges faced by the youth. At the same time, Abelena and her friends held on to traditions and identities that defined them, especially their Spanish and ties with Mexico, while gaining the linguistic and other skills that enabled them to succeed in school and beyond. In effect, they maintained the complexity of their identities and agency even as they regarded school structures as trying to bind them to marginalized futures. In this sense, this case illustrates how the stigmatizing differencing of youth can largely be the work of adults, a practice revealed in other studies about urban youth and those who police them.[18] But it also underscores the capacity of youth to bring their evolving sense of identities and collective agency forward to counter adult orderings of them, sometimes with the aid of trusted adults and sometimes not.

The Polyvocality of Rules: Agency and Difference in Putting the Power of the System to Work

During our first three years of fieldwork, how youth at NWHS positioned themselves in relationship to adult authority and school rules displayed decidedly different responses that ranged from compliance (playing by the rules) to instrumentality (playing the rules) to repression (played by the rules) to resistance (playing against the rules). Like all the repertoires of trouble handling we discussed in previous chapters, some rule-oriented responses we identified aligned, while others were in tension with each other. Patricia Ewick and Susan Silbey argue that such "polyvocality" facilitates the durability of a rule-oriented system by enabling people to exercise agency to work through their troubles.[19]

While Ewick and Silbey focus on legality, our findings extend their thinking to include other sources of normative ordering, particularly repertoires of conciliatory-remedial and moralistic practices that we uncovered among youth. Second, conditions of social trust are likely to influence the predominance and distribution of some repertoires of trouble handling over others. This dynamic at NWHS led to a proclivity toward conciliatory-remedial compared to moralistic and rule-oriented trouble responses. In settings where social trust is unstable, polyvocality may operate more as Ewick and Silbey expect. But in settings characterized by sustained social trust, trouble responses aligned with the underlying expectations of trust may contribute to agency and improvisation in handling trouble. Finally, this chapter points to how social difference, such as race and gender, intersected with different types and levels of social trust as NWHS youth positioned themselves and were positioned in relation to authority and school rules.

Some youth did, under certain conditions and with particular social identities, put the power of the system to work on their behalf when dealing with interpersonal troubles at NWHS during this historical period. When their ties to other youth were loose and trouble broke out on the frontstages of the school, some NWHS students made strategic calculations that playing by the rules brought advantages over their nemeses or ensured that school authorities and rules did not come down on them. In these contexts, youth turned for help to an adult at the school with whom they had close ties. Both the freshman football player who authored case 6.1, "Didn't Want to Get Kicked off the Team," and the star basketball player who authored case 6.3, "If A Scout Sees Me Fighting," wrote about turning to their coaches on the backstages to buffer themselves against troubles that could undermine their long-term ambitions. They illustrated a particular image of playing by the rules as involving rational calculation of the risks faced in their peer relations for turning toward the system. To play by the rules also involved more overt actions that symbolized trust in the school yet carried risks with peers, as illustrated by Alanza's actions in case 6.2, when she silenced two rowdy male students disrupting her class. In that situation, the overall desire of the class to support a teacher, uphold a collective moral identity as "hard working," and support the school as a trusted place that works all came to together to legitimate Alanza's actions in the eyes of her peers.

As noted in this chapter and chapter 3, black and Latino male youth imagined themselves playing by the rules in their youth-authored stories at lower rates than their peers, accounting for only seven stories out of 103 in which youth wrote about dealing with the system. In each of these seven stories (illustrated by case 6.5 above), the author weighed whether to pursue a moralistic beat down of a peer in light of consequences of doing so vis-à-vis peers and the possibilities of school discipline. These stories underscore how black and Latino male youth straddled informal and official control dynamics as they reflected on possible courses of action. The complexity of their decision making in this regard outstripped that of their nonwhite female and male white peers. Part of the reason for this complexity relates to the greater frequency with which they directly encountered official school authority but also experienced the pull of street culture's distrust of state institutions. Recall that black and Latino male students wrote more often about discrimination by school staff and school discipline than either young women or white males.

Youth of color from high-poverty neighborhoods live in a world rife with institutional distrust and criminal injustice, from which the campus climate of social trust only partially shields them. These dynamics enabled young Latino and black males, especially, to gain tacit knowledge as repeat players but also bear the burdens that such routine encounters entail. Many young women of color face the same burdens in many urban US schools, especially African Americans, who receive exclusionary disciplinary sanctions at higher rates than white or other female youth of color.[20] At NWHS, however, we did not detect these disparities in either official disciplinary statistics or through our fieldwork among female students of color. Latina and black female youth faced other challenges, including gender norms of "appropriate" femininity even as they were called upon to negotiate the rough and tumble of peer expectations, and conflicts that could be especially difficult for immigrant female youth who were branded academically incapable when their chief constraints were not cognitive but linguistic.

Some who played by the rules did not view the system with fear but rather regarded it as sufficiently complex and malleable that it could be played to their advantage. Youth bested other youth who just as easily could go to school authorities on their own behalf regarding the trouble at hand. The storyteller of case 6.1, for instance, did not claim to be more in the right than his antagonist; rather, he talked with the coach first about the altercation on the basketball court with another player. Dalton, in case 6.4, had considerable experience with the disciplinary system and knew how to mobilize a teacher to sanction a couple of youths who teased him about his appearance because he knew how to play the rules. Despite his regular encounters with official school control, his general social privilege as a white male may have aided his credibility with respect to the teacher who came to his aid.

Teachers and staff also knew how to play the rules as they negotiated the school bureaucracy, and how to create trouble for youth or to come to the aid of students who were in trouble with the system. Ms. Goldstein (case 6.7), for example, helped Roberta and her friends mobilize against a discriminatory teacher. Youth also recognized actions by teachers and administrators as discriminatory but often, as previous research has shown, lumped their grievances.[21] Prior to the turn of the century, however, we did not witness overt mass mobilization by students. This would change, first with the advent of safe schools and then with broader state and national politics in the latter half of the first decade of the twenty-first century.

Coda: Safe Schools Anxieties

In the early summer of 1999, students, as well as some teachers, began expressing collective anxiety, if not foreboding, about a variety of changes then just beginning to come into view on campus that would come to be known simply as safe schools. We experienced this foreboding first-hand as we conducted a mapping exercise.

During one class session, a white male senior sitting in the back of the class said very loudly that the "school looks like a prison" and held up a sketch map to show the class (see figure 6.1). His classmate, a black male eleventh grader, drew the map. He depicted the campus as a single rectangle with barbed wire around it, a few stick figures (one, holding what appears to be a gun, saying, "shot that kid"), and the word "PRISON" drawn in large letters running across one side. Several students voiced complaints about the construction then just beginning on campus. Two students volunteered that they included the parking lots in their maps because they were "part of the school" but that they "aren't really working right now." A Latina senior added that the "school is wasting a lot of money with fencing and security stuff and there's a lot of other stuff in classrooms that need fixing, like the AC." A Latino senior nodded his head affirmatively, saying the school "could've spent their money on sports equipment and club activities" or "other stuff for classrooms." He added that the school "don' care

Figure 6.1. Youth-sketched map entitled "Prison," 2000

no more what students think now." He also alluded to the disappearance of "lunch activities," such as "basketball" and "ping pong," which he said could lead to "trouble" because people "just sit around with nothing to do." As students turned in their maps, a white male senior agreed with his classmate who depicted the school as a prison, saying "the school seems more and more like a prison." He added that the "removal of the [student] lockers and clearing of trees" on school grounds reminded him of a "youth farm" where he once had to go when he "got busted for pot."

These physical transformations of the school, harbingers of carceral-like safe schools, registered strongly on students as the changing architecture undermined the ability to hang out and move around—hallmarks of anchored fluidity—and students across the campus became highly sensitive to how changes in the physical and social geography of the school could generate more trouble and conflict. Cynthia, for example, picked up on these concerns as she sat down with a small, mixed group of sophomore young women on the grass near one of the buildings and then later, with

Abelena and her friends, to record perceptions about the changes afoot on campus—problems unlike any of those we had thus far analyzed in that they recounted an overall sense of looming social problems that would afflict the entire school rather than a set of interpersonal troubles. A black sophomore mentioned the campus was moving toward "one lunch period" and a closed campus, which she believed could result in "problems" because "you'll have all the kids crowded in together in the cafeteria" and "it's crowded already." Another Latina sophomore added, and the rest of the group agreed, that "you could really get some problems" with the new schedule.

In the cafeteria a few days later, Cynthia found Abelena, Victoria, and Gabriela eating lunch and asked them about the ongoing changes to the campus. Gabriela noted that moving to a "single lunch period" from the historical double-lunch period, with ninth and tenth graders during the first hour and eleventh and twelfth graders during the second, was "stupid" and "all the kids can barely fit in the cafeteria as it is." They all wondered if there would be "more competition for tables" in the cafeteria and whether they would "be pushed out of the cafeteria by other students." Cynthia found Gabriela eating in the "Q" quad, and she echoed the group, noting that many of the diversions students "enjoy" during the lunch hours, such as ping pong, basketball, or sitting in empty classrooms and eating a "quiet lunch," would be gone. She also mentioned that the administration had not consulted students about the changes, that it would be "a good thing" if the administration discussed with the students what "is about to happen." She observed generally that "This is not how it works here. It seems so different now." Students, she noted, were "more stressed" because of both "construction noise" and the campus being "all closed in" now with the "new fencing going up" and "rules about where you can be on campus." With these concerns as backdrop, NWHS broke for the 1999 summer intercession and we turned our attention to catching up on two and a half years of team-collected field data already in hand. We did not yet fully realize the full meaning of youths' warning signs about the emergent interruption in the period of substantial trust and alignment among youth and adult controls.

SEVEN

Safe Schools

Two months into the 1999 fall semester, a violent brawl broke out during lunch as students poured in and out of the cafeteria and sat about in their many groups crowded on the main and "Q" quads. We learned about the "October Fight" from eyewitness accounts of students, teachers, security guards, and administrators who were directly involved or witnessed the events.

Case 7.1 "The October Fight"

Dot, a security guard born and raised in New West whose parents came from Mexico, watched from a distance as three males walked through the densely packed main quad toward the "Q" quad. Teo, a ninth grader born and raised in New West, whose father hailed from Mexico and his mother from El Salvador, walked out in front of the group. He was flanked on one side by Santiago, a wiry, US-born Latino sophomore, and on the other by Armando, stout like Teo but several inches shorter, who came to the United States from Mexico when he was a toddler. As they walked through the open gate between the main quad and the "Q" quad, the crowding of students increased, which slowed the group's progress. After a few minutes, they came to a metal picnic table at which sat six male youth from Mexico. The youth at the table ranged in age from ninth graders to seniors. Some were eating lunch while others chatted and one youth appeared to be studying a book. From her vantage point, Dot could not hear what was said but could see a heated exchange develop between Teo and Felix, one of the six youth at the table.

Teo, according to several boys who knew him, believed he could make a name for himself by fighting and besting Felix. Always well dressed and interested in all things electronic, Felix often was in the company of Roberta and Gabriela (see case 4.2) and at the center of discussions in the "Q" quad with other students newly-arrived from Mexico. Although two years older at seventeen, Felix stood a head shorter than Teo, who was nearly six feet tall. Unknown to Teo was Felix's other passion, boxing, for which he trained at a gym in another part of the city. According to Felix in a later interview, when Teo and his companions arrived at the picnic table outside the "Q" quad, Felix did not immediately notice them amidst the crush of youth in the quad. Teo, in a loud voice, called Felix and the other youth sitting with him "wetbacks," lacing his ethnic epithet with profanity and then spitting at them in a loud, aggressive manner. Dot had taken up a position on a low-rise wall surrounding a planter on the edge of the "Q" quad so that she could see over the crowd. According to her, Felix looked up from his lunch with his "face totally beet red" and yelled, "What the hell?!" Dot said he immediately got up "and started hitting Teo . . . as quick as a cat. Teo was taking a beating. Combinations [a boxing term for multiple punches] to the face and blood all a sudden everywhere." For a moment, Dot noted, she simply tried to get a sense of "who was involved" and in doing so came away with a detailed sense of how the incident unfolded in its first minute or two. Santiago and Armando "jumped in" to the fight, she said, trying to pull Felix off Teo. She could see Armando kicking Felix in his ribs, which caused Felix to hit his head on the picnic table, opening up a gash on his right temple that began bleeding. She then lost sight of Teo, who disappeared for a moment under the picnic table as Armando continued kicking Felix, and Santiago attempted to hold Felix's arms so he could not hit Teo. Three of the youth who had been sitting at the picnic table with Felix scattered into the crowd while two other male students sitting at the table joined the melee, tackling Santiago, who swung wildly and hit one of the three youth squarely in the nose, pushing his head hard against the bench attached to the picnic table. The youth fell over backwards off the picnic table bench and fell on the ground and did not move as the fight swirled around him.

Amidst shouts in English and Spanish, Dot called on her walkie-talkie for backup and could see Teo attempting to squirm away under a table. She then saw Felix, who had worked himself free of Santiago, pull Teo out from under the table to continue hitting him in the head and body. After calling for back-up, Dot began pushing through the crowd to the fight. She estimated that only a "minute" had elapsed since Felix started hitting Teo, but the inside of the dense crowd of students, she said, was "chaos." Two male teachers who had been walking the perimeter of the main and "Q" quads before the fight also pushed their way through the crowd, joined by Principal Samuels, who had been in the "Q" building for a lunchtime meeting. As Principal

Samuels reached the periphery of the fight, Santiago, she recounted, "hit and pushed [me] to the ground." Javier and Robert, two more security guards, arrived on the scene in a security cart and pushed through the crowd with Dot to separate the fighters, standing between them and several other boys who had pushed in as well. According to Dot, they stood "in boxing stances" ready to fight, although it was not clear whom they expected to fight. The fighter who fell to the ground had since rolled over and was holding his arm with blood coming down his face to his shirt.

By the time the fight ended, students had crowded in from the main quad to the "Q" quad. Javier noted to Cynthia that "it looked like half the school was there." Blood stained the ground around the picnic table where Felix been sitting. Dot caught a glimpse of Teo, already on the ground and bleeding a lot from his head, but then lost sight of him as she "bear hugged" Felix to "pull him away." Dot's call for back-up security also led Mr. Amado, an assistant principal in the main office, to call the New West Police Department (the regular NWPD security resource officer—SRO—was off that day) and initiate a "lock down" of the campus. With full sirens blaring, multiple NWPD units arrived minutes after the fight had been broken up, trailed by a New West Fire Department emergency medical vehicle. By that time, Dot, Javier, Robert, and Principal Samuels were escorting six of the boys who fought, plus another half dozen who looked ready to fight, to the main offices. Teo was nowhere to be seen. All six fighters required medical attention and five went to a nearby emergency room with assorted injuries, including multiple broken noses, a broken arm, broken and bruised ribs, a severely gouged eye, facial and scalp cuts and bruises, and unidentified "internal injuries" from being kicked in the stomach and sides. NWPD officers arrested three students—Felix, Santiago, and Armando—but ultimately dropped the charges. The school held disciplinary hearings for all six fighters and an "education and warning" session for the additional half dozen who appeared ready to fight. All six fighters received multiple-day out-of-school suspension (OSS). No one knew what became of Teo, although the NWPD questioned several students about him and visited his neighborhood to questions residents about him. Several youth at the scene reported to Cynthia that they saw Teo running from the "Q" quad in the aftermath of the fight as school staff and the NWPD rounded up the fighters. He never returned to NWHS.

In the days after the violence, Dot reported how Felix had told her that "something got into" him when Teo called him a "wetback" and "spit" at him and his friends. Felix told Cynthia that at one point in the fight he remembered stopping momentarily and thinking, "What am I doing? Why am

I doing this?" Felix continued, "These things don't happen here [at NWHS]. Off campus, all the time. I just ignore it." For his part, Armando told Dot (relayed to Cynthia) that Felix "started it all" and had a "beef" with Teo for insulting him and his "neighborhood." Yet no one close to Teo or Felix could remember a specific instance when Teo and Felix interacted, only "stories from Teo." As Santiago put it to Cynthia, he and Armando walked with Teo to the "Q" quad to find Felix to "see what's up with him [Felix]" and so "nuthin' happens." Felix told Cynthia in a separate conversation that he "never saw Teo or the other guys" before that day. None of our fieldworkers had observed Teo or Santiago in the "Q" quad at the same time, although Armando did take ESL classes there. Felix added, "That guy [Teo] was lookin' to make a rep as a badass. I'm a Mexicano trying to make it in this country. That's all."

By the time of the Fight, our team had been on campus continually for more than two years, and, as noted in previous chapters, uncovered group tensions, especially between US-born Latinos and newly arrived students from Mexico, but few physical altercations and nothing that escalated to a melee of this magnitude. The trouble response string for case 7.1 shares some similarities with typical moralistic strings, such as beginning with verbal insults either real or imagined, while departing from them in other ways, notably the lack of any attempt to work out trouble prior to escalation, third-party escalation, and the savagery of the violence.

"What's Going on Here?"

Over time, the Fight became a catalyst for deepening our knowledge about youth conflict at NWHS. In this chapter, we tell two intertwined stories—one story about what happened when a high-poverty school experienced an interruption to the school structure and climate facilitating control practices that served as a bedrock to peaceable relations, and the other story about how we came to understand the Fight. Both stories have their beginnings when Michael learned about the Fight via a phone call from Mrs. Robinson late on the day it occurred. As soon as he got off the phone, he emailed Cal, Cynthia, Christine, and Madelaine.[1] Below appear excerpts from the intense flurry of emails the fieldwork team exchanged that day.

To: [NWHS] Fieldwork Team
Fr: Michael Musheno
Re: What's going on here?
Date: 10/1/99

Colleagues–

Yesterday there was a significant breakout of violence on the campus involving several Latino youth. . . . I am perplexed as to what happened given our
sense of everyday conflict among youth on campus. The collective violence
seems unlike anything we've seen on campus during our time there. . . . I
am second-guessing myself. . . . We need to learn as much as we can about
the Fight.

To: [NWHS] Fieldwork Team
Fr: Calvin Morrill
Re: Re: What's going on here?
Date: 10/1/99

I agree with Michael that we should immediately learn as much as we can
about the Fight. . . . [It] doesn't seem to fit with our findings up to now
about how youth define and act on conflict. More puzzling is that in our
years on campus, we haven't witnessed anything remotely like this. . . . Is
this part of a broader pattern of hostilities among Mexicanos and other Latinos? Is this situation gang related? It's unclear. . . . Did those involved know
one another? . . . Before we make any recommendations to the school,
however, we need to have better information on what happened, some
grounded ideas about why, and be cautious with our intervention.

To: [NWHS] Fieldwork Team
Fr: Christine Yalda
Re: Re: Re: What's going on here?
Date: 10/1/99

I've noticed hostilities among Mexicanos and Chicanos around the ESL
areas [in the "Q" quad], but nothing reaching anything like Michael described. I agree with Michael that this is clearly a serious situation and that
we should be able to comment on it. I share Cal's concerns that we need
to learn more about the situation before we take any steps toward intervention.

To: [NWHS] Fieldwork Team
Fr: Cynthia Bejarano
Re: Re: Re: Re: What's going on here?
Date: 10/1/99

In reference to Cal and Christine's inquiries and comments, for a few
months, tensions seem to have been building among these groups and other
groups on campus. . . . Maybe . . . [this] . . . was just an opportunity to do
something. . . . I agree with Cal that if we do make suggestions we will have
to be very cautious in terms of representation. I don't want to further stereo-
type all "Latinos" as deviant and dangerous (and teachers and administrators
have been worried about a gang presence on campus for few months now but
I'm unclear what they're basing their fears on). I am concerned about sending out this message [about a gang presence] to teachers and administrators.

We circulated through campus in the days and weeks that followed to
gather accounts about why the Fight occurred. Several students expressed
surprise and shock that Felix was involved, given his quiet, respectful de-
meanor and his deft handling of interpersonal or intergroup tension. One
white student, who worked with Felix in the "tech lab" (a shed where a
teacher kept several old radios), remarked that he must have "gone ber-
serk" at Teo's "taunting." Several teachers linked the violence to an upsurge in gang-related activity or "turf wars," which paralleled some of what
Armando shared about Teo's "beef" with Felix. Speaking with Christine,
Mrs. Bruce, a black teacher who had taught on campus for a few years, illustrates the gang-related account: "I can't put my finger on it but I feel
the [F]ight was gang related. The kids were definitely gang members." Despite Mrs. Bruce's speculation-turned-to-certainty, we did not uncover evidence that any of the fighters affiliated or aligned with street gangs. Street
gang members attended NWHS but were not central to everyday school
life. None were involved in the Fight or claimed Felix, Teo, Santiago, or
Armando among their members and supporters.

Several students we spoke with offered accounts that discounted gang
involvement, instead accenting intra-ethnic dynamics. One student, for example, a US-born Latina named Maya, who knew Armando and Santiago
and witnessed the Fight, told Cynthia: "The [F]ight? It was a Mexicano/Chi-
cano thing. . . . Yeah, brown on brown. Not a gang thing at all. It's weird
that this would happen though. You know, sometimes we [Mexicanos and
Chicanos] get along and sometimes not. Not sure why it happened now."
We found it interesting that she referred to "we"—what sociolinguists generally call a "pronoun of solidarity"[2]—to refer to all Latinos, yet used the
term "Chicano" to distinguish US-born Latino and Mexican-born students.
She also puzzled over the intra-ethnic aspects of the conflict, seemingly uncertain herself ("it's weird") about the timing of why such tensions translated into collective violence.

Javier, a security guard who helped break up the Fight and knew the campus as well as anyone, offered a twist to the ethnic-tension explanation, implicating the school itself in an interview with Cynthia:

> Look there's personalities and identities involved, no doubt. It's bigger though, you know. . . . If the kids had activities like they used to, they could help some of the problems between these groups. . . . Tensions got pretty high over the last several months and students are more afraid of each other now because of it. . . . [T]he school only has one ping-pong table set up now; we use to have three. We don't have the lunchtime basketball games no more. . . . ESL students used the tables a lot. Other kids use the basketball. It works off some energy, you know. A lotta stuff is changed on campus with the construction and new security. Kids could go to a classroom if they din't wanna play ball and talk with each other, a teacher. Now students have nowhere to go except to be in plain sight and just stare at each other in the lunch room [cafeteria] or quads unless they in class.

Javier first referenced "personalities" (individuals) and "identities" (intra- and interethnic tensions) but then linked changes underway related to "the construction and new security" at NWHS. He then cited trouble among youth more broadly in his statement that "Tensions got pretty high over the last several months and students are more afraid of each other." Javier's account pointed us in the direction of what the Fight might tell us about the interplay of school structures, especially safe schools, and the campus climate.

Our first occasion to put forth an explanation for the Fight emerged when Mrs. Robinson asked if we might provide the school with some insight as to why the Fight occurred and how such events might be prevented. With input from the entire fieldwork team, Michael drafted a memo to NWHS teachers and administrators that attempted to put the Fight in context, drawing on what we knew from our fieldwork to date on campus. He emphasized that the bulk of our research revealed "daily interactions within and across social groups . . . [as] substantially peaceable," although "social tensions appear highest among . . . students identifying strongly with their Mexican heritage and [students] identifying strongly with popular American culture while holding onto their Latino roots." The memo also pulled our explanation of the Fight back in the direction of what we already knew, placing the event within the repertoire of moralistic trouble responses, specifically a version of an extreme, collective beat down.

At the same time, the extreme escalation of the Fight did not comport with the interactional dynamics in beat downs we observed up to that time, particularly the common practice of youth going up to the precipice of violence only to deflect further escalation by backing down, as we documented in chapter 5. Perhaps the Fight represented a social convulsion of ethnic tensions, precipitated by Teo's hostility and Felix's inability to steel himself to manage one more anxiety-ridden, stigmatizing interaction without retaliating—the proverbial straw that broke the camel's back. But this explanation did not speak to the timing of the incident, nor why third-party peers did not attempt to intervene to keep the peace as we commonly observed on campus, as illustrated in chapters 3–5. Felix appeared equally surprised at what happened, recounting a seemingly rational self-reflection as he pummeled Teo ("Why am I doing this?"), all the while asserting his identity as a member of a morally upstanding group ("I'm a Mexicano trying to make it in this country"). Violent experiences and after-the-fact accounts of violence typically contain ambiguous, conflicting tropes, as Randall Collins observes, including fear and surprise.[3] Yet this event and its accounting seemed different in scale and scope.

By 2002, with the campus firmly under an administration uninterested in our project and most of the fieldwork team members moving on to new opportunities and unrelated projects, Cal and Michael began a new phase of inquiry, reanalyzing and triangulating our data while treating the Fight as a critical reference point. We returned to the field, initially conducting observations from a distance, scouting the nearby strip mall and bus stops where students historically congregated before, during, and after the school day, and gradually increased our observations on campus while interacting with teachers and staff we came to know. We also deepened our knowledge of campus history and collected institutional data in an attempt to better contextualize both the Fight and our first few years of fieldwork. Christine continued collecting field data through 2002 in support of the team project as well as her dissertation, observing and conducting interviews with students and teachers alike.[4] Her work, coupled with our renewed field and institutional research, revealed that NWHS was becoming heavily invested in carceral-like safe schools school control technologies sweeping the United States during the early twenty-first century.

In the parlance of analytic induction, we came to regard the Fight as a "deviant" case capable of generating new pathways of inquiry rather than an event that could be explained completely at the interactional level of analysis.[5] We reassessed and expanded our approach, underscoring the school as a contested place in the crux of local- and national-level change in educational and legal fields. NWHS students comprised one set of agents responding to trouble, carving out physical and social niches while interfacing with teachers and staff who operated in the immediacy of their school lives. But they performed identities and acted on trouble while having limited capacities to shape or interrupt adult authority, agency, processes, and policies in the broader fields of law and education. Treating NWHS as an active organizational place with a historical legacy led us to new questions about the Fight and its potential link to dramatic changes in control practices on campus.

We strengthened our commitment to this new line of inquiry as we worked backward through our data to the point when we began fieldwork on campus and then forward through the years subsequent to the event. Our purpose was to interpretively recover what links might exist between the Fight, safe schools, and everyday practices of informal peer control. This inquiry caused us to more precisely recognize the significance of student anxieties in the late 1990s and early in the first decade of the twenty-first century concerning how renovation of the school had changed the lived space of the campus. As we noted in the coda at the end of the last chapter, student accounts of intensifying trouble with school discipline began to surface in spring 1999 coupled to youth feeling "all closed in" by the prison-like formal control then emerging on campus. Students also claimed to be "more stressed" and to fear that conditions in the campus downtown could precipitate more competition for space, with some being "pushed out of the cafeteria by other students." In effect, students were warning us that the new changes would render NWHS "a mess," their reasoning closely tracking Javier's account.

Our analysis conceived of the Fight as a particular type of trouble case, an organizational "accident"—an unplanned collective event that throws into relief social routines, social changes, and power relations typically obfuscated in everyday view.[6] The Fight offered clues into how safe schools architectural alterations and new control technologies jarred the social ordering on campus in two senses. First, these organizational efforts pushed change downward into the campus while drawing on rhetoric and practices from broader institutional movements at the local and national levels. In this sense, the Fight allowed us to begin seeing more acutely how adult authority structures and practices, instituted from the top down and the outside in, mattered for the social interactional processes through which youth handled peer trouble. Second, we tracked forward and backward from the Fight how safe schools interrupted anchored fluidity and trouble-response repertoires among youth while undermining trust and heightening the salience of ethnic and racial divisions. Taken together, these changes constituted a collective trauma and shock to the school in that they involved dramatic alterations to settled routines and meanings that had defined a good deal of campus life during the 1990s and, not without contestation or variation, earlier decades as well.[7] While these dynamics cannot establish a causal pathway to the Fight, they alerted us to the unintended consequences associated with official control changes in schools and the importance of local knowledge among youth about such changes. How did these changes tie into broader changes in the field of education and law? To answer this question, we stepped far beyond NWHS to explore the national context of the safe schools movement in facilitating carceral-like official school control in educational and criminal justice fields and then moved back to understand the local context leading up to the adoption of safe schools at NWHS.

The National Context: The Safe Schools Movement

The safe schools movement emerged during the late 1980s, bringing together strands of movements in criminal justice and education focused on crime prevention in schools, victim rights, and school peer mediation.[8] These movements helped articulate the framing of broader cultural and political economic shifts at the intersection of what David Garland calls the new "culture of control" and Jonathan Simon labels "governing through crime."[9] These shifts, embedded in the diffusion of neoliberal policies associated initially with economic deregulation and the retrenchment of social welfare, transformed the relationship between crime and social control aimed at marginalized populations in the United States, including changes in penal policies and practices, imageries of citizens, victims, and perpetrators, and an expansion of crime control frames into many walks of life.[10]

Although concerns about youth conflict and crime have been part of the US political and cultural landscape at least since the Progressive Era in the early twentieth century, the safe schools movement ushered in a new era of concern, gaining early legitimacy and visibility with President Ronald Reagan's establishment in 1984 of the National School Safety Center (NSSC) as a joint program of the Departments of Justice and Education. The NSSC provided an early clearing house for knowledge on technical aspects of securing and assessing school safety and a point of articulation for two grassroots networks in the field of education focused on school safety: parents and guardians of local youth who identified themselves and their children as victims of bullying and gang violence; and professionals working with youth and families affected by these dynamics, including school psychologists, school counselors, school nurses, and school resource officers employed by or aligned with local police departments. These networks expanded the meaning of victimization in schools in piecemeal fashion, coupling it to the binary of "victimized" versus "predatory" youth,[11] with the parents-guardians' network largely framing schools as unresponsive to the plight of the victims of school violence even as school districts drew on the NSSC to securitize campuses.

Media and scholarly attention to the "epidemic" of youth street violence initially focused safe schools on urban schools, but ultimately encompassed the vast majority of US schools. Advocacy organizations, such as School Safety Advocacy Council (SSAC) and the National Association of School Resource Officers (NASRO), emerged in the 1990s to organize networks of parents and professionals to advocate for governmental funding and organize conferences where local and state educational officials could learn the latest strategies for handling and preventing school violence.[12] The framing for these organizations' efforts drew from and extended into public education multiple crime response strategies that had gained currency in the 1980s, including "broken windows" (the urban crime control strategy of aggressive proactive stops of citizens by law enforcement for minor infractions);[13] "penalization" (hardening sanctions and expanding the scope of isolation of offenders);[14] and "crime control through environmental design" (creating "defensible space" to ward off criminal activity through spatial manipulation and "techno-security equipment").[15]

By the early 1990s, the National Educational Association (NEA) endorsed the safe schools movement and helped pass in 1994 the first of multiple, federal Safe Schools Acts, which established federal centers for the study of safety and security in schools.[16] The 1996 NEA *Safe Schools Manual* codified multiple components of "making a school safe," including (1) articulating mission statements and consistently enforcing disciplinary codes; (2) rationalizing the reporting of crime and vandalism through the use of monitoring all students (including identifying which "groups" are most likely to commit violence and other acts of disruption and limiting student movement on campus);[17] (3) creating "closed" campuses that stringently limit student entry and exit; (4) mobilizing student participation in the monitoring of violence and other forms of deviance; (5) placing "disruptive" students in "alternative school environments"; and (6) "altering the internal physical environment" of schools to establish and sustain official authority through architectural design.[18] Taken together, these components constituted a "policy domain shift"[19] in the field of education from one of teacher-centered instruction and social control to securitization *and* instruction through alterations to physical and social technologies of official school control.[20] With this institutional domain shift, safe schools became an essential frame for schools signaling organizational competence in preventing school violence.[21]

Governmental funding, federal to local, generated a robust market for crime control consultants, architectural firms, and construction firms to "securitize" schools from external intrusion and internal disorder.[22] With the Cold War ended and the Soviet Union disbanded in 1989, US defense contractors became suppliers of school security equipment (cameras, metal detectors, heavy fencing), training, and research on high-tech surveillance systems.[23] The late 1990s and early twenty-first century represented a high water mark for the safe schools industry as one-third of school districts across the nation invested more than $5 billion to renovate high schools with "improvements" related to "security and life safety."[24] Between the early to middle first decade of the twenty-first century, policies and practices either directly or indirectly evoking safe schools could be found in the vast majority of US public schools, pervasively instantiating what Aaron Kupchik calls the "new regime" of school security.[25] The movement also shifted focus from the threat of street violence in schools perpetrated by urban youth of color to responding to a string of rampage shootings in suburban schools committed by middle-class white males, with the 1999 Columbine High School shootings as a key reference point.[26] With its pervasive influence, the safe schools movement came to constitute an institutionalized field of public education, composed of the regulated and regulators, of sellers and buyers, and of victims and perpetrators.[27] The local context at NWHS looked quite a bit different than either urban schools suffering the tragedies of street violence or suburban schools facing the threat of rampage shootings.

The Local Context: NWHS as a Safe but Contested Campus

Our fieldwork represented conciliatory-remedial practices as the modal form of peer control among NWHS students from 1997 to 2000. This depiction paralleled district statistics that portrayed the campus as one of the safest, if not the safest, campuses in the district during this same time period. We sought independent confirmation of this pattern from sources not linked to the campus, district, or our ethnographic evidence. We consulted the New West Police Department (NWPD) to identify the types of calls the department received from students and school officials during school days over a fifteen-year period, 1995–2009. This represents three years prior to the implementation of safe schools (1995–1998) and nine years after its full implementation on campus in 2000. The NWPD would only release the data in the aggregate for this period but also gave us open access to dispatchers, departmental analysts, and field officers who worked beats around the high school during this period. These discussions resulted in a decision to focus on calls classified by dispatchers and officers on duty as "assault" (in which some sort of physical violence had occurred among youth or youth and adults), "incorrigible juvenile activity" (in which youth disobey an adult ostensibly responsible for them), and "suspicious activity" (in which someone appears to be planning a crime involving property or persons).[28] Figure 7.1 represents the pattern of calls during this period. In the years prior to and during our first years of fieldwork, the NWPD received an average of 7.2 calls per year, including 2.6 calls for assault, 1.6 calls for incorrigible juvenile activity, and 3.0 calls for suspicious activity. The more than seven calls per year seems to suggest more "serious" incidents than the three per year reported in district statistics during the same period until one considers the nature of the calls. According to a dispatcher and a field officer who actually handled many of the calls from NWHS (and other district schools), calls about assault typically consisted of "one or two one-on-one fights" among NWHS students and usually "one fight" among youth "unidentified by the school" (not enrolled) just off the campus, not among students and nonenrolled youth. Incorrigible juvenile activity and suspicious activity calls involved youth "unidentified by the school" on or near school grounds typically just before or after regu-

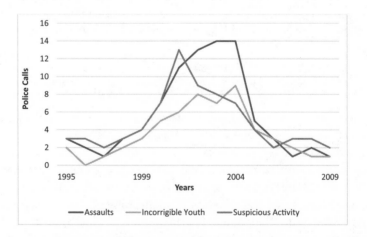

Figure 7.1. Police calls from New West High School to the
New West Police Department, 1995–2009

lar school hours. A few incorrigible youth calls also involved "drug busts" on campus. Although not precise, an estimate of the number of NWPD calls directly involving NWHS students during school hours works out to approximately three to four per year, which comports with the three serious incidents per year reported in the district statistics for the campus.

Most revealing is the pattern of NWPD police calls *after* some aspects of safe schools began to appear in the late spring and early fall of 1999. From 2000 to 2004, the average yearly number of calls to NWPD nearly quadrupled to 27.6, including 11.8 calls for assault, 8.8 calls for incorrigible juvenile activity, and 7.0 calls for suspicious activity. The character of calls about assaults changed as well during this period, shifting to "problems" involving "multiple individual youth" on campus and to "youth-teacher" altercations. The dispatcher also reported more calls coming in directly from students rather than primarily from adults, owing to the appearance of cell phones among students early in the first decade of the twenty-first century. Moreover, the NWPD received only one call from 1995 to 1999 for youth-teacher assault, which specifically related to adults intervening into the Fight. The nature of incorrigible youth and suspicious activity calls shifted in the 2000–2004 period as well, consisting of both individuals "known" and "unknown" to the school. These calls, according to the dispatcher, originated from both adults and students. In figure 7.1, there is yet another shift as the total number of NWPD calls decreases dramatically in 2005 from the previous year, returning to nearly the pre-safe schools level at 7.6 per year, including 2.6 calls for assault, 2.2 calls for incorrigible juvenile activity, and 2.8 calls for suspicious activity. Later in this chapter, we bring forward our field data to associate the spike in calls from 2000 to 2004 with a period of intensive administrative commitment to implementing safe schools at NWHS. These data do not provide evidence of a credible surge in violence, criminality, or delinquency prior to the adoption of safe schools associated with NWHS. Indeed, they appear to point in the opposite direction. Nor do they allow us to sort out whether the calls rose from 2000 to 2004 in response to increasing interpersonal physical violence on campus or a widening net of school discipline. The NWPD field officer who directly handled the calls believed that both dynamics may have been in play. What he called "tighter discipline" brought more students under scrutiny by NWHS staff and many calls were not "trivial," requiring multiple responding officers and medical personnel.

This context contrasts with the safe campus that Constance Samuels inherited when she became NWHS principal in 1998 after her predecessor left to become assistant superintendent of a neighboring school district. In her mid-fifties and white, she rose through the disciplinary side of school administration, initially in the district's more affluent suburban schools. In 1997, two years before the Fight, she joined the NWHS administration as an assistant principal of student life, focusing on discipline and extracurricular activities, the latter of which, she said in an interview with Michael, were "in dire need of fresh perspective" even as that era enjoyed the greatest expansion of student clubs in the school's history (as documented in chapter 2).

In a 1999 interview with Michael, Mrs. Samuels expressed a view of NWHS and its students that dramatically departed from our fieldwork findings and district and police department data:

> We have a dangerous mix here at [NWHS] for all sorts of problems;— minority students, especially a lot of Hispanics and African Americans, and I feel real sick about that because it is not a racial issue, it is a behavioral issue. We're talking about culturalism that's violent and threatening and without values. . . . Most of our students, 96 percent of them, want to come to school and be peaceful. For the remaining 4 percent, and they do happen to be mostly Hispanic and African American or immigrant—those are just the facts—there can be problems.

The solution to the "problems" in Mrs. Samuels's portrait of the school resonated with fears of urban street youth violence, and the rise of "get tough" criminal justice policies and laws fit well with Principal Samuels's portrait of NWHS. As she put it to Michael, the campus was in the throes of a "dangerous mix [of] . . . minority students":

> It's difficult to talk about those standards of behavior without sounding racist or generalizing or stereotyping, but I have noticed that in certain populations actually the vibes of their voices are louder. . . . There are communities where students will not look you directly in the eye because it's considered a sign of disrespect to do that. So I see more of that here because it is a diverse population of students. . . . [NWHS] is an opportunity for the school to demonstrate to the city and the state that an inner-city school need not be out of control.

These statements again expressed Mrs. Samuels's fear of student diversity, couched as forthrightness with concerns about being negatively viewed as "stereotyping." She melded these beliefs with a sense that NWHS represented a collective "opportunity" to signal competence both locally and at the state level and that such a place "need not be out of control."

In the late 1990s, the NWHS faculty divided over Principal Samuels's framing of the campus. From our interviews and observations, we estimate that approximately one-fifth of the more than seventy NWHS teachers agreed with Principal Samuels's perceptions, but that a vocal minority, known as the "responsibility group" and led by teachers like Mr. Brown, whom we met in chapter 1, provided her with strong support. Those teachers opposing Samuels portrayed the responsibility group's "worries" about the campus as unfounded. One of those in opposition, Herb Ringwall, a long-time white teacher who attended NWHS in the early 1970s, became a key bridge among students, staff, and alumni who worked to keep the school open in the 1980s and renew it in the 1990s. In an interview with Michael (prior to the Fight), he spoke about his experiences as a student in the 1970s and as a teacher in the late 1990s:

> When I went [attended NWHS], parents and administrators, maybe teachers, were concerned about a group of cowboys—kids from ranches and who worked at some of the nearby dude ranches—who would start some fights, terrorize some of the rich kids who went to school. Now it's totally different. We might have one cowboy. We have Hispanics, blacks, Asians, immigrants from all over, mainly Mexico, also a few from Russia, Vietnam. . . . You hear this all the time from parents: "I don't want my kid to go to [NWHS] because it's too dangerous." It's the eighties all over again that we fought back then. Never mind that the [NWHS] police released some crime statistics that show we've got the lowest rates of problems in the district. When people hear that, they just say, "um, well, I don't know but it still seems too rough for my kid." They mean "my white kid." It's just prejudice and we, a lot of the teachers, try to fight every day in the policies we push, how we teach class, how we treat students. The kids are good here, but even some of my colleagues and the administration are afraid even though none of them have ever been attacked. No one ever gets attacked. Look, this is the whole issue with all of the changes to the campus. It's part of the culture of fear today.

Mr. Ringwall's comments underscored how oppositional perceptions of danger/distrust and safety/trust existed side-by-side among some teachers and staff, sometimes as alternate "urban myths" about NWHS. Those, like Mr. Ringwall, who attended the high school as students and returned as teachers appeared the least swayed by these oppositional messages made vivid by safe schools ideology and practice. For teachers and staff without such biographies, these binaries tapped into fears of stranger-intruders that for many were contingent upon their time on campus and how much they invested in becoming familiar with the climate of the school, particularly from the vantage point of youth.

Mrs. Samuels's perceptions of the campus only partially fit a broader pattern we uncovered among white teachers new to the campus—an initial sense of fear and distrust followed by feelings of safety and trust. Of the seven teachers we interviewed who began teaching at NWHS in the late 1990s, five were white and fit this pattern. The other two teachers, a Latina and an African American male, did not. They reported feeling comfortable on the campus at the outset and indeed had known about NWHS as a safe campus either through other long-time teachers who recruited them to teach at the school or via other teachers they knew in the district. Megan Loften illustrated the dominant pattern among newly arrived white teachers. She joined the faculty only two years after graduating college and finishing a teaching credential. In an in-depth interview with Cal in 1999, she responded to a question about how she would compare her experiences at NWHS to where she had taught previously. She felt "scared poopooless" when she first walked onto the NWHS campus because of the preponderance of nonwhite students:

Me being a young white woman and walking around this campus . . . [where] . . . white is not the majority is a scary feeling at first. So that kind of threw me off. You don't know who belongs on campus and who doesn't. The longer I've been here, the safer I feel. This school is safe and a lot safer than a lot of schools I could work at. . . . I saw the impact I had on these kids and what they could do; I went "this is where I want to be." I really have a sense of trust in the place.

Her inability to distinguish students from nonstudents in her first year fits the pattern, particularly among new teachers without biographical ties to NWHS or urban core schools generally. Also telling is how the school as a lived experience influenced Ms. Loften's sense of NWHS students' capabilities and fed into her feel for the campus as a place of "trust."

By contrast, Principal Samuels's experiences on campus did not tie to classroom teaching (or to getting to know students through the student organizations she ostensibly supervised) but to school discipline. Since her first year on campus as assistant principal of student affairs and discipline, Mrs. Samuels had played a key role in strengthening the resolve of the responsibility group to "clamp down" on students and, in the words of one teacher, "ramped up discipline" at NWHS. In Mrs. Samuels's second year on campus (1998–99), her first as principal, the average number of yearly suspensions reached 799, nearly quintupling the average number of suspensions (both ISS and OSS combined) during the academic years 1995–1998. For 1998–1999, 65 percent of suspensions involved "insubordination," "attendance/tardy/ditching," and "behavioral disruption"; 30 percent, miscellaneous violations of the school code, including "academic misbehavior," "drugs/alcohol," and "theft"; and 5 percent, more serious interpersonal altercations categories such as "fighting," "assaults," "threats," or "weapon possession."

As several teachers and students told us, the first three categories, which accounted for two-thirds of the suspensions, gave enormous discretionary latitude to teachers and other adult authorities regarding whether youth were "insubordinate" and "disruptive" or merely spirited, and whether youth actually cheated on a test or merely daydreamed in the direction of a peer during an examination. The last set of categories involving interpersonal altercations included a range of behaviors we observed on campus, such as bumping or shouting, but rarely, as one teacher put it, "throwing punches." Even the weapon category proved elastic, as the vast majority of suspensions involved a nonweapon object (e.g., a backpack, bottle, or book) used as a weapon. As recounted in previous chapters, our fieldwork revealed that students rarely possessed knives and/or guns on or around campus, and we never uncovered their use in interpersonal altercations.

Taken together, the three suspension categories that comprised nearly two-thirds of all disciplinary infractions on campus—"insubordination," "attendance/tardy/ditching," and "behavioral disruption"—revealed ethnic and racial disparities. Students categorized by the school as African American or Latino, respectively, accounted for 32 percent and 48 percent of the suspensions in these three categories while comprising 20 percent and 42 percent, respectively, of the campus student population. Youth categorized as white accounted for 18 percent and all other ethnic and racial categories accounted for 2 percent of the remaining suspensions in these three categories while comprising 36 percent and 2 percent of the student population, respectively.[29] In 1995–1998, by contrast, disciplinary infractions approximated the distribution of ethnic categories on campus. Data from 1998–1999 suggest that ethnic and racial disparities involving the most discretionary suspension rationales had become more accentuated on campus even as many NWHS students did not view what they called system stuff as driven by ethnic and racial difference (at least as represented in the hundreds of youth-authored trouble cases we collected; see chapter 3). Some of our most astute observers, however, especially Latino and black male youth, such as Derrik (case 6.6) and Abelena and their friends (case 6.7), provided accounts and stories about ethnic and racial discrimination that picked up on these growing disciplinary disparities on campus. The campus discipline data, combined with our ethnographic evidence and the police call data, however, provide evidence that safe schools did not arrive on campus in response to a clear, growing threat of violence, although the student body increasingly experienced a discriminatory disciplinary regime beginning in 1998–1999.

In the late 1990s, the final planning for the renovation of the aging campus physical plant provided a key opportunity to affix this disciplinary regime and other safe schools practices into the social life of NWHS. In the tumultuous campaign to save and renew the school in the late 1980s and early 1990s, Mrs. Samuels's predecessor negotiated the receipt of several million dollars that was diverted to NWHS from a much larger bond issue earmarked for upgrades and new high school construction to serve youth from the more affluent neighborhoods of New West's growing suburbs. The planning for NWHS renovations had taken longer than expected, and Mrs. Samuels made it a chief priority in the first years of her administration to see it through and recast the renovations as part of the need to secure the campus, sidestepping her predecessor's campaign to frame the school as a striving, multicultural success story. In part, she justified the shift to a security frame by pointing to increasing numbers of behavioral infractions and disciplinary-related suspensions at NWHS involving "disrespect for the values of the school," drawing selectively from the school's internal disciplinary data. Her framing resonated with the national "moral panic" about urban youth violence and growing seduction of "get tough" approaches to youth control.[30] Also, her recasting the renovations as primarily about security took advantage of the availability of additional state and federal monies for securitization under the rubric of safe schools.

Alumni, veteran teachers, and students again mobilized as they had in the previous decade to push back, but they could not gain traction amidst the local and national fears about and penal responses to youth conflict. Mrs. Samuels and the responsibility group's depiction of the campus as increasingly "dangerous" drew upon broad-based fears of black and Latino youth and their presumed growth in the student population, even though their proportions of the student body remained relatively constant during the late 1990s and early in the first decade of the twenty-first century. It was not until late in the first decade of the 2000s that the slim Latino majority increased substantially, and at no time during this period was there a surge in the black student population at NWHS. Still, it was through the disciplinary and administrative control practices, imposed from the top down, that institutionalized racism gained a temporary grip at NWHS.

Mrs. Samuels, supported by the responsibility group, was successful in her framing to the school board, which authorized the safe schools renovation at NWHS as a "viable solution" for the campus—a solution that would bring "much needed upgrades" to campus security while generally improving the school's physical plant. Sustained, evidence-based discussions about academic achievement, either tied to safe schools renovations or to the school's pre-safe schools multicultural climate of inclusive trust and learning, barely made a ripple in these deliberations except, as one board member noted in a public meeting, the "obvious linkage . . . [between] . . . tough school discipline and academic achievement." The board approved the NWHS safe schools renovation plan, and construction began in mid-1999.

Renovating NWHS as a Safe School

The material centerpiece of NWHS's safe schools renovations rested in the sixth item of the 1996 NEA *Safe Schools Manual*: "altering the internal physical environment" of schools to establish and sustain official authority through architectural design. At the national level, architects and security consultants had successfully implanted "crime prevention through environmental design" (CPTED) as a core technology of safe schools.[31] Tod Schneider, an architect and national-level safe schools consultant, claimed that designing and building schools in the CPTED mold enabled the establishment of school-based "territoriality" and "authority over an environment, clarifying who is in charge, who belongs, and who is trespassing."[32] Original claims about the viability of CPTED for schools rested in two perceived threats: the intrusion of outsiders to disrupt the learning environment and victimize teachers and students and the control of insiders within the spatial confines of school grounds. To combat these threats, CPTED principles, so advocates claimed, relied upon "natural surveillance" to "limit who can gain entry to a facility and how" and internal spatial organization to enhance the observation and control of students on campuses.[33] CPTED thus resonated with dominant perspectives that view school violence as imported on to campuses by students and/or stranger-intruders who reside in nearby neighborhoods, and the need to control youth once they are on school grounds via spatial organization.[34]

Aspects of the NWHS physical plant dramatically changed during the construction on campus. Bushes, trees, and all student lockers were deemed "security hazards" and removed because they could shield students from adult observation. A "perimeter ring" of high, heavy metal fencing was installed around the campus border and internal "security gates" with heavy metal fencing divided the internal space of the campus into multiple quadrants that could be closed off and secured instantly. Large, thick one-way shaded picture windows were installed on one side of the administrative offices so that staff could watch over the campus downtown without being observed from the outside—resonant with the famous panopticon prison model designed by the eighteenth-century philosopher Jeremy Bentham, in which prisoners could be observed by a single guard without prisoners knowing they were being watched.[35] Security cameras were installed throughout the campus, concentrated in and around the downtown area. Metal detectors were installed at two main points of ingress/egress by the main office and the gymnasium (used for access to the campus for sporting events). All movable seating was replaced with fixed metal picnic tables in the quad and the outside dining area in front of the cafeteria. A photograph taken as part of the photo-narrative exercise in 1999 (figure 7.2) shows the perimeter security ring of fencing looking in from a vantage point just outside the campus. A second photograph (figure 7.3), taken

Figure 7.2. Perimeter fencing at New West High School, 2001

Figure 7.3. New West High School hallway with lockers removed, 2001

by Christine in 2001, shows a typical internal hallway stripped of student lockers and students and bathed by constant fluorescent light.[36] It offers a striking comparison to the hallway photographed by a student in 1999 as part of the photo-narrative exercise (figure 2.2). Although clean, well-lit hallways without anything adorning the walls might not seem carceral-like, Keramet Reiter points out that among the pervasive physical features of "supermax" prisons, in which incarcerated persons are confined to single cells without human contact up to twenty-two hours per day, are hallways and rooms illuminated by harsh, constant fluorescent light and "smooth walls that could be hosed down."[37] These shared attributes bear a family resemblance, as Michel Foucault famously argued, as both prisons and schools are socially and physically organized to control bodies.[38] In doing so, the physical alterations to the NWHS campus powerfully cut against the grain of the school's long-standing traditions.

Parallel to the physical transformation of the campus, an array of official social control technologies appeared, designed to "rationalize" the disciplining of youth and channel their movements aligned with other aspects of the NEA guidelines, including (1) expansion of school suspension and expulsion for "selected offenses" ranging from smoking on campus to weapon possession; (2) broader use of ISS and OSS; (3) increases in security personnel, including law enforcement personnel on campus; and (4) a dress code for students.[39] Some of the policies, such as increased use of ISS and OSS, were already being practiced before the safe schools renovations began, as we noted above. Others, such as what came to be known simply as "sweeps" and "closed campus," followed, expanding and deepening administrative authority and intensifying disciplinary control at NWHS.

Two rules operated at the core of "sweeps": any student without a "signed pass" and not in an assigned classroom during class periods or outside the designated eating area on the quad or in the cafeteria would be escorted to a room called "the tank," where they would be detained for the remainder of the class or lunch period. While in the tank, as listed in the 2001 *Falcon Guide* to student life, "students will put aside all materials, the students will not study, talk, listen to music, sleep . . . and after, they are referred for I.S.S."[40] Refusing to comply with a "sweeper" (teachers or security personnel) resulted in an automatic parent conference, followed by up to five days of OSS. Mr. Brown explained in an interview with Cal why and how the policy came about:

> Sweeps was initiated to bring some order to the school because too many kids were out of where they were supposed to be during the school day. We had some faculty meetings with Principal Samuels, who thought it was a good idea. Another teacher and I, Mr. Stone [white, middle age, teaches history] worked with the principal to put it in writing. We started with putting signs outside all classroom doors so that students who are not in their classrooms by the time the bell rang could see them when they sauntered in late. Staff were supposed to lock classroom doors when the bell rang.

The signs that went up outside classrooms once classroom doors were locked read:

> Go to the **Tank** in the Cafeteria.
> If you are excused, you **must** have a pass. Knock and slide under the door.
> There are No Exceptions!

During classroom periods, security guards set up the tank in the cafeteria and during lunch moved it to counseling rooms in building "C" near the administration offices. In that same interview, Mr. Brown reported "sweeps" was adopted with the full support of the faculty—"91–92 percent of the faculty approved the new policy"—and claimed dramatic success for the initiative in response to a question from Cal about "how it is working out": "On the first day of the policy, 169 students were swept and went to the tank. On the second day of the policy, a little more than half the [first-day total] was swept." According to Dot, a campus security guard, the number "swept" climbed back to more than one hundred students by the third day and remained at or near that level for several days before declining precipitously and then rising again. In a follow-up conversation with Mr. Brown, Cal asked him about the roller-coaster rate of "sweeps" numbers and he replied, "It's working. The number of students has dramatically declined from when we started." School authorities did not conduct a systematic analysis of "sweeps," although our fieldwork suggests that increased suspensions for 1999–2000 were rooted in noncompliance to "sweeps," which, in turn, resulted in "insubordination" and "attendance/tardy/ditching" violations. Sweeps became a self-fulfilling prophecy.

Mr. Brown's claim that nearly all the faculty supported sweeps contradicted evidence of substantial opposition to the policy among a substantial group of the faculty. Deliberations about sweeps at a faculty meeting had begun, just after Mrs. Samuels became principal, and ended without full discussion. The policies then "sat on the back burner," as one teacher put it, while Mrs. Samuels campaigned for safe schools renovations and rushed sweeps into implementation at the end of her first year as principal to demonstrate to the school board steps already underway to bring order to NWHS in advance of safe schools.[41]

For nearly a century, NWHS operated as an open campus for lunch, and students took full advantage of the opportunity to be mobile on and off campus. In the early years of the school, students walked home for lunch. Later, affluent youth could drive home or off site for lunch while less mobile youth frequented the many small businesses in close proximity that offered fast food and convenience groceries. Many remained on campus, taking advantage of the cafeteria. Prior to instituting sweeps and closing the campus, we routinely observed students engaged in anchored fluidity, moving about the campus in dyads, triads, and small cliques, near and in welcoming classrooms not in session that we identified as "sanctuaries" in chapter 2. Even students who ventured off campus to eat lunch would return to meet up with friends and find their places across the expanse of the campus.

Teachers and administrators alike agreed that what some called a "security mentality" drove the school to close the campus.[42] Typical explanations for closing campus included worries about the threat of outsiders, the desire to reduce "ditching" and tardiness, and the strong inclination of some teachers, such as the "responsibility group" and Principal Samuels, to "clamp down" on students.[43] A number of veteran teachers who had been involved in saving and renewing the school in the late 1980s and early 1990s saw the irony in these policies. Danny George, who is white and grew up in New West, agreed that the closed campus was intended to address concerns about student safety and security as well as school district liability. But, he added, "for nearly 40 years . . . the philosophy [of the school] was . . . if the kids are allowed to express themselves and get away for a bit . . . they would not fight with each other as much . . . and come back ready to learn."[44] Mr. George's description resonated with our notion of anchored fluidity, which he claimed had been encouraged by teachers for nearly forty years and contributed to, in his words, "peaceable relations among students" and "an atmosphere for learning."

Eroding Social Trust and Undermining Anchored Fluidity

In a high-poverty school, an eye insensitive to everyday peer relations could easily gravitate to clusters of youth claiming places in public view, imagining these sociospatial gatherings as young "gangsters" asserting territorial ownership. Such a view comports with the dominant view of urban youth conflict in schools and reflects campuses where street gang territoriality has in fact migrated on to school grounds.[45] When Principal Samuels spoke about youth clustering on the NWHS campus in her interview with Michael, she invoked this imagery and a harsh response to it: "[W]e have some very keen, alert, and observant faculty and security, and when we start to see territories start to develop we make them move. It will not happen here. And we will suspend long-term and have students expelled." She expanded on her statements by alluding to a report from Eastern High, which indicated that youth from different "neighborhoods and gangs" claimed territory as their own. "Keen" adult observers and aggressive sanctioning, including long-term suspensions and expulsions, she said, "will keep that from happening at [NWHS]."

By contrast, teachers who involved themselves in the campus lives of students were more likely to view peer gatherings in more nuanced ways. Prior to safe schools, for example, we routinely observed Ms. Loften interacting informally with students inside and outside her classroom. As she put it to Cal, she "gets out and walks around" but saw the clustering of students in places they call their own as a "tricky" issue:

There is always this one little Latino guy . . . who hangs out right here on the corner by the breezeway between buildings in a mixed group. And then there's always the black kids that hang out over in the little cement quad by the grassy area. Sometimes there's whites and Latinos that you can see with them. And then there's always the break-dancers that hang out over in the "M" building. I guess the goal from the administration's perspective is to break that down. . . . No matter how hard we've [the school] tried in the last two years . . . it just seems to be really visible. I don't know if they're negative. I mean I really learned that having an ethnic background is very important. And I don't feel that we're here to take that away from anybody. So to see them together and hanging out and doing their thing, that's a positive. That's good because they need community. If they're only moving around, then you can get alienated youth. If the students are in groups and able to move on their own, when they want to, that's probably healthy. Most students find their place on campus and move around the campus anyway . . . from here to there so we probably won't have alienation.

Ms. Loften was aware of the administration's desire to break up territorial claims by students, particularly when ethnic and racial identity appeared to be a defining feature. Her depiction of peer gatherings included clusters defined by ethnic and racial identities ("black kids"), those that appear ethnically mixed (one "little Latino . . . in a mixed group"), and those defined by youth-centered, mixed activities ("break dancers"). She found herself conflicted about ethnic and racial gatherings, recognizing that they were positive because of the "need to build community" yet also presented a potential source of peer alienation "if that's all there is." She also recognized anchored fluidity, observing that many youth "move around campus," which she claimed neutralized the problem of territoriality and alienation.

As depicted in chapter 2, the campus downtown was both a staging area for street-like campaigns for respect and a locale of civility on campus—a place where social trust runs thinnest on campus and hostile, confrontational moralistic trouble responses are most likely to occur, but also a place where youth enjoy diversity and the company of peers they know well. Prior to safe schools, the downtown represented one of many places youth traversed across the campus as they moved back and forth among downtown, the refuge (including sanctuary classrooms), and the fields. Beginning in the fall of 1999, downtown became one of the few places where students could hang out, perform, circulate, and cluster. Sweeps combined with surveillance, aggressive enforcement, and the closed campus chan-

neled all students to downtown when they were not in class or engaged in
official activities, particularly during lunchtime.

Christine represented the sociospatial realities of this confinement in
her observations from 2001:

> When I left campus for the day, I walked through the quad area one last
> time. It was 11:20 a.m., just minutes before the lunch hour. Students already
> were in the lunch area, apparently released from class early. When the bell
> rang, students poured into the patio area. Construction was still ongoing at
> the edges of the patio near the band room. The grassy area between the patio
> and the administration building is now huge piles of dirt. It is still fenced
> off. The patio feels incredibly cramped to me. It is dense with student bodies.
> Although I recognize individual students, as a group they appear as a nearly
> undefined mass of humanity corralled between the buildings and the fence.
> The students laugh and eat and move from table to table, full of youthful
> energy and noise. I cannot watch for long because it is hard to make sense
> of the movement. I look around and see Robert [a security guard] standing
> in front of the soda machines at the northeast corner of the patio, watching.
> He has a walkie-talkie up to his ear. Dot [another security guard] is standing
> in front of the library doors. She also has a walkie-talkie up to her ear and is
> watching the crowd intently. They clearly are "keeping watch" over the kids.
> I try to talk with her about the scene but she is barely listening. She seems
> tense, and apparently does not want to be distracted by our conversation. I
> am not sure, in all of the confusion and noise, how the guards would spot
> potential trouble. It seems to me that only once a problem escalated would
> they be able to notice it. The scene reminds me of prison guards watching
> the inmates during their recreation time. I am overwhelmed by how much
> the campus has changed in such a short time.[46]

Christine could no longer recognize individual students she had come to
know because they were "corralled between buildings and fences" and appeared as a "mass of humanity" or a "crowd." While students moved about
from table to table, she wondered how security personnel could spot trouble before it escalated or intervene when it did—a dynamic that the security guard Dot described well in relation to the Fight.

As we noted earlier, José, a security guard who intervened in the Fight,
offered one of the first slices of evidence pointing to the significance of
youth crowding in downtown during lunch as a source of heightened tensions. He realized that with confinement and heightened surveillance came
a severe reduction in activities traditionally available to occupy students'

time during lunch. Responsibility for staffing these activities largely fell on the security guards, but with full implementation of safe schools, teachers also were reassigned to surveillance duties and policing the perimeters of downtown. Recall that Javier said all that was left for the students was to be "in plain sight and just stare at each other in the lunch room." Students saw it the same way. In this excerpt from an interview conducted by Christine in 2001, a student responded to a question about what it is like on the quad on a typical day:

> During lunch, you can't listen to the radio. They took away the basketball court. All you can do is sit there. You can't have no fun at lunch. . . . [C]an't move around campus at any time, really. Now there is nothing really to do except . . . wait for something to happen.

Like the proverbial prison yard, the student recounted boredom mixed with anxiety—nothing to do except wait for the next altercation on the frontstages in and around the quad or cafeteria.

The dynamics of crowding received significant attention by social scientists, particularly in the 1970s and 1980s, when prison violence emerged as a paramount issue. The earliest work focused on the direct relationship between crowding, social density, and violence.[47] These works found less direct impact than anticipated, leading to a second generation of inquiry focusing on mediating factors, including how social control is organized under conditions of high social density. When crowding is perceived as a condition of prisons, correctional administrators concentrate the guard force on surveillance and intervention, "markedly reducing organized recreational, occupational, vocational and leisure activities."[48] The supermax prison, alluded to earlier, embodies entire organizations devoted to these principles, especially solitary confinement. The lack of activities can generate aversive reactions among incarcerated people to what they regard as crowded conditions, leading, in turn, to more aggressive and violent confrontations with one another and the prison staff.[49]

The embrace of safe schools at NWHS replicated these very conditions— "they took away the basketball courts"—and with the reduction in organized activities, there was "nothing to do except . . . wait for something to happen." In 2001 and 2002, students told Christine about continuing high tensions on campus and that fighting was escalating due to "anxiety about changes to the campus."[50] Students and teachers alike reported the elimination of informal settings in and around classrooms in the refuge that were sanctuaries—places where students clustered during lunch hour on their own or "with teachers they enjoyed."[51] Rather than creating a safe learning environment, the police call data confirm teachers and students claims about growing tension and increased, serious fighting, as students and adults alike, both on or near the campus, made the most calls for law enforcement intervention in the initial five years of "safe schools" (see figure 7.1 above). One of those calls was in response to the Fight.

When youth conflicts involved confrontations with the system, as depicted in chapter 6, black and Latino youth, much more than white students, reported being played by the administration because of their identities. Prior to this new policy, however, youth-on-youth trouble rarely revolved around students imagining trouble with one another through the lens of ethnic and racial stereotyping, even when they responded to beefs or drama with a beat down. The Fight signaled a sea change in this dynamic, as ethnic and racial identities and boundaries came to the fore in ways similar to how youth conflict is depicted in high-poverty schools where sticky identities and turf are joined, and ethnic and racial groupings of youth engage in aggressive collective confrontations fueled by honor and vengeance, places where the code of the street meets territoriality.[52]

Safe schools at NWHS dug deep and quickly, reaching into youth-centered aspects of the school climate and prompting enhanced attention to ethnic and racial identities to recast how youth on campus saw each other and calculated threats coming from one another.[53] The interpersonal troubles youth experienced with one another, sometimes tinged with racial innuendo, but almost always worked out without violence or adult awareness, could now become hostile public conflicts with racial tensions in the forefront. In an interview with Christine in 2001, a black female twelfth grader related the following experience: "It's more racial now than ever. When you're in such a small space, people mark their places. You only mix some because you're so close. They put the tables so close together. Little differences matter, you know." The small space she alluded to is the confinement of youth to downtown when not in class or moving between classes. Under these conditions, she saw people "marking" or claiming spaces as their own, defined by "racial" identities. And with everyone "so close together," she pointed out that students had to be much more aware of trouble breaking out along these lines—every "little difference matters."

Safe schools also heightened the identification of youth recently emigrated from Mexico. Sarah, a student identifying as white, chronicled interactions across ethnic and racial identity groups in an interview with Christine in 2002, pointing out the density of youth in the quad resulted in "our

Figure 7.4. Youth-made photo entitled "Confined Diversity," 1999

tables, they are like close together so you see people mixing with people, and we talk to everybody . . ." but then added that "the only group that doesn't hang out is the Mexicans" who are "stuck in Q."[54]

These perspectives again led us back to some of the visual representations made by youth, particularly the photo-narrative exercise completed in 1999 just as safe schools took hold of the campus. Jocelyn, a black female eleventh grader, eloquently defended the diversity on campus in her photo essay, but also saw inequity now associated with it. Jocelyn titled her photograph "Confined Diversity," which depicted several multicolored, discarded paint cans in a small, cluttered, fenced-in pen, where workers engaged in renovating the school had thrown construction trash.

Jocelyn wrote:

When I consider my reasons for taking this picture, many things come to mind. Such things as the difference in shapes, the contrasts of each color thus illustrating the diversity that is our school. As well as the total view and feeling that I get when looking down upon the buckets in the truck just as I was looking down on the hundreds of students that attend our school. Another way I look at this picture is as we the students are the buckets, every one of us is different in shape and color but the same in one small way. The fence in front of us and the building behind us refers to the faculty, staff, and the security guards keeping the students confined to the school premises, only allowing particular students off the premises and movements on the premises, thus illustrating the new closed campus rule the students must conform to this year.

Jocelyn used different colors of paint that have spilled out of different paint cans to identify student appearances in terms of skin color, language, and social and cultural backgrounds. Yet, in the spilling out of the paint and through her accompanying narrative, she also identified the ubiquitous commonality among students *as* students at NWHS. After interpreting her image of student diversity, she turned her attention, both visually and narratively, to students' new "confinement" and cited adult authorities as responsible for "keeping the students confined to the school premises."

In the early and middle parts of the first decade of the twenty-first century, we routinely observed multiple manifestations of the imprint of safe schools on the school, including lines of students waiting to go through metal detectors in the mornings before the school opened; pictures on student club websites made by students in 2004 and 2005 of the crowded quad during lunch with captions complaining that there was "nowhere to spread out" to conduct club business; continuing high numbers of police calls (figure 7.1), especially for assault on campus; and high numbers of student suspensions that averaged 746 per year through 2005. Students faced increasingly constrained sociospatial mobility, as anchored fluidity was severely curtailed. With boundaries in place and movement constrained, the backstage sanctuaries that teachers provided from the frontstages in downtown became less accessible. Prior to safe schools, students who ate lunch in the hallways near or in teachers' classrooms often identified with these places. One student, in conversation with Christine in 1999, said "our building . . . we know who is in our building, and who comes in, 'cause we see them all the time.[55] Teachers confirmed that student identities became intertwined with sanctuaries, as illustrated in an interview Christine conducted with Alicia James, one of the newer teachers to NWHS. Prior to "safe schools," students hung out in her classroom during lunch hour. "[T]hat's kind of a measure of liking; that they aren't going to spend just the time they're required to spend. They know it's a safe place."[56]

To reinforce the end of lunch sanctuaries, signs reading "No food or drink permitted in buildings" appeared all over campus.

All these dynamics lead back to another finding of earlier research on prison crowding and violence relevant to NWHS: Severe crowding not only creates collective anxieties, hardens ethnic and racial identifications, and strips away diversions, but also disrupts social relations supporting ongoing informal control mechanisms that incarcerated persons use to settle disputes.[57] At NWHS, safe schools translated into the interruption of anchored fluidity, which decimated the mix of student spatial movement and relational fluidity vital for conciliatory-remedial informal control. Underneath the interruption of anchored fluidity lies the erosion of institutional and intergroup trust that fed into youth anxieties about the school, peer groups, and the self. The adoption of safe schools created in part the conditions experienced in high-poverty schools where moralistic peer violence—puttin' 'em in their place in the extreme—is the norm.

Contesting and Normalizing Safe Schools

Safe schools also partly transformed the roles and identities of teachers on campus. Research on carceral-like school control in the United States during the 1990s and the first decade of the twenty-first century suggests that when faced with increased formalization and intensification of school discipline, teachers are likely to abdicate their disciplinary authority and responsibilities or fall into line to become "disciplinarians."[58] However, in his study of change in public schools, Tim Hallett argues that coping with dramatic organizational change in schools often first manifests itself through contestation over having voice in relevant decision making and beliefs that the new order is coming on line too fast, which provides grist for resistance.[59] Such dynamics, for example, appeared in an in-depth interview Christine conducted in 2001 with Danny George, a veteran white teacher. He regarded safe schools one of the "largest changes" ever in the history of NWHS. In response to a question about why the administration had adopted safe schools, particularly the safe schools zone that constricted student movement on and off campus, he questioned whether the administration understood what they had done:

I'm not sure that they fully thought through the implications of what they set up. They're basically cramming a lot of people together in a relatively small space, and I think that it has the potential of encouraging fighting.

And I'm not sure they are addressing what they need to address to end such things. Like I don't think they are being particularly good about, and again, this is my opinion, about encouraging diversity and encouraging a tolerance for diversity . . . teaching kids how to get along . . . teaching kids how to accept each other . . . I don't see them [the administration] actively doing that. So I fear that by the time it gets to be spring and the temperatures start rising again and people have been crammed together for several months that we may end up with a couple of fights.[60]

The changes, Mr. George pointed out, threatened the very idea of NWHS as an inclusive place of trust. Like Mr. George, several teachers pointed to the violation of trust and inclusion that surrounded the rapid movement to safe schools policies. Likewise, many students spoke about safe schools during the first two years of intensive embrace of its policies and practices as "disrespectful," "distrustful," and "unfair." As depicted in chapter 2, the long history of collective civic action on campus, in the form of student clubs, generated trust and opportunities to influence the school. In conjunction with supporting teachers, students enjoyed a voice in the social and cultural ordering of the school, and established channels for both critiquing and endorsing school policies. By implementing safe schools, the administration and the responsibility group excluded students from the dialogue and consolidated decision-making authority.

In the wake of these policies, both overt and covert political conflict roiled through the school staff and the student body. The first week of the sweeps policy saw students gathered in informal groups and in student clubs, especially S.T.A.N.D. (the organizing coalition of student clubs that encompassed more than a third of the student body), to discuss how to "resist." One plan focused on "flooding" the tank with hundreds of sweeps violators, "causing the system to break down." During the first week of sweeps, multiple groups of students, some organized through S.T.A.N.D., and some simply caught up in the policy, did indeed flood the tank. The numbers of students sent to the tank created multiple problems for the security guards as students spilled out into the hallways and quad, and caused a mass exodus from the cafeteria as the tank moved from there to "C" building just before lunch period. S.T.A.N.D. members also discussed a general student strike that would begin during lunch period and have students sitting on the small dirt area near the quad, refusing to go to class. But the strike never occurred as the school year ended. When word of the potential strike and flooding the tank cycled back to the administration, Mrs. Samuels addressed the student body, seeking to dampen the threat of demonstrations by telling students at a special assembly that " [W]e're not trying to punish anybody. We're trying to get some responsible behavior." She ended the assembly by pleading with students to come see her during a lunch period if they "had a problem" with sweeps or any of the other new control policies on campus, but not a single student met with her.

That students resisted new school policies drawing from their extant social organization in student clubs is not surprising, but teachers also contested the policy, improvising strategies to directly or indirectly flout the new practices and rules.[61] Some teachers, such as Mr. Rupp, who hosted one of the most popular sanctuary classrooms for eating lunch prior to sweeps, in his words, "kept losing" the sweeps signs to put on his door and then claimed that "someone must be taking the signs" when he placed them on the door. Other teachers, such as Mrs. Wright, a black veteran teacher, refused to lock her door at the bell, saying in an interview with Cal: "I don't want students to be late, but I don't want to lock 'em out either." In one instance, Principal Samuels "invited" teachers to become volunteer "tank monitors," but few volunteered, other than members of the responsibility group, creating a staffing issue for an administration that was already strapped to police both the tank and the quad. We also observed some teachers, such as Mr. Lopez, use safe schools as a teaching opportunity to critically analyze school policy and discuss how punctuality and tardiness is used against employees in the workplace. Others, like John Scott, a veteran white teacher, followed the usual rules of thumb about tardiness, not worrying about students being out of class if they looked to be engaged in "homework," which to him demonstrated "responsibility." He escorted students he found wandering around the campus back to their classrooms, talking with them along the way about what they were doing and why.[62]

Perhaps the most poignant contestation occurred when teachers with different orientations toward safe schools and sweeps confronted each other on the frontlines. One afternoon, while Cal walked with Mr. Brown up the main breezeway toward his classroom in "L" building, they encountered Gerado Barboso, a lanky Latino sophomore, well over six feet tall, wearing baggy black, ripped jeans, and a faded green t-shirt two sizes too small with "New West All-Stars" written across the chest. He sauntered toward "K" building and was poised to open the door to walk in to the hallway. Mr. Brown, who knew him from the baseball team, called, "Boso, where you supposed to be? You're getting swept, my man." Stopping instantly, Boso looked down at the ground as Mr. Brown moved toward him. But the door to "K" flung open and Mrs. Wright appeared, bustling out on to the breezeway to reach out and put her arm around Boso's waist. "He one of yours?" asked Mr. Brown. Mrs. Wright only responded with a firmly set jaw as she glared at Mr. Brown and shepherded Boso into "K," closing the door behind them. Mr. Brown looked at Cal, shrugged his shoulders, and said in a flat tone: "One less for the tank, I guess." Cal asked, "Would you have sent him to the tank?" "I don't know. Probably. He's got to learn discipline just like any other student. I'm not gonna cross Mrs. Wright. She's a tough one." The fact that Boso played on the team that Mr. Brown coached may have played a role in him not being swept or it may have been Mrs. Wright's resolve and toughness. Whatever the particular mix of motivation in this situation, it underscored the initial day-to-day tensions over the policy among the staff.

Members of the responsibility group believed that the initial contestation by youth would subside as students learned quickly to adjust their behavior to safe schools. Carl Johnson, a veteran black teacher who counted himself a member of the responsibility group, noted to Christine in an interview about how the policies "were going" that "It doesn't take the kids very long to learn."[63] Other teachers also regarded student opposition as temporary because they pointed to the seniors, who experienced open lunch and freedom of movement on campus for three years, as the ones feeling most aggrieved by the new architecture and social control technologies. Even Mr. Lopez, a teacher who openly criticized safe schools as he taught about its effects, believed this, saying that "frosh kids could care less" about the new disciplinary regime and spatial restrictions.[64] New students coming into the school had never experienced anchored fluidity, except perhaps in the narratives of their older siblings or friends who had attended NWHS. These observations on the campus parallel multiple scholars who posit that carceral-like control in schools ultimately becomes culturally embedded, gaining traction over time through the "normalizing" effects it has on both youth and adults.[65]

In fact, both obedience in the face of safe schools and contestation did become normalized at NWHS, although the high rates of police calls and disciplinary suspensions continued through 2004. At the same time, handfuls of NWHS students routinely congregated off campus in the strip mall parking lot across the street during lunch; their ability to do so was aided by security guards and teachers tiring of continually walking across the street to bring students back to campus. Students continued posting online pictures of the crowded quad in 2004 and 2005, and also boasted that "guards" sometimes allowed them "to take pictures away from the quad in empty classrooms" if a "teacher okayed it" and if "they came back" to downtown. In these pictures, we continued seeing what we documented in the late 1990s: Homogenous and ethnically and racially mixed groups— underscored by the Spanish and non-Spanish names accompanying the pictures and the skin colors of youth. These same students wrote about "eating lunch in empty classrooms" away from the quad without interference. In addition, although the school formally continued to report high suspension rates, teacher and student accounts as early as 2001 point toward teachers tiring of sending students to the tank for all-purpose offenses or ritualistically dispatching students to ISS and then having them immediately return to their classrooms. The practices of those teachers who refused to comply with safe schools normalized as tolerated exceptions, even as the numbers of those teachers engaged in noncompliance grew and colleagues in the responsibility group continued to apply pressure for adherence to the official policies.

As the everyday practices of teachers threw safe schools into question, those policies had a demonstrable effect on collective civic action on campus. Students withdrew their engagement from school clubs, perhaps influenced in part by the pullback and defensive orientation of the youth-centered teachers in response to safe schools or perhaps due to the pragmatic difficulties of finding places to meet. As we discussed in chapter 2, entries for specific clubs in *The River* reached their peak at twenty-nine in 1999. By 2002, this number dwindled to fourteen and hovered near single digits until 2006. Many of the surviving clubs focused on economic concerns, such as the "Entrepreneurs Club," or crossed religion with sports, such as the "Fellowship of Christian Athletes." Clubs organized under the umbrella of S.T.A.N.D.—tied into specific or bridging ethnic and racial student groups—were particularly hard hit as several disappeared. Those that survived appeared with pictures of their memberships in single digits rather than the dozens pictured only a few years earlier.

Organizational Recoupling in the Aftermath of Collective Trauma

Organizational researchers, Tim Hallett argues, have long regarded schools as "exemplars of institutional arguments about loose coupling"—the tendency for actual organizational practices to depart from formal policies and the broader institutional ideals on which they rest.[66] Because schools operate in uncertain environments and must tack through the constantly shifting winds of policy change, scholars argue that loose coupling enables core, practical activities, like teaching classes, to proceed unabated, at the same time facilitating the ability to signal legitimacy via ostensible compliance with new laws and policies.[67] As Hallett points out, the assumption of loose coupling in schools is so pervasive that few scholars study *how* coupling evolves, including the processes through which earlier practices recouple. Different constituents on campuses, in local communities, and in broader educational and legal fields, contest schools, placing opposing tendencies in dialectical relationships, including trust/distrust and administrative penal formal/conciliatory-remedial informal control practices. At NWHS, the 1990s represented a period of relative tight coupling with social trust, inclusion, and the sociospatial practices of informal anchored fluidity converging to encourage informal everyday responses to trouble by youth and adults alike.

As a revealing organizational accident, the Fight alerted us to the collective trauma and shock on campus induced by safe schools. After a period of sustained commitment from the top down by administrative authorities, a degree of loose coupling from safe schools occurred as, for example, security guards began allowing handfuls of youth to violate the closed campus and safe schools zone policies, and everyday contestation and noncompliance by a segment of the teaching staff normalized. Yet tight adherence to the policy also continued by a segment of teachers, particularly the responsibility group, as manifested in the high rate of suspensions. Moreover, despite normalization, the school became less safe, as indicated by the police call data and student accounts, during the relatively high-commitment period to safe schools policies on campus. Unanticipated dynamics also occurred during this same period as collective civic action in the form of student clubs declined on campus.

Loose coupling with dramatic policy changes and unanticipated consequences are routine findings in the literature on organizational change, particularly in schools.[68] Ironically, loose coupling from safe schools at NWHS began leading back in fragmented and incremental ways to a recoupling of social trust that operated as a sociocultural anchor on campus during much of the 1990s. As teachers decried and flouted safe schools, they implicitly or explicitly signaled inclusive social trust on campus. When students slipped off campus or posted online pictures of mixed groups from empty classrooms while eating lunch, they not only risked suspension and subverted the new regime but also reasserted anchored fluidity and everyday inclusive social trust shared with the frontline workforce on campus. Where did these dynamics lead the school? We turn to this question in the final chapter as we conclude our longitudinal exploration of youth conflict in the context of NWHS as an active organizational place.

EIGHT

A Contested School That Works

In this final chapter we follow what happened on the frontlines at New West High School after administrative commitment to fully implement safe schools waned, using this analysis as a point of departure to conclude our exploration of how youth navigate conflict. Throughout this book, we demonstrate *how* the historical capacity for social trust on campus— generated through bottom-up, inclusive collective civic action and top-down school structures—anchored sociospatial relations associated with the peaceable handling of interpersonal youth conflict. But these dynamics did not characterize every social interaction or place on campus in the same way. At NWHS, conciliatory-remedial peer responses to peer trouble proved difficult for young people to pull off when and where trust was uneven, such as among Mexican immigrant youth and US-born Latinos, or in the campus downtown where civility was the norm yet the code of the street also was present. Compared to previous research, black and La-tino male students reported less discriminatory school discipline when social trust ran high on campus in the 1990s. But they still faced greater challenges in this regard than their peers did. The arrival of safe schools to NWHS in the late 1990s and early in the first decade of the twenty-first century brought with it harder-edged, carceral-like control, greater anchoring of youth to hardened ethnic and racial boundaries, interruptions of peaceable informal control by students, and an erosion of social trust. How well did safe schools stick to everyday life on campus?

The Legacy of Safe Schools: Return of Social
Trust and Anchored Fluidity

Five years after leading the administrative efforts to establish safe schools on campus, Principal Samuels left NWHS in 2005 to become a school district administrator. By the end of her tenure at the school, loose coupling, rather than a hardening of safe schools policies and procedures, appeared evident on campus. Teachers who originally opposed safe schools and sweeps continued to do so, and their position on campus regained prominence. The demographics of the student body, relatively stable during the first years of the century, began changing, as well, accelerating toward a wider Latino majority toward the end of the decade. In the wake of Samuels's exit, an interim administration governed the school for a year, and the influence of the so-called faculty responsibility group waned as some teachers moved to different schools and others backed off their staunch support for safe schools and sweeps. More students went off campus for lunch, the long lines of students waiting to enter campus through metal detectors, pat-downs, diminished, and both police calls and suspensions ultimately fell to levels not seen since the mid-1990s. In 2006, Raul Molinas, an assistant principal at Eastern High, became NWHS principal. These changes compelled Cal and Michael to re-engage in more intensive fieldwork at NWHS, beginning in 2008, to further explore the legacies of safe schools on campus.

We began our explorations with focus-group interviews of students and staff. The student group comprised a cross-section of NWHS students: two Latinas (Alma and Lucia, both of whom were born in the United States to parents born in Mexico), a Latino (Esteban, who was born in Mexico and came to the United States in middle school), two white students (Tobias and Lorraine, who both claimed "Irish-German" heritage), and one black student (CC, whose family traced their arrival to New West back to the build-up of army bases in the area during World War II). Two were sophomores, three juniors, and one a senior. In addition to our ninety-minute interview that covered a variety of the same issues as our interviews with youth in the late 1990s related to peer relations, trust, and trouble on campus, we asked participants to draw sociospatial maps, replicating the directions from our original data collection. After they drew their maps, we talked with the group about what they had drawn, at one point asking if they "had to stay in the quad and cafeteria area" and, if they did move during free periods on campus, where they went. Puzzled looks broke out on the students' faces and after an awkward several seconds, Alma responded to our question about remaining in the quad and cafeteria, saying in a tone both chastising and corrective, "We can go anywhere!" Cal responded, "You can go anywhere?" And then, in rapid-fire exchanges among themselves, the group rattled off their movements about campus as they discussed their maps. Here is an excerpt from that part of the discussion:

LORRAINE: There's people in the "L" [building] all in the corner.

TOBIAS: My friend Linda, it's her and my friend Rebecca, Sara, and there's a couple of girls in that group and they sit in the "D" and they talk like every lunch.

LORRAINE: You have like those places where you go. Like last year I was in "F" and then last year there was like five of us in "F" all hanging out all the time and then this year there's like twenty kids in "F" all the time. It just liked popped up.

CC: Sometimes you have to switch areas; it's just too many people around. My group last year, we were in front of the cafeteria and there's like these seats.

ALMA: That circle thing.

CC: And we sit there and we sat there all last year. We didn't move at all. This year we were like "we have to get a different spot" because everybody was coming over there. It was like too many people so we have to move.

LUCIA: So you find a different spot. We had the corner right in front of the quad like near the stage thing and then we moved. Everybody moved from that little corner there and we moved over to like the hall.

ESTEBAN: The area around the office [administration building]?

LUCIA: Yeah.

ESTEBAN: And you just spread out.

LUCIA: That's where I hang out, just like in the field. But it's not like really close to the building.

CC: Like four girls they sit up there all the time in front of the office area but they are like dance group girls I think. They are from the dance group. Different girls coming there all the time.

LUCIA: Maybe.

CC: I know three of them. I know a lot of people, a lot of people.

In this brief exchange, participants identified six distinctive places on campus where they or their friends freely associated, split nearly evenly between what students in the late 1990s and early twenty-first century called the refuge and downtown. Two of the three places referenced were near teacher-facilitated hangouts (or sanctuaries) where students also reposed in the late 1990s to work out their troubles, often after moving off the frontstages of downtown. Lorraine referenced one of the earlier sanctuaries when she talked about people hanging in a corner of the "L" building, and Tobias referenced another when he spoke about a group that "sit[s] in 'D' and talk like every lunch." Other youth mentioned carving out space in and around the downtown where they assembled and talked. CC referenced a place on the grassy part of the quad where "four girls sit . . . in front of the office area." Participants also revealed their motivations for moving when a place became too crowded. Lorraine talked about the "F" building and how "like last year there was like five of us" and "this year there's like twenty kids. It just like popped up." CC followed Lorraine's point, adding that "sometimes you have to switch areas; it's just too many people around." Lucia picked up on the crowding and moving theme—"so you find a different spot"—with a specific example of one of her groups moving from a "little corner" to a spot "in the field," which is actually a grassy/dirt area adjacent to the concrete quad. Despite many of their moves involving short distances of a few or dozens of yards, their movement put space among their assemblies in larger crowds, cliques, and close friendship groups.

All participants' maps depicted their full participation in the lived space of the school. Their sketches reinforced their claims of being able to associate and move across the campus during free periods of the day and represented patterns paralleling what we uncovered about anchored fluidity prior to safe schools in the late 1990s. In figure 8.1, Esteban drew what upon first glance appears to be random movement but, upon closer examination, reveals a pattern of movement from downtown to the refuge, with most of his arrows ending in and around historic sanctuaries in teachers' classrooms. Esteban asserted his freedom of movement in large print—"Every Where = me"—and in figure 8.2, CC made a similar unsolicited claim on his map ("I'm pretty much everywhere"). In addition to declaring freedom of movement, CC identified the groups that formed in particular areas of the school in a way that comports with our earlier findings. Youth hanging out together are referenced with youth-centered identities (e.g., "Rockers") or as "diverse groups," whereas those in the downtown are ascribed with particular ethnic and racial identities (e.g., "lot of blacks," "Mexican"). Both Esteban and CC marked the "downtown" with "Ts" where they see most of the trouble among youth cropping up.

While students in the focus group depicted ethnic and racial identities as most salient in downtown, they saw the entire campus as "peppered," a point first raised by CC and evident in his map as well. "Peppered," in their local parlance, referenced how NWHS students recognized campus space marked by peers of different social identities as well as the continual

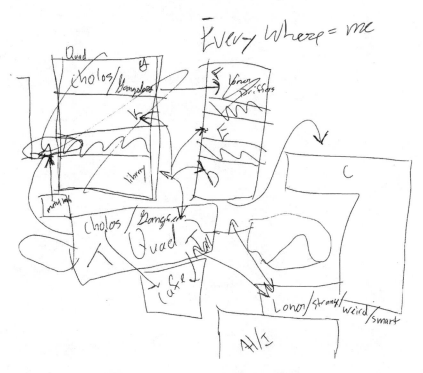

Figure 8.1. Esteban's sociospatial map of the eastern
portion of the New West High campus, 2008

movement of such markers and rituals for gaining entrance to groups and places. Lorraine put it this way: "You don't just go and hang out if somebody already hangs out there. You can wait for them to move. I mean, nobody's gonna fight you. You just know how to do it." CC added, "you need to know a certain person in that group [and then] the people will be okay with you, be cool with you." In referencing sociospatial boundaries, the students talked about "jocks" or "drama people" or "good friends" sitting together, but did not reference neighborhoods or street gangs as figuring in such lines (again, consistent with our earlier findings from the previous decade). The one exception to this pattern appeared in Esteban's map where he marked "Cholos/Gangsters" twice—once in the main quad and then again behind "L." When asked about these markings Esteban laughed, commenting, "These are some friends. Some guys are in gangs, some are wannabes dressing up, have a tricked out car, you know [in an exaggerated, drawn-out tone], Choooolos." Four of the six youth also marked their maps with groups identified explicitly as "diverse people" or "peppered

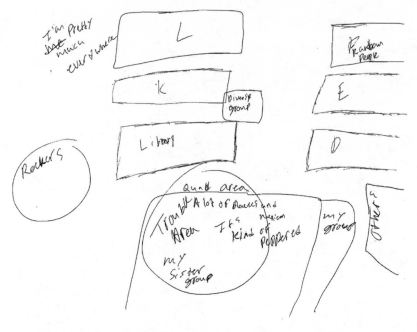

Figure 8.2. CC's sociospatial map of the quad and the main breezeway, 2008

groups," and all mentioned hanging out with mixed groups both on the quad and on other parts of campus. Moreover, on none of the maps did concentrations of youth identified as Mexican immigrants appear either in and around the "Q" quad or elsewhere on campus.

When students identified their own groups, they characterized them in terms of strong acquaintances and friendships—peers with whom they hung out—rather than invoking ethnic or racial identities. They referenced gender identities, mixed among female and male students. Without prompting, they invoked boundary crossing that suggested ethnic and racial groupings are not stuck like crazy glue, but more like flypaper. They revealed this in their depictions of "diverse groups" and the local cultural idiom of NWHS being peppered.

Gabe Preston, a white teacher whom we met in the late 1990s, confirmed the return of anchored fluidity. Early in our research, we recognized Mr. Preston as a youth-centered teacher dedicated to building inclusive social trust on campus. He established two college prep programs in 2006, shortly after Mrs. Samuels left, and split his time administering the programs and teaching science classes. One of the programs he brought to

NWHS attracted students of middling academic achievement, helping further the official NWHS mission to provide "avenues for academic achievement for everyone." One afternoon in 2008, Cal and Michael walked with Mr. Preston through campus to his science classroom, a place he has occupied since we first met him and one of the sanctuaries we identified in the late 1990s. On that afternoon, he told us he had students "interested in science hang out in my classroom eating their lunch as long as they clean up after themselves." As he told us this, we passed by one of the last remaining safe schools signs from earlier in the decade that read "No food or drink permitted in the building."

Our campus observations over the years 2009–2013 comport with the youth focus group and Mr. Preston's accounts. With students able to go anywhere on campus, we routinely observed patterns of movement and association consistent with anchored fluidity. Youth gathered in cliques and friendship groups and then moved on and off the frontstages of downtown. Downtown again appeared as social scene of groups hanging out, with constant movement among youth and between other places on campus where youth looked for niches to communicate more intimately on the backstage. On the occasions when places away from downtown became overpopulated, youth splintered, searching once again for a new place to claim for themselves. They also moved from the downtown, seeking sanctuary classrooms where teachers might be around, but not in official capacities.

In addition to disruptions to anchored fluidity, the hardening of ethnic and racial identities among youth, and aggression among the student population, the first five years of safe schools on campus created fractures among the teaching staff along the fault lines of trust and distrust of students, staff peers, and the administration. As we recount in chapter 7, during the late 1990s and early twenty-first century, a vocal subgroup of NWHS faculty designated itself the responsibility group and fell in line behind the administration's interests in facilitating exogenous forces, particularly the New West School Board and more distant authorities incentivizing safe schools in educational fields throughout the country.

To explore the legacy of safe schools among the staff, we composed a faculty focus group in 2008 of veteran teachers, an administrator, and a security guard all with a minimum of a decade experience on campus. In addition to Mr. Preston, the focus group included Drew McNamara (a veteran white teacher), Gillian Rodrigo (a Latina assistant principal fluent in Spanish), Eve Grutter (a veteran white teacher), and Catalina Marquez (a veteran Latina security guard).

We asked the group to take a long view of their impressions of NWHS students and how well they get along, from the late 1990s forward. In a representative comment, Mr. McNamara said, "The late 90s and early 2000s [was] a tough period we went through administration wise . . . [and] . . . I think we've come out of that." Mrs. Rodrigo recalled the late 1990s and early twenty-first century as a period of "crisis" for NWHS due to a lot of "worry" about "security" on campus. In response, the administration at the time "got some money and set out a lot of tough policies." Mrs. Rodrigo believed those policies resulted in "clamping down" on truancy and discipline, but also created rifts among the faculty and students. Now, she said, "We're behind each other." She also added that "these issues are no longer problems" because the current principal relaxed the tough policies and created better structures for "supporting all students," including "better screening procedures for students coming from outside the catchment area." Mr. McNamara added that Mr. Molinas's "leadership orientation" gave teachers a sense that "the administration has their back." Ms. Marquez also emphasized the solidarity among staff: "I can go to a teacher if I need to, and I know they'll support me as well as they can come to us and we'll support them. So, we're behind each other."

Front-end screening of students from outside the catchment area and student laminated IDs that must be carried at all times rendered the sweeps policy obsolete and a distant memory among the assembled adults. "Learning and Respect" (LR), a local invention that grew out of the need to apply formal school discipline without students losing academic time, replaced the tank and ISS—two staples of the safe schools era on campus. Teachers could send as few as one and as many as an entire class to the LR Center where computers, books, and multiple staff were available to aid students, together with a security guard and teachers who volunteered their class prep hour to LR students. In LR, students developed a learning plan and, according to Mr. Preston, could choose to return to the class when ready or stay in LR to advance their studies. Additional consequences, involving parent contact, occurred only if students were sent to LR several times in a given school week.

With these changes since the intensive safe schools era, NWHS remains a contested campus, albeit a place considerably closer to the one we studied a decade earlier. In 2007, Mr. Molinas and ESL instructors renamed the program English Language Learning (ELL), following new developments in California and Arizona public education, which emphasized the dynamic character of language instruction and attempted to reduce official sources of stigma for students for which English is a second language. Even so, both student and staff focus groups noted social tensions between ELL students and students of Mexican descent not in ELL. Esteban observed that while his "English is pretty good," he sometimes "catch it from other kids [Latinos] because they're different or they don't speak Spanish much." School staff also raised these tensions, noting "language barriers" and "social barriers" for youth recently emigrated from Mexico. Compounding these challenges, earlier in 2008, the Arizona Department of Education announced a mandatory four hours of English instruction per day for ELL students apart from native English speakers. We asked those assembled how NWHS was positioned to respond to this new policy and Mrs. Rodrigo spoke up first:

> We're not going to follow the law. This will create lots of conflicts and increase the isolation of ELL students. We'll figure out how to be in in complete compliance with the English language standards without locking ELL students up on one part of campus. We've got to recognize the dynamic nature of this process.

Mrs. Rodrigo's comments were intriguing on at least two counts. First, she gave a frontline blueprint for loose coupling in declaring that NWHS will not "follow the law" as the campus "figure[s] how to be in complete compliance." Second, she implicitly referenced the importance, if not the legitimacy, of local, practical knowledge regarding the social consequences of following the new state policy in lockstep fashion. Although none of the staff spoke up immediately in support of Mrs. Rodrigo's statements, everyone in the focus group nodded affirmatively in agreement. Ms. Grutter added, "We learned a lot from what happened here ten years ago. Those policies wound up favoring some students over others. It undermined trust."

After Safe Schools: "The Kids Are Well Meshed"

Several seconds of silence followed Mrs. Rodrigo and Ms. Gruttner's statements. Looking down at the table at which we were all seated, Mr. McNamara added, "Look, compared to the early 2000s, the kids are well meshed. There's not as much trouble and I agree that we don't want to do anything to upset that." His reflection tracked well with the police call data (see figure 7.1) that showed a dramatic decline in requests to the NWPD from the campus after 2005 compared to the first five years of safe schools. His comments also tracked our observations of Mexican immigrant youth not being so tightly clumped in the "Q" quad, spreading out into the main quad and spaces between classroom buildings toward the refuge.

Mr. McNamara's observation of the "well meshed" character of the student body pointed to another trend on campus, the re-emergence of collective civic action in student clubs. In 2006, the teacher-moderators who remained steadfastly supportive of clubs during the safe schools era, even as students drifted away from collective civic action and social investment in the school, began recruiting a new generation of students and teachers into what again was termed the "club scene." Supported by Mr. Molinas and scores of teachers, student club presence in *The River* grew from fourteen in 2007 to twenty-five in 2010 to forty-four in 2013, with stalwart clubs such as the Black Students Association and MEChA greatly increasing their sizes and spans of activities, signaling intense youth "ownership" of the campus and its important place in the community.

NWHS student clubs, for example, joined statewide protests against Arizona anti-immigrant bills in 2010, especially SB 1070, which required checks of citizenship documentation during routine law enforcement stops, and SB 2281, which banned the teaching of Mexican American studies courses in Arizona K-12 public schools. Collaborating with their teacher moderators, NWHS clubs organized student-led workshops, teach-ins, and other events on campus about the bills and worked with local unions and NWHS alumni to organize protests off campus regarding discrimination aimed at undocumented youth. Student clubs also directed their attention to the campus itself, again working with alumni to organize meetings with the administration and gaining a voice at New West School Board meetings to register their strong opposition to proposed Arizona legislation (never passed) that would ban undocumented youth from attending public schools. Student-teacher collective civic action, embedded in student club organizations, had been reignited at NWHS. In this sense, NWHS student clubs differed from typical school student clubs in high-poverty schools in that they were not "ghosts" with little presence or efficacy, and connected with "larger movement networks outside the school" to translate their collective civic action on campus into social change frameworks off campus.[1]

While some of the most severe elements of safe schools have not stuck to the campus, other elements have become rooted materially and normalized culturally in the school climate. Students and adults on campus alike have come to accept the presence of security cameras throughout the campus. When asked in the youth focus group about their feelings about the cameras, Esteban responded, "They are there for show," and Tobias added, "Nobody's watching in the camera room. The tapes get dumped every night. If something bad happened, you could review them I guess for a couple of days. Otherwise it doesn't matter." Screening out students from outside the catchment area who have a record of disciplinary problems, now a routine practice, has been observed in other schools where safe schools is institutionalized.[2] Moreover, the campus is closed, with the security perimeter signaling a separation between NWHS and the surrounding community, even as students found ways to hang out around the local strip malls without the "official" knowledge of school authorities (as reported at the end of chapter 7). Security guards, though no more prevalent in the first decade of the twenty-first century than they were in the late 1990s, continued as a visible presence watching and buzzing around campus on their golf carts, chatting with and engaging in surveillance of the students. A new generation of students without English language proficiency continued to be differenced by academic tracking, although, as noted above, the administration recognized how these policies, together with the new state-level requirements, could divide the student body.

In this sense, NWHS illustrates a broader pattern in research on organizations facing top-down institutional and legal pressures. Scholars using perspectives such as "inhabited institutionalism"[3] or "legal endogeneity"[4] emphasize the sustaining capacities of organizational cultures whether rooted in local public commitments or private managerial prerogatives. Policy researchers who study the diffusion of externally mandated governance plans into local organizational settings demonstrate a tendency for local administrators to adapt and reconstruct newly mandated state policies to local cultures rather than routinely implement them whole cloth.[5] And empirical studies of frontline workers, including teachers and social workers, reveal that they are far more driven to make decisions based on ties to their professions and the people they serve than to change practices with external mandates imposed on them.[6]

As for NWHS students, they again easily claimed places across the campus to form close ties while also performing their public personas on the quad. Their sociospatial lives on campus had been restored. But what do youth reveal about how they handle interpersonal peer trouble a decade after safe schools at NWHS?

Peer Trouble on Campus a Decade after Safe Schools

When our 2008 youth focus group turned to how they responded to peer trouble, participant accounts resonated with what we found in the late 1990s, as illustrated by the following representative excerpts:

CAL: Have you ever had any trouble with other students on campus?

ALMA: Not too much, you know. But sometimes trouble can come. People say stuff. At the first football game this year, this girl I had some classes with is talking crap about me saying like I kissed her and stuff and I don't go that way. I have no problem with people who do. It's like you have some rumor you're sleeping with some guy and it's not true. . . . I get a text on it. She put it on Facebook. I kept hearing this and hearing that she was talking other crap about me so at the football game at the top of the bleachers. I go up there and I'm thinking I could just push her down these bleachers right now and give her the beat down she deserves. I could post something on her too. But I don't do that. It's not how it goes here, you know. I want to know why you are talking crap about me. And she's like "I'm not, I didn't mean to, I only told one person and she put it up on Facebook." So I'm like "Look, let's solve this. Take it down. Telling one person and then it's on the Web just blasts it, you gotta know, two-four." So she's like "I'm sorry." I think she meant it too. Nothing ever happened again. But me and her go our own way now.

CC: To me, just like she said. . . . Ask the person what problems they have and who they heard from and tell them it's not true. Educate them. Talk it out. Sometimes you gotta just get away from them for a while. You can go to a different part of campus.

LORRAINE: So true. I liked this [guy] . . . and he started liking [my friend] and they went out. . . . I told them I'm not upset . . . when I was really like was upset. . . . Just deal with it, you know. Get a new attitude. Move on.

ESTEBAN: . . . . Yeah, I talk it out. I don't have much problems but if I do.

ALMA: . . . . I told her "The next time I hear you crap about me I'm not just going to confront you. I'll have somebody else confront you."

CAL: How does that work?

ALMA: . . . . Oh yeah, I can get people outside of school to give 'em a beat down if I want to. I'm friends with people who are in gangs. . . . [B]ut I'm not that kind of person. You get so mad. Sometimes you want revenge. That's not how we go here. I mean get someone to talk to them. Sometimes you need like another person to ask them that helps chill it.

TOBIAS: You need someone trustworthy.

ESTEBAN: You can't really meet those in every high school.

CAL: What do you mean?

ESTEBAN: A lot of high schools. People say things. Gossip. Hard to find those kind of people. Present company excepted. Here, there's more people you can trust than other high schools I hear about in my experience.

TOBIAS: It can be tough in high school to meet people you trust. This place is better than what my friends at other places say.

CAL: . . . . [H]ow strict is it here? . . . What about the rules?

LORRAINE: Sometimes the dress code. Like if you're half naked or something. To me that's it. Doesn't affect me much.

TOBIAS: If you do something bad you get in trouble but . . . if you like generally following the rules then you are fine.

ESTEBAN: I don't think about it too much. . . . [P]unishment the system is pretty fair here.

CC: . . . . [M]ost teachers, they treat you okay. Not going to get in you business if you doing right. That's how I see it.

MICHAEL: Earlier, some of you mentioned gangs. What do you mean by gangs?

ESTEBAN: Gangs are people . . . hustling drug paraphernalia . . . buy tons of tattoos . . . throw signs.

C: Get mad really easy about stupid stuff like where you from or what street you live on. Take respect to the end, you know. Most people don't care.

ESTEBAN: Yeah, that's really stupid.

LORRAINE: . . . . I came here my freshman year and it's worse over there [in Boston] as far as like gangs and stuff go because. . . . They go and they bring knives and guns to school. . . . It's like [Eastern High]. I have friends there. But you don't really have that here.

MICHAEL: . . . . [W]hen you leave campus what is it like around here? Where you live?

LUCIA: You go to like [13th Street], that's where everyone lives. Like everyone lives there. But if you go to [13th]. . . . it's like [14th Avenue] . . . and it's like the halfway point between one gang and another gang.

ESTEBAN: [I]t's like the worst part ever.

LUCIA: Yeah, you don't go there. . . . . I feel safe . . . here at school.

The group recounted many of the issues sparking trouble that we found a decade earlier, especially evidence of heterosexual drama, now sprinkled with same-sex drama. Parallel to our earlier findings and other previous research, youth immediately resonated with the idea of "trouble" and did not use the adult-centered term, "bullying," to describe peer conflict.[7] The term bullying, as we note in chapter 3, reifies power dynamics among young people as "victims" and "predators," rather than emphasizing the often-blurred boundaries between these roles. The repertoire we identified in the late 1990s—including conciliatory-remedial actions characteristic of workin' it out, moralistic responses characteristic of puttin' 'em in their place, and rule-oriented responses related to dealing with the system of official school authority—all emerged in the focus group. Again parallel to our earlier findings, youth reported favoring trouble responses related to bottom-up, conciliatory-remedial control, including coping ("Deal with it"), making self-direct changes ("Get a new attitude"), apologizing ("So she's like 'I'm sorry'"), complaint making to and attempts at correcting a troublesome party ("Educate them" or "let's solve this. Take it down"), temporary avoidance ("Sometimes you gotta just get away from them for a while. . . . go to a different part of campus"), or exit ("Move on"). At the same time, some participants made blustery allusions to beat downs but, like most of the actions we revealed in earlier chapters, rarely escalated to violence. Alma, for instance, talked about a trouble string seemingly careening toward violence ("push her down these bleachers now") but thought better of it, even suggesting how third-party peers could help "chill" the trouble. When asked about the strictness of rules at NWHS, students claimed the system operates on the periphery of their lives ("Don't think about it too much") and was both "fair" and proportional in responding to trouble ("If you do something bad you get in trouble").

Students in the focus group compared NWHS to other schools and the neighborhoods where they currently lived or lived prior to moving to New West, evoking images of gang turf and street violence. Lorraine made two comparisons along these lines, one to where she attended middle school in Boston and the other to Eastern High School in New West. In both comparisons, NWHS came out favorably in terms of students not bringing weapons to campus ("It's not like that here"). Lucia observed the danger of a border between two neighborhoods controlled by rival street gangs in neighborhoods where many NWHS students lived ("where everyone lives"), which Esteban reinforced with a proclamation that one should be wary of being on that neighborhood border ("you don't go there"). In response to Michael's question about the meaning of gangs in their lives, students decried the campaigns for respect waged by some gang members on campus, to quote Esteban, as "stupid." CC claimed that such public identities were not central to youth at NWHS ("Most people don't care here"). In contrast to the neighborhood that participants mentioned as riven by gang tensions and turf wars, Alma declared she felt "safe" on campus. And finally, all the participants emphasized social trust on campus. Alma, for instance, in briefly recounting how she did not violently confront a peer, noted the antiviolence norms on campus: "It's not how it goes here, you know." In the midst of a conversation about mobilizing third parties to help chill other young people, Tobias mentioned that such actions required peers who are "trustworthy," to which Esteban interjected a world-weary observation that high schools, for the most part, do not yield such relationships. When asked to elaborate, Esteban differentiated NWHS from other high schools "in his experience," adding, "Here, there's more people you can trust than other high schools." Tobias added another favorable comparison for NWHS: "This place is better than what my friends at other places say."

Social media emerged as a new contingency that did not exist in young people's lives during the late 1990s. Alma, for example, noted how texting and posting on Facebook about a claimed kiss "blasts it" to a broad audience with twenty-four-hour access. While claiming not to be homophobic, she felt she must directly confront the young woman making these claims, directing her to tell a third party to remove the posting from Facebook. Here we see how face-to-face youth "personal communities" become intertwined with virtual public communities, intensifying emotions and the stakes of identity.[8] Yet, at NWHS, the repertoire of peer trouble responses given voice by the 2008 youth focus group did not sound much different in the digital era than similar groups a decade earlier. Perhaps this continuity resulted from what Internet researcher danah boyd observes is the "seamless" character of social media in young people's lives; that is, social media offers an additional channel through which to connect and respond to trouble with peers rather than providing entirely new mechanisms of control.[9] If social media did not offer new repertoires of peer control, it might still enhance particular parts of trouble-response repertoires available to youth. Alma noted, for example, that she could engage in retribution against her peer by "posting something on her." The fact that such postings can be anonymous may enhance the feasibility of spreading malicious gossip or creating anonymous, hidden transcripts that harm peer reputations. Such practices commonly occur in digital environments among high school youth across the United States and in other countries,[10] although, similar to our research a decade earlier, youth in our focus group and other conversations with both youth and adults on campus in the early 2010s did not reveal these practices as modal at NWHS. More generally, our arguments raise questions about how social trust and anchored fluidity might operate in the digital era. We address these considerations toward the end of this chapter.

Intertwining Informal and Formal Control

In the following typical fieldnote excerpts from 2013, Michael represented two sets of interactions among students and school staff, the first in the library and the second in a classroom after school:

As usual, I was given space on one of the large tables in the main reading room of the library to stack and review the collection of yearbooks. My table was closest to the main entrance and just to my left stood the librarian staff desks, situated with a clear view of the doors and nearly all the reading tables. Mrs. Ruth, a black staffer who attended NWHS and had been working on campus for over a decade, occupied the desk with the clearest panoramic view of the quad and its surroundings. Classes had just let out and a group of five males came through the doors talking. They immediately quieted down as they approached Mrs. Ruth's desk. All wore baggy jeans and two had on hoodies. It was difficult to tell their ethnicities, although three had decidedly dark, olive skin tones compared to the other two, and, as they walked through the door, I picked up some Spanish passed between two of the olive-skinned youth. In all, they appeared to be a "mixed" group. They asked Mrs. Ruth if they could take a table because their rides were running late and it was blistering hot where they usually get picked up. She pointed to a table a few beyond my location and they gathered around a computer interacting quietly for about twenty minutes before they thanked Mrs. Ruth and headed out the door. She told me the boys come by periodically at the end of the school day because their rides are unreliable and that she rarely had to "shush" them. She thought they shared an interest in some video games and came from the same neighborhood. "I don't let them play any video games but it's fine if they talk quietly about whatever they're interested in and don't disturb any other students."

Randy Nielsen came by to see if I had any questions about ten minutes later. I did and my questions led him to take me on a walk to get the phone numbers of two retired teachers whom he believed were better situated to answer than he. First, he took me to Principal Molinas, who was still in touch with the retired teachers. Mr. Molinas was in his office sitting around a small conference table dressed in a NWHS sweatshirt and sweat pants with Mr. Prescot, who had on a blue NWHS polo shirt, and two students, both of whom looked to be black (judging from their skin color and hair styles) also dressed in "NWHS" sports sweats. Mr. Molinas told Randy and me they were plotting how to get the referees on their side for a big basketball game scheduled for next week. We all laughed and Mr. Molinas directed us to another teacher, Ms. Perez, to run down the phone numbers.

Mr. Nielsen and I met Ms. Perez in her "K" classroom. More than a half hour after the final bell of the day had rung, she remained at her desk, marking student papers while seven students, a mix of young men and women of differing ethnic backgrounds (skin tones varying from light, almost pink, to very dark brown), huddled in a set of desks near the front of the room. They interacted in an animated way about the upcoming elections of what appeared, judging from a flier they had, to be a meeting of the officers of the "Public History" club. Some had their phones out and were texting, periodically interjecting into the conversation, while others were completely captivated by the conversation in real time. As Ms. Perez finished giving us the numbers for the retired teachers, she turned to the youth, saying, "OK, it's time to wrap it up, and remember, you need to expand your membership." With the retired teachers' phone numbers in hand, Mr. Nielsen and I walked down the main breezeway back to the library. Students moved past us in small clusters, smiling and talking with each other and glancing at us with an occasional nod to Mr. Nielsen. On a side path that led to the cafeteria, I observed a security guard in his cart with one leg dangling over the cart and four students gathered around, with one, a female, sitting on the curved frame that covered one of the cart's front wheels. She talked with another student while the other two chatted with the security guard.

These observations reveal several instances of informal and formal social control at NWHS operating conjunctively. The frontline staff assumed full responsibility over the places of the school where students gathered, were unobtrusive in monitoring student interactions in those places, and consequently gave students the social room to work on their interpersonal relations. Students, in turn, showed respect for the places they occupied and an awareness of the boundaries of their actions in context. Administrators and security personnel embraced the perspective that adult controls were substantially in the hands of the school's frontline personnel, the teachers and staff who worked directly with students in the social and educational learning environments of the school.

Mrs. Ruth, the library staffer, ensured that every student who entered the facility checked in with her, visually and usually verbally. Her authority at the ready, she rarely needed to "shush" students. Mrs. Ruth had a good feel for what the students did at each of the tables and frequently interacted with them about their projects. As long as their discussions did not distract others or they did not abuse their access to library resources ("I don't let them play any video games"), she afforded them room to make the library a place to engage socially. The students, in turn, showed an awareness of the social order of the library and only occasionally needed reminders, almost always through subtle gestures or familiar nonverbal cues, like Mrs. Ruth's style of quieting a group with a stare and single finger to her lips. Mutual respect held sway, and care was taken to teach students the ways of the library without embarrassment or put-downs when youth disturbed the environment. In only one instance during multiple field visits during this period did we observe the appearance of a security guard who, along with another library staff member, escorted a young man and two young women outside when their argument continued after the usual admonishments. Otherwise, the social order of the library was in the hands of the staff *and* students who passed through its doors, with adult authority on the ground having the final say. This form of control, what we call conciliatory-remedial control, operated from the middle out and the bottom up, where youth had the social and physical space to define their everyday interactions and staff on the campus frontlines had established local norms of appropriate conduct that students understood and viewed as legitimate.

The brief observation of the history teacher, Ms. Perez, and her students in the classroom after hours revealed a similar dynamic, even as the setting contributed to subtle differences in the way adult and youth controls played out. The students engaged in animated and loud conversation, even slightly heated interactions, with Ms. Perez ostensibly paying little attention. After all, the school day had ended, and Ms. Perez knew precisely what the students were discussing, including enjoying a close working relationship with them. The students toned down their discussion when we first arrived to collect phone numbers. As the three adults stood nearby making small talk, the youth circled back to their relational exchanges at about the same level of animation. Just as we were about to leave, Ms. Perez signaled her authority by telling them it was time to "wrap it up" and reminded them she was listening by noting that they "need to expand the membership"—an implicit suggestion not only to concentrate on the election of new officers but also to continue generating new rank-and-file members.

Taken together, these observations reveal patterns of control active at NWHS that makes it a contested school that works. Both Ms. Perez and Mrs. Ruth conveyed their authority over school places, while using informal means to control environments of student social interaction and learning. Youth recognized adult authority while carving out places of their own to assemble, interact, and move through with purpose. Adult and youth control practices pulled in the same direction with little effort needed to address the blending of the formal with the informal—the blending itself blurred the boundaries between the two.

When we describe NWHS as a "contested school that works," we mean a school with an emplaced identity that can absorb with purpose and safety new generations of students who bring distinctive interests and identities with them, sometimes different from those of previous generations. It is a place where both the adults and youth of the school feel secure, and the mission of educational and social learning is accomplished cooperatively from the middle out and the bottom up. Inclusive student collective civic action is an important part of this story, providing places where youth can meaningfully mix and come together to achieve common goals of both their clubs and the school as a whole. As noted above, student clubs also operate off campus, directly opposing the last decade of state-level anti-immigration legislation and policing. The school administration, with substantial membership drawn from the teaching ranks, serves as a buffer between the school and its external environment, including the school district and state school authorities. Students claim the school as their place, as well, having substantial freedom of movement and assembly to work their relationships and work out their troubles with one another.

By contested, we mean that the school both stimulates and adapts to different interests and inequalities among US-born Latinos and Mexican-immigrant youth; black males vis-à-vis the administration; and competing visions of youth conflict and strategies of control held by adults rippling through campus, the local community, and in broader educational and legal fields. Our final phase of fieldwork revealed an alignment of vision and interests at NWHS that parallels the school we began studying more than a decade earlier.

Against this backdrop, we devote the remainder of this chapter to moving beyond the window of NWHS to advance a series of social themes important to the study of youth conflict and public education derived from a synthesis of our analyses in conversation with salient literature. Each points the way for further inquiry. At the same time, these themes may offer some direction to those on the frontlines striving to make public education work and provide space for youth to exercise their agency in building peaceable relations amidst diversity.

Constituting Moral Authority on the Frontlines

Over the past few decades, scholars and pundits concerned with the fate of US public education have decried the demise of moral authority on the frontlines of schools—the capacity of teachers, in particular, to respond to student misbehavior while sustaining order and rich learning environments on their campuses. Richard Arum, for example, empirically traces the decline of frontline moral authority in schools to the affirmation of individual student rights, for which the Supreme Court decision in *Goss v. Lopez* regarding due process in school disciplinary procedures proved a watershed moment. The court's decision in 1975 ushered in decades of educational litigation about due process that challenged the legitimacy of school discipline.[11] Other scholars have focused on moral authority on the frontlines of high poverty schools. Martín Sánchez-Jankowski, for example, advances the perspective that urban public schools are "sites of struggle" between high-poverty neighborhoods and state mandates. In schools heavily structured by carceral logic and practices—"state schools"—the efficacy of frontline moral authority can sidestep basic academic training and efforts to socialize youth into self-control, relying on naked coercion, often literally at the end of a metal detection wand or gun.[12] In schools captured by local communities—"neighborhood schools"—staff can draw moral authority from living and having standing in surrounding neighborhoods, but much of the time they are beholden to what some would recognize as "street" values.[13] John Devine, who worked in the high-poverty schools of New York City as a tutor, mentor, and researcher, argues that struggles between the state and the community on high-poverty high school campuses is "camouflaged by a discourse of denial" both by scholarly and administrative interests.[14] Devine, like us, recognizes urban schools as having lives of their own, but in the schools where he operated as a participant-observer, the norm of violence was, in part, made real by teachers who removed from their responsibility "the body of the student" and steered clear of "imparting ('imposing is the more usual verb') . . . standards of conduct or values on students or, certainly, in entering into direct confrontations about etiquette or behavior."[15]

We observed a very different kind of frontline moral authority at NWHS, where what we call youth-centered teachers abounded, highly attentive to the body and mind of their students. These teachers cared about students' lives, learning, and comportment and regarded the entire campus, not just the classroom, as their place. Such teachers were crucial for facilitating a campus where youth feel safe and wanted while having the freedom of movement and places to go to work things out among themselves. They are important everyday architects of a social order and instantiate a social trust that evolves from the bottom up, where students deal with their troubles with one another, and from the middle out, where adults provide sanctuaries for youth to hang out and engage one another and, at the same time, have the credibility and will to intervene when they see issues escalate.

Throughout this and previous chapters, we met youth-centered teachers who keep their ears to the ground, such as Mrs. Robinson in chapter 1. In chapter 7, we introduced Ms. Loften, an early-career faculty member who joined the teaching staff of NWHS with some trepidation because of the school's "ghetto" reputation. By her second year, she routinely walked around the entire campus, making her own decisions about whether and how to step in to gatherings of students in places they claimed as their own. In this chapter, we briefly met Ms. Perez and Mrs. Ruth, already strong presences on campus, who reflected the increasingly diverse generation of younger teachers at NWHS who also are youth-centered and crucial to sustaining the architecture of a social order from the middle out.

In chapter 7, we bought forward the illustrative voice of Mr. George, a veteran white teacher and a graduate of NWHS, who openly opposed safe schools in the late 1990s and early in the first decade of the twenty-first century. He observed that Principal Samuels did not understand the consequences of her decisions, warning that cramming students together on the quad was a potential tinderbox of trouble, and he asserted that the sweeps policy could harm the long-standing diversity project of the school, a place that "teach[es] kids how to accept each other." Earlier in this chapter, we drew attention to Mr. Preston, who was proud to be a part of an administration that worked to restore the centrality of the teaching staff to the structures and climate of NWHS in the aftermath of safe schools. Mr. Preston proved a crucial player by enabling the reconstitution of a school that works from the inside. He provided places of learning and social interaction for his students, serving as a catalyst for students to go directly to university science programs or through the state's community college system. While Mr. Preston operated as an inside player in the development of a harmonized order at NWHS, Mr. Nielsen, the head of IT services and the school's archivist, operated a crucial conduit to the larger community, providing human intelligence about how the school was fairing to alumni who are now influential citizens in New West. His actions mobilized alumni for as minor a task as providing us with historical materials on the school and for as major a task as saving the school from being closed in the 1980s and helping to reconnect student collective civic action to the community in the 2010s.

These teachers illustrate John Devine's formulation that the vocation of teaching requires that teachers assume major responsibility for the moral climate of the entire school and exercise power for "emancipatory ends, for creating a unified communitas with a harmony of rules based on a respect for diversity."[16] To achieve that, teachers must teach, but also be mentors, spiritual guides, and disciplinarians, "articulating and enforcing the behavioral standards and limits for an adolescent."[17]

In her classic study of the "good high school," Sara Lawrence Lightfoot observes teachers who have a "fearless and empathetic regard of students," including those "young people who tend to baffle and offend the rest of us."[18] She notes the easy rapport such teachers enjoyed with students as they moved through public settings, like the cafeteria or up the outdoor steps into school buildings, using humor, conversation, and occasional prodding to move students along. Lightfoot observes these teachers handling animated outbursts of students directed both at them and among youth, and is amazed by "their understanding, diagnosis, and quick interpretations of adolescent needs."[19] She notes these teachers' awareness of individual student and group differences, grounded in empathetic assessments, as they make judgments about whether and how to insert themselves when they move across the entire territory of a school to contribute to climates of school wholeness and an ordered harmony.[20]

While Lightfoot includes urban high schools from the 1980s that were judged as "good," research by Ron Astor, Heather Ann Meyer, and William Behre focuses on high schools that on a host of factors are considered unsafe.[21] In these schools, the largest contingent of teachers had pulled back to their classrooms, similar to what other researchers have noted, leaving large sections of school grounds untended by adults, spaces where the safety of youth was at risk. Still, they, too, find the equivalents of Lightfoot's fearless teachers. Their "model teachers" are identified by students as expecting quality work, making efforts to ensure students' attendance, caring about their lives, and willing to intervene when youth trouble appeared to point in the direction of aggression and potential violence, "regardless of location or time."[22] These observations parallel those by Victor Rios in his ethnography of Oakland urban youth of color. Although he depicts urban public high schools as an integral part of the "youth control complex," he also credits teacher-mentors as crucial to his mobility from a high-poverty background to university professor and to moving from "negative credential status to positive credential status."[23]

The evidence from NWHS and general meditations on teachers underscore frontline moral authority as what Steven Maynard-Moody and Michael Musheno call "pragmatic improvisation"—a creative constitution and application of "practical knowledge and judgments" of frontline workers in the face of "uncertainty."[24] This perspective resonates with contemporary pragmatist social theory, repurposed from John Dewey, to focus on the ways that experiential obstacles, or trouble in the sense that we use it in this book, give rise to creative, practical problem solving.[25] Pragmatist frontline moral authority and the empathetic agency it entails are contingent upon institutional practices and broader cultural contexts.[26] Schools narrowly reflective of state or neighborhood interests limit what teachers can know, imagine, or enact in their routine practices, especially how they make sense of and evaluate the everyday interactions they have with youth. Collectively sustained social trust and anchored fluidity constitute contexts that broaden available cultural schemas for understanding youth, which facilitate creative solutions to a school order attentive to social equity. When social trust is instantiated from the bottom up, teachers and students consistently collaborate, and this carries over, as we noted above, in the blending of informal and formal social control.

Slowing Down Social Time amid Difference and Digital Life

Still left open is the relationship on a theoretical level between trust, sociocultural difference, and conflict. To specify this relationship at a more general level we turn to Donald Black's concept of "social time," which he defines as the "fluctuation of every dimension of social space."[27] Black argues that movements in social time—interpersonal relationships forming or dissolving, people rising or falling in status and material positions comprising social hierarchies, or cultural differences growing or shrinking—are associated with moral evaluations and social conflict. He posits that the faster the speed and greater the disjunctions of social time, the greater the rate of social conflict and likelihood that it will assume moralistic orientations. Radical changes in social time not only generate more conflict but also increase the chances that responses will be most severe.[28] This formulation, for example, helps make sense of the persistent finding by social scientists that settings experiencing dramatic change in ethnic and racial diversity are fraught with conflict, a lack of cooperation, and low social trust.[29]

At NWHS, students and adults slowed social time through bottom-up collective civic action in student clubs that gave a sense of common identity and social trust, and through middle-out pragmatist moral authority exercised by teachers that facilitated students solving problems on a daily basis. Taken together, social trust buttressed anchored fluidity, which meant that small changes in social time constantly occurred as relationships, social status, and cultural difference were also in flux. These changes in social time brought into contact youth of different cultural orientations, especially ethnic and racial identities, languages, and popular styles.

From a non-Latino standpoint, the cultural differences between US-born Latinos and Mexican immigrant youth would seem to be less, for example, than those between black and white youth. Yet we found much less social tension between peers of these latter identifications than between Latino youth of different origins and identities. And when trouble broke out between these Latino youth across this point of difference, it usually played out through the antagonists' deployment of control repertoires that were minimally conciliatory-remedial rather than aggressively moralistic. This pattern suggests that how one interprets fluctuations in relationships, status, and cultural difference matters in moral evaluation. In this regard, distrust can act as a catalyst speeding up social time, making change seem more jarring, perhaps even a harbinger of danger.[30] Trust, by contrast, can act as a deaccelerant, slowing down social time, not only leading to less negative moral evaluations but also affecting even the valence of such evaluations.

Under conditions of robust social trust, fluctuations in social time associated with anchored fluidity can be perceived as normatively appropriate and a pleasurable part of social life rather than a harbinger of trouble. Although the quad at NWHS generated peer conflict and moralistic trouble responses, more often than not it took on the character of Elijah Anderson's sense of a cosmopolitan canopy—a place to enjoy diversity and comity among one's peers and get some food. The quad we came to know parallels closely Anderson's original representations of cosmopolitan canopies, such as the Reading Terminal Market in Philadelphia, in which he emphasizes such contexts as gathering places where social differences are crossed and enjoyed, people can get a bite to eat, and gestures of civility are displayed.[31]

Beyond this overall sense of the relationship between social trust and social time, the timing and clustering of controls in a trouble string can matter for the pace of social time in handling trouble. Conciliatory-remedial trouble responses, for example, tended to slow down social time as relationships were rebuilt, status differences diminished, or cultural differences bridged. As we demonstrated in chapters 3 and 4, youth at NWHS often clustered together multiple practices of conciliatory-remedial control, which slowed down social time. When youth clustered moralistic (emphasizing honor) or rule-oriented responses together, social time sped up, and with it, the possibility for ever more severe responses to trouble.

How does social time among young people play out online? This question is an important concern because youth increasingly conduct significant parts of their social lives online. As we noted earlier, at NWHS it appears that many of the dynamics of peer control we uncovered in the late 1990s still inhered in the 2010s. At the same time, social media may distort aspects of face-to-face social time and be associated with more conflict and moralistic responses to it. That is, changes in relationships, social status, or cultural differences can appear instantly, be broadcast to broader audiences, and persist twenty-four hours per day over long periods of time.[32] The anonymity of such postings not only removes crucial social information necessary for a complete representation of social time and constitution of social trust, but also can lead to inferential errors regarding what changes in social time mean to whom.[33] Social media also can expand the frontstage and make finding meaningful backstages more difficult. Adding to the distortion of social time may be difficulties in sustaining social trust in social interactions involving social media.[34]

Clearly, social media platforms tempt youth to deploy moralistic trouble responses hidden from reasoned engagement yet exposed to frontstage audiences in compressed time that can illicit responses from aggrieved parties with the same insensitivities in the same breakneck speed. Trouble responses related to goin' undercover are particularly ripe for use via social networking sites. It is possible to imagine such practices, spinning rapidly and expanding in scope, doing injury to social trust.

Yet there are also qualities of how youth deploy social networking sites (SNS) that make it a complementary medium for enacting anchored fluidity.[35] Foremost, youth use social media sites to enrich their interactions with those to whom they already have strong social ties, giving them a virtual backstage for communication away from face-to-face sites dominated by frontstages, illustrated by the downtown at NWHS.[36] In these safe havens, youth form and reinforce a sense of self-identity and strong affinity with their closest friends. Like our observations of youth moving their troubles away from the gaze of downtown audiences, youth have learned how to partition information for certain subsets of their friends when using SNS even as they worry about how to deal with information slipping to those who are not really friends.[37] Finally, anchored fluidity, our discovery that youth at NWHS move around socially and spatially with relative ease, is achievable through the use of social network sites. Youth recognize that SNS offers space to construct and perform a host of identities and "resist being fixed as rigid, unchanging subjects."[38] When experimenting with identities, they communicate with trusted friends, but also engage in these performances to build and enhance social relationships with youth who are less well known to them. As with the face-to-face practices of anchored fluidity, youth use of social networking can operate as a source of connectivity and empowerment from the personal through intergroup levels.[39] The historic capacity of NWHS to generate social trust may moderate the trouble-generating effects of social media to some extent, as our youth focus group and more recent observations suggest, but future research will need to tease out the complex interplay between trust, social time, and social control among youth on- and offline.

Sustaining Social Resilience in a Neoliberal-Paternal Era

As we presented our research on youth conflict to multiple audiences over the years, someone almost invariably would ask how youth at NWHS remain "so resilient" given the challenges they face. Resilience, in some sense, represents the flip side of the resignation and stress young people can experience growing up in a poor neighborhood and attending a high-poverty school.[40] At the individual level, resilience, as Peter Hall and Michèle Lamont write, refers to "better coping skills, or multiple domains of the self or stress-response characteristics that mitigate the negative effects of risk factors." By contrast, Hall and Lamont draw attention to "social resilience," which describes how collectivities "sustain their well-being in the face of challenges to them." Well-being encompasses both material and symbolic aspects, including senses of dignity and belonging. Rather than static, social resilience is dynamic in that it must be constantly attended to and made sense of, yet does not necessarily mean a return to an a priori state of equilibrium, but can lead to new social arrangements adaptive to changing conditions.[41] Empirically, individual and social resilience integrally intertwine as resilient contexts empower individual persons, enhancing their sense of self-efficacy.[42]

Social resilience has always been important for marginalized populations, especially poor communities of color, but especially so during the past few decades as neoliberal ideas ascended both in the United States and throughout the world. As Wendy Brown reminds us, neoliberalism does not refer to a settled, coherent set of policy positions, but rather is a loose, plastic ideology privileging economistic, market rationality as the central lens of governance, a way to see all social problems and their solutions.[43] Although ostensibly about rolling back state protections for the marginalized and rolling out laissez-faire economics, Joe Soss, Richard Fording, and Sanford Schram argue that in practice "[N]eoliberals have not dismantled the activist state; they have embraced its authority while working to redirect to transform it."[44] Governing the poor thus has occurred along two intersecting dimensions, the first privileging market rationality and the second involving intensifying paternalistic "monitoring, incentives for right behavior, and penalties for noncompliance."[45] For the urban poor, especially young men of color, paternalism belies authoritarian orientations and practices, Löic Wacquant argues, represented by violent penal policies and criminalization, all within a "trope of [failed] individual responsibility."[46]

Instead of seeing poor families, schools, and communities, neoliberal-paternal policy makers see individual actors driven by poor choices, which, at the individual and collective levels, need "law and order" and "mass incarceration." At a global level, international agencies encourage governments to privatize public services, including utilities, schools, prisons, and hospitals, while social welfare shifts to "workfare" programs and incentives that compel individuals of lesser privilege to become more "self-reliant" as they negotiate carceral control.[47] At the individual level, neoliberalism is associated with different conceptions of the person and group, in effect according communal and democractic solidarity less value while elevating the value of individuality.[48] Some of these trends existed long before the rise of neoliberalism paternalism, while others operate as expedient rationales for neoconservative and authoritarian movements exercising their political will and social power. Moreover, multiple collective political actors have opposed and embraced neoliberal-paternal thinking, ranging from the purely secular to extremist religious movements. It is beyond the scope of this book to assess the ultimate impact of such thinking and polices. Suffice to say that the cacophony of ideas, policies, and practices under the rubric of neoliberal paternalism has exacerbated social inequities of all kinds, transforming state protections and dramatically expanding carceral capacity and control for poor populations of color.[49]

Scholars have begun studying how social resilience can be sustained at the macro-level in the neoliberal-paternal era, but much less attention has been devoted to the local level. Particularly salient in this regard are high-poverty public schools, which are targets of, but also can be bulwarks against, the deleterious consequences of such policies. In chapter 2, we focused on anchored fluidity and inclusive collective civic action, including the long-standing tradition of young women of color being recognized for high academic achievement and holding leadership positions in student organizations and government. These same mechanisms are important for sustaining social resilience both directly and indirectly through their relationships to social trust. They operate directly in that they enable adaptation and indirectly because through social trust, schools are able to sustain collective identities that operate as bellwethers in difficult times. To be clear, trust and anchored fluidity do not substitute for significant, material public investment into schools and programs, including the recruitment, socialization, and sustained support of high-quality teachers and administrators, who can enhance the life opportunities of youth. They also do not substitute for fair, inclusive structures of official school discipline that reject carceral control. But material investment and fair disciplinary structures, although crucial, are not enough to produce social resilience and to empower youth with academic and social skills, dignity, and self- and collective efficacy. Moreover, our analyses also point to another important mechanism for sustaining durable social resilience: the capacity of youth actively engaged with frontline staff to navigate conflict in peaceful and equitable ways through an everyday governance of schools that operates with relative autonomy.

At NWHS, being able to get along with and trust diverse peers, as well as adults, was a long-standing source of student identity and pride. These inclinations carried over with regard to how youth worked out trouble (aided by a portion of the teachers and at various junctures by the administration). This pattern illustrates what Laura Nader calls a "harmony model" of social control: "an emphasis on conciliation, recognition that resolution of conflict is inherently good . . . [and that] harmonious behavior is more civilized than disputing behavior."[50] Top-down harmony models can generate repression and injustice, as illustrated by repressive school discipline systems or on a global stage when more powerful countries for economic gain impose reconciliation to pacify less-powerful peoples.[51] When harmony models emerge from the bottom up, however, they become a resource for preserving local autonomy and creative solutions to conflict.[52] In our observations, NWHS is a place unto its own. On a daily basis, youth workin' out trouble with peers provide just such a resource, signaling, as one black female senior put it, how youth "can take care of their own business." In this way, everyday governance remains largely in the hands of students and teachers, with the mobilization of formal authority and control less visible, feeding into the school's cohesion and constraining imposition by external authorities. It is this relative autonomy—bolstered by the pragmatist frontline moral authority of teachers and the slowing down of social time—that enabled the school to recouple control with trust in the second half of the first decade of the twenty-first century after its experiences with full administrative commitment to safe schools in the first half of the same decade. And it is this relative autonomy that will facilitate the campus to further learn from and adapt to ongoing change in the local community and in the broader fields of education and law.

Taking Stock

Older and newer generations of youth and adults at NWHS continuously engage their agency and mobilization skills in the accomplishment of a place—a high-poverty school that is a local tradition operating continuously for over a century.[53] Its institutional glue is inclusive social trust, both *within* the school, a relational characteristic of faith in the reliability and integrity of teachers and based in collective civic action in student clubs, and *of* the school, a political characteristic of faith in the reliability and integrity of the organization's value to its external constituencies and stakeholders—its legitimacy.

Emerging from its latest struggle with safe schools and reclaiming its place in the local community during the period that dominates our ethnography, we documented how youth navigate conflict on their own terms, while NWHS teachers kept their ears to the ground. NWHS is a place where local equities are secured from the everyday of trouble and conflict through youth largely slowing down social time to work it out.[54] It is a place where students have the backs of teachers, as chronicled in chapter 7 when Alanza successfully challenged two young male peers, who like herself were born in Mexico, to stop disrespecting Ms. Lopato, a teacher, and make space for the class to better learn English. It is a place where teachers have the backs of students, revealed in chapter 7 when Mrs. Wright pulled into her classroom a student who was about to be swept up by Mr. Brown, a strong advocate of safe schools. It is a place where teachers engaged in collective dialogue with one another, as evidenced in an adult focus group, when all assembled agreed to circumvent a state policy that would further distance the new wave of ELL students from the rest of the school's student population.

No single study can do justice to all the complexities of youth conflict in high-poverty schools. What we hope to have accomplished is a textured analysis that moves the dialogue beyond the tropes of gang violence and school dysfunction to represent youth conflict up close and on the frontlines as lived by youth and adults. We also hope to have advanced a research agenda into the sociospatial lines of action that link inclusive social trust with the practices of informal and formal control. This research agenda, which encourages sampling on degrees of social trust rather than violence, will generate insight into the dynamics of youth conflict, particularly the roles played by local knowledge and improvisation on the part of youth and adults, while also shedding new light on social conflict in settings beset by material poverty yet rich in resilience.

Additional Notes on Data Collection, Analysis, Writing, and Generalizability

This appendix discusses the intricacies of our data sets and analytical strategies beyond our overview and discussion in chapter 1. We report our strategies for handling the challenges of conducting group fieldwork, triangulating multiple data sets, and constituting a longitudinal design. We also begin dredging methodological channels for scholars of youth studies, educational policy, sociology, and sociolegal studies to put our questions, findings, and conceptual framing to further study while pursuing their own. To these ends, we provide additional details on interviews, youth-authored trouble cases, sketch map and photo-narrative exercises, and archival and institutional evidence. Our discussion closes with an overview of our data analysis strategies, consulting with participants, field writing, and perspective on generalizability.

Interviews

In the late 1990s and 2000s we conducted individual taped in-depth, semi-structured, and focus group interviews with NWHS students and staff. On campus, we purposively sampled informants for these interviews based on the knowledge about campus we gained from our initial fieldwork. In the late 1990s, thirty-four student participants in the interviews ranged across different grade levels, including nine ninth graders, six sophomores, ten juniors, and nine seniors, with three more young women than men comprising the overall sample. In terms of ethnic and racial identities, we approximated the demographic composition of the campus with fourteen Latinos (with more Mexican-immigrant than Mexican-descent youth), ten white students, seven black students, two Asian students, and one Native

American student. Participants ranged from students considered by their peers to be "in the mix" on campus to those considered more marginal.

Interviews ranged from one-half hour to ninety minutes. The logic of our interviews focused on specific activities, peer relations, and practices as a way to reveal how differentially positioned youth make sense of their daily lives. This type of strategy, as Amy Best argues and as we noted in chapter 1, enables researchers to examine the "contested" meanings and socially constructed character of young people's lives.[1] The interviews first focused on youth biographies, such as when they came to New West and the campus and whether they held jobs of any kind on or off campus. We then turned to sociospatial and sociocultural relations on campus, including specific experiences in peer relations involving different kinds of social bases (e.g., race/ethnicity, activities, friendships) and how youth use on- and off-campus space. We then asked students about their observations of and personal experiences with interpersonal and intergroup trouble. With these concrete events and practices as a backdrop, we then asked youth about their general impressions of a range of issues. This two-pronged strategy facilitated understanding how youth accounted for routine and nonroutine practices compared to what they expected in particular contexts. The protocols for all interviews appear at the end of this appendix.

The narrative photo exercise in 1999 (discussed in the next section) also occasioned four youth focus-group interviews of eleventh and twelfth graders in groups of six to eight students each with two-thirds of the group young women but again approximating the overall ethnic and racial composition of the school. Nearly all the students who participated in the narrative photo project participated in these interviews. In our focus-group interviews, each lasting approximately ninety minutes, we explored many of the same themes as in the in-depth interviews but had students relate those themes to the pictures they made of the campus.

In-depth interviews with fourteen teachers, three nonteaching staff (two security guards and a school counselor), and two administrators enabled us to gain a perspective on how adults on campus view youth and youth trouble and conflict while gaining a deeper sense of the intersection of adult biography with each informant's current work situation. As with the youth interviews, we sampled purposively and broadly, including "rookie" and "veteran" teachers; those in the mix with respect to school policy and those on the peripheries; and those teachers who, like Carol Robinson, "keep their ears to the ground" with respect to youth culture on campus and those who attempt "to tune out the noise." We interviewed nearly an equal number of men and women, again representing the demographic composition of the faculty: nine white staff, five Latino staff, and three African American staff. Interviews ranged from forty to ninety minutes. Teacher interviews began with biographical questions, specific questions about interactions with youth, specific questions about trouble and conflict among and with youth, and general impressions of the campus climate and structures. Administrator interviews focused on biographical questions and then on the history of NWHS, on specific administrative decisions regarding particular policies and formal procedures on campus, and then general impressions.

Focus group interviews in 2008 replicated as much as possible our procedures from a decade earlier. The student focus group contained two sophomores, two juniors, and two seniors; was equally divided among male and female youth; and was representative of the demographic composition of the student population, with three Latinos, two white students, and one black student. The staff focus group contained five teachers and one administrator, equally divided among men and women, including two Latinos and one African American. Each focus group lasted approximately ninety minutes.

A technique we developed in the context of in-depth and focus group interviews of youth involved what we call "object-response interviewing." In this type of interviewing, we asked young people about the maps and photos they made and then used our discussion about the artifact as a means for accessing broader topics, including abstract and sensitive issues. Although not referred to as object-response interviewing, Bernard Harcourt used this strategy to discuss emotion and violence in the lives of incarcerated youth through their responses to photographs of guns that Harcourt supplied, and Philippe Bourgois used it to discuss social inequality and the "brutal facts shaping daily life on [the inner-city] street" through responses by young male drug dealers and users to drug paraphernalia.[2] Certainly the selection of objects in such interviews matters a great deal, and in our case so does the process of calling for their production, given that the choreography of these processes involves people differentially positioned in terms of power relations. Later in the appendix, we explain the process deployed to get students to photograph NWHS and write narratives about the imagery they captured.

Christine, Cynthia, and Michael used object-response interviewing in focus groups with participants in the photo-narrative exercise (of four to six students each, representing a cross-section of the photography class and skewed toward female students) in late 1999 with four questions guiding the discussion: Why did you take these pictures? Why did you take pictures of these people? Why did you take pictures of these places? What would you have liked to take a picture of but did not? The discussions ranged far beyond responses to these questions, revealing additional insights into youth sociospatial practices, perceptions of sociocultural diversity on campus, and the safe schools policies then just being adopted on campus.

We supplemented semistructured interviews with innumerable "conversational interviews" that occurred during the course of interactions with youth and adults on NWHS and with actors associated with the school both on and off campus. Conversational interviews occurred throughout our entire time in the field and proved especially important for our research during the first decade of the twenty-first century as we assessed our preliminary findings during the pre-safe schools era compared to what we found in the era of relaxed safe schools. We not only asked questions but also practiced "interviewing by comment," through which team members used a statement rather than a question to elicit information from a participant in the study. This technique stands somewhere between naturalistic "perspectives in action" by participants and "perspectives of action" expressed through responses to specific questions in semistructured interviews.[3] To be effective, interviewing by comment requires a great deal of contextual knowledge so as not to offend or confuse a participant, especially in older adult-youth interactions. However, in some instances when fieldwork team members experienced slight, unintended social awkwardness from an interview-by-comment, unpacking what happened with both the participant and later with the fieldwork team led to useful insights.

Youth-Authored Trouble Cases

Youth-authored trouble cases provided glimpses into the imaginations of youth as represented in their own words, reflecting the rich storytelling we encountered on the NWHS campus and evident in many other settings where youth cultures are practiced.[4] Our approach drew from techniques used to study the sociocultural and legal contours of decision making in everyday conflict among adults and frontline workers in public organizations.[5] We collected written trouble cases from ninth graders because of the particular social and cognitive challenges faced by youth as they transition from middle- to high school and pursued a smaller sample of twelfth graders for comparison.[6]

Specifically, we collected two sets of youth-authored trouble cases from ninth graders taking first-semester required English classes in 1997 and 1998 and followed that up in 1999 by collecting a smaller sample youth-authored cases from students in twelfth grade required English classes.

Team members administered the exercise with a brief introduction from a teacher that students would later be analyzing some subset of the youth-authored cases as part of a literature assignment. Students responded to a prompt that instructed them to "write a story about trouble or conflict that you experienced with another student, including who was involved, where it happened, and what, if any resolution came of the situation." Participation in the exercise was voluntary; students who opted out could read as part of their regular weekly reading assignments. Students were further instructed not to mention any personal names (some did anyway) and not to identify themselves (some did anyway). Of the 606 students in the ninth grade English classes in which we fielded the exercise, 526 participated (87 percent response rate), and of the 71 twelfth graders, 51 participated (72 percent response rate).[7] Taken together, these procedures yielded 497 and 42 codable narratives from ninth and twelfth graders, respectively. We dropped 29 and 9 cases, respectively, from the ninth and twelfth grade samples because they were either unintelligible or focused on actions prior to high school. We did not discern any systematic demographic differences between the youth who authored cases that we dropped from the sample and those whose narratives we included.

Sketch Map and Photo-Narrative Exercises

We designed another set of data collection strategies to acquire students' visual representations of NWHS, specifically their sketch maps and photographs. Our mapping exercise emulated methods in previous research used to understand how youths and adults see and use the physical and social contours of their worlds.[8] We sought maps drawn by eleventh graders because they were well embedded in the school, possessed a temporal lens of its social geography, and likely had the greatest range of connections to other grade levels below and above them. Participants drew maps on blank sheets of paper, seeking to maximize our ability to see the ways they draw the physical and social spaces of the campus as their places.

During the fall of 1998, we drew our samples for these exercises from required English classes because they are the most representative of the demographics in the school. Students wishing to opt out of the exercise were given the opportunity to read or catch up on other assignments. Typically with teachers not present, we asked students to "draw the places they know well on campus and place themselves and the social groups on their maps that they typically see during free periods." The exercise yielded 114 maps for analysis. At the conclusion of the mapping exercises, Cal and Michael administered the open-ended question on social trust (reported in chapter 2). Cal also engaged in object-response conversational interviewing with youth about their maps, yielding additional insights into how youth made sense of space and peer relations on campus. As part of the 2008 focus group, we replicated the mapping exercise from 1998 and discussed how the school works for students.

A second visual data set emerged from the photo-narrative exercise designed by Cynthia and Raul Flores, a teacher with strong student ties who planned to teach an elective photography class. Our idea was that the photos would not simply illustrate material aspects of the campus but would, rather, potentially yield analytic insights into peer relations, space, and trouble on campus.[9] Cynthia approached the team about Mr. Flores's willingness to engage the students in a group photography project related to our inquiry in exchange for receiving financial support to develop an outlet for exhibiting the photographs. Michael and Cynthia conveyed the ideas for a photography project in an email to Mr. Flores:

To: Miguel Flores
Fr: Michael Musheno and Cynthia Bejarano
Re: Commissioning a Photo-Essay Exhibit
Date: 02/17/99

Dear Mr. Flores–

We hope you are well!
We're writing about an idea for a project related to the youth study that we think you and your students might be interested. We're interested in observing the school setting through the "eyes" of students, and would like to capture what their perceptions are of everyday life at school. One way we've thought of doing this to have the students make photos of what school life means to them, and provide them with cameras to use throughout the school day. Our hope is that they will photograph people and places that are important to them. In addition to the students' photos, it would be helpful to have them include a brief essay summary of why they took a particular picture and what it means to them. Perhaps more importantly, we would like them to title the photo in a way that provides insight into how and what the student sees in the picture.

All the best,
Michael Musheno and Cynthia Bejarano

Twenty-four students participated in the class project in the spring of 1999, producing over two hundred black-and-white photos. Students curated the photos for the ones they found most meaningful and wrote titles and a brief essays about what each selected photograph meant to them. Some students wrote their narratives and titles in both Spanish and English. Drawing on the resources of a local university, a group of photographs and accompanying narratives selected by Mr. Flores, Cynthia, and Michael were professionally enlarged, framed, mounted and displayed in a community exhibit in late 1999 at the university research center where the youth conflict team was based. Soon after, a staff person at the center developed an electronic version of the photo-essay exhibit, placing it online.

Archival and Institutional Data

Michael sampled yearbooks every five years to collect information on student demographics (for years prior to when official information was available from the NWHS and the district) and the presence and activities of student clubs over a century of the school's operation. He also added to this information a review of the school newspaper, beginning in the 1940s, for evidence of student club activities on campus and student club diaries, a few of which were stored in the campus administrative offices. Finally, drawing on the historical records of the city, Michael collected local governmental documents and stored newspaper articles about NWHS to help corroborate information about key events in the school's history, such as the founding of the first student clubs on campus, the near-closing of the school in the 1980s, and the renewal of the school in the 1990s. Cal and Michael together used this information to construct an archive of collective civic action on and around campus over the century during which the school has been in operation. Christine complemented this evidence with data from her dissertation about changes in the official governance of the school over the past half-century.[10] Cal constructed an additional small online archive of publicly accessible NWHS student websites and social media posts, 2003 through 2013.

Campus-related police call data, covering 1995–2010, came directly from the New West Police Department. Michael also conducted interviews with the dispatchers, departmental analysts, and field officers who took and handled most of the calls during the first five years of safe schools at NWHS, 2001–2005, and who had high familiarity with the school during the duration of our study. These interviews focused on the types of people making the calls (students or adults) and the circumstances of the call (an incident in progress or one that that was reported to the caller by another person).

Online institutional data included (1) official data on NWHS student demographics from 1990 (when this data was first made available online) to 2013; (2) documents from the NWHS and New West School District websites, 1999–2008, concerning relevant school activities and notices; and (3) obituaries and other notices in local newspapers to provide background information for actors in the early years of the school that we identified through the *River* yearbooks.

Data Analysis

The challenge of analyzing the multiple data streams we amassed was twofold: We needed to develop a strategy for processing evidence within *and* across different data sets. Our overall approach to coding was iterative and recursive as we pursued answers to research questions with which we entered the field and developed while in the field and through comparative data analysis. This analytic strategy resonates with qualitative "abductive analysis," described by Stefan Timmermans and Iddo Tavory, which occupies a middle ground between purely inductive analysis (building theory from the ground up without a priori theoretical commitments) and deductive analysis (exploring research questions or testing hypotheses strongly framed by existing theory). In abductive analysis, the coding and recoding of fieldwork evidence occurs in the dynamics of both preexisting and evolving theoretical goals, as well as revisiting multiple kinds of data, which can lead to unexpected and alternative explanations for the patterns observed.[11] We pursued this strategy operationally through first *intradataset coding* that keys on particular data sets and then by *transdataset coding*, through which we used the same coding categories across different data sets. With regard to trans-dataset coding, we engaged in two coding logics. The first searched for continuities across data sets, which is a hallmark of triangulation, and a second was attentive to discontinuities, which is a hallmark of analytic induction whereby one searches for negative cases to revise one's emerging propositions.[12]

Our initial intradataset coding efforts centered on the observational fieldnotes generated as early as our first few months in the field. As is standard in most ethnographic fieldwork, Cal, Cynthia, Jerlyn, and Michael began reading the fieldnotes as a data set during our first months in the field and open coding them.[13] Using the qualitative data analysis software "The Ethnograph," we developed an initial mixed typology of emic and etic codes with the following master categories: (1) types/issues of trouble; (2) trouble responses; (3) types of actors (adults or youth); (4) types of peer relations; (5) social identities of actors; (6) places on and off campus; (7) trust (added after our short survey on "how the school works for you," encompassing interpersonal, intergroup, place, and institutional); and (8) time (day, week, and point in the academic year; duration of a social process). We also began constructing ethnographic trouble cases, adding detail to the cases as we continued our fieldwork. Information for ethnographic trouble cases not corroborated by at least two sources was placed in files linked to the cases awaiting further verification. With Christine working as the project's data manager, she and Cynthia used our initial coding as a way to begin gaining a wide-angle sense of what data we had collected and plan for future field visits. Quite early in our analysis, we noted that youth handled everyday trouble on campus quite contrary to dominant representations of high-poverty youth practices, often pushing away from intimidation, aggression, and violence without the direct involvement of adults.

As our fieldwork continued, we began a more intensive effort to code the first wave of youth-authored cases because we believed this data offered opportunities for understanding how youth retrospectively make sense of their reasoning strategies in handling peer trouble and conflict, as well as offering us a less capacious data environment than the fieldnotes in which we could begin making initial statements about preliminary findings. We deployed some of the coding categories emerging from the open coding of our ethnographic fieldnotes, but we approached the youth-authored cases as narratives, per se, and our efforts resulted in a publication that coded the youth-authored cases for their "narrative style," which provides insight into how youth understand their decision making in managing peer conflict.[14] That typology laid foundations for the repertoire of trouble responses and normative orientations that youth constitute in their daily management of peer trouble as depicted in this book.

Cal and Michael revisited the initial coding categories with the additional ethnographic and other data they collected in the first decade of the twenty-first century and settled on the tripartite trouble-response repertoire of workin' it out (conciliatory-remedial responses), puttin' 'em in their place (moralistic responses), and dealing with the system (rule-oriented responses), which enabled analysis of trouble responses across both types of cases—observed and youth-authored. We used this scheme to create conditional matrices from our original coding scheme, paying particular attention to how the repertoire varied by youth relationships, space on/off campus, social identity, and time. Finally, we constructed a visual schematic, specifically what we call a trouble string, which captures the sequencing and clustering of trouble responses and then constructed trouble strings for all the cases.

As noted in chapter 3, we developed a coding system for visually representing trouble strings that enabled us to decompose each case into the interactional sequences through which youth and adults handled trouble. Each node in a string represents a particular trouble response. The shape of the node—circle for conciliatory-remedial, triangle for moralistic, or square for rule-oriented—represents the normative orientation of the trouble response. The numerals within nodes represent the positioning of a trouble response in a string. A horizontal line between nodes represents a transition from one trouble response or cluster to another. A larger node represents a critical turning point in a string. A shadowed node above a string represents a potential trouble response mentioned by a participant that did not occur. Horizontally intersecting nodes represent trouble responses that overlapped interactionally. Vertically intersecting nodes represent trouble responses with multiple, simultaneous normative orientations. The letters within nodes correspond to third-party involvement ("YT" for youth third parties or "AT" for adult third parties) or a geographical move from where the trouble first emerged ("G"). In chapter 3, we presented and discussed an example representative of trouble strings in which conciliatory-remedial orientations predominated. Below, we offer two more examples: the first from a representative ethnographic case discussed in chapter 5 in which moralistic responses predominate (figure A.1) and the second from a representative ethnographic case discussed in chapter 6 in which rule-oriented responses predominate (figure A.2).

To ensure coding consistency with regard to trouble responses and strings, Cal and Michael conducted two different assessments of reliability, approximating standard procedures typically used in large, team-based qualitative coding projects.[15] The first assessment focused on coding trouble responses, using pairs of UC Berkeley graduate and undergraduate sociolegal students, respectively, as coders. Cal and Michael, together with three pairs of student coders (four undergraduate and two graduate students), analyzed twenty segments of text from ethnographic and youth-authored cases (representing 10 percent of the ethnographic and 2 percent of the youth-authored cases) that contained a broad range of trouble responses culled from ninth and twelfth grade cases.

Cal and Michael included themselves as a coding pair because they subsequently performed the bulk of coding. Together, they achieved near perfect agreement in their coding of the segments, and the student pairs

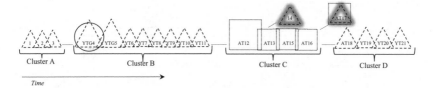

Figure A.1. Trouble string for trouble case 5.4, "Jumped In"

Key

1 –	moralistic/hostile accusation ("taking" the pendant)
2 –	moralistic/hostile accusation ("bitch")
3 –	moralistic/exit ("hung up")
YTG4 –	conciliatory-remedial and moralistic/lumping and physical fight ("letting it slide" and "beat down")
YTG5 –	moralistic/hostile accusation ("thief and whore")
YT6 –	moralistic/hostile denial ("liar bitch")
YT7 –	moralistic/nonverbal threat ("got in her face)
YT8 –	moralistic/third-party partisan support ("jumped in")
YT9 –	moralistic/ ("What's your fuckin' problem?!")
YT10 –	moralistic/physical fighting (blows to the face and flinging to the ground)
YT11 –	moralistic/physical fighting (kicking in thigh and torso)
AT12 –	rule-oriented/third-party settlement (security guard intervenes)
AT13 –	rule-oriented/third-party discipline ("interviews" with the principal)
14 –	moralistic/verbal threat ("I'm gonna give him a beat down too")
AT15 –	rule-oriented/third-party discipline ("disciplinary hearings")
AT16 –	rule-oriented/third-party discipline ("group hearings")
AT17 –	moralistic and rule-oriented/third-party violent discipline ("whip my ass")
YT18 –	moralistic/accusation ("disappointment and sadness")
YT19 –	moralistic/exit ("don't want to be friends with fighters")
YT20 –	moralistic/exit ("needed to get with some sane people")
YT21 –	moralistic/exit ("need to be with people who aren't so into drama")

among themselves achieved a 0.81 Cohen's kappa coefficient. We met with the students and discovered that the disagreements between Cal and Michael's coding, on the one hand, and the students, on the other, principally arose from classifying particular phrases differently. For example, what the students sometimes coded as "talking it out," Cal and Michael deemed "hostile accusations." By teasing out these differences, we discovered that in some instances, Cal and Michael read emotional expressions of mild anger present in ethnographic and youth-authored cases as evidence of a "hostile accusation." We used this information to modify our coding rules, limiting coding hostile accusations to situations in which a claim that someone has actually done something wrong is made rather than merely implied by the emotions present. Interestingly, we were pleased to find that all coding pairs could make reliable inferences about subtler behaviors, such as "temporary avoidance" or "deflection." The second reliability assessment occurred less formally with regard to coding the trouble

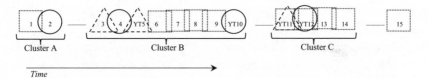

Figure A.2. Trouble string for trouble case 6.2, "Mrs. Lopato, Alanza, and the *Payasos*"

Key

1 –	rule-oriented/non-compliance ("No comprendo . . .")
2 –	conciliatory-remedial/coping (. . . barely paused and then simply spoke a little louder . . .)
3 –	rule-oriented/resistance ("¡Orale!")
4 –	conciliatory-remedial/coping
YT5 –	moralistic/covert accusation (whispering *payaso*)
6 –	rule-oriented/nonverbal discipline (giving the "look")
7 –	rule-oriented/resistance (periodic disruptions)
8 –	rule-oriented/nonverbal discipline (giving the "look")
9 –	rule-oriented/resistance (periodic disruptions)
YT10 –	conciliatory-remedial/self-directed changes (reading the text)
YT11 –	moralistic and rule-oriented/command ("¡Cálmate!")
YT12 –	conciliatory-remedial and rule-oriented/third-party friendly support and active compliance (nonverbally affirms support for teacher)
13 –	rule-oriented/nonverbal discipline (giving the "look")
14 –	rule-oriented/active compliance (participation and no further disruption)
15 –	rule-oriented/verbal discipline (what they did in class should not occur in hers or any other class they attend; "*No de nuevo en esta o en cualquiera otra clase*")

strings. Cal produced a document with all ninety-four ethnographic cases coded as trouble strings (sequences of trouble responses). He and Michael then discussed the string coding, coming to agreement on the sequencing and clustering of trouble responses. We used a similar approach with regard to coding the youth-authored cases as strings but because of their large number randomly selected a ten percent subsample to discuss coding inconsistencies.

Our analyses of the sketch maps involved two phases. First, early in the first decade of the twenty-first century, Cal and Mary Nell Trautner, then a doctoral student in sociology at the University of Arizona, developed a coding scheme for analyzing the maps as a whole and the identity labels placed on the maps by youths. They then grouped the identity labels from each individual map into areas identified by students (i.e., downtown, refuge, or fields) to gain a sense of their spatial distribution on campus. Cal revisited the coding scheme and conducted a reliability analysis with UC Berkeley and UC Irvine undergraduate students who coded the labels for their identity groupings and location on campus. Cal selected a 20 percent random sample of identity labels and achieved a 0.93 Cohen's kappa with regard to the identity grouping labels and a 0.88 Cohen's kappa with regard to spatial coding.

As Cal and Michael returned to NWHS for more embedded ethnographic observations and interviewing in 2008, they revisited the team's initial understandings of the 1999 October Fight, which had, as discussed in chapter 7, called into question what we believed we knew about youth conflict at NWHS. We used the Fight as a point of departure for engaging in a deep, retrospective analysis of our evidence—what we call an "ethnographic archaeology"—in light of our observations of the school in the years since the occurrence of the fight. In some sense this term resonates with what Michel Foucault means by the "archaeology of knowledge," which involves the examination of historically discursive traces (texts) in archives to understand power and disciplinary relations in the past and present.[16] More relevant to our approach is abductive analysis and historical contextualization through which we sought to understand the "deviant" case of the Fight in light of the broader history of the school and how it transformed in the twenty-first century.

This "dig" compelled us to re-examine data streams we knew well and explore those we had not fully engaged previously, particularly the social maps and photographs. Taken together, these visual images deepened not only our sense of what we came to call anchored fluidity, but also our sense of the school as a disrupted place where both physical spaces and disciplinary practices had undergone an abrupt transformation with regard to official channels of power and discipline, beginning in late 1999. The maps contain a range of students' vantage points with respect to this disruption and the persistence of the spatial components of anchored fluidity. Although we first focused our attention on the sociospatial maps, which yielded the identity labels, some of the most interesting maps, such as the example in chapter 7, do not represent the physical environs of the school in any literal way but are quite instructive as to how students began to see safe schools modifications to the campus.

Our ethnographic archaeology also reconnected us with Christine's dissertation work on the temporal evolution of the legal, disciplinary, and control apparatus employed at NWHS.[17] The account we offer in chapter 7 for why the Fight occurred departed from the gang-centered account offered by the administration and the pure ethnic tension perspective offered by some youth. Our account built on the insights of both youth and security guards regarding the linkages between the changes afoot on campus and the Fight, and insights from a nexus of literatures that focus on institutional arrangements of power as they are enacted, sustained, and altered by ongoing local relations and social movements.

Through the lens of the Fight as an organizational accident, we began to tease out how the transformation to the campus disrupted the everyday ways youth imagine and act on conflict. It is also through this lens—as well as the long view afforded by our longitudinal engagement with NWHS—that we were able to link everyday experience on campus with broader institutional transformations of punitive control aimed at youth. Thus, our archaeology revealed the power relations implicated in the tacit knowledge of youth and adults that undergird everyday practices and discourses on campus with the logics, ideas, and architectures of the safe schools movement.

With this new perspective and our focus on the question of why the Fight occurred, some data sets took on greater significance than we had previously afforded them, such as the quick-response, open-ended survey on how NWHS "works" for students and the observations in the early to middle years of the first decade of the twenty-first century by Cal and Michael. The former data pointed strongly to the campus as a contested place of trust while the latter pointed to a school under siege, so to speak, by a disciplinary regime both undermining everyday sociospatial practices, particularly anchored fluidity, and tilting toward social distrust. Our discovery that the disciplinary regime had taken hold of NWHS in the early to middle years of the first decade of the twenty-first century in turn provided a baseline for ultimately allowing us to see that the school had experienced a relaxation of safe schools control during 2005–2008 with a successive change in administration. Although we found evidence that the repertoire of trouble responses and anchored fluidity had reemerged in the latter half of the first decade of the twenty-first century, our final round of fieldwork also compelled us to better understand the historical contexts of our research in the late 1990s, as well as the safe schools period and its subsequent relaxation on campus.

Consulting with Participants

We consulted with participants during all periods of our fieldwork to assess the validity of our inferences via member checks. Such consultations can be useful to manage potential observational and interpretive errors and to place evidence in contextualized frames of reference.[18] At NWHS, such checking occurred through interviewing-by-comment moments in conversational interviews with both youth and adults when a researcher would interject a vernacular term (e.g., "hustlin'" or "workin' it out") to see whether and how a student would react to the researcher's usage. In most instances, such checks did not elicit clarifying comments from youth or adults, although in some instances we gained a deeper understanding of the meanings of a term or how the meaning had changed since we first picked it up in our fieldnotes or interviews. Consultations with youth and adults proved particularly useful with regard to particular events, such as the October Fight, as we gathered and informally assessed different narrative accounts about what happened and why. Consultations also proved useful with regard to our archival data, since as late of 2013, when we were near the end of our fieldwork, there were still staff on campus whose direct experience spanned multiple decades of the school's operations.

Writing

For the past three decades, sociological and anthropological fieldworkers have recognized and reflected on the importance of ethnographic writing at every stage of fieldwork.[19] Writing is the means of representing both what one has learned in the field and how one has made sense of it. At the heart of any ethnographic fieldwork project are field jottings and fully realized fieldnotes. For solo fieldworkers, such notes can take on an idiosyncratic, almost diary-like aura and appear in many different forms.[20] The idiosyncrasies of such experiences can certainly be represented in different ways, but they must be accessible in a team fieldwork context to team members who have had similar and different experiences in the field. Along these lines, members of the fieldwork team agreed to organize fieldnotes into a tripartite structure. "Observational" notes consisted of "tellings of the day's experiences and observations in the field . . . perhaps telling about an interaction, next transition to a different location, now sketching in the scene of the new context."[21] Of particular importance in observational notes was providing interactional detail among people and groups and the words they use to describe their actions to each other. Because members of the fieldwork team were positioned systematically over long periods of time at different places, times, and events on- and off campus, observational notes provided both in-depth looks at particular episodes of interaction and panoramic views. Fieldworkers also included asides and commentaries in their notes, which we dubbed "analytic notes," that expressed early inferential hunches of the meaning of what was being observed, sometimes linking those observations with other events. Finally, fieldworkers included what we called "methodological notes" about how tactics used in the field to position one's self for observation or comments used in conversational interviewing either constrained or yielded various streams of evidence. Included in methodological notes were reflections of how one's social identity limited or facilitated interactions and observations, including how it might affect the hunches expressed in the fieldworker's analytic notes. We also encouraged each other to include impressionistic or confessional emotional responses to what was observed, which could appear throughout fieldnotes.[22] The longer we stayed in the field, the more we agreed that representations of our personal experiences might be more useful as a reflective and reflexive commentary on what we had represented in our observational notes. We recognized the potential distancing of the "knower" from the "known" that this strategy might unintentionally produce, but it enabled us to interrogate more effectively the role of fieldworkers' situated experiences in the field and on the team in shaping our evidence.

Our team approach meant that our fieldnotes immediately entered into the "negotiated order" of the fieldwork team—a working set of contingent agreements around our roles and tasks on the project.[23] As noted in chapter 1, Cal and Michael led the group and made a number of key decisions regarding the project, articulating these decisions with a series of negotiated agreements among all members on the team. At the center of this negotiated order were "interpretive zones" that enabled the team to process changing conditions in the field as represented in fieldnotes and other written documents, including developing modes of inquiry that we could not have anticipated individually at the outset of the research project.[24] The team carried with it a built-in capacity for reflexivity that compelled us to evaluate how our individual and collective identities shaped our positioning in the field and the inferences we made about our fieldnotes.

Because we recognized our notes as representations of complex social worlds, we remained conscious of where we collectively and individually stood, so to speak, and how this influenced what we saw and inferred. We interrogated each other on these differences in the negotiated order formed by our face-to-face meetings, analytic memos that raised empirical questions and developed theoretical leads. These dynamics enabled group and solo publications with very different intellectual orientations.[25] And two members of the team drew on material collected by the fieldwork team and their analytic memos to write doctoral dissertations.[26]

In turning to the writing of this manuscript, we, Cal and Michael, wrote dozens of analytic memos back and forth to each other that first focused on particular data sets and then added evidence, in a stepwise fashion, to integrate insights from the analyses of the fieldnotes, youth-authored cases, interviews, maps and photos, and archival and institutional data. Interspersed with our memos were various intra- and transdataset coding projects. In this way, our memos became the lynchpins that both reflected and guided transdataset analyses as well as further data collection in the archives and with the New West Police Department. Ultimately, we linked our memos together and formulated conference papers and presentations made at multiple universities and academic conferences. The feedback we received both aligned with our ideas and sometimes pushed back, causing us to reformulate our thinking.

The writing of this manuscript proceeded as much ethnographic writing does—linking our research questions that evolved over the course of the project with evidence-centered fieldnote excerpts and other slices of textual and visual evidence.[27] We wrote this manuscript holding to the goal of producing a unified authorial voice between us. Our authorial voice ultimately went where the evidence we amassed, analyzed, and triangulated took us, with much of it emerging from the bottom up (through the many voices of youth and adults across time) while giving close attention to a wide range of scholarship that we think adds perspective to what we discovered in the field.

Generalizability

We are confident in our findings. But we are well aware that an oft-mentioned weakness of case studies is their lack of generalizability. From a conventional, positivistic social science perspective, the findings from a single social context, process, network, or place, whether bounded or not, cannot be considered representative of an underlying population.[28] In chapter 1, we briefly lay out features of the campus that appear similar and different from most high-poverty public high schools in the United States. These qualities render NWHS particularly intriguing for reopening discussion of attributes common to public schools whose students come from poor neighborhoods. It also is a strategic site for encouraging study of those attributes, however contested, that are important for creating schools that work, places where supportive formal control and trust are evident. More broadly, the generalization critique offers an unsatisfying metric for judging case studies, especially relational case studies, because of their other virtues.

Among the chief virtues of case studies is a deep contextualization that enables researchers to identify potential mechanisms of contingency and context and the roles that firsthand experiences with local meaning and practices play in constituting such mechanisms.[29] The identification of such mechanisms, like anchored fluidity, and their relation to context, in this case to the maintenance and creation of social trust, may be especially important in attempts to transfer case study findings from one setting to another.[30] Relational case studies may be especially useful in this regard because they focus on relationships among actors, groups, organizations, places, and fields. Matt Desmond argues that rather than conventional generalization, relational ethnographic studies should seek to "connect all parts of a [social] system unique to the specific contexts of the field-work."[31] In some sense, this methodological directive evokes what Howard Becker calls "breadth . . . trying to find out something about every topic the research touches on, even tangentially."[32] In our study, connection and breadth meant an expansionary effort to uncover the full array of mechanisms that young people used to manage peer trouble and conflict, and then linking those mechanisms to school, a key place in which they interact, as well as to the local community and to broader fields in both contemporary and historical contexts.

Yet another potential contribution of case studies is their capacity to reveal how fundamental values and normative orders operate in empirical settings—in our approach, social trust or distrust—and how such values are realized, sustained, or interrupted, as well as their unanticipated consequences.[33] Case studies based on ethnographic observation over long periods of time, such as our study, also include opportunities for theoretical development, including extension, revision, and discovery because of the richness of the data they marshal and the openness to unexpected findings.[34]

Finally, ethnographically based case studies carry the possibility for expanding "the universe of human discourse," in Clifford Geertz's words, or what Richard Shweder calls representing "what it is like to be a differentially situated human being."[35] Young people create and navigate different, yet overlapping, social worlds with adults and are differentially situated relevant to them. Perhaps the greatest virtue of our research, then, is its capacity to enlarge the discursive space to meaningfully consider how young people from poor neighborhoods attempt to solve interpersonal problems in schools that were not designed with them in mind but which they have made their own.

Interview Guides

Topical Guide for In-Depth Youth Interviews

Sociospatial Relations

1   Tell me about some of the social groups you see hanging out on campus. Are they based on race, class, activities, clubs?

2   Where do you fit in on campus? Who do you hang out with? What do you do when you hang out?

3   Where do you hang out at school during lunch or free periods? Do you always hang out with the same people or does it depend on what you're doing?

4   When you first came to NWHS did you know older students? Why was this relationship important to you?

5   Is there a group or are there groups that other students recognize as at the top of the pecking order among students? If there is such a group, who are they? How did they get to the top?

Trouble

6   What kinds of situations are there on campus where people aren't getting along?

7   Can you think of a situation where you were not getting along with a group of students but later (in the year) you started hanging out with them? Can you give me an example from your experience without giving names? How was the trouble handled?

8   Have you ever been faced with a situation that might turn violent but didn't? If so, what happened? Why didn't it turn violent? How did you know what to do? How did you learn to do this? Did anyone tell you how do this? Did you observe it?

Relations with Adults

9   Do you know a teacher on campus that you respect? How did you get to know him/her? Why do you respect that teacher? Do students respect teachers in general? How do they show their respect?

Work and Neighborhood

10 Have you ever or do you currently work after school? If so, where? Why do you work? What does work mean to you?

11 What's your neighborhood like? Where are most of the people from who live there?

Topical Guide for In-Depth Faculty/Staff Interviews

Background

1 How long have you worked at NWHS? Where did you work before? What subjects have you taught? What positions have you held?
2 How did you come to be a teacher? What other interests do you have outside of being a teacher?
3 Did you go to school in New West? Did you go to NWHS? What was it like when you were growing up? In school?
4 What is life like at NWHS? What changes have you observed in the school since you've worked here? In the neighborhoods? In the students? In your colleagues?
5 How would you compare the culture at NWHS with other schools you know?
6 Would you want to attend NWHS today if you were choosing a high school? Why or why not? Would you choose NWHS for your children?

Students

7 How would you describe the students at NWHS?
8 How would you describe your relationship to students?
9 What do students talk about on campus? What interests them? What are they concerned about?

Trouble

10 Where do you see/hear trouble among students taking place on campus on a typical day? Are there "trouble spots" around the school?
11 What is the trouble usually about? Can you give me an example?
12 Are there "trouble students"? Can you give me an example?
13 How do youth typically handle peer trouble? Can you give me an example?
14 What was the worst conflict between students that you remember? What happened? Who was involved? Where did it take place? What did you do? Who else was involved (allies, back-up, vulnerability, school authorities, police)? While it happened, how did you feel? What was the immediate

outcome? (Educational moment? Suspension?) What was the long-term outcome? Is the situation ongoing?

15 When these situations occur, is there a protocol that you follow (e.g., confrontation, counseling, negotiation, mediation, unilateral punishment, group sanction)?

16 What was the worst conflict between a student and a teacher that you remember? (Repeat follow-up questions from #14 and #15.)

17 When do you think conflict is good? Bad? Can you give me an example?

Topical Guide for Youth Focus Group Interviews

Sociospatial Relations

1 Do you tend to stay in your groups most of the time, move across groups a lot, or some of both? If you're moving, tell us about that. Why do you move?

2 During free periods, do you sit in the same place every day? Move around campus?

3 When you and your friends are hanging out on campus, do you feel like you are being monitored? Who might be doing so, and why?

Trouble

4 What kinds of situations are there on campus where people aren't getting along?

5 Can you think of a situation where you were not getting along with a group of students, but later (in the year) you started hanging out with them? Can you give me an example from your experience without giving names? How was the trouble handled?

6 Is there disagreement over the "ownership" of particular places on campus? Are there normal "hang-out" spots that are contested by several groups? If so, how are they contested?

7 Have you ever been faced with a situation that could have turned violent but didn't? If so, what happened? How was violence averted?

8 Can you think of a situation when two groups of students that were not getting along started hanging out together later in the year? How did the situation change?

9 What about the opposite situation? Did two groups of students who typically hang out together end up separating during the year? Why did this happen?

Topical Guide for Faculty Focus Group Interviews

Students

1 What are the most important relationships you have with students?
2 How would you describe the relationships between students and teachers at NWHS? Has this changed at all during your time teaching here?
3 What are students talking about these days? What are they interested in? What concerns them?
4 How would you describe the students at NWHS?

Trouble

5 Where do you see/hear trouble taking place between students? Are there "trouble spots" around campus? What is the trouble usually about? How does the trouble usually get resolved? Can you give us an example?
6 During the fall of 1999, there was violent incident involving two groups of Latino students after which the school was locked down and police were called to campus. There were some significant student injuries and even the principal was slightly hurt. To your knowledge, have there have been any incidents of this magnitude since then? Could you describe them, if so?

Security and Surveillance

7 The NWHS campus, like a lot of schools in the state and country, underwent a dramatic transformation in the first part of the 2000s with respect to security, including physical changes and disciplinary practices. If you think back to those days, from your perspective, how did that transformation affect the way you dealt (or deal now) with students on campus? How did it affect you, particularly the way you view the campus and your place in it?
8 Has the student population changed over the last ten years, and if so, how? How have the demographic changes influenced safety and security on campus?

Trouble Issue and Response Aggregate Data

Table B.1   Focal trouble issues by trouble case sources

Source→ Focal trouble issue ↓	Youth-authored trouble cases	Ethnographic trouble cases	Row totals
"Drama"	44.53% (240)	38.29% (36)	43.60% (276)
"Beefs"	24.68% (133)	15.96% (15)	23.38% (148)
"System stuff"	14.66% (79)	27.66% (26)	16.59% (105)
"Racial stuff"	11.69% (63)	13.83% (13)	12.01% (76)
"Hustling" "Not paying up" "Rip-offs"	4.44% (24)	4.26% (4)	4.42% (28)
Column totals	100.0% (539)	100.0% (94)	100.0% (633)

Note: By percentage. Figures in parentheses are absolute frequencies of focal issues.
$X^2 = 4.876$; $df = 3$; $p < 0.20$.

Table B.2 Focal trouble issues by writer's ethnoracial identity in youth-authored trouble cases

Writer's ethno-racial identity → Trouble issue ↓	African American/ Black	Asian/Pacific Islander/Native American	Latino	White/ Anglo	Row totals
"Drama"	34.0% (35)	48.8% (21)	37.2% (68)	55.2% (116)	44.53% (240)
"Beefs"	21.4% (22)	37.2% (16)	22.9% (42)	25.2% (53)	24.68% (133)
"System stuff"	21.4% (22)	9.3% (4)	14.2% (26)	12.9% (27)	14.66% (79)
"Racial stuff" (with peers)	19.4% (20)	4.7% (2)	19.7% (36)	2.4% (5)	11.69% (63)
"Hustling" "Not paying up" "Rip-offs"	3.9% (4)	— (0)	6.0% (11)	4.3% (9)	4.44% (24)
Column totals	100.0% (103)	100.0% (43)	100.0% (183)	100.0% (210)	100.0% (539)

Note: By percentage. Figures in parentheses are absolute frequencies of focal issues. $X^2 = 54.8910$; $df = 12$; $p < 0.001$.

Table B.3 Focal trouble issues by writer's sex in youth-authored trouble cases

Writer's sex → Focal trouble issue ↓	Females	Males	Row totals
"Drama"	55.5% (158)	32.3% (82)	44.5% (240)
"Beefs"	8.4% (24)	42.9% (109)	24.7 (133)
"System stuff"	19.3% (55)	9.4% (24)	14.7% (79)
"Racial Stuff"	11.9% (34)	11.5% (29)	11.6% (63)
"Hustling" "Not paying up" "Rip-offs"	4.9% (14)	3.9% (10)	4.5% (24)
Column totals	100.0% (285)	100.0% (254)	100.0% (539)

Note: By percentage. Figures in parentheses are absolute frequencies of focal issues. $X^2 = 85.7805$; $df = 6$; $p < 0.001$.

Table B.4 Focal trouble issues by writer's grade level in youth-authored trouble cases

Writer's grade level → Focal trouble issue ↓	Ninth grade	Twelfth grade	Row totals
"Drama"	45.12% (222)	38.30% (18)	44.53% (240)
"Beefs"	24.39% (120)	27.66% (13)	24.67% (133)
"System stuff"	13.62% (67)	25.53% (12)	14.66% (79)
"Racial stuff"	12.60% (62)	2.13% (1)	11.69% (63)
"Hustling" "Not paying up" "Rip-offs"	4.27% (21)	7.14% (3)	4.45% (24)
Column totals	100.0% (492)	100.0% (47)	100.0% (539)

Note: By percentage. Figures in parentheses are absolute frequencies of focal issues. $X^2 = 10.9464$; $df = 4$; $p < 0.05$.

Table B.5 Trouble responses by youth-authored and ethnographic trouble cases

Source → Trouble responses ↓	Youth-authored trouble cases (case n = 539)	Ethnographic trouble cases (case n = 94)	Row totals
"Working it out" (conciliatory-remedial)	19.94% (661)	47.81% (557)	28.29% (1218)
"Puttin' 'em in their place" (moralistic)	62.14% (2059)	31.39% (252)	53.68% (2311)
"Dealing with the system" (rule-oriented)	17.92% (594)	20.80% (182)	18.03% (776)
Column totals	100.0% (3314)	100.0% (991)	100.0% (4305)

Note: Figures in cells are absolute frequencies of trouble responses. $X^2 = 243.2097$; $df = 2$; $p < 0.001$.

Table B.6 Focal trouble issues and responses in youth-authored trouble cases

Focal trouble issue → Trouble responses ↓	"Drama"	"Beefs"	"System stuff"	"Racial stuff"	"Hustling" "Not paying up" "Rip-offs"	Row totals
"Working it out" (conciliatory-remedial)	25.42% (367)	14.91% (134)	7.35% (33)	26.25% (105)	18.03% (22)	19.94% (661)
"Puttin' 'em in their place" (moralistic)	68.07% (983)	75.19% (676)	19.82% (89)	59.75% (239)	59.02% (72)	62.14% (2059)
"Dealing with the system" (rule-oriented)	6.51% (94)	9.90% (89)	72.83% (327)	14.00% (56)	22.95% (28)	17.92% (594)
Column totals	100.0% (1444)	100.0% (899)	100.0% (449)	100.0% (400)	100.0% (122)	100.0% (3314)

Note: Figures in parentheses are absolute frequencies of trouble responses. $X^2 = 230.5425$; $df = 8$; $p < 0.001$.

Table B.7 Focal trouble issues by trouble responses in ethnographic trouble cases

Focal Trouble Issue → Trouble responses ↓	"Drama"	"Beefs"	"System stuff"	"Racial stuff"	"Hustling" "Not paying up" "Rip-offs"	Row totals
"Working it out" (conciliatory-remedial)	67.33% (340)	56.29% (94)	39.13% (72)	47.47% (47)	11.11% (4)	47.81% (557)
"Puttin' 'em in their place" (moralistic)	23.76% (120)	30.54% (51)	19.02% (35)	23.23% (23)	63.89% (23)	31.39% (252)
"Dealing with the system" (rule-oriented)	8.91% (45)	13.17% (22)	41.85% (77)	29.30% (29)	25.00% (9)	20.80% (182)
Column totals	100.0% (505)	100.0% (167)	100.0% (184)	100.0% (99)	100.0% (36)	100.0% (991)

Note: Figures in parentheses are absolute frequencies of trouble responses. $X^2 = 150.9686$; $df = 8$; $p < 0.001$.

Table B.8 Trouble responses by writer's sex in youth-authored trouble cases

Writer's sex → Trouble responses ↓	Female	Male	Row totals
"Working it out" (conciliatory-remedial)	23.65% (399)	16.10% (262)	19.93% (661)
"Puttin' 'em in their place" (moralistic)	56.26% (949)	68.22% (1110)	62.14% (2059)
"Dealing with the system" (rule-oriented)	20.09% (339)	15.68% (255)	17.93% (594)
Column totals	100.0% (1687)	100.0% (1627)	100.0% (3314)

Note: By percentage. Figures in parentheses are absolute frequencies of trouble responses. $X^2 = 10.9267$; $df = 2$; $p < 0.01$.

Table B.9 Trouble responses in youth-authored trouble cases by writer's self-reported ethnic or racial identity

Writer's ethnoracial identity → Trouble responses ↓	African American/ Black	Asian/Pacific Islander/ Native American/ other	Latino	White/ Anglo	Row totals
"Working it out" (conciliatory-remedial)	20.91% (217)	29.35% (27)	20.77% (226)	17.43% (191)	19.93% (661)
"Puttin' 'em in their place" (moralistic)	62.13% (645)	50.00% (46)	61.67% (671)	63.59% (697)	62.14% (2059)
"Dealing with the system" (rule-oriented)	16.96% (176)	20.65% (19)	17.56% (191)	18.98% (208)	17.93% ·(594)
Column totals	100.0% (1038)	100.0% (92)	100.0% (1088)	100.0% (1096)	100.0% (3314)

Note: By percentage. Figures in parentheses are absolute frequencies of trouble responses. $X^2 = 2.2910$; $df = 6$; $p > 0.8$.

Table B.10 Trouble responses by principals' sex in ethnographic trouble cases

Principals' sex → Trouble responses ↓	Only males	Only females	Different sex	Row totals
"Working it out" (conciliatory-remedial)	40.91% (127)	46.81% (155)	52.00% (275)	47.59% (557)
"Puttin' 'em in their place" (moralistic)	36.36% (76)	34.04% (76)	28.00% (100)	31.93% (252)
"Dealing with the system" (rule-oriented)	22.73% (54)	19.15% (48)	20.00% (80)	20.48% (182)
Column totals	100.0% (257)	100.0% (279)	100.0% (455)	100.0% (991)

Note: By percentage. Figures in parentheses are absolute frequencies. $X^2 = 1.3934$; $df = 4$; $p > 0.08$.

Table B.11 Trouble responses by principals' ethnic or racial identification in ethnographic trouble cases

Principals' ethnoracial identification → Trouble responses ↓	Same	Different	Row totals
"Working it out'" (conciliatory-remedial)	60.15% (240)	53.55% (317)	47.59% (557)
"Puttin' 'em in their place" (moralistic)	25.06% (100)	25.68% (152)	31.92% (252)
"Dealing with the system" (rule-oriented)	14.79% (59)	20.78% (123)	20.48% (182)
Column totals	100.0% (399)	100.0% (592)	100.0% (991)

Note: By percentage. Figures in parentheses are absolute frequencies. $X^2 = 0.4250$; $df = 2$; $p > 0.50$.

Table B.12 Trouble responses by grade level in youth-authored trouble cases

Grade level → Trouble responses ↓	Ninth grade (case n = 497)	Twelfth grade (case n = 42)	Row totals
"Working it out" (conciliatory-remedial)	15.65% (461)	54.20% (200)	19.94% (661)
"Puttin' 'em in their place" (moralistic)	67.20% (1979)	21.68% (80)	62.14% (2059)
"Dealing with the system" (rule-oriented)	17.15% (505)	24.12% (89)	17.92 (594)
Column totals	100.0% (2945)	100.0% (369)	100.0% (3314)

Note: By percentage. Figures in parentheses are absolute frequencies. $X^2 = 68.1621$; $df = 2$; $p < 0.001$.

NOTES

CHAPTER ONE

1. Acland 1995; Devine 1996; Morrill, Yalda, Adelman, Musheno, and Bejarano 2000, 521–522; Bushman et al. 2016; Sánchez-Jankowski 2016, 2.

2. Zhang, Musu-Gillette, and Oudekerk 2016, v. The term "safe schools" is associated with two different meanings and movements that developed in the United States during the 1980s and 1990s and continue to the present day. The criminal justice–leaning safe schools movement focuses on the prevention of school crime and violence via carceral-like discipline and security policies. The sexual orientation and gender identity (SOGI) safe schools movement seeks to create inclusive spaces for all youth and reduce harassment of LGBTQ students in schools via direct interventions and training, as well as state and federal policies (Russell et al. 2016). The former movement grew out of collaborations in the 1980s among victim rights advocates in the field of criminal justice and parents and professionals in the field of education. The latter movement—organized through the Gay, Lesbian and Straight Education Network (GLSEN)—emerged among teachers and students in the field of education in the 1990s. The interplay between these two movements is beyond the purview of the present work, although their underlying logics appear to differ substantially. An instantiation of GLSEN, called the "Gay-Straight Alliance," began in the late 1990s at our focal research site, New West High School (NWHS). Our use of the term safe schools relates to policies implemented at NWHS that stemmed from the criminal justice–leaning safe schools movement, which we discuss in chapter 7.

3. The names of all NWHS students, staff, and school collectivities are pseudonyms.

4. Gottfredson 2001; Gottfredson et al. 2005; Chen 2008.

5. Anderson 1999a, 37; Horowitz 1983; Fagan and Wilkinson 1998; Mateu-Gelabert and Lune 2007; Jones 2010.

6. Jones 2010. See also, Morris 2015.

7. Anderson 1999a, 95–98.

8. Rios 2017, 48-49. He draws these conclusions from his study of an alternative school for educating urban youth who were unsuccessful in their local high schools or in trouble with the law. He found that youth had capacities to code switch and recognized the importance of education, but that the interactional and spatial contexts of the school brought out the worst in these young people.

9. Elliot, Hamburg, and Williams 1998; Sánchez-Jankowski 2008.
10. Sánchez-Jankowski 2008; Harding 2010.
11. Sánchez-Jankowski 2016. For an earlier take on similar dynamics, see Pinderhughes 1997.
12. Gottfredson et al. 2005.
13. Chen 2008, 303–4.
14. Ferguson 2000; Casella 2003; Rios 2011; Shedd 2015; Brown 2016; Morris 2015
15. Paulle 2013.
16. Casella 2003.
17. Crenshaw, Ocen, and Nanda 2015; see also Brown 2016 and Morris 2015.
18. Crenshaw, Ocen, and Nanda 2015, 28–34.
19. Emerson and Messenger 1977; Black 1976, 1993, 2011; Nader and Todd 1978; Black and Baumgartner 1983; Merry 1979, 1990; Morrill 1995; Emerson 2008, 2011, 2015; Danby and Theobald 2012. These developments also resonate with agentic perspectives on urban youth conflict that explore how young people of color avoid interpersonal street violence (Sharkey 2006; Dill and Ozer 2015).
20. Seron and Silbey 2004, 39; Llewellyn and Hoebel 1941.
21. Emerson 2015. Earl (2009) argues that the concept of "trouble" can apply across multiple levels of analysis, from the interactional to the institutional.
22. Black 1984, 4.
23. Felstiner, Abel, and Sarat 1980; Albiston, Edelman, and Milligan 2014.
24. Nader and Todd 1978; Black 1993.
25. Crosnoe and Johnson 2011; Emerson 2008.
26. Wästerfors 2011.
27. Although the concept of trouble string focuses on social interaction, it does not, strictly speaking, derive from Collins's (2004) idea of "interactional ritual chains," which consist of situated social interactions that mobilize emotion to produce group solidarity and symbols of group membership. Trouble strings can lead toward or away from solidarity and symbols of group membership dependent upon the sequences and contexts of the trouble responses enacted. The concept shares a sense of movement with the idea in physics of "strings," which refer to subatomic, fundamental objects without subparts that vibrate and move in different ways to give matter its ostensible character (Becker, Becker and Schwarz 2007). However, we do not conceptualize trouble strings as fundamental objects without subparts. On the contrary, linked trouble responses constitute trouble stings. The trouble string concept more directly resonates with the idea of meaningful lines of action, which refer to how people build and make sense of alternative activities through social interaction, contingent upon institutional and cultural contexts (Swidler 1986). We also draw from several processual approaches to social conflict, especially interactional perspectives on trouble (Emerson and Messenger 1977), anthropological perspectives on the disputing process (Nader and Todd 1978), and sociolegal approaches on the transformational processes of meaning through which people mobilize legal, quasi-legal, and extralegal mechanisms to settle disputes (Felstiner, Abel, and Sarat 1980). The concept of trouble string is particularly consonant with Emerson's (2015, 163) concept of "response cycle," although it differs somewhat in being especially sensitive to changes in types of trouble responses and interruptions both in social and geographical space. Our approach also draws from "social sequence analysis," which researchers use to understand the temporal pathways through which relational events unfold between individuals, organizations, and

fields (Abbott 1995). Black and Baumgartner (1983), Morrill (1995, 23), and Emerson (2015, 15) all discuss variations in and contingencies of bilateral and trilateral lines of action in trouble handling.

28. Emerson (2011) refers to these orientations as "conflict-resonant" and "deviant-resonant," respectively. Black (1976, 4–6) refers to normative orientations as "styles of social control," whereas Morrill (1995, 20–22) calls them "grievance schemas." On conciliatory orientations, see Black (1976, 4–6) and Horwitz (1990, 65–78). On orientations that move toward minimalistic responses, see Baumgartner (1988).

29. Emerson 2011; see also Katz 1988; Dunn and Schweitzer 2005; Collins 2008, 20.

30. More than fifty years of research has been devoted to this claim, including Macaulay 1963; Felstiner 1974; Black 1993; Nader and Todd 1978; Baumgartner 1988; Horwitz 1990; Morrill, Johnson, and Harrison 1998.

31. Fine 2001, 162–63; Adler and Adler 1998; Weiss and Fine 2000.

32. Garot 2009.

33. Black and Baumgartner 1983; Baumgartner 1988; Horwitz 1990, 65–78; Black 1993; Cooney 1998.

34. On parallel dynamics among adults, see Black and Baumgartner 1983; Cooney 1998.

35. On the emplacement of social conflict, see Sampson 2012, 2013.

36. Our use of the concept of climate encompasses traditional usages (e.g., Cohen et al. 2009) and resonates with interactional approaches to group cultures in organizations (Fine and Hallett 2014).

37. Nasir et al. 2013, 297.

38. Hall and Jefferson 1976; Hebdige 1979; Massey 1998; Venkatesh and Kassimir 2007; Jones 2009.

39. On trust as a positive ethos for school reform, see Bryk and Schneider 2002; on trust and school safety, see Williams and Guerra 2011; on trust as a cognitive basis for building durable interpersonal relationships and faith in institutions, see: Erikson 1968; Giddens 1991; Putnam 2000.

40. Harding 2010, 101; Scott 2008.

41. Hagan, Shedd, and Payne 2005; Harding 2010; Rios 2011; Shedd 2015.

42. Bejarano 2005.

43. Gottfredson et al. 2005.

44. Foucault 1977, 138; Harcourt 2001, 18–19, 162–63; Kupchik 2010, 38–39.

45. Sampson, McAdam, MacIndoe, and Weffer-Elizondo 2005; Sampson 2012, 184; Smith 2007.

46. Gordon 2010, 69–70; HoSang 2006.

47. These ideas in part play off intergroup contact theory first developed by Allport (1954) and more recently tested in a meta-analytic framework by Pettigrew and Tropp (2006). Allport's original idea was that intergroup social prejudice based on ethnicity or race can be reduced by interpersonal contact organized around equal status, common goals, collaboration, and the support of official authorities. Pettigrew and Tropp (2006) argue that these conditions are not necessary for the reduction of prejudice via social contact and can be extended beyond racial and ethnic prejudice.

48. Eliasoph 2012, 232.

49. Ibid., 233. On collective efficacy and collective civic action, see Sampson (2012, 179–209).

50. Putnam 2007; Seron 2016, 23.

51. On situational trust in urban settings, see Bell (2016).
52. Swidler 2001, 134.
53. Males 1999; HoSang 2006; Nasir et al. 2013.
54. Anderson 1999a; Harding 2010; Jones 2010; Paulle 2013; Rios 2011; Sánchez-Jankowski 2008, 2016.
55. To be FRL eligible, students must live in a household with a total income up to 130 percent of the poverty threshold (see www.fns.usda.gov/nslp/national-school -lunch-program-nslp/). The US poverty threshold for a household of four with two children under the age of eighteen in 1997 was $16,276 and in 2013 was $23,624 (see www.census.gov/hhes/poverty/data/threshold/).
56. Milem et al. 2013, 24.
57. Lawrence 2006, 1.
58. Snow and Anderson 1991, 152.
59. Desmond 2014.
60. Best 2007, 4.
61. Gerstl-Pepin and Gunzenhauser 2002, 139.
62. Snow, Morrill, and Anderson 2003; Lofland et al. 2005.
63. Eric Margolis (a sociologist of education) and William Fabricius (a developmental psychologist) participated as early members of the team. Eric and Bill soon stepped away from the project in 1998 to pursue other projects. Billy left the project in 1998 to continue with his PhD in anthropology, and Jerlyn left the project in 1999, when she completed her master's degree.
64. Kusenbach 2003.
65. Best 2007, 11.
66. Bonacich 1990, 449; Morrill 1995, 238.
67. Delgado 2006, 9; Best 2007.
68. Pink 2013, 96.
69. For a general review of intersectionality as it relates to social inequality and power relations, see Collins (2015).
70. On language and power, generally, see Conley and O'Barr (1998). Berrey (2015, 18) observes that "Through discourse, people with authority exercise power. Their conceptual categories, symbols, and linguistic devices enable them to control or limit others' actions."
71. Omi and Winant (2015, 105) describe this process as part of "racial formation"—the often confused, contradictory, and unintended ways of "defining racial groups" and racial hierarchies.
72. On the social construction of race and other social categories, see Obasogie (2014).
73. Compare Perry's (2002) observations on the "normalization" of "whiteness" in a white-dominated high school.
74. Based on US census data, Lee and Bean (2012) find "multiracial" identification is more common among those identifying as Asian, Latino, or white and less common among those identifying as black. Lee and Bean argue that this pattern not only points to a growing multiracial society but also to a growing black/nonblack divide in twenty-first-century US society.
75. On heteronormativity in US high schools, see Pascoe (2011).
76. We draw the term "neoliberal-paternal" from Soss, Fording, and Schram (2011), which we discuss in chapter 8.
77. Goffman 1983, 6.

CHAPTER TWO
1. Anderson 1999a; Astor, Meyer, and Behre 1999; Harding 2010; Sánchez-Jankowski 2008, 2016.
2. Adler and Adler 1998; Akerlof and Kranton 2002; Brown and Klute 2003; Bearman, Moody, and Stovel 2004; Massey 2005; Crosnoe and Johnson 2011, 445.
3. Whyte 1980, 24–53.
4. Goffman 1959, 110–12.
5. Adult staff members often attempted to create backstages to consult with youth about delicate matters.
6. Anderson 2011.
7. Anderson 1999a, 72.
8. The mapping exercise resembled "indigenous maps" that are drawn by indigenous peoples rather than emanating from sources of institutional authority (Chapin, Lamb, and Threlkeld 2005).
9. The term "sociospatial" derives from the work of urban sociologists who emphasize the interplay of social, cultural, and spatial features of everyday life (Gottdiener, Hutchison, and Ryan 2014). Maps not coded as sociospatial include what we call "symbolic" maps (n = 6), in which youth mix irreverence, anxiety, and uncertainty with critiques aimed at school authority, and "site" maps (n = 31) that suggest the solidity of geographical space and display draft-like details, without demarcating people, closest to the official orientation in figure 2.3.
10. Brown and Klute 2003.
11. Details on our coding procedures can be found in appendix A.
12. This example was recorded on a microcassette tape recorder.
13. Multiple researchers have studied the social constraints of gender, race, and ethnicity on relational fluidity among urban youth in and apart from schools. Sánchez-Jankowski (2008) demonstrates how relational fluidity among youth in urban schools varies by the historical demography of their surrounding neighborhoods. Harding (2010) finds that in disadvantaged neighborhoods youth can be constrained to close friends on the blocks where they grew up and whom they do not fear. Moody (2001) underscores how school structures that involve participants from different ethnic and racial peer crowds can lead to greater relational fluidity across sociocultural lines and more diverse friendship networks. Macleod (1987) finds little fluidity between groups of black and white working-class males, except under extraordinary circumstances.
14. Carter 2005.
15. Bejarano 2005, ix.
16. Moody 2001; Giordano 2003.
17. Carter 2012.
18. Twenty-one of the groups contain only male youth; twenty only female youth; and twenty-five both males and females.
19. Anderson (1999b) notes that being a part of an "own" can vary across situations and individuals and may not refer to homogeneous mindsets or collective interests.
20. Benton-Cohen 2009, 7; Gómez 2007, 4; Powers 2008, 470.
21. Powers 2008, 470.
22. Ibid., 470–71.
23. Faris and Felmlee 2011; West et al. 2010; Bushman et al. 2016.
24. Carter (2012, 9) adapts the concept of cultural flexibility ("stepping out of one's

skin") from Zerubavel (1991) who argues generally that minds that are flexible can lead to richer social lives and more tolerant societies.

CHAPTER THREE

1. Harding 2010.
2. On drama involving romantic relationships, see Marwick and boyd (2011).
3. Harding 2010, 101–2.
4. Pascoe 2011, 7.
5. Marwick and boyd 2011, 2 (see also boyd 2014, 128–52).
6. Marwick and boyd 2011, 5.
7. Harding 2010.
8. Sánchez-Jankowski (2008, 321) documents these processes in high-poverty areas of Los Angeles and New York. One could argue that NWHS youth might deny gang or turf defense to protect themselves and their peers. As we note elsewhere, gang members did attend NWHS, but our evidence leads away from significant gang involvement, per se, in trouble on campus.
9. Harding 2010, 18–19.
10. In this sense, system trouble involving race or ethnicity parallels the concept of "systemic" or "institutional racism" (Feagin 2006).
11. Rios 2011, 72–73.
12. McFarland (2001, 655) notes that at the beginning of school years, a high school classroom is an "uncertain terrain" on which teachers attempt to establish their control such that youth will focus primarily on academics. If that control is not established early on, teachers can face increasing disruptions and may have to use carceral-like tactics to gain back control.
13. See appendix A for details on data collection and coding of youth-authored and ethnographic trouble cases.
14. Morrill, Yalda, Adelman, Musheno, and Bejarano 2000. On institutional contexts and storytelling more generally, see Polletta et al. (2011).
15. On sociological narrative analysis, see Polletta et al. (2011).
16. Calavita and Jenness 2015, 187.
17. See table B.1 in appendix B. By focal, we mean the primary issue at stake in each story or case. In most youth-authored and ethnographic cases, we could easily identify focal issues. Where we could not easily do so, we consulted with youth and had multiple independent coders assess which issue was focal. For the purposes of this analysis, our coding resulted in a total of 633 issues, one for each youth-authored story and trouble case.
18. Anderson 1999a; Garot 2009; Milner 2004.
19. Pinderhughes (1997, 129) cites these figures from the 1990 "Study of High School Students and Educational Staff on Prejudice and Race Relations."
20. Fisher, Wallace, and Fenton 2000, 689. This study uses the "Adolescent Discrimination Distress Index" and is based on a purposive sample of 177 students in an "urban, ethnically diverse" high school with approximately equal distributions of youth identifying as "African American," "Latino," "of Chinese or Korean heritage," or "non-Latino white."
21. See table B.2 in appendix B. These categories preclude us from representing students who identify as "mixed" or with different Latino identifications. Qualitative data in subsequent chapters facilitate taking into account these subtleties.
22. Hagan, Shedd, and Payne 2005.

23. Morrill, Edelman, Tyson, and Arum (2010, 671) found in their multistate study of twenty-five urban high schools that 34 percent of black and 28 percent of Latino youth reported perceived racial discrimination by teachers.

24. See table B.3 in appendix B for details.

25. Adelman and Kil 2007; Brown and Klute 2003; Giordano 2003.

26. Of the fifty-five female students who wrote about system stuff, thirty-four (62 percent) wrote about academic issues and the rest about disciplinary problems. Of the twenty-four male students who wrote about system stuff, eighteen (75 percent) wrote about disciplinary problems and the rest about academic issues.

27. Crenshaw, Ocen, and Nanda 2015.

28. See table B.4 in appendix B.

29. On emotional linkages that tie persons, acts, and social control together, see Pasquetti (2013). While we benefit significantly from Emerson's formulation of "conflict-resonant" (2008, 2011, 2015), we do not refer to conciliatory-remedial responses as conflict-resonant because for youth and adults at NWHS (if not more generally in US high schools), "conflict" carries a meaning that pushes toward the moralistic and hostile, which is more akin to a "deviant-resonant" sense of trouble.

30. On relational work, see Zelizer (2012).

31. Emerson (2008, 493) identified this type of trouble response as a "self-directed change."

32. Emerson 2008, 500; Conley and O'Barr 1998, 84.

33. On the social functions of apology, see Tavuchis (1993).

34. On temporary avoidance, see Baumgartner 1988; Felstiner 1974; Morrill 1995.

35. We draw the concepts of the third-party partisan/supporter and third-party friendly peacemaker from Black and Baumgartner (1983).

36. In Hirschman's (1970) formulation, this moment is called "voicing," and in the dispute transformation model, it is referred to as "grievance expression" (Felstiner, Abel, and Sarat 1980).

37. This observation parallels Emerson's (2008, 486) regarding the conciliatory and remedial functions of interpersonal, dyadic responses to trouble.

38. Katz (1988) refers to this dynamic as "moral transcendence," which in its most extreme form is associated with moralistic homicide (Black 1983).

39. In this sense, "puttin' 'em in their place" resonates with Katz's (1988, 81–82) analysis of how "badasses" handle trouble.

40. Anderson 1999a; Harding 2010; Jimerson and Oware 2006; Jones 2010.

41. Scott 1990.

42. This process resonates with the classic idea of "exit" articulated in Hirschman (1970).

43. Rios (2011, 145–46) argues that youth who are channeled more toward the streets are not resentful of youth who want to do well in school. Tensions arise over schooling, on and off campus, between youth differently situated in relation to education due to adult actions. It is under these conditions that "snitching" takes place and where retaliation is likely. We did not observe these divisive practices at NWHS.

44. Ewick and Silbey 1998, 57–107.

45. Ibid., 134–37.

46. On resistance to bureaucratic power and law, see: Ewick and Silbey 2003; Morrill, Zald, and Rao 2003.

47. See table B.5 in appendix B.

48. In appendix B, see tables B.6 and B.7.
49. In appendix B, see tables B.8 and B.9 for youth-authored cases; see tables B.10 and B.11 for ethnographic cases.
50. The period covered is 1997–2000 (Robers et al. 2014, 96). Serious violent incidents are defined as "rape, sexual assault, robbery, and aggravated assault."
51. See table B.12 in appendix B for details. We also note that the length of youth-authored cases across the ninth (234 words) and twelfth grade (258 words) did not differ dramatically.
52. Crosnoe and Johnson 2011; Nasir, McLaughlin, and Jones 2009.
53. See Rios (2011) and Jones (2010) on how parents and other adult figures in high-poverty areas engage in both instilling positive values toward education and negotiating the dangers of the streets.
54. Freeman, Romney, and Freeman 1987, 322.
55. Harding 2010, 72.
56. This story was tape recorded with the student's oral consent.
57. Of the nine physical fights we uncovered during our fieldwork in 1997–2000, five occurred in moralistic-dominant strings and four in mixed strings. Of the six moralistic string fights, two ended with adult interventions to stop hostilities and four with such interventions as "mop-up operations" after much of the action had ended. One of the mixed string fights ended with adult intervention and the other two ended when the parties reconciled on their own.
58. Macaulay 1963; Black 1976; Nader and Todd 1978; Felstiner, Abel, and Sarat 1980; Morrill 1995; Morrill, Harrison, and Johnson 1998; Garot 2009; Emerson 2015.
59. Although we run the risk of left or right censoring in a trouble string—that is, that a string may not contain a complete set of responses that occurred before or after the represented string begins or ends—we are confident that our fieldwork adequately represents when trouble surfaces and when it dissipates (again, without necessarily a definitive resolution).
60. Anderson 1999a; Fagan and Wilkinson 1998.
61. Emerson and Messinger 1977; Fagan and Wilkinson 1998; Emerson 2015.
62. Emerson 2015, 163.
63. Wästerfors (2011) observes this tendency in the way male youth interweave "going concerns" like meals and classes into interpersonal disputes in a school for "troublesome boys."
64. Anderson 1999a; Fagan and Wilkinson 1998; Harding 2010; Jones 2010; Rios 2011.
65. Harding 2010.

CHAPTER FOUR

1. Anderson 1999a; Harding 2010; Jones 2010; Jimerson and Oware 2006; Stewart and Simons 2010.
2. Garot 2009; Harding 2010.
3. Putnam 2000, 136.
4. Roloff and Cloven 1990.
5. Jones 2010, 8–9.
6. Costa et al. 2014.
7. On social identity and in- and out-group dynamics, see Tajfel (1974). On in- and out-group dynamics and social conflict, see Pruitt and Kim (2004).
8. Harding 2010; Rios 2010; Papachristos, Hureau, and Braga 2013.
9. Black 1993.

10. Goffman 1967, 9–10.
11. Goth youth culture emerged in Britain during the early 1980s and made its way to the United States in the late 1980s and early 1990s, identified with a strain of post-punk music that popularized theatrical performances of music emphasizing dark costuming and other accoutrements, such as thick black eyeliner worn by both men and women (Brill 2007). Goth youth culture also came to be associated with various high school rampage shootings in the 1990s, although it is unclear, aside from a few of the white males involved in the violence dressing in all-black with other black adornments (e.g., eye liner, nail polish, tattoos, and piercings), what their relationship was to broader goth culture (Newman 2004).
12. Devine 1996; Kupchik 2010.
13. Cumming, Cumming, and Edell 1965.
14. Bell 2016.
15. On handguns as archetypical symbols of urban youth violence, see Harcourt (2001).
16. Some of the punctuated character of youth-authored cases may be an artifact of asking students to "write a story," which suggests a conventional chronological narrative with a beginning, middle, and end. That youth also conformed to similar senses of narrative in their oral stories outside the classroom suggests how deeply embedded such forms are in the imagination of youth.
17. Garot (2009) discusses the ambivalence and emotional dissonance that youth feel in the aftermath of engaging in moralistic violence against peers.
18. Felstiner 1974; Black 1976; Baumgartner 1988; Morrill 1995.
19. The dynamics described here also contrast those described by Merry (1979, 920) in which lower-income urban residents resorted to courts and more confrontational strategies first before engaging in avoidance, which carried high social costs in the tight-knit neighborhoods she studied. Under the conditions we describe at NWHS, the opportunities for temporary avoidance reduce its costs.
20. Kolb 1992, 64.
21. Duck 2010; see also Zelizer (2012) on relational work and Guerrero, Eloy, and Wabnik (1993) on relational maintenance.

CHAPTER FIVE

1. This approach to trust is analogous to what Anderson (1999a) calls "code switching" among young black men in inner-city Philadelphia or what Jones (2010) calls "working the code," which captures the challenges young women in inner-city Philadelphia face as they move between "good" and "ghetto" orientations. More generally, these dynamics refer to a subclass of interactional dynamics that Erving Goffman (1969) called "strategic interaction"—the calculative, game-like aspects of face-to-face communication and control.
2. Anderson 1999a, 97; Garot 2009, 76.
3. Katz 1988, 22.
4. Harding 2010; Jones 2010. Williams and Guerra (2011) report from a 2006–2008 survey of 7,299 youth in fifth, eighth, and eleventh grades in seventy-eight Colorado schools that lowered expectations among youth that adults and youth will intervene into problematic peer altercations in public is associated with rates of self-reported instances of "bullying perpetration."
5. Garot 2009, 83.
6. Anderson 1999a, 68–69.
7. Jackson-Jacobs 2013, 24; see also Katz 1988, 114–63.

8. Collins 2008, 350–51; see also Katz 1988, 114; Garot 2007.
9. Collins 2008, 19–20.
10. Under some conditions, the term "vato loco" (crazy dude) can refer to a male youth who is known as a particularly violent and somewhat unpredictable individual, hence someone to respect or even to seek out for protection from peer-based, interpersonal predation. In the NWHS context, "crazy" literally means someone who cannot be trusted and should be avoided as almost mentally ill.
11. Jimerson and Oware 2006, 46.
12. Jones 2010, 155.
13. Ibid., 154.
14. Ibid., 100.
15. Goffman 1961, 175.
16. Goffman 1963.
17. Merry 1983, 279, 296.
18. Jones 2010.

CHAPTER SIX
1. Durkheim 1903 [1961], 149.
2. Merry 1990, 142.
3. Galanter 1974.
4. Bumiller 1988, 82–83.
5. Jones 2010.
6. Bourdieu and Passeron 1977.
7. Rios 2011, 145.
8. Kupchik 2010, 178.
9. Barajas and Pierce 2001.
10. Crenshaw, Ocen, and Nanda 2015.
11. Rios 2011, 162.
12. Kupchik 2010, 178.
13. Morrill, Edelman, Tyson, and Arum 2010, 684; Welch and Payne 2010.
14. Crenshaw 1991; Best et al. 2011.
15. Goffman 1961, 304–5.
16. Nolan 2011, 119–34.
17. Gau and Brunson 2010; Venkatesh and Murphy 2007; Gilliom 2001; Conley and O'Barr 1990.
18. Rios 2011; Oberweis and Musheno 2001.
19. Ewick and Silbey 1998, 30–31.
20. Losen and Skiba 2010; Brown 2016; Morris 2015.
21. Morrill, Edelman, Tyson, and Arum 2010.

CHAPTER SEVEN
1. Jerlyn Jones and Billy Gray both had moved on to other pursuits by this time.
2. Brown and Gilman 1960.
3. Collins 2008, 73–82.
4. Yalda 2002
5. Lofland et al. 2005.
6. Molotch and Lester 1974, 109–10.
7. Although environmental disasters, such as Hurricane Katrina (Eyerman 2015), floods, earthquakes, or fires (Erikson 1976), are usually associated with collective

trauma, they also can occur as a result of wholly human-made catastrophes, such as financial crises, population change, wars, genocides, and national elections (Gross 2016; Onwuachi-Willig 2016). Collective traumas also are associated with shocks to social systems. Fligstein and McAdam (2012, 19–20) argue that such shocks can be destabilizing and interrupting, leading to intense "episodes of contention."

8. McEvoy 1999.
9. Garland 2002; Simon 2007.
10. Wacquant 2001.
11. Morrill, Yalda, Adelman, Musheno, and Bejarano 2000.
12. For example, the 2014 National School Safety Conference, organized by the School Safety Advocacy Council, occurred at Walt Disney World in Florida and featured a variety of speakers drawn from law enforcement focused on strengthening official responses to both rampage violence and everyday youth disruption in schools.
13. Harcourt 2001.
14. Simon 2007, 207–32.
15. Newman 1973; Casella 2006.
16. Kingery, Coggeshall, and Alford 1999; McEvoy 1999; Verdugo 1999.
17. As the safe schools movement gained momentum, American courts ironically focused on constraining the ability of teachers and administrators to exercise discipline (Arum 2005).
18. Trump (1998) summarized these features in his best-selling *Practical School Security*.
19. Laumann and Knoke 1988.
20. Simon 2007, 214–17.
21. Simon 2007, 207–32; Kupchik 2010, 13–41; Monahan and Torres 2010, 1–18.
22. Monahan 2010.
23. Casella 2006.
24. Agron and Anderson 2000.
25. Kupchik 2010.
26. Newman 2004; Bushman et al. 2016.
27. On institutionalized fields, see Meyer and Rowan (1977) and DiMaggio and Powell (1983).
28. In a taped interview with Michael, Charles Brennan, a senior analyst for the NWPD, explained the logic of these call categories: "Fights are basically understood as two people in mutual conflict, often prior to either being physical. So, fights are often related to events occurring or unfolding in real time. Assaults reference physical altercations that may be occurring in real time or that are later reported by a person who is a party to an altercation—as in 'I see two people hitting each other' versus 'I was assaulted earlier this evening.' Suspicious activity is a broader category and often requires the call taker to question a person closely about potential bias. For example, if a person living in a neighborhood that is white sees an African American riding their bike around in the neighborhood, the call taker may decide that the person is biased and give the call a very low priority. On the other hand, if a citizen says they are watching a Latino male walk down the street looking inside the windows of each parked car, the call taker may categorize the call as suspicious activity and enter a high-priority response. Incorrigible juvenile references a parent or someone responsible for a youth reporting difficulty with the youth as distinct from juveniles disturbing the peace, which refers to a third party seeing someone else's kid engaging in questionable behavior like kids throwing rocks at a passing train."

29. Yalda 2002, 300–301. Suspensions of students for "fighting/assaults/threats/weapon possession" did not evince any ethnoracial pattern.
30. Zimring 1998, 2014.
31. Schneider 2006. See also: Newman 1973; Musheno, Levine, and Palumbo 1978; Astor, Meyer, and Behre 1999.
32. Schneider 2006, 251. As such, CPTED advocates represented what Gans (2002, 329) calls "spatial determinism."
33. Schneider, Walker, and Sprague 2000, 222.
34. Lyons and Drew 2006, 42–44; Laub and Lauritsen 1998.
35. Foucault 1977.
36. Yalda 2002, 184.
37. Reiter 2016, 21.
38. Foucault 1977.
39. Yalda 2002, 126–27, 97–177, 218–45, 260–68. On the replication of these changes across the country, see: Nolan 2011, 19–38; Kupchik 2010, 13–41; Simon 2007, 207–32; Lyons and Drew 2006, 1–3.
40. Yalda 2002, 190–91.
41. Ibid., 193.
42. Ibid., 200–201.
43. Ibid., 201.
44. Ibid., 200–201.
45. Devine 1996; Sánchez-Jankowski 2008; Harding 2010.
46. Yalda 2002, 208.
47. Nacci, Teitelbaum, and Prather 1977; McCain, Cox, and Paulus 1980.
48. Ellis 1984, 301.
49. Ibid., 301–302.
50. Yalda 2002, 209.
51. Ibid., 207.
52. Sánchez-Jankowski 2008; Harding 2010.
53. Pinderhughes (1997) reveals the significance of adult attitudes and adult socialization of youth to interracial and ethnic violence among youth in urban neighborhoods of New York City. He also points to cultural buildup over time, or localized "cultural messages about the meaning of ethnic and racial differences" (16), and how such messaging can encourage both ethnoracial tolerance and intolerance.
54. Yalda 2002, 206.
55. Ibid.
56. Ibid., 207.
57. Eckland-Olson 1986.
58. Devine 1996; Kupchik 2010, 38–39.
59. Hallett 2010, 63–65.
60. Yalda 2002, 204.
61. Maynard-Moody and Musheno 2012.
62. Yalda 2002, 197.
63. Ibid., 194.
64. Ibid., 192.
65. Monahan 2005; Simmons 2011.
66. Hallett 2010, 53.
67. Meyer and Rowan 1977; Edelman 2016.
68. Morrill 2008.

CHAPTER EIGHT

1. Gordon 2010, 69–70.
2. Kupchik 2010.
3. Hallett and Ventresca 2006.
4. Edelman 2016.
5. Soss, Fording, and Schram 2011.
6. Maynard-Moody and Musheno 2000, 2003, 2012; Oberweis and Musheno 2001; Gilliom 2001.
7. boyd 2014, 128–153; Aalsma and Brown 2008; Cuadrado-Gordillo 2012.
8. boyd 2014, 83.
9. Ibid., 84.
10. Kowalski et al. 2014.
11. Arum 2005, 5.
12. Sánchez-Jankowski (2008, 302–4) notes that urban school authorities have other purposes, specifically teaching literacy and other skills needed for labor market success, such as the "norms and etiquette of adult American society," but that social control and the restriction of freedom is an overall message.
13. Anderson 1999a, 13; Sánchez-Jankowski 2008, 299–342; Paulle 2013, 213.
14. Devine 1996, 38.
15. Ibid., 10.
16. Ibid., 221.
17. Ibid., 235. In his articulation of power and discipline, Devine calls for a "new panopticon" (220–21) while taking seriously the "classical" panopticon and the oppressive disciplinary practices of urban schools (75–100).
18. Lightfoot 1983, 342.
19. Ibid., 343.
20. Ibid., 344–45. Her notion of the "good high school" is depicted earlier (23–26).
21. Astor, Meyer, and Behre 1999.
22. Ibid., 24.
23. Rios 2011, 162.
24. Maynard-Moody and Musheno 2012, 19; Maynard-Moody and Musheno 2003.
25. Emirbayer and Maynard 2011, 228.
26. Giddens 1979; Sewell 1992.
27. Black 2011, 4; Phillips and Cooney 2015, 731–734.
28. Black 2011, 9.
29. Putnam 2007.
30. This point is alluded to by Merry (1979), who argues that cultural difference in urban settings under conditions of social distrust can lead to perceptions of dangerousness across different sociocultural groups and more hostile conflict.
31. Anderson 2011.
32. Jones, Mitchell, and Finkelhor 2013, 54.
33. Phillips and Cooney 2015, 727.
34. Sabatini and Sarracino 2014.
35. Torin Monahan suggested this idea in his prepublication review of this book for the University of Chicago Press.
36. Adams 2007; Livingstone 2008.
37. Raynes-Goldie 2010.
38. Westlake 2008, 23.
39. Regan and Steeves 2010.

40. Paulle 2013.
41. Hall and Lamont 2013, 13.
42. Bandura 1977.
43. Brown 2015.
44. Soss, Fording, and Schram 2011, 6.
45. Ibid., 2.
46. Wacquant 2010, 197.
47. Hall and Lamont 2013, 6.
48. Ibid., 5; Brown 2015.
49. Hall and Lamont 2013, 3–12.
50. Nader 1990, 2.
51. Nader 1995. A version of top-down harmony models swept through American schools during the 1980s and 1990s in the "peer mediation movement," which attempted to teach students conflict management skills based in reconciliation regardless of the context and power asymmetries to which those skills were being transplanted (Burrell, Zirbel, and Allen 2006).
52. In this sense, we see restorative justice structures (Menkel-Meadow 2007) in which youth reconcile interpersonal peer trouble through open dialogue as a useful alternative for school based conflict management and discipline if such programs are sensitive to the social contexts, including repertoires of social control, into which they are implemented. Absent such sensitivity, we view such programs as deleterious and potentially dangerous for both adults and youth.
53. For a detailed treatment of places as accomplishment, see Molotch, Freudenburg, and Paulsen (2000).
54. The production of local equities acknowledges the bottom-up, middle-out view that we hold toward the production of social ordering and is evidenced when asymmetrical power dynamics give way to mutual dialogue and where parties at any level of an organizational hierarchy have the capacity to exercise agency in remedying differences (Maynard-Moody and Musheno 2012; Musheno and Maynard-Moody 2015).

APPENDIX A

1. Best 2007, 10–11.
2. Harcourt 2006; Bourgois 1995, 2.
3. Snow, Zurcher, and Sjoberg 1982; Lofland et al. 2005, 88.
4. Gaines 1990; MacLeod 1987; Morrill, Yalda, Adelman, Musheno, and Bejarano 2000; White and Wyn 2008.
5. Ewick and Silbey 1998; Morrill, Yalda, Adelman, Musheno, and Bejarano 2000; Oberweis and Musheno 2001; Maynard-Moody and Musheno 2003.
6. Jessor and Jessor 1977; Benner and Graham 2009; Nasir, McLaughlin, and Jones 2009. Our interests in collecting youth-authored cases about conflict converged with the interests of two of our NWHS teacher collaborators, ultimately resulting in their creation of what they called the ninth grade "Conflict Resolution Workbook" blending youth-authored trouble cases and American literature to explore and shape entering students' understandings, experiences, and options when faced with peer conflict. The use of the workbook ended after one year in the wake of Arizona adopting top-down testing standards for each grade that left little room for enhancements to local curricula.
7. Ninth grade ELL Spanish-speaking students without the levels of English-language

proficiency necessary to take required English courses did not write cases. For these students, we relied on gathering cases through informal and in-depth interviews in Spanish.

8. Lynch 1977; Tamm and Granqvist 1995; Astor, Meyer, and Behre 1999; Chapin, Lamb, and Threlkeld 2005.
9. Becker 1995; Pink 2013.
10. Yalda 2002.
11. Timmermans and Tavory (2012); Lara-Millán and Van Cleve (2017).
12. Katz 2001; Lofland et al. 2005, 161–62.
13. Lofland et al. 2005, 195–219; Emerson, Fretz, and Shaw 2011, 171–99.
14. Morrill, Yalda, Adelman, Musheno, and Bejarano 2000.
15. Hruschka et al. 2004.
16. Foucault 1972.
17. Yalda 2002.
18. Lofland et al. 2005, 94–95.
19. Clifford and Marcus 1986; Geertz 1988; Van Maanen 1988; Emerson, Fretz, and Shaw 2011.
20. Emerson, Fretz, and Shaw 2011.
21. Emerson, Fretz, and Shaw 2011, 74.
22. Van Maanen 1988.
23. Strauss 1978.
24. Wasser and Bresler 1996, 13.
25. Adelman and Yalda 2000; Bejarano 2005; Adelman and Kil 2007.
26. Bejarano 2005; Yalda 2002. Bejarano (2005) transformed her dissertation into a book on urban youth culture and border identities.
27. Emerson, Fretz, and Shaw 2011, 207.
28. On generalizability in case studies, see Snow and Anderson 1991, 164–166.
29. Snow and Anderson 1991.
30. Thacher 2006.
31. Desmond 2014, 573.
32. Becker 1996, 65.
33. Thacher 2006.
34. Snow, Morrill, and Anderson 2003.
35. Geertz 1973, 14; Shweder 1996, 17.

REFERENCES

Aalsma, Matthew C., and James R. Brown. 2008. "What is Bullying?" *Journal of Adolescent Health* 43:101–2.

Abbott, Andrew. 1995. "Sequence Analysis: New Methods for Old Ideas." *Annual Review of Sociology* 21:93–113.

Abrego, Leisy. 2011. "Legal Consciousness of Undocumented Latinos: Fear and Stigma as Claims Making for First and 1.5 Generation Immigrants." *Law & Society Review* 45:337–69.

Acland, Charles R. 1995. *Youth, Murder, Spectacle: The Culture Politics of "Youth in Crisis."* Boulder, CO: Westview Press.

Adams, Helen. 2007. "Social Networking and Privacy: A Law Enforcement Perspective." *School Library Media Activities Monthly* 23:33–34.

Adelman, Madelaine, and Sang Hea Kil. 2007. "Dating Conflicts: Rethinking Dating Violence and Youth Conflict." *Violence against Women* 13:1296–318.

Adelman, Madelaine, and Christine Yalda. 2000. "Seen but Not Heard: The Legal Lives of Young People." *POLAR: Political and Legal Anthropology Review* 2:37–58.

Adler, Patricia A., and Peter Adler. 1998. *Peer Power: Preadolescent Culture and Identity.* New Brunswick, NJ: Rutgers University Press.

Agron, Joe, and Larry Anderson. 2000. "School Security by the Numbers." *School Security 2000,* supplement to *American School & University* and *Access Control & Security Systems Integration,* edited by Joe Agron and Larry Anderson, 6–17.

Akerlof, George A., and Rachel E. Kranton. 2002. "Identity and Schooling: Some Lessons for the Economics of Education." *Journal of Economic Literature* 40:1167–201.

Albiston, Catherine, Lauren B. Edelman, and Joy Milligan. 2014. "The Dispute Tree and the Legal Forest." *Annual Review of Law and Social Science* 10:105–31.

Allport, Gordon W. 1954. *The Nature of Prejudice.* Cambridge, MA: Addison-Wesley.

Anderson, Elijah. 1999a. *Code of the Street: Decency, Violence, and the Moral Life of the Inner City.* New York: W. W. Norton.

———. 1999b. "The Social Situation of the Black Executive: Black and White Identities in the Corporate World." In *The Cultural Territories of Race: Black and White Boundaries,* edited by Michèle Lamont, 3–29. Chicago: University of Chicago Press.

———. 2011. *The Cosmopolitan Canopy: Race and Civility in Everyday Life.* New York: W.W. Norton.

Arnett, Jeffrey Jensen. 2012. *Adolescence and Emerging Adulthood: A Cultural Approach.* 5th ed.. Upper Saddle River, NJ: Pearson Prentice Hall.

Arum, Richard. 2005. *Judging School Discipline: The Crisis of Moral Authority.* Cambridge, MA: Harvard University Press.

Astor, Ron Avi, Heather Ann Meyer, and William J. Behre. 1999. "Unowned Places and Times: Maps and Interviews about Violence in High Schools." *American Educational Research Journal* 36:3–42.

Balliet, Daniel, and Paul A. M. Van Lange. 2013. "Trust, Conflict, and Cooperation: A Meta-Analysis." *Psychological Bulletin* 139:1090–112.

Bandura, Albert. 1977. "Self-Efficacy: Toward a Unifying Theory of Behavioral Change." *Psychological Review* 84:191–215.

Barajas, Heidi, and Jennifer Pierce. 2001. "The Significance of Race and Gender in School Success among Latinas and Latinos in College." *Gender and Society* 15 (6): 859–78.

Baumgartner, M. P. 1988. *The Moral Order of a Suburb.* New York: Oxford University Press.

Bearman, Peter S., James Moody, and Katherine Stovel. 2004. "Chains of Affection: The Structure of Adolescent Romantic and Sexual Networks." *American Journal of Sociology* 110:44–91.

Becker, Howard S. 1995. "Visual Sociology, Documentary Photography, and Photojournalism: It's (Almost) All a Matter of Context." *Visual Studies* 10:5–14.

———. 1996. "The Epistemology of Qualitative Research." In *Ethnography and Human Development: Context and Meaning in Social Inquiry,* edited by Richard Jessor, Anne Colby, and Richard A. Shweder, 53–71. Chicago: University of Chicago Press.

Becker, Katrin, Melanie Becker, and John H. Schwarz. 2007. *String Theory and M-Theory: A Modern Introduction.* Cambridge, UK: Cambridge University Press.

Bejarano, Cynthia L. 2005. *¿Qué Onda? Urban Youth Cultures and Border Identity.* Tucson, AZ: University of Arizona Press.

Bell, Monica C. 2016. "Situational Trust: How Disadvantaged Mothers Reconceive Legal Cynicism." *Law & Society Review* 50:314–47.

Benner, Aprile D., and Sandra Graham. 2009. "The Transition to High School as a Developmental Process among Multiethnic Urban Youth." *Child Development* 80:356–76.

Benton-Cohen, Katherine. 2009. *Borderline Americans: Racial Division and Labor War in the Arizona Borderlands.* Cambridge, MA: Harvard University Press.

Berrey, Ellen. 2015. *The Enigma of Diversity: The Language of Race and Limits of Racial Justice.* Chicago: University of Chicago Press.

Best, Amy L. 2007. "Introduction." In *Representing Youth: Methodological Issues in Critical Youth Studies,* edited by Amy L. Best, 1–35. New York: New York University Press.

Best, Rachel, Lauren B. Edelman, Linda Hamilton Krieger, and Scott R. Eliason. 2011. "Multiple Disadvantages: An Empirical Test of Intersectionality Theory in EEO Litigation." *Law & Society Review* 45:991–1025.

Black, Donald. 1976. *The Behavior of Law.* New York: Academic Press.

———. 1983. "Crime as Social Control." *American Sociological Review* 48:34–45.

———. 1984. "Social Control as a Dependent Variable." In *Toward a Theory of Social Control,* vVolume 1: *Fundamentals,* edited by Donald Black, 1–36. Orlando, FL: Academic Press.

———. 1993. "The Elementary Forms of Conflict Management." In *The Social Structure of Right and Wrong,* 74–94. San Diego, CA: Academic Press.

———. 2011. *Moral Time.* Oxford, UK: Oxford University Press.

Black, Donald, and M. P. Baumgartner. 1983. "Toward a Theory of the Third Party." In

Empirical Theories about Courts, edited by Keith O. Boyum and Lynn Mather. 84–114. New York: Longman.

Bonacich, Phillip. 1990. "Communication Dilemmas in Social Networks: An Experimental Study." *American Sociological Review* 55:448–59.

Bortner, M.A. and Linda A. Williams. 1997. *Youth in Prison: We the People of Unit Four.* New York: Routledge.

Bourdieu, Pierre, and Jean-Claude Passeron. 1977. *Reproduction in Education, Society and Culture.* London: Sage Publications.

Bourgois, Philippe. 1995. *In Search of Respect: Selling Crack in El Barrio.* Cambridge, UK: Cambridge University Press.

boyd, danah. 2014. *It's Complicated: The Social Lives of Networked Teens.* New Haven, CT: Yale University Press.

Brill, Dunja. 2007. "Gender, Status, and Subcultural Capital in the Goth Scene." In *Youth Cultures: Scenes, Subcultures, and Tribes*, edited by Paul Hodkinson and Wolfgang Deicke. 111–26. New York: Taylor & Francis.

Brown, B. Bradford, and Christa Klute. 2003. "Friendships, Cliques, and Crowds." In *Blackwell Handbook of Adolescence*, edited by Gerald R. Adams and Michael D. Berzonsky, 330–48. Malden, MA: Blackwell.

Brown, Kenly. 2016. "Institutional Production of Anti-Black Violence in Public Schools." Unpublished paper, Department of African American Studies and African Diaspora Studies, University of California, Berkeley.

Brown, Roger, and Albert Gilman. 1960. "The Pronouns of Power and Solidarity." In *Style in Language*, edited by Thomas A. Sebeok, 253–77. Cambridge, MA: MIT Press.

Brown, Wendy. 2015. *Undoing the Demos: Neoliberalism's Stealth Revolution.* Brooklyn, NY: Zone Books.

Bryk, Anthony S., and Barbara Schneider. 2002. *Trust in Schools: A Core Resource for Improvement.* New York: Russell Sage Foundation.

Bumiller, Kristin. 1988. *The Civil Rights Society: The Social Construction of Victims.* Baltimore, MD: Johns Hopkins University Press.

Burrell, Nancy A., Cindy S. Zirbel, and Mike Allen. 2006. "Evaluating Peer Mediation Outcomes in Educational Settings: A Meta-Analytic Review." In *Classroom Communication and Instructional Processes: Advances through Meta-Analysis*, edited by Barbara Mae Gayle, Raymond W. Press, Nancy A Burrell, and Mike Allen, 113–28. Malwah, NJ: Earlbaum.

Bushman, Brad J., Katherine Newman, Sandra L. Calvert, Geraldine Downey, Mark Dredze, Michael Gottfredson, Nina G. Jablonski, Ann S. Masten, Calvin Morrill, Daniel B. Neill, Daniel Romer, and Daniel W. Webster. 2016. "Youth Violence: What We Know and What We Need to Know." *American Psychologist* 71:17–39.

Calavita, Kitty, and Valerie Jenness. 2015. *Appealing to Justice: Prisoner Grievances, Rights, and Carceral Logic.* Oakland, CA: University of California Press.

Carter, Prudence L. 2005. *Keepin' It Real: School Success Beyond Black and White.* New York: Oxford University Press.

———. 2012. *Stubborn Roots: Race, Culture and Inequality in US and South African Schools.* New York: Oxford University Press.

Casella, Ronnie. 2003. "Punishing Dangerousness through Preventive Detention: Illustrating the Institutional Link between School and Prison." *New Directions for Youth Development* 99:55–70.

———. 2006. *Selling Us the Fortress: The Promotion of Techno-Security Equipment in Schools.* New York: Routledge.

Chapin, Mac, Zachary Lamb, and Bill Threlkeld. 2005. "Mapping Indigenous Lands." *Annual Review of Anthropology* 34:619–38.

Chen, Greg. 2008. "Communities, Schools, and School Crime: A Confirmatory Study of Crime in US High Schools." *Urban Education* 43:301–18.

Clifford, James, and George E. Marcus, eds. 1986. *Writing Culture: The Poetics and Politics of Ethnography*. Berkeley, CA: University of California Press.

Cohen, Jonanthan, Elizabeth M. McCabe, Nicholas M. Michelli, and Terry Pickeral. 2009. "School Climate: Research, Policy, Practice, and Teacher Education." *Teachers College Record* 111:180–213.

Collins, Patricia Hill. 2015. "Intersectionality's Definitional Dilemmas." *Annual Review of Sociology* 41:1–20.

Collins, Randall. 2004. *Interactional Ritual Chains*. Princeton, NJ: Princeton University Press.

———. 2008. *Violence: A Micro-Sociological Theory*. Princeton, NJ: Princeton University Press.

Comaroff, John, and Jean Comaroff. 1992. *Ethnography and the Historical Imagination*. Boulder, CO: Westview Press.

Conley, John and William O'Barr. 1990. *Rules vs. Relationships: The Ethnography of Legal Discourse*. Chicago: University of Chicago Press.

———. 1998. *Just Words: Law, Language and Power*. Chicago: University of Chicago Press.

Cook, Karen S. 2001. "Trust in Society." In *Trust in Society*, edited by Karen S. Cook, xi–xxviii. New York: Russell Sage.

Cooney, Mark. 1998. *Warriors and Peacemakers: How Third Parties Shape Violence*. New York: New York University Press.

Costa, Albert, Alice Foucart, Sayuri Hayakawa, Melina Aparici, José Apesteguia, Joy Heafner, and Boaz Keysar. 2014. "Your Morals Depend on Language." *PLOS ONE* 9:1–7.

Crenshaw, Kimberlé Williams. 1991. "Mapping the Margins: Intersectionality, Identity Politics, and Violence against Women of Color." *Stanford Law Review* 43:1241–99.

Crenshaw, Kimberlé Williams, Priscilla Ocen, and Jyoti Nanda. 2015. *Black Girls Matter: Pushed Out, Overpoliced, and Underprotected*. New York: African American Policy Forum, Center for Intersectionality and Social Policy Studies, Columbia University.

Crosnoe, Robert, and Monica Kirkpatrick Johnson. 2011. "Research on Adolescence in the Twenty-First Century." *Annual Review of Sociology* 37:439–60.

Cuadrado-Gordillo, Isabel. 2012. "Repetition, Power Imbalance, and Intentionality: Do These Criteria Conform to Teenagers' Perception of Bullying? A Role-Based Analysis." *Journal of Interpersonal Violence* 27:1889–910.

Cumming, Elaine, Ian Cumming, and Laura Edell. 1965. "Policeman as Philosopher, Guide and Friend." *Social Problems* 12:276–86.

Danby, Susan, and Maryanne Theobald. 2012. "Introduction: Disputes in Everyday Life—Social and Moral Orders of Children and Young People." *Sociological Studies of Children and Youth* 15:xv–xxiv.

Delgado, Melvin. 2006. *Designs and Methods for Youth-Led Research*. Thousand Oaks, CA: Sage Publications.

Desmond, Matthew. 2014. "Relational Ethnography." *Theory and Society* 43:547–79.

Devine, John. 1996. *Maximum Security: The Culture of Violence in Inner-City Schools*. Chicago: University of Chicago Press.

de Wied, Minet, Susan J. T. Branje, and Wim H. J. Meeus. 2007. "Empathy and Conflict Resolution in Friendship Relations among Adolescents." *Aggressive Behavior* 33:48–55.

Dill, LeConté J., and Emily J. Ozer. 2015. "'I'm Not Just Runnin' the Streets': Exposure to

Neighborhood Violence and Violence Management Strategies Among Urban Youth of Color." *Journal of Adolescent Research* 31:1–21.

DiMaggio, Paul M., and Walter W Powell. 1983. "The Iron Cage Revisited: Institutional Isomorphism and Collective Rationality in Organizational Fields." *American Sociological Review* 48:157–60.

Dornbusch, Sanford M. 1989. "The Sociology of Adolescence." *Annual Review of Sociology* 15:233–59.

Dornbusch, Sanford M., Kristan L. Glasgow, and I-Chun Lin. 1996. "The Social Structure of Schooling." *Annual Review of Psychology* 47:401–29.

Duck, Steve. 2010. *Rethinking Relationships*. Thousand Oaks, CA: Sage.

Dunn, Jennifer R., and Maurice E. Schweitzer. 2005. "Feeling and Believing: The Influence of Emotion on Trust." *Journal of Personality and Social Psychology* 88:736–48.

Durkheim, Émile. 1903 [1961]. *Moral Education: A Study in the Theory and Application of the Sociology of Education*. New York: Free Press.

Earl, Jennifer. 2009. "When Bad Things Happen: Toward a Sociology of Troubles." In *Access to Justice (Sociology of Crime, Law and Deviance, Volume 12)*, edited by Rebecca L. Sandefur, 231–54. Bingley, UK: Emerald Group Publishing.

Eckland-Olson, Sheldon. 1986. "Crowding, Social Control, and Prison Violence: Evidence from the Post-Ruiz Years in Texas." *Law & Society Review* 20:389–421.

Edelman, Lauren B. 2016. *Working Law: Courts, Corporations, and Symbolic Civil Rights*. Chicago: University of Chicago Press.

Eliasoph, Nina. 2012. *Making Volunteers: Civic Life after Welfare's End*. Princeton, NJ: Princeton University Press.

Elliot, Delbert S., Beatrix H. Hamburg, and Krik R. Williams. 1998. "Violence in American Schools: An Overview." In *Violence in American Schools: A New Perspective*, 3–28. Cambridge, UK: Cambridge University Press.

Ellis, Desmond. 1984. "Crowding and Prison Violence: Integration of Research and Theory." *Criminal Justice and Behavior* 11:277–308.

Emerson, Robert M. 2008. "Responding to Roommate Troubles: Reconsidering Informal Dyadic Control." *Law & Society Review* 42:483–512.

———. 2011. "From Normal Conflict to Normative Deviance: The Micro-Politics of Trouble in Close Relationships." *Journal of Contemporary Ethnography* 40:3–38.

———. 2015. *Everyday Troubles: The Micro-Politics of Interpersonal Conflict*. Chicago: University of Chicago Press.

Emerson, Robert M., Rachel I. Fretz, and Linda L. Shaw. 2011. *Writing Ethnographic Fieldnotes*, 2nd ed. Chicago: University of Chicago Press.

Emerson, Robert M., and Sheldon L. Messinger. 1977. "The Micro Politics of Trouble." *Social Problems* 25:121–34.

Emirbayer, Mustafa, and Douglas W. Maynard. 2011. "Pragmatism and Ethnomethdology." *Qualitative Sociology* 34:221–61.

Erikson, Erik. H. 1968. *Identity, Youth, and Crisis*. New York: W. W. Norton.

Erikson, Kai T. 1976. *Everything in Its Path: Destruction of Community in the Buffalo Creek Flood*. New York: Simon & Schuster.

Ewick, Patricia, and Susan S. Silbey. 1998. *The Common Place of Law: Stories from Everyday Life*. Chicago: University of Chicago Press.

———. 2003. "Narrating Social Structure: Stories of Resistance to Legal Authority." *American Journal of Sociology* 108: 1328–72.

Eyerman, Ron. 2015. *Is This America? Katrina as Cultural Trauma*. Austin, TX: University of Texas Press.

Fagan, Jeffrey, and Tom R. Tyler. 2005. "Legal Socialization of Children and Adolescents." *Social Justice Journal* 18:217–42.

Fagan, Jeffrey, and Deanna L. Wilkinson. 1998. "Guns, Youth Violence, and Social Identity in Inner Cities." In *Youth Violence*, edited by Michael Tonry and Mark H. Moore, 105–88. Chicago: University of Chicago Press.

Faris, Robert, and Diane Felmlee. 2011. "Status Struggles: Network Centrality and Gender Segregation in Same- and Cross-Gender Aggression." *American Sociological Review* 76:48–73.

Feagin, Joe R. 2006. *Systemic Racism: A Theory of Oppression*. New York: Routledge.

Felstiner, William L. F. 1974. "Influences of Social Organization on Dispute Processing." *Law & Society Review* 9:63–94.

Felstiner, William L. F., Richard L. Abel, and Austin Sarat. 1980. "The Emergence and Transformation of Disputes: Naming, Blaming, Claiming. . . ." *Law & Society Review* 15:631–54.

Ferguson, Ann Arnett. 2000. *Bad Boys: Public Schools in the Making of Black Masculinity*. Ann Arbor, MI: University of Michigan Press.

Fine, Gary Alan. 1984. "Negotiated Orders and Organizational Cultures." *Annual Review of Sociology* 10:239–62.

———. 2001. *Gifted Tongues: High School Debate and Adolescent Culture*. Princeton, NY: Princeton University Press.

Fine, Gary Alan, and Tim Hallett. 2014. "Group Cultures and the Everyday Life of Organizations." *Organization Studies* 35:1773–1792.

Fisher, Celia B., Scyatta A. Wallace, and Rose E. Fenton. 2000. "Discrimination Distress During Adolescence." *Journal of Youth and Adolescence* 29:679–95.

Fligstein, Neil, and Doug McAdam. 2012. *A Theory of Fields*. New York: Oxford University Press.

Foucault, Michel. 1972. *The Archaeology of Knowledge*. New York: Pantheon Books.

———. 1977. *Discipline and Punish: The Birth of the Prison*. New York: Vintage.

Freeman, Linton C., A. Kimball Romney, and Sue C. Freeman. 1987. "Cognitive Structure and Informant Accuracy." *American Anthropologist* 89:310–25.

Gaines, Donna. 1990. *Teenage Wasteland: Suburbia's Dead End Kids*. Chicago: University of Chicago Press.

Galanter, Marc. 1974. "Why the 'Haves' Come Out Ahead: Speculations on the Limits of Legal Change." *Law & Society Review* 9:95–160.

Gans, Herbert J. 2002. "The Sociology of Space: A Use-Centered View." *City & Community* 1:329–39.

Garland, David. 2002. *The Culture of Control: Crime and Social Order in Contemporary Society*. Chicago: University of Chicago Press.

Garot, Robert. 2007. "Non-Violence in the Inner-City: Decent and Street as Strategic Resources." *Journal of African American Studies* 10:94–111.

———. 2009. "Reconsidering Retaliation: Structural Inhibitions, Emotive Dissonance, and the Acceptance of Ambivalence among Inner-City Young Men." *Ethnography* 10:63–90.

Gau, Jacinta, and Rod K. Brunson. 2010. "Procedural Justice and Order Maintenance Policing: A Study of Inner-City Young Men's Perceptions of Police Legitimacy." *Justice Quarterly* 27 (2): 255–79.

Geertz, Clifford. 1973. *The Interpretation of Cultures*. New York: Basic Books.

———. 1988. *Works and Lives: The Anthropologist as Author*. Stanford, CA: Stanford University Press.

Gerstl-Pepin, Cynthia I., and Michael G. Gunzenhauser. 2002. "Collaborative Team Ethnography and the Paradoxes of Interpretation." *Qualitative Studies in Education* 15:137–54.

Giddens, Anthony. 1979. *Central Problems in Social Theory: Action, Structure, and Contradiction in Social Analysis*. Berkeley and Los Angeles: University of California Press.

———. 1991. *Modernity and Self-Identity: Self and Society in the Late Modern Age*. Stanford, CA: Stanford University Press.

Gilliom, John. 2001. *Overseers of the Poor: Surveillance, Resistance, and the Limits of Privacy*. Chicago: University of Chicago Press.

Giordano, Peggy C. 2003. "Relationships in Adolescence." *Annual Review of Sociology* 29:257–81.

Giordano, Peggy C., Stephen A. Cernkovich, and Donna D. Holland. 2003. "Changes in Friendship Relations over the Life Course: Implications for Desistance from Crime." *Criminology* 41:293–327.

Goffman, Erving. 1959. *The Presentation of Self in Everyday Life*. New York: Anchor Books.

———. 1961. *Asylums: Essays on the Social Situation of Mental Patients and Other Inmates*. New York: Anchor.

———. 1963. *Stigma: Notes on the Management of Spoiled Identity*. New York: Simon & Schuster.

———. 1967. *Interaction Ritual: Essays on Face-to-Face Behavior*. New York: Anchor Books.

———. 1969. *Strategic Interaction*. Philadelphia, PA: University of Pennsylvania Press.

———. 1983. "The Interaction Order." *American Sociological Review* 48:1–17.

Golden-Biddle, Karen, and Karen Locke. 2007. *Composing Qualitative Research*. 2nd ed. Thousand Oaks, CA: Sage Publications.

Gómez, Laure E. 2007. *Manifest Destinies: The Making of the Mexican American Race*. New York: New York University Press.

Gordon, Hava Rachel. 2010. *We Fight to Win: Inequality and the Politics of Youth Activism*. New Brunswick, NJ: Rutgers University Press.

Gottdiener, Mark, Ray Hutchison, and Michael T. Ryan. 2014. *The New Urban Sociology*. 5th ed. Boulder, CO: Westview Press.

Gottfredson, Denise C. 2001. *Schools and Delinquency*. Cambridge, UK: Cambridge University Press.

Gottfredson, Gary D., Denise C. Gottfredson, Allian Ann Payne, and Nisha C. Gottfredson. 2005. "School Climate Predictors of School Disorder: Results from a National Study of Delinquency Prevention in Schools." *Journal of Research in Crime and Delinquency* 42:412–44.

Gould, Roger V. 2003. *Collision of Wills: How Ambiguity about Social Rank Breeds Conflict*. Chicago: University of Chicago Press.

Gross, Neil. 2016. "Are Americans Experiencing Collective Trauma?" *New York Times*, Sunday Review, December 16.

Guerrero, Linda K., Silvie Eloy, and Alisa I. Wabnik. 1993. "Linking Maintenance Strategies to Relationship Development and Disengagement: A Reconceptualization." *Journal of Social and Personal Relationships* 10:273–82.

Hagan, John, and Bill McCarthy. 1997. *Mean Streets: Youth Crime and Homelessness*. Cambridge, UK: Cambridge University Press.

Hagan, John, Carla Shedd, and Monique R. Payne. 2005. "Race, Ethnicity, and Youth Perceptions of Criminal Injustice." *American Sociological Review* 70:381–407.

Hall, Peter A., and Michèle Lamont. 2013. "Introduction." In *Social Resilience in the Neoliberal Era*, edited by Peter A. Hall and Michèle Lamont, 1–31. Cambridge, UK: Cambridge University Press.

Hall, Stanley. 1904. *Adolescence—Its Psychology and Its Relations to Physiology, Anthropology, Sociology, Sex, Crime and Religion*. New York: D. Appleton & Co.

Hall, Stuart, and Tony Jefferson, eds. 1976. *Resistance through Rituals: Youth Subcultures in Post-War Britain*. London: Routledge.

Hallett, Tim. 2010. "The Myth Incarnate: Recoupling Processes, Turmoil, and Inhabited Institutions in an Urban Elementary School." *American Sociological Review* 75:52–74.

Hallett, Tim, and Marc J. Ventresca. 2006. "Inhabited Institutions: Social Interactions and Organizational Forms in Gouldner's *Patterns of Bureaucracy*." *Theory and Society* 35:213–36.

Harcourt, Bernard. 2001. *The Illusion of Order: The False Promise of Broken Windows Policing*. Cambridge, MA: Harvard University Press.

———. 2006. *Language of the Gun: Youth, Crime, and Public Policy*. Chicago: University of Chicago Press.

Harden, Jacalyn D. 1988. "African American Students as Translators of Cultural Pluralism: An Ethnography." Master's thesis, Arizona State University.

Harding, David J. 2010. *Living the Drama: Community, Conflict, and Culture among Inner-City Boys*. Chicago: University of Chicago Press.

Hebdige, Dick. 1979. *Subculture: The Meaning of Style*. London: Meuthen & Co.

Hirschfield, Paul J., and Katarzyna Celinska. 2011. "Beyond Fear: Sociological Perspectives on the Criminalization of School Discipline." *Sociology Compass* 5:1–12.

Hirschman, Albert O. 1970. *Exit, Voice, and Loyalty: Responses to Decline in Firms, Organizations, and States*. Cambridge, MA: Harvard University Press.

Horowitz, Ruth. 1983. *Honor and the American Dream: Identity and Culture in a Chicano Community*. New Brunswick, NJ: Rutgers University Press.

Horwitz, Allan V. 1990. *The Logic of Social Control*. New York: Plenum.

HoSang, Daniel. 2006. "Beyond Policy: Ideology, Race and the Reimagining of Youth." In *Beyond Resistance! Youth Activism and Community Change*, edited by Shawn Ginwright, Pedro Noguera, and Julio Cammarota. 3–19. New York: Routledge.

Hruschka, Daniel J., Deborah Schwartz, Daphne Cobb St. John, Erin Picone-Decaro, Richard A. Jenkins, and James W. Carey. 2004. "Reliability in Coding Open-Ended Data: Lessons Learned from HIV Behavioral Research." *Field Methods* 16:307–31.

Jackson-Jacobs, Curtis. 2013. "Constructing Physical Fights: In Interactionist Analysis of Violence among Affluent, Suburban Youth." *Qualitative Sociology* 36:23–52.

Jessor, Richard, and Shirley L. Jessor. 1977. *Problem Behavior and Psychosocial Development: A Longitudinal Study of Youth*. New York: Academic Press.

Jimerson, Jason B., and Matthew K. Oware. 2006. "Telling the Code of the Street: An Ethnomethodological Ethnography." *Journal of Contemporary Ethnography* 35:24–50.

Jones, Gil. 2009. *Youth*. Cambridge, UK: Polity Press.

Jones, Lisa M., Kimberly J. Mitchell, and David Finkelhor. 2013. "Online Harassment in Context: Trends from Three Youth Internet Surveys (2000, 2005, 2010)." *Psychology of Violence* 3:53–69.

Jones, Nikki. 2010. *Between Good and Ghetto: African American Girls and Inner-City Violence*. New Brunswick, NJ: Rutgers University Press.

Jordan, Larry. 1983. "Social Construction as Tradition: A Review and Reconceptualization of the Dozens." *Review of Research in Education* 10:79–101.

Katz, Jack. 1988. *The Seductions of Crime: Moral and Sensual Attractions in Doing Evil*. New York: Basic Books.

———. 2001. "Analytic Induction Revisited." In *Contemporary Field Research: Perspectives and Formulations*, 2nd ed., edited by Robert M. Emerson, 331–34. Prospect Heights, IL: Waveland Press.

Kingery, Paul M., Mark B. Coggeshall, and Aaron A. Alford. 1999. "Weapon Carrying by Youth: Risk Factors and Prevention." *Education and Urban Society* 31:309–33.

Kolb, Deborah M. 1992. "Women's Work: Peacemaking in Organizations." In *Hidden Conflict in Organizations: Uncovering Behind-the-Scenes Disputes*, edited by Deborah M. Kolb and Jean M. Bartunek, 63–91. Newbury Park, CA: Sage Publications.

Kowalski, Robin M., Gary W. Giumetti, Amber N. Schroeder, and Micah R. Lattanner. 2014. "Bullying in the Digital Age: Critical Review and Meta-Analysis of Cyberbullying Research Among Youth." *Psychological Bulletin* 140:1073–137.

Krisberg, Barry. 2008. "The Politics of the War against the Young." In *After the War on Crime: Race, Democracy, and a New Reconstruction*, edited by Mary Louise Frampton, Ian Haney López, and Jonathan Simon, 187–206. New York: New York University Press.

Kupchik, Aaron. 2010. *Homeroom Security: School Discipline in an Age of Fear*. New York: New York University Press.

Kusenbach, Margarethe. 2003. "Street Phenomenology: The Go-Along as Ethnographic Research Tool." *Ethnography:* 4:455–85.

Lara-Millán, Armando, and Nicole Gonzalez Van Cleve. 2017. "Interorganizational Utility of Welfare Stigma in the Criminal Justice System." *Criminology* 55:59–84.

Laub, John H., and Janet L. Lauritsen. 1998. "The Interdependence of School Violence with Neighborhood and Family Conditions." In *Violence in American Schools*, edited by Delbert S. Elliot, Beatrix A. Hamburg, and Kirk R. Williams, 127–58. Cambridge, UK: Cambridge University Press.

Laumann, Edward O., and David Knoke. 1988. *The Organizational State: Social Change in National Policy Domains*. Madison, WI: University of Wisconsin Press.

Lawrence, Richard. 2006. *School Crime and Juvenile Justice*. 2nd ed. Oxford, UK: Oxford University Press.

Lee, Jennifer, and Frank D. Bean. 2012. "A Postracial Society or a Diversity Paradox? Race, Immigration, and Multiraciality in the Twenty-First Century." *Du Bois Review* 9:419–37.

Lightfoot, Sara Lawrence. 1983. *The Good High School: Portraits of Character and Culture*. New York: Basic Books.

Lincoln, Yvonna S., and Egon G. Guba. 1985. *Naturalistic Inquiry*. Beverly Hills, CA: Sage Publications.

Livingstone, Sonia. 2008. "Taking Risky Opportunities in Youthful Content Creation: Teenagers' Use of Social Networking Sites for Intimacy, Privacy, and Self Expression." *New Media and Society* 10:393–411.

Llewellyn, Karl. N., and E. Adamson Hoebel. [1941] 1983. *The Cheyenne Way: Conflict and Case Law in Primitive Jurisprudence*. Norman, OK: University of Oklahoma Press.

Lofland, John., David A. Snow, Leon Anderson, and Lyn H. Lofland. 2005. *Analyzing Social Settings*. 4th ed. Belmont, CA: Wadsworth.

Lofland, Lyn H. 1998. *The Public Realm: Exploring the City's Quintessential Social Territory*. New York: Aldine de Gruyter.

Losen, Daniel J., and Russel Skiba. 2010. *Suspended Education: Urban Middle Schools in Crisis*. Atlanta, GA: Southern Poverty Law Center.

Lynch, Kevin, ed. 1977. *Growing up in Cities: Studies of the Spatial Environment of Adolescence in Cracow, Melbourne, Mexico City, Toluca, and Warszawa*. Cambridge, MA: MIT Press.

Lyons, William, and Julie Drew. 2006. *Punishing Schools: Fear and Citizenship in American Public Education.* Ann Arbor, MI: University of Michigan Press.

Macaulay, Stewart. 1963. "Non-Contractual Relations in Business: A Preliminary Study." *American Sociological Review* 28:55–67.

MacLeod, Jay. 1987. *Ain't No Makin' It: Aspirations and Attainment in a Low-Income Neighborhood.* Boulder, CO: Westview Press.

Males, Mike A. 1999. *Framing Youth: 10 Myths about the Next Generation.* Monroe, ME: Common Courage Press.

Marwick, Alice, and danah boyd. 2011. "The Drama! Teen Conflict, Gossip, and Bullying in Networked Publics." Paper presented at "A Decade in Internet Time: Symposium on the Dynamics of the Internet and Society," Oxford University Internet Institute.

Massey, Doreen. 1998. "The Spatial Construction of Youth Cultures." In *Cool Places: Geographies of Youth Cultures,* edited by Tracey Skelton and Gill Valentine, 121–29. London: Routledge.

———. 2005. *For Space.* Los Angeles, CA: Sage.

Mateu-Gelabert, Pedro, and Howard Lune. 2007. "Street Codes in High School: School as an Educational Deterrent." *City & Community* 6:173–91.

Maynard-Moody, Steven, and Michael Musheno. 2000. "State Agent or Citizen Agent: Two Narratives of Discretion." *Journal of Public Administration Research and Theory* 10:329–58.

———. 2003. *Cops, Teachers, Counselors: Stories from the Front Lines of Public Service.* Ann Arbor, MI: University of Michigan Press.

———. 2012. "Social Equities and Inequities in Practice: Street-Level Workers as Agents and Pragmatists." *Public Administrative Review* 72:16–23.

McCain, Garvin, Verne C. Cox, and Paul B. Paulus. 1980. *The Effect of Prison Crowding on Inmate Behavior.* Washington, DC: US Department of Justice.

McEvoy, Alan. 1999. "The Relevance of Theory to the Safe Schools Movement." *Education and Urban Society* 31:275–85.

McFarland, Daniel A. 2001. "Student Resistance: How the Formal and Informal Organization of Classrooms Facilitate Everyday Forms of Student Deviance." *American Journal of Sociology* 107:612–78.

Menkel-Meadow, Carrie. 2007. "Restorative Justice: What Is It and Does It Work?" *Annual Review of Law and Social Science* 3:161–87.

Merry, Sally Engle. 1979. *Urban Danger: Life in a Neighborhood of Strangers.* Philadelphia, PA: Temple University Press.

———. 1983. "Rethinking Gossip and Scandal." In *Toward a Theory of Social Control,* volume 1: *Fundamentals,* edited by Donald Black, 271–302. Orlando, FL: Academic Press.

———. 1990. *Getting Justice and Getting Even: Legal Consciousness among Working-Class Americans.* Chicago: University of Chicago Press.

Meyer, John W., and Brian Rowan. 1977. "Institutionalized Organizations: Formal Structure as Myth and Ceremony." *American Journal of Sociology* 83:340–63.

Milem, Jeffrey F., W. Patrick Bryan, Diana B. Sesate, and Stephanie Montaño. 2013. *Arizona Minority Student Progress Report 2013: Arizona in Transition.* Tucson, AZ: University of Arizona Center for the Study of Higher Education.

Milner, Murray. 2004. *Freaks, Geeks, and Cool Kids: American Teenagers, Schools, and the Culture of Consumption.* New York: Routledge.

Molotch, Harvey, William Freudenburg, and Krista E. Paulsen. 2000. "History Repeats Itself, but How? City Character, Urban Tradition, and the Accomplishment of Place." *American Sociological Review* 65:791–823.

Molotch, Harvey, and Marilyn Lester. 1974. "News as Purposive Behavior: On the Strategic Use of Routine Events, Accidents, and Scandals." *American Sociological Review* 39:101–12.

Monahan, Torin. 2005. *Globalization, Technological Change, and Public Education*. New York: Routledge.

———. 2010. *Surveillance in a Time of Insecurity*. New Brunswick, NJ: Rutgers University Press.

Monahan, Torin, and Rudolfo D. Torres. 2010. "Introduction." In *Schools Under Surveillance: Cultures of Control in Public Education*, edited by Torin Monahan and Rudolfo D. Torres, 1–18. New Brunswick, NJ: Rutgers University Press.

Moody, James R. 2001. "Race, School Integration, and Friendship Segregation in America." *American Journal of Sociology* 107:679–716.

Morrill, Calvin. 1995. *The Executive Way: Conflict Management in Corporations*. Chicago: University of Chicago Press.

———. 2008. "Culture and Organization Theory." *ANNNALS of the American Academy of Political and Social Science* 619:15–40.

Morrill, Calvin, Lauren B. Edelman, Karolyn Tyson, and Richard Arum. 2010. "Legal Mobilization in Schools: The Paradox of Rights and Race." *Law & Society Review* 44 (3–4): 651–730.

Morrill, Calvin, Michelle Johnson, and Tyler Harrison. 1998. "Voice and Context in Simulated Everyday Legal Discourse: The Influence of Sex Differences and Social Ties." *Law & Society Review* 32:639–65.

Morrill, Calvin, Mayer N. Zald, and Hayagreeva Rao. 2003. "Covert Political Conflict in Organizations: Challenges from Below." *Annual Review of Sociology* 29:391–415.

Morrill, Calvin, and Daniele S. Rudes. 2010. "Conflict Resolution in Organizations." *Annual Review of Law and Social Science* 6:627–51.

Morrill, Calvin, Christine Yalda, Madelaine Adelman, Michael Musheno, and Cindy Bejarano. 2000. "Telling Tales in School: Youth Conflict and Culture Narratives." *Law & Society Review* 34:521–65.

Morris, Monique W. 2015. *Pushout: The Criminalization of Black Girls in Schools*. New York: The New Press.

Musheno, Michael. 1980. "On the Hazards of Selecting Intervention Points: Time-Series Analysis of Mandated Policies." *Policy Studies Journal* 8:1134–44.

———. 1995. "Legal Consciousness on the Margins of Society: Struggles Against Stigmatization in the AIDS Crisis." *Identities: Global Studies in Culture and Power* 1–2:101–22.

Musheno, Michael, James Levine, and Dennis Palumbo. 1978. "Television Surveillance and Crime Prevention: Evaluating an Attempt to Create Defensible Space in Public Housing." *Social Science Quarterly* 58:647–58.

Musheno, Michael, and Steven Maynard-Moody. 2015. "'Playing the Rules': Discretion in Social and Policy Context." In *Understanding Street-Level Bureaucracy*, edited by Peter Hupe, Michael Hill, and Aurélien Buffat, 169–85. Bristol, UK: Policy Press.

Nacci, Peter L., Hugh E. Teitelbaum, and Jerry Prather. 1977. "Population Density and Inmate Misconduct Rates in the Federal Prison System." *Federal Probation* 41:26–31.

Nader, Laura. 1990. *Harmony Ideology: Justice and Control in a Zapotec Mountain Village*. Stanford, CA: Stanford University Press.

———. 1995. "Civilization and Negotiations." In *Understanding Disputes: The Politics of Argument*, edited by Pat Caplan, 39–64. Oxford, UK: Berg Publishers.

Nader, Laura, and Harry F. Todd, eds. 1978. *The Disputing Process: Law in Ten Societies*. New York: Columbia University Press.

Nasir, Na'ilah Suad, Milbrey W. McLaughlin, and Amina Jones. 2009. "What Does It Mean to Be African American? Constructions of Race and Academic Identity in an Urban Public High School." *American Educational Research Journal* 46:73–114.

Nasir, Na'ilah Suad, Cyndy R. Snyder, Niral Shah, and Kihanna Miraya Ross. 2013. "Racial Storylines and Implications for Learning." *Human Development* 55:285–301.

Newman, Katherine S. 2004. *Rampage: The Social Roots of School Shootings.* New York: Basic Books.

Newman, Oscar. 1973. *Defensible Space: Crime Prevention through Urban Design.* New York: Macmillan.

Nolan, Kathleen. 2011. *Police in the Hallways: Discipline in an Urban High School.* Minneapolis: University of Minnesota Press.

Obasogie, Osagie K. 2014. *Blinded by Sight: Seeing Race Through the Eyes of the Blind.* Stanford, CA: Stanford University Press.

Oberweis, Trish, and Michael Musheno. 2001. *Knowing Rights: State Actors' Stories of Power, Identity and Morality.* Hampshire, UK: Ashgate/Dartmouth Press.

Omi, Michael, and Howard Winant. 2015. *Racial Formation in the United States.* 3rd ed. New York: Routledge.

Onwuachi-Willig, Angela. 2016. "The Trauma of the Routine: Lessons on Cultural Trauma from the Emmett Till Verdict," *Sociological Theory* 34:335–57.

Papachristos, Andrew V., David M. Hureau, and Anthony A. Braga. 2013. "The Corner and the Crew: The Influence of Geography and Social Networks on Gang Violence." *American Sociological Review* 78:417–47.

Pascoe, C. J. 2011. *Dude, You're a Fag: Masculinity and Sexuality in High School.* Berkeley, CA: University of California Press.

Pasquetti, Silvia. 2013. "Legal Emotions: An Ethnography of Distrust and Fear in the Arab Districts of an Israeli City." *Law & Society Review* 47:461–92.

Paulle, Bowen. 2013. *Toxic Schools: High-Poverty Education in New York and Amsterdam.* Chicago: University of Chicago Press.

Perry, Pamela. 2002. *Shades of White: White Kids and Racial Identities in High School.* Durham, NC: Duke University Press.

Pettigrew, Thomas F., and Linda R. Tropp. 2006. "A Meta-Analytic Test of Intergroup Contact Theory." *Journal of Personality and Social Psychology* 90:751–83.

Phillips, Scott, and Mark Cooney. 2015. "The Electronic Pillory: Social Time and Hostility toward Capital Murders." *Law & Society Review* 49:725–59.

Pinderhughes, Howard. 1997. *Race in the Hood: Conflict and Violence among Urban Youth.* Minneapolis: University of Minnesota Press.

Pink, Sarah. 2013. *Doing Visual Ethnography.* London: Sage Publications.

Polletta, Francesca, Pang Ching Bobby Chen, Beth Gharrity Gardner, and Alice Motes. 2011. "The Sociology of Storytelling." *Annual Review of Sociology* 37:109–30.

Powers, Jeanne M. 2008. "Forgotten History: Mexican American School Segregations in Arizona from 1900–1951." *Equity & Excellence in Education* 41:467–81.

Pruitt, Dean G., and Sung Hee Kim. 2004. *Social Conflict: Escalation, Stalemate, and Settlement.* 3rd ed. New York: McGraw Hill.

Putnam, Robert D. 2000. *Bowling Alone: The Collapse and Revival of American Community.* New York: Simon & Schuster.

———. 2007. "*E Pluribus Unum*: Diversity and Community in the Twenty-First Century. The 2006 Johan Skytte Prize Lecture." *Scandinavian Political Studies* 30:137–74.

Raynes-Goldie, Kate. 2010. "Aliases, Creeping, and Wall Cleaning: Understanding Privacy in the Age of Facebook." *First Monday* 15:4–10.

Regan, Priscilla, and Valerie Steeves. 2010. "Kids R Us: Online Social Networking and the Potential for Empowerment." *Surveillance and Society* 8:151–65.

Reiter, Keramet. 2016. *23/7: Pelican Bay Prison and the Rise of Long-Term Solitary Confinement*. New Haven, CT: Yale University Press.

Rios, Victor M. 2011. *Punished: Policing the Lives of Black and Latino Boys*. New York: New York University Press.

———. 2017. *Human Targets: Schools, Police, and the Criminalization of Youth*. Chicago: University of Chicago Press.

Robers, Simone, Jana Kemp, Amy Rathbun, Rachel E. Morgan, and Thomas D. Snyder. 2014. *Indicators of School Crime and Safety: 2013* (NCES 2014–042/NCJ 243299). Washington, DC: National Center for Education Statistics, US Department of Education, and Bureau of Justice Statistics, Office of Justice Programs, US Department of Justice.

Roloff, Michael E., and Denise H. Cloven. 1990. "The Chilling Effect in Interpersonal Relationships: The Reluctance to Speak One's Mind." In *Intimates in Conflict: A Communication Perspective*, edited by Dudley D. Cahn, 49–76. Hillsdale, NJ: Lawrence Erlbaum.

Rosenbloom, Susan Rakosi, and Niobe Way. 2004. "Experiences of Discrimination among African American, Asian American, and Latino Adolescents in an Urban High School." *Youth & Society* 35:420–51.

Ruiz, Vicki L. 2001. "South by Southwest: Mexican Americans and Segregated Schooling, 1900–1950." *OAH Magazine of History* 15:23–27.

Russell, Stephen T., Jack K. Day., Salvatore Ioverno, and Russell B. Toomey. 2016. "Are School Policies Focused on Sexual Orientation and Gender Identity Associated with Less Bullying? Teacher's Perspectives." *Journal of School Psychology* 54:29–38.

Sabatini, Fabio, and Francesco Sarracino. 2014. "E-Participation: Social Capital and the Internet." Munich Perosnal RePEc Archive.

Sampson, Robert J. 2012. *Great American City: Chicago and the Enduring Neighborhood Effect*. Chicago: University of Chicago Press.

———. 2013. "The Place of Context: A Theory and Strategy for Criminology's Hard Problems." *Criminology* 51:1–31.

Sampson, Robert J., Doug McAdam, Heather MacIndoe, and Simón Weffer-Elizondo. 2005. "Civil Society Reconsidered: The Durable Nature and Community Structure of Collective Civic Action." *American Journal of Sociology* 111:673–714.

Sánchez-Jankowski, Martín. 2008. *Cracks in the Pavement: Social Change and Resilience in Poor Neighborhoods*. Berkeley, CA: University of California Press.

———. 2016. *Burning Dislike: Ethnic Violence in High Schools*. Oakland, CA: University of California Press.

Schneider, Tod. 2006. "Violence and Crime Prevention through Environmental Design." In *Safe and Healthy School Environments*, edited by Howard Frumkin, Robert J. Geller, and I. Leslie Rubin, 251–69. New York: Oxford University Press.

Schneider, Tod, Hill Walker, and Jeffrey Sprague. 2000. *Safe School Design: A Handbook for Educational Leaders: Applying the Principles of Crime Prevention through Environmental Design*. Eugene, OR: University of Oregon, College of Education, ERIC Clearinghouse on Educational Management.

Scott, James C. 1990. *Domination and the Arts of Resistance: Hidden Transcripts*. New Haven, CT: Yale University Press.

Scott, W. Richard. 2008. *Institutions and Organizations: Ideas and Interests*. 3rd ed. Los Angeles, CA: Sage Publications.

Seron, Carroll. 2016. "The Two Faces of Law and Inequality: From Critique to the Promise of Situated, Pragmatic Policy." *Law & Society Review* 50:9–33.

Seron, Carroll, and Susan S. Silbey. 2004. "Profession, Science, and Culture: An Emergent Canon of Law and Society Research." In *The Blackwell Companion to Law and Society*, edited by Austin Sarat, 30–59. Malden, MA: Blackwell Publishing.

Sewell, William H. 1992. "A Theory of Structure: Duality, Agency, and Transformation." *American Journal of Sociology* 98:1–29.

Sharkey, Patrick. 2006. "Navigating Dangerous Streets: The Sources and Consequences of Street Efficacy." *American Sociological Review* 71:826–46.

Shedd, Carla. 2015. *Unequal City: Race, Schools, and Perceptions of Injustice*. New York: Russell Sage.

Shweder, Richard A. 1996. "True Ethnography: The Lore, the Law, and the Lure." In *Ethnography and Human Development: Context and Meaning in Social Inquiry*, edited by Richard Jessor, Anne Colby, and Richard A. Shweder, 15–32. Chicago: University of Chicago Press.

Simmons, Lizbet McCrary. 2011. "Buying into Prison, and Selling Kids Short." *Modern American* 6:51–56.

Simon, Jonathan. 2007. *Governing Through Crime: How the War on Crime Transformed American Democracy and Created a Culture of Fear*. New York: Oxford University Press.

Skelton, Tracey, and Gil Valentine, eds. 1998. *Cool Places: Geographies of Youth Cultures*. London: Routledge.

Small, Mario Luis. 2002. "Culture, Cohorts, and Social Organization Theory: Understanding Local Participation in a Latino Housing Project." *American Journal of Sociology* 108:1–54.

Smith, Sandra Susan. 2007. *Lone Pursuit: Distrust and Defensive Individualism among the Black Poor*. New York: Russell Sage.

Snow, David A., and Leon Anderson. 1991. "Researching the Homeless: The Characteristic Features and Virtues of the Case Study." In *A Case for the Case Study*, edited by Joe R. Feagin, Anthony M. Orum, and Gideon Sjoberg, 148–73. Chapel Hill, NC: University of North Carolina Press.

Snow, David A., Calvin Morrill, and Leon Anderson. 2003. "Elaborating Analytic Ethnography." *Ethnography* 4:181–200.

Snow, David A., Louis A. Zurcher, and Gideon Sjoberg. 1982. "Interviewing by Comment: An Adjunct to the Direct Question." *Qualitative Sociology* 5:285–311.

Soss, Joe, Richard C. Fording, and Sanford F. Schram. 2011. *Disciplining the Poor: Neoliberal Paternalism and the Persistent Power of Race*. Chicago: University of Chicago Press.

Spradley, James P. 1980. *Participant Observation*. New York: Holt, Rinehart, and Winston.

Stewart, Eric A., and Ronald L. Simons. 2010. "Race, Code of the Street, and Violent Delinquency: A Multilevel Investigation of Neighborhood Street Culture and Individual Norms of Violence." *Criminology* 48:569–605.

Strauss, Anselem. 1978. *Negotiations*. San Francisco, CA: Jossey-Bass.

Swidler, Ann. 1986. "Culture in Action: Symbols and Strategies." *American Sociological Review* 51:273–86.

———. 2001. *Talk of Love: How Culture Matters*. Chicago: University of Chicago Press.

Tajfel, Henri. 1974. "Social Identity and Intergroup Behaviour." *Social Science Information* 13:65–93.

Tamm, Maare E., and Anna Granqvist. 1995. "The Meaning of Death for Children and Adolescents: A Phenomenographic Study of Drawings." *Death Studies* 19:203–22.

Tavuchis, Nicholas. 1993. *Mea Culpa: A Sociology of Apology and Reconciliation*. Stanford, CA: Stanford University Press.

Thacher, David. 2006. "The Normative Case Study." *American Journal of Sociology* 111: 1631–76.

Timmermans, Stefan, and Iddo Tavory. 2012. "Theory Construction in Qualitative Research: From Grounded Theory to Abductive Analysis." *Sociological Theory* 30:167–86.

Trump, Kenneth S. 1998. *Practical School Security: Basic Guidelines for Safe and Secure Schools*. Thousand Oaks, CA: Corwin.

Tyson, Karolyn. 2013. *Integration Interrupted: Tracking, Black Students, and Acting White after "Brown."* New York: Oxford University Press.

Tyson, Karolyn, William Darity, and Domini Castellino. 2005. "It's Not 'A Black Thing': Understanding the Burden of Acting White and Other Dilemmas of High Achievement." *American Sociological Review* 24:582–605.

Van Maanen, John. 1988. *Tales from the Field: On Writing Ethnography*. Chicago: University of Chicago Press.

Venkatesh, Sudhir Alladi, and Ronald Kassimir. 2007. "Youth and Legal Institutions: Thinking Globally and Comparatively." In *Youth, Globalization, and the Law*, edited by Sudhir Alladi Venkatesh and Ronald Kassimir, 3–16. Stanford, CA: Stanford University Press.

Venkatesh, Sudhir Alladi, and Alexandra K. Murphy. 2007. "Policing Ourselves: Law and Order in the American Ghetto." In *Youth, Globalization, and the Law*, edited by Sudhir Alladi Venkatesh and Ronald Kassimir, 124–57. Stanford, CA: Stanford University Press.

Verdugo, Richard R. 1999. "Safe Schools: Theory, Data, and Practices." *Education and Urban Society* 31:267–74.

Wacquant, Loïc. 2001. "The Penalisation of Poverty and the Rise of Neo-Liberalism. *European Journal of Criminal Policy and Research* 9:401–12.

———. 2010. "Crafting the Neoliberal State: Workfare, Prisonfare, and Social Insecurity." *Sociological Forum* 25:197–230.

Wasser, Judith Davidson, and Liora Bresler. 1996. "Working in the Interpretive Zone: Conceptualizing Collaboration in Qualitative Research Teams." *Educational Researcher* 25:5–15.

Wästerfors, David. 2011. "Disputes and Going Concerns in an Institution for 'Troublesome' Boys." *Journal of Contemporary Ethnography* 40:39–70.

Weiss, Lois, and Michele Fine. 2000. "Spaces for Identity Work." In *Speed Bumps: Excavating Race, Class, and Gender among Urban Youth*, edited by Lois Weiss and Michele Fine, 1–3. New York: Teachers College Press.

Welch, Kelly, and Allison Ann Payne. 2010. "Racial Threat and Punitive School Discipline." *Social Problems* 57:25–48.

West, Patrick, Helen Sweeting, Robert Young, and Shona Kelly. 2010. "The Relative Importance of Family Socioeconomic Status and School-Based Peer Hierarchies for Morning Cortisol in Youth: An Exploratory Study." *Social Science and Medicine* 70:1246–53.

Westlake, E. J. 2008. "Friend Me if You Facebook: Generation Y and Performative Surveillance." *TDR: The Drama Review* 52:21–40.

White, Rob, and Johanna Wyn. 2008. *Youth and Society: Exploring the Social Dynamics of Youth Experience*. 2nd ed. New York: Oxford University Press.

Whyte, William H. 1980. *The Social Life of Small Urban Spaces*. New York: Project for Small Urban Spaces.

Williams, Kirk R. and Nancy G. Guerra. 2011. "Perceptions of Collective Efficacy and Bullying Perpetration in Schools." *Social Problems* 58 (1): 126–43.

Willis, Paul. 1977. *Learning to Labor: How Working Class Kids Get Working Class Jobs*. New York: Morningside.

Yalda, Christine A. 2002. "Just Kids? The Role of Legality in Governing a Public High School." PhD diss., School of Justice Studies, Arizona State University, Tempe, Arizona.

Zelizer, Viviana A. 2012. "How I Became a Relational Economic Sociologist and What Does That Mean?" *Politics & Society* 40:145–74.

Zerubavel, Eviatar. 1991. *The Thin Line: Making Distinctions in Everyday Life*. New York: Free Press.

Zimring, Franklin E. 1998. American Youth *Violence*. Oxford, UK: Oxford University Press.

——. 2014. "American Youth Violence: A Cautionary Tale." In *Choosing the Future for American Juvenile Justice*, edited by Franklin E. Zimring and David S. Tanenhaus, 7–36. New York: New York University Press.

Zhang, Anlan, Lauren Musu-Gillette, and Barbara A. Oudekerk. 2016. "Indicators of School Crime and Safety: 2015." Washington, D.C.: National Center for Educational Statistics.

COURT CASES

Brown v. Board of Education of Topeka, 347 U.S. 483 (1954)

In re Gault, 387 U.S. 1 (1967)

Miller v. Alabama, 132 S. Ct. 2455 (2012)

People ex rel. Gallo v. Acuña, 14 Cal. 4th 1090 (1997)

Roper v. Simmons, 543 U.S. 551 (2005)

Tinker v. Des Moines Independent Community School District, 393 U.S. 503 (1969)

INDEX

moral authority on the front lines, 218; constituting, 218–21

moralistic orientations, 10–11; social time, social conflict, and, 221

moralistic string fights, 264n57

moralistic strings, 124. *See also* moralistic trouble strings

moralistic trouble responses, 87, 90, 103, 120, 123, 137, 238, 239f, 240f; anchored fluidity and, 84, 117; attempts to interrupt the flow of, 119–20; attitudes toward students who engage in, 71; conciliatory-remedial trouble responses and, 9–10, 68t, 75f, 76, 77, 77f, 81–84, 84t, 88, 105, 114, 120, 157, 212, 222, 238, 253t–56t; examples of, 81, 82, 94, 103, 105, 110, 112, 115–16, 137; gender and, 76, 115–16, 124, 136–37; goin' undercover and, 68t, 72, 118, 129, 132; grade level and, 77; October Fight and, 168; social media and, 223; social time and, 222–23; social trust and, 14, 114, 116–18; trouble response strings and, 165; violence and, 10, 84, 88. *See also* "puttin' 'em in their place"

moralistic trouble strings, 120, 148; in which young women are the primary players, 136–37. *See also* moralistic strings; "puttin' 'em in their place"

moral transcendence, 263n38

movement. *See* space and movement

"movin' around," 29

moving when a place becomes too crowded, motivations for, 202

"movin' on," 27, 68t, 71–73, 135. *See also* anchored fluidity

multicultural navigator, 44

multiracial identity, 26, 260n74

Nader, Laura, 9, 226

Nasir, Na'ilah Suad, 11

National Educational Association (NEA), 172

National School Safety Center (NSSC), 171–72

neoliberalism: nature of, 224, 225; scope of the term, 224

neoliberal-paternal era, sustaining social resilience in a, 224–27

"New West High School" (NWHS), 1; as a contested school that works, 216–17, 227; hallway with lockers removed, 183f (*see also* lockers); maps of (*see* sociospatial map(s)); overview, 1, 15–17; renovating NWHS as a safe school, 181–86; as a safe but contested campus, 173–81. *See also specific topics*

object-response interviewing, 231–32

October Fight (1999), 24, 162–69, 188, 190, 243; adults intervening in, 175; description and characteristics of, 167; differing perspectives on, 167–69, 241; informal peer control and, 170; insights gained from, 24, 165–71, 198, 241–42; as an organizational accident, 170, 198, 242; reasons it occurred, 167–71, 241–42; safe schools and, 24, 170–71, 190, 198; security guard who helped break up, 168

off-campus suspension, 73. *See also* out-of-school suspension

on-campus suspension, 73. *See also* In School Suspension

organizational accident, October Fight as an, 170, 198, 242

organizational recoupling in the aftermath of collective trauma, 197–98

out-of-school suspension (OSS), 17, 127, 164. *See also* off-campus suspension

Oware, Matthew, 124

peacekeeping. *See* keeping the peace

peer control, 24, 104, 112, 136, 137, 143, 173, 223. *See also* educating; informal control

peer mediation movement, 270n51

peer pressure, 119, 120, 136

peer relations, 10. *See also specific topics*

peer trouble: voices of, 2–5. *See also specific topics*

perimeter ring/perimeter fence, 182, 182f

Pettigrew, Thomas F., 259n47

photo-narrative exercises, 34, 182, 182f, 183, 191, 230, 231, 233–35

Pierce, Jennifer, 149

played by the rules, getting, 68t, 74, 150–53; definition and nature of, 150, 156

THE CHICAGO SERIES IN LAW AND SOCIETY
Edited by John M. Conley and Lynn Mather

Series titles, continued from front matter:

The Internationalization of Palace Wars: Lawyers, Economists, and the Contest to
Transform Latin American States
by Yves Dezalay and Bryant G. Garth

Free to Die for Their Country: The Story of the Japanese American Draft Resisters in
World War II
by Eric L. Muller

Overseers of the Poor: Surveillance, Resistance, and the Limits of Privacy
by John Gilliom

Pronouncing and Persevering: Gender and the Discourses of Disputing in an African
Islamic Court
by Susan F. Hirsch

The Common Place of Law: Stories from Everyday Life
by Patricia Ewick and Susan S. Silbey

The Struggle for Water: Politics, Rationality, and Identity in the American Southwest
by Wendy Nelson Espeland

Dealing in Virtue: International Commercial Arbitration and the Construction of a
Transnational *Legal Order*
by Yves Dezalay and Bryant G. Garth

Rights at Work: Pay Equity Reform and the Politics of Legal Mobilization
by Michael W. McCann

The Language of Judges
by Lawrence M. Solan

Reproducing Rape: Domination through Talk in the Courtroom
by Gregory M. Matoesian

Getting Justice and Getting Even: Legal Consciousness among Working-Class Americans
by Sally Engle Merry

Rules versus Relationships: The Ethnography of Legal Discourse
by John M. Conley and William M. O'Barr